NATURAL RESOURCES: MANAGEMENT, ECONOMIC DEVELOPMENT AND PROTECTION

NATURAL RESOURCES: MANAGEMENT, ECONOMIC DEVELOPMENT AND PROTECTION

JEANETTE B. PAULING
EDITOR

Nova Science Publishers, Inc.
New York

For permission to use material from this book please contact us:
Telephone 631-231-7269; Fax 631-231-8175
Web Site: http://www.novapublishers.com

LIBRARY OF CONGRESS CATALOGING-IN-PUBLICATION DATA

Library of Congress Cataloging-in-Publication Data
Natural resources : management, economic development, and protection / Jeanette B. Pauling (editor).
p. cm.
ISBN 978-1-60456-982-7 (hardcover)
1. Natural resources--Management. 2. Economic development--Environmental aspects. 3. Conservation of natural resources. I. Pauling, Jeanette B.
HC85.N384 2009
333.7--dc22

2008037244

Published by Nova Science Publishers, Inc. ✢ New York

CONTENTS

PREFACE

'Natural resources' are naturally occurring substances that are considered valuable in their relatively unmodified (natural) form. A natural resource's value rests in the amount of the material available and the demand for it. There are 2 types of natural resources: renewable and non-renewable. Natural Resources include soil, timber, oil, minerals, and other goods taken more or less from the Earth. Both extraction of the basic resource and refining it into a purer, directly usable form, (e.g., metals, refined oils) are generally considered natural-resource activities, even though the latter may not necessarily occur near the former. A nation's natural resources often determine its wealth in the world economic system. In recent years, the depletion of natural capital and attempts to move to sustainable development have been a major focus of development agencies. This is of particular concern in rainforest regions, which hold most of the Earth's natural biodiversity - irreplaceable genetic natural capital. Conservation of natural resources is the major focus of natural capitalism, environmentalism, the ecology movement, and Green Parties. Some view this depletion as a major source of social unrest and conflicts in developing nations. This new book gathers and presents important research in the field.

Chapter 1 - The Alentejo region, in the South of Portugal, between Tage river and the Algarve, represents almost one third of the Portuguese territory and only 5% of the population. Its socio-economic situation is more unfavourable then the country average and the tendency is to become worst.

This region is strongly specialized in the activities related with agriculture, forestry and hunting, which is certainly linked with the existence of the *Montado* ecosystem all over the region. According to the Agricultural Census data (INE, 1999), almost 43% of the Alentejo farms' total surface is occupied with shrubs and forests, mainly composed by *Quercus suber sp.* and *Quercus ilex sp.*. Almost 80% of this forest and shrubs' area is used to seed cereals or pastures under the trees, which shows the undeniable socio-economic interest of the *Montado* ecosystem agro-forestry exploitation in the region.

In this ecosystem, and beside the agro-forestry activities, there are many upstream and downstream economic activities linked with rural life. But this is a very vulnerable ecosystem, with a particular flora and fauna, where we can find many endangered species, and many areas where erosion risks are very high, not only due to heavy animal header but also to intensification and cultural practices.

With this work, we try to analyse the viability of the traditional *Montado* ecosystem, studying the effects of agricultural policy in the competitiveness and sustainability of this system.

We use a Policy Analysis Matrix to evaluate the agricultural systems competitiveness and their economic efficiency. The agricultural systems are classified concerning their contribution for the economic growth, in function of income levels and policy effects.

Chapter 2 - The federal government owns about 671.8 million acres (29.6%) of the 2.27 billion acres of land in the United States. Four agencies administer 628.4 million acres (93.5%) of this land: the Forest Service in the Department of Agriculture, and the Bureau of Land Management, Fish and Wildlife Service, and National Park Service, all in the Department of the Interior. Most of these lands are in the West, including Alaska. They generate revenues for the U.S. Treasury, some of which are shared with states and localities. The agencies receive funding from annual Interior and Related Agencies appropriations laws, trust funds, and special accounts.

The lands administered by the four agencies are managed for a variety of purposes, primarily related to preservation, recreation, and development of natural resources. Yet, each of these agencies has distinct responsibilities for the lands and resources it administers. The Bureau of Land Management (BLM) manages 261.5 million acres, and is responsible for 700 million acres of subsurface mineral resources. BLM has a multiple-use, sustained-yield mandate that supports a variety of uses and programs, including energy development, timber harvesting, recreation, grazing, wild horses and burros, cultural resources, and conservation. The Forest Service (FS) manages 192.5 million acres also for multiple use and sustained yields of various products and services, for example, timber harvesting, recreation, grazing, watershed protection, and fish and wildlife habitats. Most of the lands are designated national forests, but there are national grasslands and other lands. National forests now are created and modified by acts of Congress. Both the BLM and FS have several authorities to acquire and dispose of lands.

The Fish and Wildlife Service (FWS) manages 95.4 million acres, primarily to conserve and protect animals and plants. The 793 units of the National Wildlife Refuge System include refuges, waterfowl production areas, and wildlife coordination units. Units can be created by an act of Congress or executive order, and the FWS also may acquire lands for migratory bird purposes. The National Park Service (NPS) manages 79.0 million acres of federal land (and oversees another 5.4 million acres of nonfederal land) to conserve and interpret lands and resources and make them available for public use. Activities that harvest or remove resources generally are prohibited. The National Park System has diverse units ranging from historical structures to cultural and natural areas. Units are created by an act of Congress, but the President may proclaim national monuments.

There also are three special management systems that include lands from more than one agency. The National Wilderness Preservation System consists of 105.2 million acres of protected wilderness areas designated by Congress. The National Wild and Scenic Rivers System contains 11,303 miles of wild, scenic, and recreational rivers, primarily designated by Congress and managed to preserve their free-flowing condition. The National Trails System contains four classes of trails managed to provide recreation and access to outdoor areas and historic resources.

Chapter 3 - There is consensus in the international community that development and poverty alleviation in rural Africa are among the most urgent global agendas for the 21st century. Many rural Africans have traditionally depended on natural resources. Land use patterns are highly heterogeneous across diverse agro-ecological/farming systems and even within the systems, some being more extensive, while others being more intensive. These days a range of factors, including increasing population pressure and global climate change, has made it impossible for development through conventional extensive technologies or degradational pathways to be sustainable as a viable strategy. To achieve both development and environmental goals, sound agricultural intensification technologies through more intensive and efficient use of inputs internal to systems, or conservation pathways, must be identified and tailored to specific local needs and conditions to be adopted by rural households, while enabling policy and infrastructure should be availed by government and development agencies.

This chapter investigates the challenges that Africa has faced in rural development and natural resource management and seeks guidance for policies and research. Firstly, the chapter gives an overview of the current state of heterogeneous agro-ecological and farming systems and the development challenges posed by population growth and climate change in rural Africa. We propose a conceptual framework to guide empirical research in effectively examining the multi-dimensional aspects of the evolution of farming systems/resource management and review how the framework is applied at meso-level in the recent literature. Secondly, a case study from a Rift Valley community in western Kenya is presented to show micro-level evidence of diverse portfolios of technology options in a semi-arid environment.

It turns out that some conservation pathways may exist to promote more sustainable development in rural Africa, possibly through the better integration of system components, i.e., crop and livestock, and the inclusion of agroforestry into the farming systems. Concurrently, there are also degradational pathways entailing substantial trade-offs between promoting economic development vs. conserving natural resources. To promote conservation development pathways, policies not only need to identify optimal technology portfolios best suited to local conditions and exploit the complementarities among system components but also to provide education with farmers to augment their human capital assets and to promote stable non-farm/off-farm income opportunities to enable investment in resource management. The chapter concludes by synthesising the findings for policy implications and by presenting another emerging challenge of rising food/fuel prices and a subsequent future research agenda.

Chapter 4 - Riparian landscapes are natural habitats of unique ecological and scenic values, which are highly sensitive to human intervention and impact. Yet, due to their qualities, and especially the presence of water, they are also usually attractive for recreation purposes. This is more so in arid and semi-arid zones like Israel. Nevertheless, in the past, the importance of riparian landscapes in Israel did not receive adequate attention in policy and planning. As a result, over the years they were exposed to various negative impacts, including pollution by industrial and agricultural effluents, exploitation of water for agricultural and other purposes, and land use conflicts. Although in recent years with the growing awareness of their ecological and recreational potential, considerable efforts are being invested in the rehabilitation of deteriorated riparian landscapes, their protection is still deficient.

This chapter reviews and examines policy tools used for the protection of riparian landscapes in Israel, based mainly on regulations, reports and existing literature. It concludes by offering some lessons for policy-making in general and suggestions for improving the protection of riparian landscapes in Israel in particular.

Chapter 5 - Forest certification provides a means to ensure that forests are managed to achieve economic, environmental, and social goals that are the foundation of sustainable forest management and sustainable development. We collected data on forest certification for the major systems in the Americas, including the Forest Stewardship Council (FSC) in Argentina, Brazil, Chile, and the United States, and the Sustainable Forestry Initiative (SFI) in the United States and Canada, Sistema Brasileiro de Certificação Florestal (Cerflor) in Brazil, and Sistema Chileno de Certificación Forestal (Certfor) in Chile. Repoorted average total costs varied considerably depending on forest ownership size, certification system, and country. Median average total costs ranged from \$6.45 to \$39.31 per ha per year for small tracts of less than 4,000 hectares. The large ownerships of 400,000 ha or more had median costs of \$0.07 to \$0.49 per ha per year. Mean costs were greater than median costs, due to large expenses for a few firms. Regression results indicated that average total costs for certification were a function of ownership size, but did not vary significantly among certification systems or country, although the sample of reporting firms was small for finding statistical differences. Opinions about benefits of forest certification generally classed firm strategic or management reasons highest, organizational learning factors second, signaling stewardship to external groups third, and improved prices or markets last, but all broad groups were considered important benefits of certification. The largest perceived disadvantages of forest certification were its time and audit costs, and no other disadvantage was rated more than somewhat important. Certified forest firms had relatively evenly mixed opinions about whether certification benefits exceeded costs, but a large majority stated that they would continue forest certification in the future.

Chapter 6 - The objective of this study is to provide a theoretical framework to jointly analyze the role of natural resources and intangible capital in the process of economic development, addressing a simple mechanism that can explain why natural resource abundance may lower income and welfare. The model extends the development theory of relative incomes of Parente and Prescott to include intermediate goods production which require the use of a natural input. The model relative income predictions are consistent with the economic development observations of some Latin American countries.

Chapter 7 - Restoration is increasingly recognised as an important tool in the resource manager's toolkit. From an anthropocentric view, the restoration of damaged, degraded or destroyed ecosystems aims to reinstate the flow of ecosystem goods and services that contribute to human well being. The application of micro-economic tools can provide input into decision making with respect to ecosystem restoration. This chapter develops a framework that highlights when and how economic input fits into restoration decision making and discusses a series of challenges with the economic analysis of restoration projects. The first elements of the framework links a series of micro-economic tools – ex-ante and ex-post cost–benefit, cost–effectiveness and cost–utility analyses – to the different stages of the adaptive restoration process, while the second element provides guidance for selection among the tools. The practical application of the tools in a restoration context is expected to be challenging from a number of perspectives: lack of costing data, incomplete understanding of ecosystems, substitution and complementarity among restoration projects, non-market multidimensional outcomes, long timeframes, and potential for irreversibilities.

Chapter 8 - According to climate change assessments, less precipitations and higher temperatures can be expected in the Iberian Peninsula and other Mediterranean zones. Besides, an increment in droughts and other extreme events can be expected as well. Such climatic conditions require an effort to optimize irrigation technologies and to improve water management efficiency. There are currently available water-use and crop-growth simulation models, which can be combined to climate scenarios and weather generators in order to recommend, through many simulations, the most reliable irrigation management. The Preliminary Assessment of the Impacts in Spain due to the Effects of Climate Change and the National Plan for Adaptation to Climate Change recommend the use of such simulation tools in Spanish climate-change impact assessments. Those tools, however, have not been used yet to support irrigation decision-making in our country. In that sense, the EU-funded proposal AGRIDEMA, leaded by Spain, has been addressed to introduce such tools, connecting the tools "providers" from Universities and high-level research centres, with their "users", located in agricultural technological or applied-research centres. AGRIDEMA comprised courses and Pilot Applications of the tools. Local researchers knew in the AGRIDEMA courses how to access to GCM data and seasonal forecasts, they receive also basic knowledge on weather generators, statistical and dynamical downscaling; as well as on available crop models as DSSAT, WOFOST, CROPSYST, SWAP and others. About 20 pilot assessments have been conducted in several European countries during AGRIDEMA, applying the modelling tools in particular cases.

The AGRIDEMA results are commented, mentioning particularly the Pilot Assessments that were held in Spain and in the Mediterranean area. Furthermore, several "users" opinion regarding the available climate and crop-growth simulation tools are also pointed out. Those opinions can be used as important feedback by the tools "developers". An illustrative example on how modelling tools can help to manage Sugarbeet irrigation under present and future climate conditions in Spain is also shown. Several future research directions are pointed out, as followed from the shown example and the AGRIDEMA results. Those research directions agree with the actions recommended in the Spanish National Plan for Adaptation to Climate Change, as well as in the European and international guidelines. Stakeholder will adopt climate-change mitigation options only if they realize the reliability of such options on their specific cases. To achieve this, the "users" of the modelling tools must develop local demonstration proposals, aimed to model calibration and validation, etc. Particularly, some demonstration proposals should be aimed to recommend productive and efficient irrigation water managements under the adverse climate conditions that Spanish farmers will eventually face in the next years.

Chapter 9 - This chapter reviews three approaches to water management i) supply-side, ii) demand-side and, iii) integrated. Tools and applications for each approach are reviewed in order to understand their reach in the solution of water-related problems. The paper focuses on management tools which are also applicable on the scale of urban areas.

Recent formulations take into account a holistic understanding of water resources that provides environmentally and socially acceptable solutions. The solutions proposed explore a combination of technologies and strategies, depending on the aims of projects, their local and national context, and the available data. The involvement of decision-makers, stakeholders and other end-users is essential for the specification of relevant issues and the development of useful tools to support decisions.

The challenges that face central and northern Mexico are reviewed. The limitations of conventional practices of water management in Mexico point to the need for a paradigm change, from increasing supply to reducing demand. The change toward more integrated management is a complex and difficult task, given the traditional dominance of centralized and technocratic management. The benefits of holistic management approaches are discussed, as are the obstacles that have limited their adoption so far.

In: Natural Resources
Editor: Jeanette B. Pauling

ISBN 978-1-60456-982-7

Chapter 1

COMPETITIVENESS EVALUATION FOR THE ALENTEJO AGRICULTURE AMONG THE *MONTADO* ECOSYSTEM

Rui Fragoso*

Assistant Professor in the Management Department and Member of the Institute of Mediterranean Agrarian Sciences, Évora University, Largo dos Colegiais, 2, 7000 Évora, Portugal

Maria de Belém Martins†

Assistant Professor in the Faculty of Natural Resources Engineering, Algarve University and Member of the Studies and Advanced Research Center in Management and Economy, Algarve University, Campus de Gambelas, 8005-139 Faro, Portugal

Maria Raquel Lucas‡

Associate Professor with requirements for Full Professor in the Management Department and Member of the Studies and Advanced Research Center in Management and Economy, Évora University, Largo dos Colegiais, 2, 7000 Évora, Portugal

ABSTRACT

The Alentejo region, in the South of Portugal, between Tage river and the Algarve, represents almost one third of the Portuguese territory and only 5% of the population. Its socio-economic situation is more unfavourable then the country average and the tendency is to become worst.

This region is strongly specialized in the activities related with agriculture, forestry and hunting, which is certainly linked with the existence of the *Montado* ecosystem all over the region. According to the Agricultural Census data (INE, 1999), almost 43% of

* rfragoso@uevora.pt
† mbmartins@ualg.pt
‡ mrlucas@uevora.pt

the Alentejo farms' total surface is occupied with shrubs and forests, mainly composed by *Quercus suber sp.* and *Quercus ilex sp.*. Almost 80% of this forest and shrubs' area is used to seed cereals or pastures under the trees, which shows the undeniable socio-economic interest of the *Montado* ecosystem agro-forestry exploitation in the region.

In this ecosystem, and beside the agro-forestry activities, there are many upstream and downstream economic activities linked with rural life. But this is a very vulnerable ecosystem, with a particular flora and fauna, where we can find many endangered species, and many areas where erosion risks are very high, not only due to heavy animal header but also to intensification and cultural practices.

With this work, we try to analyse the viability of the traditional *Montado* ecosystem, studying the effects of agricultural policy in the competitiveness and sustainability of this system.

We use a Policy Analysis Matrix to evaluate the agricultural systems competitiveness and their economic efficiency. The agricultural systems are classified concerning their contribution for the economic growth, in function of income levels and policy effects.

INTRODUCTION

As all southern Iberian Peninsula, the Alentejo region in the South of Portugal, between Tage River and the Algarve, is dominated by a savannah-like ecosystem, the *Montado*, which is a typically Mediterranean ecosystem cultural adaptation to generally poor productive areas (annex 1). Stevenson (1985a,b), Stevenson and Moore (1988) and Stevenson and Harrison (1992) documented the long-term (ca. 6000 years) evolution of these production systems with human intervention and continued human influence. After the tenth century A.D., written history demonstrates the management regulations that influenced vegetation composition and derived products, as well as the early occurrence of stakeholder conflicts related to grazing or acquiring oak wood for naval construction (cf. Joffre et al. 1999). The function of *Montado* ecosystem is maintained via the flow of carbon fixed in photosynthesis, which supports tree and herbaceous respiration and growth, and, thereby, the accumulation of biomass during annual cycles as well as over longer periods (Tenhunen et al, 2007).

Covering a large geographic area, *Montado* ecosystem is exploited for three main uses: forestry, agriculture, and extensive grazing, in proportions that vary according to local conditions (more or less productive land) and historical circumstances. It is an agro-forestry-pastoral ecosystem that consists of scattered tree cover (60–100 trees per ha) dominated by evergreen oaks (cork oak, *Quercus suber,* and holm oak, *Quercus ilex spp. rotundifolia*), with pastures and agricultural fields (clover, wheat, barley, oats) as undercover, usually in a rotation scheme that includes fallows (Pinto-Correia 1993, Lourenço et al. 1998). It is a high diversity system (De Miguel 1999, Carrión et al. 2000), and the varying tree density suggests that these human-made agro-ecosystems have adjusted to local climate (Joffre et al. 1999). Shrubs sprout frequently (e.g., *Cistus, Erica, Lavandula,* and *Ulex* ssp.), and are either cleared out or artificially kept at low densities (Lourenço et al. 1998, Pinto-Correia and Mascarenhas 1999). According to Pereira and Fonseca (2003), humans and nature contribute in equal parts to the making of *Montado* ecosystem: the environment providing the raw ecological material, and humans decoding and exploiting it. Biodiversity, species distribution, management practices (animal husbandry, agriculture and forestry) and, cultural landscape, would be expected to vary among *Montado*, specially according their natural resources use.

With cork as one of the country's largest agricultural exports, the Alentejo region represents almost one third of the Portuguese territory and only 5% of the population (Lucas *et al.*, 2005). Additional biological products are the acorn crops, foliage of pruned branches and herbaceous understory biomass that provide fodder to animals, the animals themselves, pruned branches and cut invading shrubs as firewood or for charcoal production, cereal crops planted after understory clearing, and tannins for industry (Tenhunen, 2007). Alentejo socio-economic situation is more unfavourable then the country average as it can be seen in the Figure 1.

In 2001, the Gross Domestic Product (GDP) *per capita* in Alentejo assigned a life level 20% below the country's average and the Families Disposable Gross Income (FDGI) was almost 13% below the average. Alentejo population has registered a negative evolution in the last decades and it presents the lowest population density in the country and an ageing index substantially over the national one. As expected, the economic activity rate is below the national average (almost 3% below) and the unemployment rate is above the average (almost 2% above) (Lucas *et al.*, 2005).

The Gross Added Value (GAV) analysis allow the conclusion that in 2001 the primary sector represented 16,4% of Alentejo economy. This contribution, almost exclusively coming from agriculture, forestry and hunting, is almost four times above the contribution of primary sector for national GAV. In what concerns the population employed, we can observe that in spite of a predominance of activities linked with the tertiary sector (61% of the employment), the population employed in the primary sector (13%) is almost three times more then in the country average (Lucas et al., 2005).

These indicators demonstrate the Alentejo's strong specialization in the activities related with agriculture, forestry and hunting, which is certainly linked with the existence of the *Montado* ecosystem all over the region.

For this reason, the Common Agricultural Policy (CAP) has a strong effect in the region, deepened by the fact that the CAP reforms, beginning in 1992, had huge consequences on the Portuguese agriculture, which has adopted this policy in counter-cycle, has it is recognized by several authors (Estácio, 1983; Pearson, 1987; Pinto, 1984; and Soares, 1985).

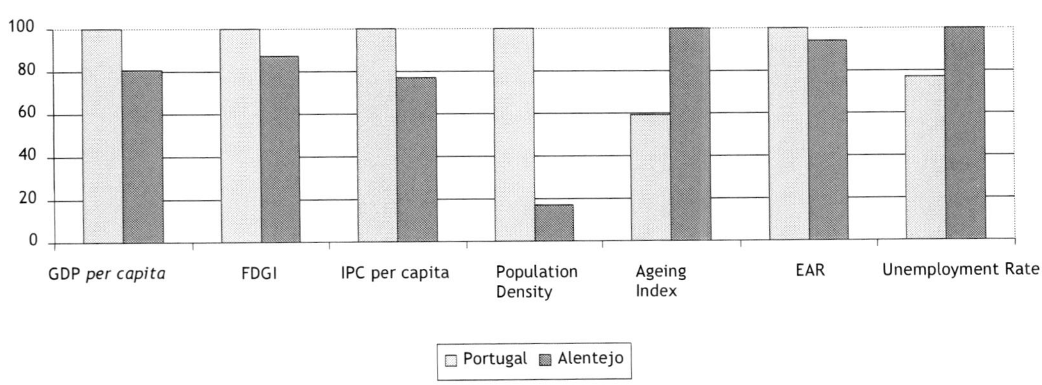

Fonte: Lucas *et al.*, 2005.

Figure 1. Socio-economic indicators in the Alentejo and Portugal.

The 1992 CAP reform was meant to answer the budgetary problems of CAP and the pressures with GATT international negotiations in Uruguay Round. Although this reform maintains the fundamental principles of CAP, the main objectives are now to struggle the agricultural production in order to re-balance markets and to diminish the agricultural expenses while considering the Community responsibilities, as a major actor on world exchanges, and maintaining a sufficient number of persons linked to land, to preserve the environment and the European family model of agriculture.

These objectives implied substantial changes on the political instruments that support the markets, which deeply affected the Common Market Organizations (CMO) of cereals, cattle, important for the Alentejo. The accompanying measures also created with this reform, namely the agro-environmental measures and the agricultural lands forestation, labelled a more territorial and more concerned with environmental problems CAP.

The 2000 Agenda review meant to reinforce the objectives of 1992 reform, namely the competitiveness, the multifunctionality and the sustainability of the EU agriculture. The growing importance of sustainability and multifunctionality objectives allowed the implementation of CAP 2nd pillar, which means the integration of rural development on agricultural policy – the CAP is no longer mainly a sector policy and integrates the territory as one of its main concerns, which was due to mean that the expenses with agricultural policy should give a clear contribution to landscape planning and nature conservation.

Finally, in 2003, the mid-term review of CAP was approved. This review pursues the objectives of Agenda 2000 in what concerns competitiveness reinforcement and the promotion of multifunctionality and sustainability, but strongly changes the CAP instruments. The main change is the institution of a farm specific payment that substitutes the support to agricultural income trough direct payments to grand cultures, cattle or sheep. To promote competitiveness, sustainability and multifunctionality and turn the CAP a more flexible policy the specific support regimens to certain products were changed, the eco-conditionality was introduced, which implies obligations concerning the environment and the rural development supports were reinforced, explicitly supporting also non-agricultural activities in rural areas.

The CAP adoption, with all its changes, led to profound structural adjustments in Portuguese agriculture and especially in Alentejo agriculture. The agricultural income evolution can be characterized by the evolution of GAV at markets prices and at base price and the evolution of Factors Income (FI). Data used is the three years average for the 1986 based series (1986-1996) and the 1995 base series (1995-1999) in the National Statistical Bureau Economic Accounts of Agriculture. The results in these two series are not comparable because the 1986 base series is based on the methodology of the European Accounting System of 1979 and the 1995 base series is based on the European Accounting System of 1995. For this reason, the main aggregates for agricultural income are distinct for the 1986/88 to 1994/96 period and for the 1995/97 to 1997/99 period.

Factors Income (FI), that represents the available income to pay for land, labour, capital and profits, shows a better average evolution for Alentejo than for the rest of the country. In 1986/88, the FI in Alentejo was 257.5 millions € and eight years latter it was 500 millions €, which represents an average annual increase of 8.7%. During that period, the FI in Continental Portugal also raised, but only at an annual average of 7.4%. In the 1995/97 to 1997/99 period the nominal values of FI has maintain, since growing rates revealed low variation amplitudes, namely -0.7% and 0.7%, respectively.

Table 1. Gross Added Value (GAV) and Factors Income (FI) for Continental Portugal and Alentejo (annual averages 1986/88 to 1994/96 at market prices – 1986 serie), calculated at market prices

	Alentejo			Continental Portugal			Alentejo/Continent		
	86/88	94/96	Annual Rate	86/88	94/96	Annual Rate	86/88	94/96	Annual Rate
GAV (millions €)	252	311	2.7	1532	2318	5.3	0.16	0.13	0.50
FI (millions €)	257	500	8.7	1488	2625	7.4	0.17	0.19	1.18
GAV/AWU (thousand €)	3.2	7.3	10.8	1.6	4.0	12.4	2.05	1.83	0.87
FI/A WU(€)	3.3	11.8	17.2	1.5	4.6	14.6	2.15	2.59	1.18

Source: Adapted from Marques, 2005.

Table 2. Gross Added Value (GAV) and Factors Income (FI) for Continental Portugal and Alentejo (annual averages 1995/97 to 1997/99 at market prices – 1995 serie), calculated at market prices

	Alentejo			Continental Portugal			Alentejo/Continent		
	95/97	97/99	Annual Rate	95/97	97/99	Annual Rate	95/97	97/99	Annual Rate
GAV (millions €)	412	392	-2.5	2673	2645	-0.5	0.15	0.15	4.60
FI (millions €)	387.5	382	-0.7	2359	2392	0.7	0.16	0.16	-1.04
GAV/AWU (thousand €)	8.2	8.3	0.3	4.2	4.7	5.8	1.97	1.77	0.05
FI/A WU(€)	7.8	8.1	2.1	3.7	4.2	7.1	2.10	1.91	0.30

Source: Adapted from Marques, 2005.

Productivity of agricultural work, measured by the relation between GAV and work (measured in Annual Working Units – AWU) was 3.2 thousands € for the years 1986/88 in Alentejo. This was two times the average value for Continental Portugal (1.6 thousand €). Between 1986/88 and 1994/96 the productivity of agricultural work raised much more then GAV, due to an annual growing rate of 10.8% in Alentejo and 12.4% in Continental Portugal. In the period 1995/97-1997/99 the productivity of agricultural work stabilized in Alentejo but continued to grow in Continental Portugal, although in a much more lower rate, as indicated by the average rates of 0.3% and 4.7%, respectively. We must say, anyway, that in the end of these two periods the productivity of agricultural work was still much higher in Alentejo then in Continental Portugal.

In what concerns the FI by AWU the evolution was even more favourable, mainly in the period 1986/88 to 1994/96 and especially in Alentejo, where annual growing rate was 17.2%.

In the period 1986/88 to 1994/96, between Portuguese accession to EEC and full application of CAP 1992 reform, GAV from agriculture has raised less then income available to pay for land, labour and capital, this evolution being more sensible in Alentejo then in Continental Portugal. This is undoubtedly due to the raise in factors productivity that was not a direct consequence of a raise in products value but of the factors' reduction and more efficient use. The very strong raise on labour productivity is a good example of this point. It doesn't reflect the raise on agricultural GAV but the reduction of agricultural population that is due to the important socio-economic modifications the country has gone through during the last decades. In the period 1995/97 to 1997/99, the growth rates of the agricultural production structure's economic indicators do not show great changes, which can imply the conclusion the major adjustments were made in the previous period.

These evolution of agricultural income indicators reflects important structural changes, namely on the final agricultural production (FAP) and on the production specialization pattern for Portuguese and Alentejo agriculture. The FAP evolution and the production specialization pattern can be analysed by sub-sector, considering the values of the final production location coefficient in each sub-sector. This coefficient relates the relative importance of a considered sub-sector production value on the final agricultural production of Alentejo to the same sub-sector relative importance in Continental Portugal, i.e.:

$$(X_{u,A} / X_{t,A}) / (X_{u,C} / X_{t,C})$$

where $X_{u,A}$ is the agriculture's sub-sector u production value in Alentejo; $X_{t,A}$ is the value of agricultural final production of Alentejo; $X_{u,C}$ is the agriculture's sub-sector u production value in Continental Portugal; and $X_{t,C}$ is the value of agricultural final production of Continental Portugal.

A location coefficient above 1 reveals Alentejo specialization in a given sub-sector. According to this, in 1986/88 Alentejo showed a specialization of its agricultural pattern on the sub-sectors of cereals and rice, industrial crops, olive oil and sheep and goats.

Between 1986/88 and 1994/96 crop production in Alentejo lost importance to animal production. The changes that occurred allowed the enlargement of Alentejo's specialization basis to the sub-sectors of swine production and fruits. Between 1995/97 and 1997/99, Alentejo FAP raised 1.9%/year, almost 0.9% above Continental Portugal average. This increase was mainly due to crop production. In what concerns specialization patterns, there were not major changes between the two periods.

According to the Agricultural Census data (INE, 1999), the farms' total surface in Alentejo was mainly (89%) Usable Agricultural Surface (UAS) and almost 43% of the Alentejo farms' total surface is occupied with shrubs and forests, mainly composed by *Quercus suber* and *Quercus ilex spp. rotundifolia*. Almost 80% of this forest and shrubs' area is used to seed cereals or pastures under the trees, which shows the undeniable socio-economic interest of the *Montado* ecosystem agro-forestry exploitation in the region.

In Portugal, 31.9% of the farms raise swine. In Alentejo, this number falls to 20.4%, which means that this region has 5.5% of the farms with swine and 19.3% of the Portuguese swine. The allocation of these swine by the NUTS III regions of Alentejo is linked to some intensive exploitation of swine that happens in Central and Litoral Alentejo and a very extensive production system that occurs in the pastures under *Quercus suber* and *Quercus ilex spp. rotundifolia* trees.

In this ecosystem, and beside the agro-forestry activities, there are many upstream and downstream economic activities linked with rural life. This is a very vulnerable ecosystem – here a particular flora and fauna can be found, with many endangered species, and there are many areas where erosion risks are very high, not only due to heavy animal header but also to intensification and cultural practices.

The sustainable development of this ecosystem implies the study, development and diffusion of models and technologies adapted to solve the problems of the various actors we can find there (public administration, producers associations, rural owners and others). As the available information is not sufficient to realize efficiently the integrated management of the ecosystem resources, this research tries to evaluate its socio-economic situation in what concerns the viability of the actual production systems and the effects of agricultural policy in its competitiveness and sustainability, contributing to decision-making and adequate policy definition.

METHODOLOGY

In the agro-forestry sector, it can be stated that the production unit is the farm, or the agricultural enterprise. Barros et Estácio (1972) define an agricultural enterprise as an organization where, using limited work and land resources, the decisions are directed to develop a defined production system, with which it is aimed to obtain a sustainable economic result. The production systems of the *Montado* ecosystem, having a set of specificities that often complement the agro-forestry system, should be evaluated in the production unit's micro-economic context.

From the production system's study, the socio-economic characterization of a production technology is obtained. Nevertheless, it is not possible to establish the relations between the production factors work and capital with the factor entrepreneur, not even to capture the effects of complementary productions, as it is the case of cross elasticities in the factors' demand that occurs between animal production activities and crop production activities. In these cases, there are systems which products are simultaneously a profit for crop activities and a cost for animal activities. In extensive animal production, fodder crops and cereals by-products are produced by crop activities with the objective of being an intermediate consumption of animal activities and its economic valuation results indirectly of animal production profits.

The competitiveness of activities can be studied with different methodologies. There are several examples of econometric models, such as the applications to competitiveness analysis followed by Mattas (1990) and Bureau & Butuault (1990) for European Community agriculture and in Maza *et al* (1992) for sheep production. Mathematical programming models were made by Jaraba & Thompson, 1980, Baysan, 1984, Martin, 1989, Abreu, 1987, Marques, 1988, Marques *et al,* 1995, Lucas, 1995 and Martins & Marques, 2006, and policy analysis matrixes can be found in Pearson & Meyer, 1974, Santana, 1986, Fox, 1987, Pearson *et al,* 1987, Avillez & Queiroz, 1987, Avillez *et al.* 1988, Pearson & Monke, 1989 and Venturini, 1989.

The policy analysis matrix (PAM) proposed by Pearson & Meyer in 1974 has been used frequently in the agriculture competitiveness analysis (Winter-Nelson, 1991, Michalek, 1995, Ezeala-Harrison, 1997, Kydd J. *et al.*, 1997, Fang *et al.,* 2000, Mohanty *et al.* 2003, Pearson, *et al.*, 2003, Drew *et al.*, 2005, Andrés *et al.*, 2007, Ramanovich, 2007), as it is a simple method to integrate chronologically the technological aspects of agro-forestry production, the factors demand and the products supply. The concepts of agricultural enterprise and farm allow the framework to be established in the scope of economic analysis. Considering these two concepts, socio-economic models of *Montado* exploitation are established, permitting to obtain socio-economic indicators to the characterization and analysis of the economical policy effects that are coherent with the evolution of the adopted solutions.

The analysis of economic viability of these models considers their capacity to face production costs, both in short and long term, as well as the invested capitals, costs and profits structure. This analysis will allow the evaluation of competitiveness and economic sustainability using a PAM.

For these reasons, PAM has been the methodology adopted to evaluate the competitiveness of *Montado* agro-forestry production systems (MAPS) and their efficient contribution to the economy burdening, as well as the institutional income transferences, due both to Common Agricultural Policy and to the national policies that support the agro-forestry sector and rural development.

With the PAM methodology, a matrix of cost, profits and results is built for each MAPS, first including the policies effects and afterwards without this inclusion. In Table 3 it is shown the simplified structure of the used PAM.

The Net Return (NR) column summarizes the balance between profits and costs. This balance can be done either at private prices or social prices or considering the institutional net income transferences.

The NR at private prices (NR_{pp}) (C or D) is given in the first matrix row by subtracting the costs at market prices (B) from the profits at market prices (A). The result, C in our matrix, shows how the MAPS react to the income transferences determined by CAP. This result allows the evaluation of NR at private prices in the actual socio-economic context. The D element of our matrix isolates the effect that CAP rural development policies have in the considered MAPS.

The NR_{pp} represents the Entrepreneurial Net Return per used surface unit, which means it represents the return for the entrepreneur own resources, such as land, capital and entrepreneurial capacity. This means that a positive NR_{pp} indicates the MAPS generates profits that cover the production factors' real costs, in its particular socio-economic context. It also measures the risk farmer faces. A positive NR_{pp} means the farmer has some capacity to face income risks, determined by the prices, the technology or the resources.

The NR at social prices (NR_{sp}) (G) is given in the second matrix row by subtracting the costs at social prices (F) from the profits at social prices (E). The result shows the MAPS profitability in an open economy, without the effects of the income transferences determined by CAP and the national policies that support the sector. In this case, a positive NR indicates that the set of agro-forestry activities developed in the MAPS are economically efficient, as they are profitable even in an open market, with free prices.

Table 3. Policy Analysis Matrix

Analysis	Profits	Costs	Net Return	Net Return*
Private prices	A or A'	B	C	D
Social prices	E	F	G	G
Policy effects and market failures	H	I	J	L

Notes: Net Return (NR) at private prices C = A – B.

Net Return (NR) at social prices G = E – F.

NR* without CAP; national support at private prices D = A' - B.

Source: Adapted from Pearson, 1987.

In our PAM the difference between the first row, at private prices, and the second row, at social prices, highlights both the effect of the institutional income transference policies and eventual market failures. Public supports to production, income and rural development are given by the matrix element H, which is obtained by the difference between A and E. If H is positive, this means profits at private prices (A) are above the profits at social prices (E). In this situation, production and income are institutionally supported because domestic prices are above import prices, because of low competitiveness of internal production or because there are payments for the services done to the community, which is what happens with the supports of the CAP second pillar.

Public support to factors use are given by the matrix element I, resulting from the difference between B and F, respectively the factors costs at private prices and the factors costs at social prices. A positive value for I shows there are subsidies that increase the competitiveness of agro-forestry production – to overcome the fact that domestic prices for production factors are higher then world prices or the fact that domestic production factors have too high opportunity costs.

The net effects of all the income transference policies (J) is the difference between all the production support, income and rural development policies (H) and the policies that support the use of production factors (I). The L element, in the matrix, shows the net effect of the rural development policy of the CAP second pillar and the net effect of the income transference public policies can also be calculated by the difference between NR_{pp}, C and D, and the NR_{sp}, G.

The social evaluation of results implies profits and costs to be calculated at scarce prices, i.e., at opportunity costs. This analysis supposes that if social prices are considered in economic decisions we can obtain an optimal resources distribution and as a consequence an efficient contribution from the sector, or activity, to economic growth.

Nevertheless, the problem of social analysis is exactly the social prices' calculation, which are no more then shadow prices for the resources. When it is impossible to obtain shadow prices, social prices can always be approximated. A very common example of social prices approximation is the use of CIF (cost, insurance and freight) international prices for undisclosed agricultural products and FOB (free on board) international prices to production factors that are sold in international markets.

The main reason for the impossibility of using these international prices is exactly the specificity of the *Montado* ecosystem and its MAPS. Some of the products produced are exclusive of this ecosystem and are differentiated from their similars, as it is the case of Alentejano swine breed, for which it is not possible to find a price in international markets.

As Portuguese economy is an open economy, internal market prices are also strongly influenced by imports and so the relation between national prices for agricultural products and production factors and their origin prices are influenced only by transport costs and commercialization margins. This is the reason to consider as social prices for agricultural products and production factors the prices in national market deducted from their commercialization margins.

The previous explanations are valid for those production factors that are available at international markets. The next question concerns the primary production factors, such as land, capital and labour that are usually not transacted at those markets. These factors requires a different approach – they must be valuated by their opportunity costs, i. e., the value that reflects the income that could be achieved with an additional unit of the considered factor, used in its best alternative use.

And a last remark in what concerns land. In the long-run, when all the other factors become variable, land is assumed to be the only that remains fixed. So, it is sometimes a very hard and unsuccessful task to determine the land's best agro-forestry production alternative income. Many times the results are envisaged and so it is the calculus of social price. As an alternative, the renting market price can be used and this was the option taken in this work.

Social cost of improvements and fixed capital was evaluated by current interest rate, which was considered to be, on average, 2% yearly. This rate reflects an average return for this capital that is similar to the one of a great majority of risk-less financial applications, a little bit above the net interest rate for bank deposits and slightly over the inflation rate.

Operating capital has always an interest rate above fixed capital. In this case, it was considered a rate of 4%, which results from the arithmetic average of annual interest rates for long-term deposits and campaign loans.

In what concerns work, the social cost is given by the average indicators for the sector's work remuneration, obtained with a survey's data, and also accounts for the opportunity cost of non-remunerated work.

The PAM doesn't account for market failures, which means it is considered that they are not significant and/or they are significantly corrected by public policies. This previous consideration allows a direct relation between social benefits and the distortion effects of institutional income transference's policies.

RESULTS

This work was developed in two phases. First, the problem was to identify the representative MAPS, based on the dominant patterns of a convenience sample of 30 agro-forestry farms. For this study, the Évora University's Unit of Macroecology and Conservation accounted the agro-ecological factors, the Technical-Economic Orientation (TEO) derived from the production value origin and the kind of agro-forestry production activities' developed and also some aspects of agricultural economy, such as MAPS economic dimension, agro-forestry area and annual work volume. The result was the identification of 6 representative MAPS, which characteristics are the following (table 4):

The second phase was the study of competitiveness and economic efficiency, which was preceded by a viability analysis.

The viability analysis comprises an appraisal of the MAPS in terms of the invested capital, production costs, profits and incomes. Tables 5 to 8 present the structural results for those issues respectively.

MAPS invested capitals by area unit vary between 1115 € and 4774 €. The smaller value occurs on type A MAPS and the greater one to type C MAPS. Capital applications by area unit are generally lower on MAPS with larger areas. It is remarkable that MAPS type A, D and F, mainly with big and medium agro-forestry farms have the lowest investment level per unit, always under 2000 €/ha. MAPS type B and C are more intensive in what concerns capital investment, with values always above 4000 €/ha.

Table 4. Alentejo representative *Montado* Agro-Forestry Production Systems (MAPS)

MAPS	Soil occupation	Animal activity	Forest characteristics	Climatic factors	Agricultural economy aspects	Nº of Farms (%)	Surface (%)
A	Pastures under trees	Cattle and swine	Weak forest. Predominance of *Quercus ilex spp. rotundifolia*	Inner zones, with low level of precipitation	Big farms: 1366 ha UAS and 6 AWU	16,7	20,5
B	Gras and grazings activities, under trees or not	Cattle	*Quercus ilex spp. rotundifolia* with high density	Inner zones, with low level of precipitation	Medium and small farms: 377 ha UAS and 2,42 AWU	26,7	31,8
C	Olive oil and vineyards systems and gras and grazings activities	Cattle and sheep	*Quercus ilex spp. rotundifolia* and *Quercus suber* with high density	Littoral zones with good level of precipitation	Small farms: 177 ha UAS and 6,43 AWU	13,3	6,8
D	Gras and grazings activities, under trees or not	Cattle and swine	*Quercus ilex spp. rotundifolia* with low density	High inner zones with good level of precipitation	Medium to big farms: 798 ha UAS and 4,21 AWU	23,3	33,7
E	Cereals and pastures, under trees or not	Cattle	*Quercus suber* with high density	Inner zones near littoral with good level of precipitation in Winter	Small farms: 107 ha UAS and 1,15 AWU	10	3,1
F	Cereals and pastures, under trees or not	Cattle	*Quercus ilex spp. rotundifolia* and *Quercus suber* with high density	Inner zones with low level of precipitation	Small to médium farms: 448 ha UAS and 3,05 AWU	10	4,1

Source: k-means analysis, done by the Évora University's Unit of Macroecology and Conservation.

When evaluating the level of invested capital by the annual working volume -measured in Annual Working Units (AWU) -, it can be seen that the majority of MAPS have a level between 235 and 287 €/AWU. Only MAPS type B and C are very different, the first one because it has a very higher value of 648 €/AWU and the second one because it has a much lower value of 132 €/AWU. The first case represents a production system where work use is much higher then on all the others MAPS, which is certainly related with the presence of vineyards and olive oil orchards that require working levels above the extensive systems based on cattle production or above systems completely mechanized based on crops production. On the contrary, in the second case, the production system is less exigent in what concerns working units.

Table 5. Invested capitals' structure for the representative MAPS

	Units	MAPS					
		A	B	C	D	E	F
Total assets or applied capital per ha UAA	€/ha	1155	4151	4774	1487	2523	1772
Total assets per AWU	thousand €/AWU	263	648	132	282	235	261
Fixed capital weight on total assets	€/€	0.91	0.96	0.92	0.90	0.88	0.85
Exploitation capital weight on total assets	€/€	0.09	0.04	0.08	0.10	0.12	0.15
Land weight on total fixed capital	€/€	0.35	0.62	0.72	0.48	0.44	0.39
Improvements weight on total fixed capital	€/€	0.16	0.07	0.10	0.15	0.06	0.26
Machinery and equipment weight on total fixed capital	€/€	0.05	0.20	0.14	0.19	0.35	0.16
Breeding cattle weight on total fixed capital	€/€	0.44	0.10	0.04	0.18	0.16	0.19

Source: Survey results.

The fixed capital (i.e. the production structure) weight in total invested capital it is a particularly important indicator to evaluate the system's capacity to generate net results. In general, almost 90% of MAPS's invested capital is fixed. The remaining 10% can eventually be linked with a weak capacity of generating net results. This financial structure's rigidity is one of the factors blocking structural changes. So, big structural adjustments can only happen if farmers appeal to indebtedness or sell patrimony.

Table 6. MAPS cost structure indicators

	Units	MAPS					
		A	B	C	D	E	F
Total real costs per ha UAA	€/ha	125	311	517	199	411	338
Fixed costs weight	€/€	0.31	0.47	0.57	0.45	0.43	0.52
Variable costs weigth	€/€	0.69	0.53	0.43	0.55	0.57	0.48
Depreciation weight on fixed costs	€/€	0.42	0.88	0.45	0.53	0.64	0.37
Work weight on fixed costs	€/€	0.58	0.11	0.53	0.31	0.22	0.37
Environmental costs	€/ha	79	126	125	90	182	131

Source: Survey results.

Table 7. MAPS profits structure indicators

	Units	DAPS					
		A	B	C	D	E	F
Total profits per ha UAA	€/ha	192	899	1032	279	613	426
Production value weight in total profits	€/€	0.64	0.57	0.82	0.50	0.33	0.48
Subsidies weight in total profits	€/€	0.36	0.43	0.18	0.50	0.67	0.52
First pillar weight in total subsidies	€/€	0.74	0.96	0.75	0.93	0.97	1.00
Second pillar weight in total subsidies	€/€	0.26	0.04	0.25	0.07	0.03	0.00

Source: Survey results.

Table 8. MAPS Entrepreneurial Gross and Net Return (EGR; ENR) per factor unit

	Units	MAPS					
		A	B	C	D	E	F
EGR / UAA	€/ha	83	716	646	127	313	153
ENR / UAA	€/ha	67	589	514	79	202	88
EGR / AUW	thousand €/AWU	19	112	18	24	29	22
ENR / AWU	thousand €/AWU	15	92	14	15	19	13
EGR/short-term costs	€/€	1.8	4.9	2.7	1.8	2.0	1.6
ENR/total costs	€/€	1.5	2.9	2.0	1.4	1.5	1.3

Source: Survey results.

On the fixed capital structure of all the MAPS agricultural and forestry lands have a high weight, always above 35% of total fixed capital. MAPS type C and F also have a high weight for capital invested in improvements (26% of fixed capital) and we also have to underline the high weight on fixed capital represented by breeding cattle on MAPS type A (44%), D (18%), and F (19%).

The costs structure analysis reflects the management actions took in each MAPS. The evaluation is made both in what concerns costs per area unit and also in what concerns the decisions took by the entrepreneur and consequently the associated costs.

The total real cost per area unit has a direct relation with agro-forestry production technology: it reflects the intensity in the use of capital by agro-forestry production.

The real cost per unit is between 125 €/ha on type A MAPS and 517 €/ha on type C MAPS. The gap between these values reflects distinct organization structures, land dimension and production technologies.

The lower values, under 200 €/ha, occur in big and medium agro-forestry farms with gras and grazings of inner zones (types A and D). In these MAPS, *Montado* has a very important role on reducing feeding costs, mainly in what concerns swine production.

The higher values occur in MAPS type C (517 €/ha) and E (411 €/ha). These are smaller MAPS, where scale economies are less evident, and that have production options are more capital demanding, as it is the case of vineyards (C) and durum wheat (E). Finally, production costs on MAPS type B (311 €/ha) and F (338 €/ha) are also high. These costs reflect not only the problem of scale economies, but particularly the use of more intensive production technologies, as it is the case of fodder activities (B) and durum wheat (F).

Almost all of these MAPS also have a high proportion of fixed costs in total costs, being over 50% in MAPS type C and F.

An excessive use of chemicals, mainly nitrates, pesticides, heavy machinery and high animal heads/ha is linked to a negative environmental impact of agro-forestry activities, namely water and soils contamination and soils erosion, which has as consequence the degradation of soils' structure. These environmental effects are diffuse and generally long-term effects, which makes their evaluation a complex task.

One of the methods that can be used for this evaluation is the assessment of costs with these polluting elements, such as agro-chemicals, fuels, energy or related elements.

For instance, agro-chemicals costs reflect the usage intensity of fertilizers and phyto-drugs on the agro-forestry production technology. So, a production system with higher costs with these factors might mean higher polluting effects, due to nitrates lixiviation and percolation and to pesticides residues in the soil. Its responsibility on soils and surface waters contamination is higher then a production system with lower costs in these factors.

Costs with fuels and energy are linked with the use and power of agricultural machinery (tractors, irrigation systems, etc.). Higher costs with these factors reveal a higher number of agricultural operations or the use of heavier and powerful equipment, more polluting and with worst effects in what concerns erosion and soil structure degradation.

The same method can be used to evaluate the environmental effects of animal herds. The indicator used for this was the cost with bought feed. This makes an indirect evaluation of animal herds effects. A production system with an adequate (in number of animals/ha) herd, in what concerns the environment, should allow the animals to be fed mainly from the farm products. In these circumstances, cost with bought feed is, of course, lower then in systems with higher number of animals/ha.

Results point to an environmental cost of the agro-forestry activity between 79 €/ha (MAPS type A) and 182 €/ha (MAPS type E). The first ones are the most extensive and bigger and on the other hand are the MAPS of small and medium farms, with production systems mainly cereals-pastures. It must be underlined that on these production systems (E and also F) the environmental cost is higher then in MAPS type C, with vineyards, olive orchards and gras and grazings.

Profits are the compensation for management actions took inside each MAPS to realize the agro-forestry activities. Of course, these compensations depend on many factors, such as farm dimension, resources quality and production technology. All these factors are differently reflected on production costs. There effects are particularly felt on the produced quantities and product quality, which influences the production value.

The profits level, beside being dependent on socio-structural characteristics that define each MAPS, also depends on the agents' participation on the different agro-forestry products markets and on the institutional income transferences. These are mainly due to CAP first and second pillars' subsidies, which corresponds to the incentives to production and income and incentives to rural development.

Total profits have the higher values on MAPS type C (1032 €/ha) and B (899 €/ha) and the lower values on MAPS type A (192 €/ha) and D (279 €/ha). In the middle, MAPS type E (613 €/ha) and F (426 €/ha) can be found.

In MAPS type C, profits come mainly from the production of wines VQPRD (quality wines produced in a determined region) and DOC (controlled denomination of origin). Subsidies in this case represent only 18% of total profits and are particularly linked with CAP first pillar. Nevertheless, CAP second pillar subsidies, linked with rural development actions, represent in this MAPS 25% of the institutional income transferences.

MAPS type B, E and F have the majority of their profits coming from cattle production and the subsidies linked to this production. These subsidies represent, respectively, 43%, 67% and 52% of these MAPS total profits, which shows these MAPS great dependence on public supports, 90% of which come from CAP's first pillar.

On MAPS type A and B, swine production represents a significant part of profits (almost 40%). Beside swine, cattle, with its associated subsidies, are the other important production.

On type A MAPS, subsidies represent 36% of total profits. Although the majority of these subsidies come from the first pillar, subsidies from the second pillar are also important (26%), especially compared with all the other MAPS. In the second case, the weight of supports on total profits is 50% and subsidies coming from CAP first pillar clearly dominate, being 96% of total public supports received by this MAPS.

Economic results are presented for short and long-term per surface unit (€/ha), annual working units (€/AWU) and in the form of cost/benefit ratio (€/€). This results presentation allows the evaluation of how real costs are covered and so the retribution for the entrepreneur own factors, which means it allows the evaluation of the economic viability of each MAPS and, simultaneously, the evaluation and discussion of the factors land, work and capital productivity, both in short and long-term.

All the studied MAPS have positive levels of real costs coverage. This indicates that, in any case, it is possible to achieve some return for the entrepreneur own factors, leading to the conclusion that these systems are viable from an economic point of view, considering the actual agricultural policy institutional framework.

MAPS type B is the one that better remunerates the entrepreneur own factors. ENR is 589 €/ha, 82 mil €/AWU and 2.9 €/€, referred to land, work or capital, respectively. These values are substantially higher then those obtained for the other MAPS. This difference has its origin in the efficiency of production costs, especially in cattle production, with low levels of working units (2.42 AWU) and good fertility rates. Another determining factor is subsidies that on average reach 400 €/ha.

After MAPS type B, type C is the one that has the highest values of ENR in what concerns productivity of land and capital. Most of the UAA is directed to the production of animal fodder activities. Nevertheless, vineyards are clearly the main economic activity, which justifies the good results in what concerns land and capital productivity.

The lower levels of the entrepreneur own factors retribution occurs in the big agro-forestry farms with extensive gras and grazings of the inner zones, classified as MAPS type A and B. The average productivity of land, work and capital, measured by ENR is 67 to 79 €/ha, 15 thousand €/ha and 1.5 €/€. In these cases, one should expect high average productivity for land and capital, since costs are relatively low when compared with other MAPS, but that doesn't happen because the production profits are also low, even considering the institutional income transferences.

Table 9. Results of the Policy Analysis Matrix for MAPS

	Profits	Costs	Net Return	Net Return*
Type A MAPS				
Private prices	192	125	67	16
Social prices	123	167	-43	-43
Policy effects and market failures	69	-41	110	59
Type B MAPS				
Private prices	899	311	589	216
Social prices	511	411	100	100
Policy effects and market failures	389	-100	489	116
Type C MAPS				
Private prices	1032	517	514	374
Social prices	846	801	45	45
Policy effects and market failures	185	-283	469	329
Type D MAPS				
Private prices	279	199	79	-50
Social prices	140	268	-128	-128
Policy effects and market failures	139	-69	208	78
Type E MAPS				
Private prices	613	411	202	-195
Social prices	202	502	-300	-300
Policy effects and market failures	410	-91	502	105
Type F MAPS				
Private prices	426	338	88	-134
Social prices	204	447	-243	-243
Policy effects and market failures	222	-109	331	109

* Net Return considering the effects of the CAP second pillar policies.

Source: Survey results.

The competitiveness and economic efficiency was studied using the PAM described earlier.

Table 9 presents the PAM results for the representative MAPS in Alentejo. The first Net Return column includes the actual policies effects (CAP first and second pillars) and the second Net Return column isolates the effects of Rural Development policy (CAP second pillar).

For A type MAPS, which represents the big agro-forestry farms of extensive gras and grazings of inner zones with low levels of precipitation, Net Return (NR) at private prices is 67 €/ha. This return is above social costs, estimated as 41 €/ha. Considering only the rural development policy measures of CAP second pillar, NR falls to 16 €/ha. Social prices analysis shows a negative NR, which indicates that profits generated by type A MAPS, in an open economy, are not enough to pay for all its production factors.

For B type MAPS, which correspond to medium and small farms with gras and grazings activities, under trees or not of inner zones, with low level of precipitation, NR at private prices is 589 €/ha, lowering to 216 €/ha when considering only the rural development policies impact. Social analysis also shows a positive NR (100 €/ha). The results allow the conclusion that type B MAPS generates profits that are enough to face all its costs, needing no public policy transferences.

C type MAPS, that portray small farms of littoral zones with good level of precipitation and a forest of *Quercus ilex spp. rotundifolia* and *Quercus suber* with high density, have a NR at private prices of 514 €/ha, decreasing to 374 €/ha when considering only the rural development policies. These results are largely over the social cost of factors (283 €/ha), the NR at social prices being 45 €/ha. So this MAPS, with an adequate return to all production factors without the effect of public policies, are economically sustainable.

In type D MAPS, medium to big farms with gras and grazings activities, under trees or not in high inner zones with good level of precipitation and a low density cover of *Quercus ilex spp. rotundifolia* the NR is 79 €/ha when we consider the global effect of public policies at private prices. This value is 10 €/ha above the social cost of factors but if only rural development policies are to be maintained the NR will decrease to a negative value (-50 €/ha). These MAPS generate enough profits to properly remunerate all its production factors considering the actual institutional policies but they present a negative profitability when only the rural development policies are considered. Its competitiveness is mainly linked to subsidies received via the policies of CAP first pillar.

With a NR at private prices of 202 €/ha, type E MAPS (that include small farms with cereals and pastures, under trees or not and important spots of *Quercus suber* with high density in the inner zones near littoral with good level of precipitation in Winter) in the actual policy context remunerate all the factors, including opportunity costs. Isolating the effects of rural development policy, NR becomes not only smaller then the 91 €/ha estimated for social costs, as it becomes negative (-195 €/ha). With an effective negative contribution to general economic growth, viability and competitiveness of these MAPS are guaranteed by supports to production and income given by CAP first pillar.

In the actual context of public policies that support the agro-forestry sector, in MAPS type F, that represent small to medium farms of cereals and pastures, under trees or not, with cattle and high densities on spots of *Quercus ilex spp. rotundifolia* and *Quercus suber*, a NR of 88 €/ha is obtained, smaller then the 109 €/ha estimated for social costs. In this case, profits cover the real costs of production but don't remunerate the resources opportunity costs. Isolating the effect of rural development policies, NR assumes a negative value (-134 €/ha).

To make results interpretation easier a classification of MAPS according to NR levels and agricultural policies measures effects was adopted:

- *Competitive and Efficient Systems* – NR is positive at private *and* social prices.
- *Competitive and Dependent on Subsidies Systems* – NR is negative at social prices but positive at private prices, being also generally above the social cost of resources; when rural development policies with environmental or territorial impacts are evaluated, the NR at private prices lowers under the social cost of resources.
- *Competitive and Environmentally Sustainable* – NR is negative at social prices, being positive and above the social cost of resources at private prices when only rural development policies are evaluated.

- *Viable and Dependent on Subsidies* - NR at social prices is negative being positive at private prices although under the social cost of resources. NR at private prices it is also negative when only the rural development policies are considered.
- *Viable and Environmentally Sustainable* – NR at social prices is negative being positive at private prices although under the social cost of resources when only the rural development policies are considered
- *Economically Impracticable* – NR is negative both at social as at private prices.

Table 10 presents the MAPS classification that shows, in what concerns competitiveness and sustainability, the results of PAM presented in Table 9.

Among Competitive and Efficient MAPS, type B and C can be found. These MAPS remain competitive even without institutional policies of income transference, being able to compete in international markets and efficiently contributing to the agro-forestry sector and economy growth.

Among Competitive and Dependent on Subsidies MAPS, type A, D and E can be found. In this case, competitiveness is maintained mainly due to direct subsidies to production and income, its maintenance being threatened by CAP evolution, being desirable its structural conversion to competitive and environmentally sustainable MAPS or, less likely, to competitive and efficient MAPS.

Finally, the group of Viable and Dependent on Subsidies MAPS, represented by type F. These MAPS are not competitive, as they don't remunerate their resources at opportunity cost level and there viability is linked to CAP's direct supports to production and income. Being more vulnerable then competitive and dependent on subsidies MAPS, its maintenance depends on its adjustment capacity, namely costs reductions and productions recovery.

Table 10. Classification of DAPS according its competitiveness and sustainability

Socio-Economic Models for *Montado* Agro-forestry Production Systems (DAPS)	
Competitive and Efficient	*Type B*, medium and small farms with gras and grazings activities, under trees or not of inner zones, with low level of precipitation; *Type C*, small farms of littoral zones with good level of precipitation and a forest of *Quercus ilex spp. rotundifolia* and *Quercus suber* with high density;
Competitive and Dependent on Subsidies	*Type A*, big agro-forestry farms of extensive gras and grazings of inner zones with low levels of precipitation; *Type D*, medium to big farms with gras and grazings activities, under trees or not in high inner zones with good level of precipitation and a low density cover of *Quercus ilex spp. rotundifolia*; *Type E*, small farms with cereals and pastures, under trees or not and important spots of *Quercus suber* with high density in the inner zones near littoral with good level of precipitation in Winter;
Viable and Dependent on Subsidies	*Type F*, small to medium farms of cereals and pastures, under trees or not, with cattle and high densities on spots of *Quercus ilex spp. rotundifolia* and *Quercus suber*;

Source: Table 9.

Table 11. PAM aggregate results for Alentejo

MAPS	Farms (%)	Total Área (%)
Competitive and Efficient	40	38,6
Competitive and Dependent on Subsidies	50	57,3
Viable and Dependent on Subsidies	10	4,1

Source: Table 4 and Table 10.

Table 11 presents the aggregated results of PAM to all Alentejo, depending on the number of farms and its area.

Competitive and Dependent on Subsidies MAPS are dominant in Alentejo, representing half of the agro-forestry farms of the region and almost 60% of its area. On the second place, we have the Competitive and Efficient MAPS, with almost 40% of the farms and area. Finally, there are the Viable and Dependent on Subsidies MAPS, representing almost 10% of the farms and 4% of the area. So, the competitiveness of the main part of Alentejo agro-forestry farms depends on institutional supports to production and income, given by CAP's first pillar. Nevertheless, it must be underlined that a majority is sustainable from an economic point of view and has an effective contribution to economic growth, even without the support of income transference public policies.

CONCLUSION

The identification and economic evaluation of *Montado* socio-economic models led to the analysis of representative MAPS's viability, competitiveness and economic efficiency. The viability analysis had the main objective of evaluate how real costs were covered by profits and which was the remuneration of the producer's own resources – land, capital and entrepreneurship capacity, reflected in the directive work function and on the capacity to assume risks. This analysis was based on indicators that evaluate the applied capitals' structure, the costs and profits structure and the Net Entrepreneurial Return. To evaluate the competitiveness and economic efficiency of MAPS a Policy Analysis Matrix (PAM) was used. This methodology allows the simultaneous evaluation the MAPS competitiveness and their efficient contribution to economic growth, as well as the institutional income transferences.

It can be said, in general, that the technical-economic orientation of MAPS is more directed to animal production, especially cattle and swine. Soil occupation is determined by the climatic factors that are specific of each region, the forest characteristics and the kind of animal breeds in presence. The more favourable economic framework in what concerns public supports determines the animal production's importance, which is also linked with the competitive advantages of the territory, where acorn production and large areas of increased and spontaneous pastures play a crucial role on the animals' feeding costs reduction.

The capital applied per surface unit is in general lower on the MAPS with higher surfaces. Almost 90% of these capitals are assets, which conduct to a low short-run liquidity; this fact might become a blocking factor to eventual structural changes. In these assets' structure agriculture and forestry land have a very high weight.

The higher real costs of production occur on smaller MAPS, which is linked to important scale economies on the bigger MAPS that are also oriented to extensive production systems. The environmental costs of MAPS varies between 79 and 182 €/ha, from bigger and more extensive MAPS to small and medium MAPS with production systems cereals-pastures.

The institutional income transferences represent a significant part of MAPS incomes, which reveals a strong dependence on public supports. These supports are mainly from CAP's first pillar. The studied MAPS profits are enough to cover their respective production real costs allowing some return to the entrepreneur own factors, leading to the conclusion that they are economically viable on the actual institutional policy framework.

In what concerns competitiveness and economic efficiency, Alentejo has a predominance of MAPS that are competitive but dependent on subsidies – half of agro-forestry farms of the region with more then 100 ha and almost 2/3 of its surface are in this situation. Competitive and efficient MAPS are represented by 40% of the agro-forestry farms with more then 100 ha and almost 40% of its surface. At last, there are some MAPS that are viable, but dependent on subsidies, represented by 10% of the agro-forestry farms with more then 100 ha and more or less 4% of the Alentejo's surface.

It can be concluded that the competitiveness of the majority of Alentejo's MAPS depends on institutional subsidies to production and income, from CAP's first pillar. It would be desirable that these MAPS could benefit, in the future, of supports linked with CAP's second pillar, which would imply some adjustments to adequate technologies and production options to a territorial perspective of rural development and environmental resources preservation. In general, these adjustments are possible to do as in the majority of these MAPS agro-forestry production is already oriented to extensive production systems - with production costs relatively low and products with recognized quality standards that have a valuing potential in the market -, and the technologies used allow the maintenance of the ecosystem environmental conditions. Regarding the new CAP paradigm, the multifunctionality of European agriculture, these ecosystems maintenance is likely to be supported for their undeniable value as carbon fixers and biomass accumulators. They are also a success example of the link that can be established between humans and nature, with the environment providing the raw ecological material, and humans decoding and exploiting it and leading to differences on biodiversity, species distribution, management practices and, of course, cultural landscape.

ANNEX 1.

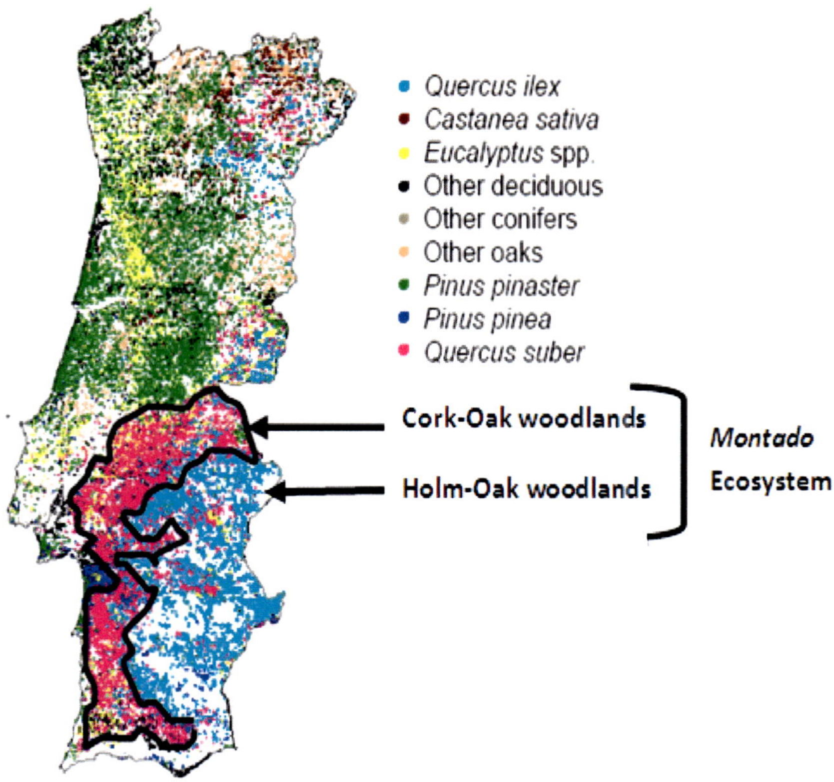

Distribution of the *Montado* Ecosystem in Portugal.

REFERENCES

Abreu, J. V. 1987. Sheep as a competitive livestock enterprise in Missouri. Columbia, *Master thesis*, Missouri University.

Avillez, F. & A. Queiroz. 1987. A competitividade da beterraba sacarina no contexto da agricultura dos vales do Tejo e Sorraia. *Revista de Ciências Agrárias*, vol. n.º3: 5-21.

Avillez, F. & Carrilho. 1988. A. Situação actual e competitividade futura das explorações agrícolas portuguesas. Évora, *Actas do Seminário EEC Agricultural Markets and Policy*, 19.1-19.44.

Baysan, T. 1984. Resource shifts under tariff liberazation and Turkey's comparative advantage in agriculture. *European Review of Agricultural Economics*, 11 (3).

Bureau, J. & J. P. Butuault. 1990. Competitivité des agricultures et advantages nationaux de prix dans la CEE : différentiels de productivité et PPA spécifiques sur la base des coûts de production des grands produits agricoles. *VIth European Congress of Agricultural Economists*, Hague, pp.93-106.

Carrión, J. S., I. Parra, C. Navarro, & M. Munera. 2000. Past distribution and ecology of the cork oak (*Quercus suber*) in the Iberian Peninsula: a pollen-analytical approach. *Diversity and Distributions* 6:29–44.

De Miguel, J. M. 1999. Naturaleza y configuración del paisaje agrosilvopastoral en la conservación de la diversidad biológica en España. *Revista Chilena de Historia Natural* 72:547–557.

Drew, W., J. Alavalapati, & P. Nair. 2005 Determining Agroforestry Profitability Using the Policy Analysis Matrix. A Case Study from Pohnpei, Federated States of Micronesia. *Valuing Agroforestry Systems, Advances in Agroforestry* Book Series, Alavalapati and Mercer (Eds), Volume 2, Kluwer Academic Publishers, Springer Netherlands.

Ezeala-Harrison, F. 1997. Agricultural Policy in Kenya: Applications of the Policy Analysis Matrix, *Canadian Journal of African Studies / Revue Canadienne des Études Africaines*, Vol. 31, No. 1 (1997), pp. 186-188.

Fang, C. & J. Beghin 2000. Food Self-sufficiency comparative advantages and Agricultural Trade: A police Analysis matrix for Chinese Agriculture, *Working Paper* 99-WP 223, Center for Agricultural and Rural Development and Department of Economics, Iowa State University, USA.

Fox, R. 1987. *Extensive farming in Alentejo in Portuguese Agriculture in Transition.* Ithaca, USA, Scott R. Pearson Eds, Cornell University Press.

Jaraba, C. & R. Thompson. 1980. Agricultural comparative advantage under international price uncertainty: the case of Senegal. *American Journal of Agricultural Economics*, 188-198.

Joffre, R., S. Rambal, & J. P. Ratte. 1999. The *Montado* system of southern Spain and Portugal as a natural ecosystem mimic. *Agroforestry Systems* 45:57–79.

Kydd J., R. Pearce, & M. Stockbridge. 1997. The Economic Analysis of Commodity Systems: Extending the Policy Analysis Matrix to Account for Environmental Effects and Transactions Costs. *Agricultural Systems*, Volume 55, Number 2, October, pp. 323-345(23)

Lourenço, N., T. Pinto-Correia, M.R. Jorge, & C. R. Machado. 1998. Farming strategies and land use changes in southern Portugal: land abandonment or extensification of the traditional systems? *Mediterrâneo* 12/13:191–208.

Lucas, M. 1995. A competitividade da produção de borrego no Alentejo. *PhD thesis*, Universidade de Évora, Évora, Portugal,

Lucas, M.; R. Fragoso & L. Coelho. 2005. Caracterização Sócio-Económica da Região Alentejo", *Relatório da 2ª fase do Projecto Interreg Desarollo de un sistema de información para la gestión ambiental y económica del ecosistema Montado/Montado en Extremadura y Alentejo.*

Marques, C. 1988. Portuguese Entrance Into The European Community: Implications For Dryland Agriculture In The Alentejo Region. 274 p. *PhD Tesis*. Purdue University. West Lafayette, U.S.A.

Marques, C., M. B. Martins & R. Lucas. 1995. A reforma da PAC e a competitividade da agricultura regional. *Feira do Alentejo/95- 12ª Ovibeja*, Beja, 23 de Março.

Marques, C, R. Fragoso & M. R. Lucas. 2005. Agricultura e Recursos Agro-Alimentares. *Plano Regional de Inovação do Alentejo*, Edição CCDR-Alentejo Comissão de Coordenação e Desenvolvimento Regional do Alentejo, ISBN 972-644-112-9, pp 15-81.

Martin, F. P. 1989. Food security and comparative advantage in Senegal: a micro-macro approach, *PhD thesis*, Michigan State University, USA.

Martins, M. B. & C. Marques. 2006. Methodological Aspects of a Mathematical Programming Model to Evaluate Soil Tillage Technologies in a Risky Environment. *European Journal of Operational Research*, Vol. 177/1 pp. 556-571.

Mattas, K. 1990. Competitiveness of EC'S agriculture an intra-EC analysis. *VIth European Congress of Agricultural Economists,* Hague, pp. 108-120.

Maza, M. T., Olaizola, Manrique & Hamrouni, S. 1992. Influence of production and economic factors on the comparative advantages of sheep production systems in the EEC, Dep. Agricultura y Economia Agraria, Universidad de Zaragoza, Zaragoza.

Michalek J. 1995. An application of the policy analysis matrix for an evaluation of agricultural policies in the Slovak republic, *Oxford Development Studies*, Volume 23, Issue 2, pages 177 - 196.

Mohanty, S., Fang, Cheng & J. Chaudhary 2003. Assessing the Competitiveness of Indian Cotton Production: A Policy Analysis Matrix Approach. *The Journal of Cotton Science* 7:65–74 (2003) 65, http://journal.cotton.org.

Pearson, S. & R. Meyer. 1974. Comparative advantage among African coffee producers. *American Journal of Agricultural Economics*, 56: 310-313.

Pearson, S., F. Avillez, J. W. Bentley, T. Finan, R. Fox, T. Josling, Longworthy, E. Monke and S. Tangermann. 1987. *Portuguese Agriculture in Transition*. Nova Icrque and Ithaca, Cornell University Press.

Pearson, S. & E. Monke. 1989. *The Policy Analysis Matrix for Agricultural Development*. 279 p. Ithaca and London, Cornell University Press.

Pearson, S., C. Gotsch & S. Bahri 2003. Applications of the Policy Analysis Matrix in Indonesian Agriculture. http://www.stanford.edu/group/FRI/indonesia/newregional/newbook.htm#_ftn1

Pereira, P. M. & M. Pires da Fonseca. 2003. Nature vs. nurture: the making of the montado ecosystem. *Conservation Ecology* 7(3): 7. [online] URL: http://www.consecol.org/vol7/iss3/art7/

Pinto-Correia, T. 1993. Threatened landscape in Alentejo, Portugal: the montado and other agro-sylvo-pastoral systems. *Landscape and Urban Planning* 24:43–48.

Pinto-Correia, T., & J. Mascarenhas 1999. Contribution to the extensification / intensification debate: new trends in the Portuguese montado. *Landscape and Urban Planning* 46:125–131.

Ramanovich, M. 2007. Policy Analysis Matrix: an analysis of dairy sector in Belarus. paper presented at MACE Summer School, July, Budapest.

Santana, E. 1986. A produção leiteira açoreana face à concorrência internacional: as vantagens comparativas, *PhD thesis*, Universidade dos Açores, Angra do Heroísmo.

Stevenson, A. C. 1985a. Studies in the vegetational history of S.W. Spain. I. Modern pollen rain in the Doñana National Park, Huelva. *Journal of Biogeography* 12:243-268

Stevenson, A. C. 1985b. Studies in the vegetational history of S.W. Spain. II. Palynological investigations at Laguna de las Madres, SW Spain. *Journal of Biogeography* 12:293-314

Stevenson, A. C. & R. J. Harrison. 1992. Ancient forests in Spain: a modelfor land-use and dry forest management in South-west Spain from 4000 BC to 1900 AD. *Proceedings of the Prehistoric Society* 58:227-247.

Tadeo, A., E. Martinez & V. Estruch 2007. Assessing profitability in rice cultivation using the policy analysis matrix and profit-efficient data, *Papeles de trabajo del Instituto de Estudios Fiscales. Serie economía*, ISSN 1578-0252, N° 10, pags. 3-24.

Tenhunen, J., Geyer, R., Banza, J., Besson, C., Carreiras, J., Dinh, NQ, Herd, A., Mirzae, H., Otieno, D., Owen, K., Pereira, J. S., Reichstein, M., Ribeiro, N., Schmidt, M., Wenigmann, M., & Xiao, X. 2007. Assessing Ecology, Vulnerability and Ecosystem Services of Mediterranean Oak Woodlands, Non Published paper.

Venturini, L. 1989. Teorie del commercio internazionale e determinanti della competitivitá: un quadro conceptuale per l'analisi degli scambi agro-alimentari, *Rivista di Economia Agraria*, vol. 44 (1): 3-24.

Winter-Nelson, A. 1991. *Applications of the Policy Analysis Matrix* (PAM). Workpackage, NO. 91-[4], /00058474, The Economic Development Institute of the World Bank.

In: Natural Resources
Editor: Jeanette B. Pauling

ISBN 978-1-60456-982-7

Chapter 2

FEDERAL LAND MANAGEMENT AGENCIES: BACKGROUND ON LAND AND RESOURCES MANAGEMENT*

Carol Hardy Vincent

SUMMARY

The federal government owns about 671.8 million acres (29.6%) of the 2.27 billion acres of land in the United States. Four agencies administer 628.4 million acres (93.5%) of this land: the Forest Service in the Department of Agriculture, and the Bureau of Land Management, Fish and Wildlife Service, and National Park Service, all in the Department of the Interior. Most of these lands are in the West, including Alaska. They generate revenues for the U.S. Treasury, some of which are shared with states and localities. The agencies receive funding from annual Interior and Related Agencies appropriations laws, trust funds, and special accounts.

The lands administered by the four agencies are managed for a variety of purposes, primarily related to preservation, recreation, and development of natural resources. Yet, each of these agencies has distinct responsibilities for the lands and resources it administers. The Bureau of Land Management (BLM) manages 261.5 million acres, and is responsible for 700 million acres of subsurface mineral resources. BLM has a multiple-use, sustained-yield mandate that supports a variety of uses and programs, including energy development, timber harvesting, recreation, grazing, wild horses and burros, cultural resources, and conservation. The Forest Service (FS) manages 192.5 million acres also for multiple use and sustained yields of various products and services, for example, timber harvesting, recreation, grazing, watershed protection, and fish and wildlife habitats. Most of the lands are designated national forests, but there are national grasslands and other lands. National forests now are created and modified by acts of Congress. Both the BLM and FS have several authorities to acquire and dispose of lands.

The Fish and Wildlife Service (FWS) manages 95.4 million acres, primarily to conserve and protect animals and plants. The 793 units of the National Wildlife Refuge System include

* Excerpted from CRS Report 1-60021-151-8, dated August 2, 2004.

refuges, waterfowl production areas, and wildlife coordination units. Units can be created by an act of Congress or executive order, and the FWS also may acquire lands for migratory bird purposes. The National Park Service (NPS) manages 79.0 million acres of federal land (and oversees another 5.4 million acres of nonfederal land) to conserve and interpret lands and resources and make them available for public use. Activities that harvest or remove resources generally are prohibited. The National Park System has diverse units ranging from historical structures to cultural and natural areas. Units are created by an act of Congress, but the President may proclaim national monuments.

There also are three special management systems that include lands from more than one agency. The National Wilderness Preservation System consists of 105.2 million acres of protected wilderness areas designated by Congress. The National Wild and Scenic Rivers System contains 11,303 miles of wild, scenic, and recreational rivers, primarily designated by Congress and managed to preserve their free-flowing condition. The National Trails System contains four classes of trails managed to provide recreation and access to outdoor areas and historic resources.

ABBREVIATIONS

RSI: Resources, Science, and Industry;
INF: Information Research;
ALD: American Law

INTRODUCTION [1]: SCOPE AND ORGANIZATION

This article provides an overview of how federal lands and resources are managed, the agencies that manage the lands, the authorities under which these lands are managed, and some of the issues associated with federal land management. The article is divided into nine sections. The introduction provides a brief historical review and general background on the federal lands. "Federal Lands Financing" describes revenues derived from activities on federal lands; the appropriation processes and the trust funds and special accounts that fund these agencies; federal land acquisition funding, especially from the Land and Water Conservation Fund; and programs that compensate state and local governments for the tax-exempt status of federal lands. The next sections pertain to the four major federal land management agencies: the Forest Service (FS) in the Department of Agriculture, and the Bureau of Land Management (BLM), Fish and Wildlife Service (FWS), and National Park Service (NPS), all in the Department of the Interior. The sections relate each agency's history; organizational structure; management responsibilities; procedures for land acquisition, disposal, and designation, where relevant; current issues; and statutory authorities. The final sections provide essentially the same information for the three major protection systems that are administered by more than one agency and hence cross agency jurisdictions: the National Wilderness Preservation System, the National Wild and Scenic Rivers System, and the National Trails System. Relevant CRS reports are listed following each section. The article concludes with an appendix of acronyms used in the text, and another defining selected terms used.

BACKGROUND

The federal government owns and manages approximately 671.8 million acres of land in the United States — 29.6% of the total land base of 2.27 billion acres. [2] Table 1 identifies the acreage of federal land located in each state and the District of Columbia. The figures range from 5,318 acres of federal land in Rhode Island to 243,847,037 federal acres in Alaska. Further, while a dozen states contain less than ½ million acres of federal land, another dozen have more than 10 million federal acres within their borders. Table 1 also identifies the total size of each state, and the percentage of land in each state that is federally owned. These percentages point to significant variation in the size of the federal presence within states. Specifically, the figures range from 0.5% of Connecticut land that is federally owned to 91.9% of land in Nevada that is federally owned. All 12 states where the federal government owns the most land are located in the West (including Alaska).

Four agencies administer about 628.4 million acres (93.5%) of the 671.8 million acres of federal land. [3] These four agencies are the Forest Service, Bureau of Land Management, Fish and Wildlife Service, and National Park Service. [4] The BLM has jurisdiction over approximately 261.5 million acres (38.9%) of the federal total. The FS has jurisdiction over approximately 192.5 million acres (28.7%) of the total federal acreage. The FWS administers approximately 95.4 million acres (14.2%). The National Park Service (NPS) administers about 79.0 million acres of federal land (11.8%), and oversees another 5.4 million acres of nonfederal land, for a total of about 84.4 million federal and nonfederal acres. Figure 1 shows the percent of land managed by each agency, and Table 2 displays the acreage for each of these four agencies in each state, the District of Columbia, and the territories. The lands administered by these four agencies are managed for a variety of purposes, primarily relating to the preservation, recreation, and development of natural resources. Although there are some similarities among the agencies, each agency has a distinct mission and special responsibilities for the lands under its jurisdiction.

The majority of the 671.8 million acres of federal lands are in the West, a result of early treaties and land settlement laws and patterns. Management of these lands is often controversial, especially in states where the federal government is a predominant or majority landholder and where competing and conflicting uses of the lands are at issue.

HISTORICAL REVIEW

The nation's lands and resources have been important in American history, adding to the strength and stature of the federal government, serving as an attraction and opportunity for settlement and economic development, and providing a source of revenue for schools, transportation, national defense, and other national, state, and local needs.

Table 1. Federally Owned Land by State, as of September 30, 2003

State	Total Acreage in State	Acreage of Federally Owned Land in State	% of Land Federally Owned in State
Alabama	32,678,400	1,202,614	3.7
Alaska	365,481,600	243,847,037	66.7
Arizona	72,688,000	36,494,844	50.2
Arkansas	33,599,360	3,955,959	11.8
California	100,206,720	46,979,891	46.9
Colorado	66,485,760	23,174,340	34.9
Connecticut	3,135,360	15,212	0.5
Delaware	1,265,920	29,488	2.3
District of Columbia	39,040	10,284	26.3
Florida	34,721,280	4,605,762	13.3
Georgia	37,295,360	2,314,386	6.2
Hawaii	4,105,600	671,580	16.4
Idaho	52,933,120	35,135,709	66.4
Illinois	35,795,200	651,603	1.8
Indiana	23,158,400	534,126	2.3
Iowa	35,860,480	302,601	0.8
Kansas	52,510,720	641,562	1.2
Kentucky	25,512,320	1,706,562	6.7
Louisiana	28,867,840	1,501,735	5.2
Maine	19,847,680	164,003	0.8
Maryland	6,319,360	192,692	3.0
Massachusetts	5,034,880	105,973	2.1
Michigan	36,492,160	3,638,588	10.0
Minnesota	51,205,760	3,534,989	6.9
Mississippi	30,222,720	2,101,204	7.0
Missouri	44,248,320	2,237,951	5.1
Montana	93,271,040	29,239,058	31.3
Nebraska	49,031,680	1,458,802	3.0
Nevada	70,264,320	64,589,139	91.9
New Hampshire	5,768,960	830,232	14.4
New Jersey	4,813,440	180,189	3.7
New Mexico	77,766,400	26,518,360	34.1
New York	30,680,960	242,441	0.8
North Carolina	31,402,880	3,602,080	11.5
North Dakota	44,452,480	1,333,375	3.0
Ohio	26,222,080	457,697	1.7
Oklahoma	44,087,680	1,331,457	3.0
Oregon	61,598,720	30,638,949	49.7
Pennsylvania	28,804,480	724,925	2.5
Rhode Island	677,120	5,318	0.8
South Carolina	19,374,080	1,236,214	6.4
South Dakota	48,881,920	2,314,007	4.7

Tennessee	26,727,680	2,016,138	7.5
Texas	168,217,600	3,171,757	1.9
Utah	52,696,960	35,024,927	66.5
Vermont	5,936,640	450,017	7.6
Virginia	25,496,320	2,617,226	10.3
Washington	42,693,760	13,246,559	31.0
West Virginia	15,410,560	1,266,422	8.2
Wisconsin	35,011,200	1,981,781	5.7
Wyoming	62,343,040	31,531,537	50.6
Total	**2,271,343,360**	**671,759,298**	**29.6**

Source: U.S. General Services Administration, Overview of the United States Government's Owned and Leased Real Property: Federal Real Property Profile as of September 30, 2003. See Table 16, GSA website at [http://www.gsa.gov/gsa/cm_attachments/GSA_DOCUMENT/Annual%20Report %20%20FY2003-R4_R2M -n11_0Z5RDZ-i34K-pR.pdf], visited March 8, 2004. The data do not include trust properties or Department of Defense land outside the United States.

The formation of our current federal government was particularly influenced by the struggle for control over what were known as the "western" lands — the lands between the Appalachian Mountains and the Mississippi River claimed by the original colonies. Prototypical land laws enacted by the Continental Congress, such as the Land Ordinance of 1785 [5] and the Northwest Ordinance of 1787, [6] established the federal system of rectangular land surveying for disposal and set up a system for developing territorial governments leading to statehood. During operation of the Articles of Confederation, the states that then owned the western lands were reluctant to cede them to the developing new government, but eventually acquiesced. This, together with granting constitutional powers to the new federal government, including the authority to regulate federal property and to create new states, played a crucial role in transforming the weak central government under the Articles of Confederation into a stronger, centralized federal government under our Constitution.

The new Congress, which first met in 1789, enacted land statutes similar to those enacted by the Continental Congress. Subsequent federal land laws reflected two visions: reserving some federal lands (such as for national forests and national parks) and selling or otherwise disposing of other lands to raise money or to encourage transportation, development, and settlement. From the earliest days, these policy clashes took on East/West overtones, with easterners more likely to view the lands as national public property, and westerners more likely to view the lands as necessary for local use and development. Most agreed, however, on measures that promoted settlement of the lands to pay soldiers, to reduce the national debt, and to strengthen the nation. This settlement trend accelerated after the Louisiana Purchase in 1803, the Oregon Compromise with England in 1846, and cession of lands by treaty after the Mexican war in 1848. [7]

During the mid- to late 1800s, Congress passed numerous laws that encouraged and accelerated the settlement of the West by disposing of federal lands. Examples include the Homestead Act of 1862 [8] and the Desert Lands Entry Act of 1877.

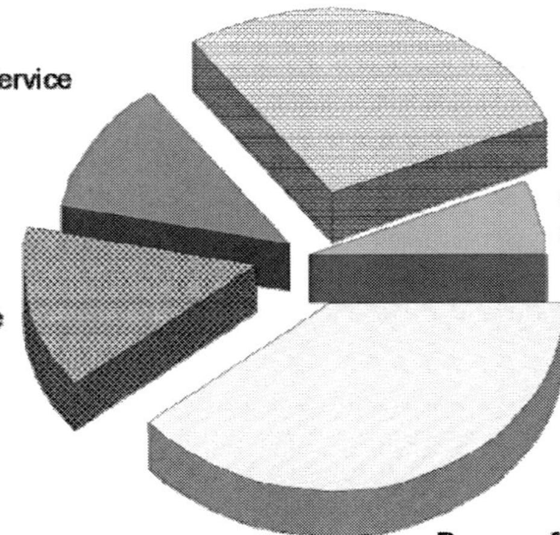

Note: Percentages do not add to 100% due to rounding.

Figure 1. Agency Jurisdiction Over Federally Owned Land in the United States.

Approximately 815.9 million acres of the public domain lands were transferred to private ownership between 1781 and 2002. Another 328.5 million acres were granted to the states generally, and an additional 127.5 million were granted in Alaska under state and native selection laws. [9] Most transfers to private ownership (97%) occurred before 1940; homestead entries, for example, peaked in 1910 at 18.3 million acres but dropped below 200,000 acres annually after 1935, until being totally eliminated in 1986. [10]

Certain other federal laws were "catch up" laws designed to legitimize certain uses that already were occurring on the federal lands. These laws typically acknowledged local variations and customs. For example, the General Mining Law of 1872 recognized mineral claims on the public domain lands in accordance with local laws and customs, and provided for the conveyance of title to such lands. In addition, early land disposal laws allowed states to determine the rights of settlers to use and control water. The courts later determined, however, that the federal government could also reserve or create federal water rights for its own properties and purposes.

Although some earlier laws had protected some lands and resources, such as timber needed for military use, other laws in the late 1800s reflected the growing concern that rapid development threatened some of the scenic treasures of the nation, as well as resources that would be needed for future use. A preservation and conservation movement evolved to ensure that certain lands and resources were left untouched or reserved for future use. For example, Yellowstone National Park was established in 1872 [11] to preserve its resources in a natural condition, and to dedicate recreation opportunities for the public. It was the world's first national park, [12] and like the other early parks, Yellowstone was protected by the U.S. Army — primarily from poachers of wildlife or timber. In 1891, concern over the effects of timber harvests on water supplies and downstream flooding led to the creation of forest reserves (renamed national forests in 1907).

Table 2. Acreage Managed by Federal Agencies, by State

State	Forest Service	National Park Service	Fish and Wildlife Service	Bureau of Land Management
Alabama	665,978	16,917	59,528	111,369
Alaska	21,980,905	51,106,274	76,774,229	85,953,625
Arizona	11,262,350	2,679,731	1,726,280	11,651,958
Arkansas	2,591,897	101,549	361,331	295,185
California	20,741,229	7,559,121	472,338	15,128,485
Colorado	14,486,977	653,137	84,649	8,373,504
Connecticut	24	6,775	872	0
Delaware	0	0	26,126	0
Dist. of Col.	0	6,949	0	0
Florida	1,152,913	2,482,441	977,997	26,899
Georgia	864,623	40,771	480,634	0
Hawaii	1	353,292	299,380	0
Idaho	20,465,345	761,448	92,165	11,846,931
Illinois	293,016	12	140,236	224
Indiana	200,240	11,009	64,613	0
Iowa	0	2,708	112,794	378
Kansas	108,175	731	58,695	0
Kentucky	809,449	94,169	9,078	0
Louisiana	604,505	14,541	545,452	321,734
Maine	53,040	76,273	61,381	0
Maryland	0	44,482	45,030	548
Massachusetts	0	33,891	16,797	0
Michigan	2,865,103	632,368	115,244	74,807
Minnesota	2,839,693	142,863	547,421	146,658
Mississippi	1,171,158	108,417	226,039	56,212
Missouri	1,487,307	63,436	70,859	2,094
Montana	16,923,153	1,221,485	1,328,473	7,964,623
Nebraska	352,252	5,909	178,331	6,354
Nevada	5,835,284	777,017	2,389,616	47,874,294
New Hampshire	731,942	15,399	15,822	0
New Jersey	0	38,505	71,197	0
New Mexico	9,417,693	379,042	385,052	13,362,538
New York	16,211	37,114	29,081	0
North Carolina	1,251,674	394,833	423,948	0
North Dakota	1,105,977	71,650	1,566,026	59,642
Ohio	236,360	20,552	8,875	0
Oklahoma	399,528	10,200	170,032	2,136
Oregon	15,665,881	197,301	572,590	16,125,145
Pennsylvania	513,399	51,239	10,048	0
Rhode Island	0	5	2,179	0
South Carolina	616,970	27,488	162,958	0
South Dakota	2,013,447	263,644	1,300,465	274,960

Table 2. (Continued)

State	Forest Service	National Park Service	Fish and Wildlife Service	Bureau of Land Management
Tennessee	700,764	362,133	116,966	0
Texas	755,363	1,184,046	534,319	11,833
Utah	8,180,405	2,099,083	112,027	22,867,896
Vermont	389,200	21,513	33,230	0
Virginia	1,662,124	336,950	132,989	805
Washington	9,273,381	1,933,972	344,956	402,355
West Virginia	1,033,882	62,707	18,595	0
Wisconsin	1,525,978	74,010	236,470	159,982
Wyoming	9,238,067	2,393,281	101,857	18,354,151
Territories	28,149	33,179	1,766,965	0
Total	**192,511,012**	**79,005,557**	**95,382,237**	**261,457,325**

Sources: For FS: See the FS website at [http://www.fs.fed.us/land/staff/lar/LAR03/table4.htm], visited April 1, 2004. Data are current as of September 30, 2003. They reflect land managed by the FS that is within the National Forest System, including national forests, national grasslands, purchase units, land utilization projects, experimental areas, and other land areas, water areas, and interests in lands.

For NPS: U.S. Dept. of the Interior, National Park Service, Land Resources Division, *National Park Service, Listing of Acreage by State, as of 12/31/2003*, unpublished document. The data consist of all federal lands managed by the NPS. For information on acreage by type of unit as of September 30, 2003, see the NPS website at [http://www2.nature.nps.gov/stats/acresum03cy.pdf], visited April 1, 2004.

For FWS: U.S. Dept. of the Interior, Fish and Wildlife Service, *Annual Report of Lands Under Control of the U.S. Fish and Wildlife Service, as of September 30, 2002*. They comprise all land managed by the FWS, whether the agency has sole, primary, or secondary jurisdiction, and include acres under agreements, easements, and leases. For more information, see the FY2002 Annual Report of Lands on the FWS website at [http://realty.fws.gov/brochures.html], visited April 1, 2004.

For BLM: U.S. Dept. of the Interior, Bureau of Land Management, *Public Land Statistics, 2002*, and are current as of September 30, 2002. The data consist of lands managed exclusively by BLM, including certain types of surveyed and unsurveyed public and ceded Indian lands as well as withdrawn or reserved lands. For more information, see the BLM website at [http://www.blm.gov/natacq/pls02/], visited April 1, 2004.

The creation of national parks and forest reserves laid the foundation for the current development of federal agencies with primary purposes of managing natural resources on federal lands. For example, in 1905, responsibility for management of the forest reserves was joined with forestry research and assistance in a new Forest Service within the Department of Agriculture. The National Park Service was created in 1916 [13] to manage the growing number of parks established by Congress and monuments proclaimed by the President. The first national wildlife refuge was proclaimed in 1903, although it was not until 1966 that the refuges coalesced into the National Wildlife Refuge System. The Grazing Service (Department of the Interior, first known as the Grazing Division) was established in 1934 to administer grazing on public rangelands. It was combined with the General Land Office in 1946 to form the Bureau of Land Management (BLM). [14]

In addition to the conservation laws and activities noted above, emphasis shifted during the 20th century from the disposal and conveyance of title to private citizens to the retention and management of the remaining federal lands. Some laws provided for sharing revenues from various uses of the federal lands with the states containing the lands. Examples include the Mineral Leasing Act of 1920, [15] which provides for the leased development of certain federal minerals, and the Taylor Grazing Act of 1934, which provides for permitted private livestock grazing on public lands. [16]

During debates on the Taylor Grazing Act, some western Members of Congress acknowledged the poor prospects for relinquishing federal lands to the states, but language included in the act left this question open. It was not until the passage of the Federal Land Policy and Management Act of 1976 (FLPMA, P.L. 94-579, 43 U.S.C. §§1701, et seq.) that Congress expressly declared that the remaining public domain lands generally would remain in federal ownership. [17] This declaration of policy was a significant factor in what became known as the Sagebrush Rebellion, an effort that started in the late 1970s to take state or local control of federal land and management decisions. To date, judicial challenges and legislative and executive attempts to make significant changes to federal ownership have proven unsuccessful. Current authorities for acquiring and disposing of federal lands are unique to each agency, and are described in subsequent chapters of this article.

Issues

Since the cession to the federal government of the western lands of several of the original 13 colonies, many issues and conflicts have recurred. Ownership continues to be debated, with some advocating increased disposal of federal lands to state or private ownership, and others supporting retention of federal lands by the federal government. Still others promote acquisition by the federal government of additional land, including through an increased, and more stable, funding source. A related issue is determining the optimal division of resources between federal acquisition of new lands and maintenance of existing federal lands and facilities.

Another focus is whether federal lands should be managed primarily to produce national benefits or benefits primarily for the localities and states in which the lands are located. Who decides these issues, and how the decisions are made, also are at issue. Some would like to see more local control of land and a reduced federal role, while others seek to maintain or enhance the federal role in land management to represent the interests of all citizens.

The extent to which federal lands should be made available for development, preserved, and opened to recreation has been controversial. Significant differences of opinion exist on the amount of traditional commercial development that should be allowed, particularly involving energy development, grazing, and timber harvesting. How much land to accord enhanced protection, what type of protection to accord, and who should protect federal lands are continuing questions. Whether and where to restrict recreation, either generally or for such uses as motorized off-road vehicles, also is a focus of debate.

The debate over land uses perhaps has intensified with the increase over the decades in visitors to federal lands. Current agency figures on visitor use point to recreation as a fast-growing use of agency lands overall. For FY2003, recreation visits totaled 265 million for the

National Park System, 53 million for BLM lands, and 39 million for the National Wildlife Refuge System. For FY2002, recreation visits to the National Forest System totaled 211 million.

CRS Reports and Committee Prints [18]

CRS Issue Brief IB10076, *Bureau of Land Management (BLM) Lands and National Forests*, coordinated by Ross W. Gorte and Carol Hardy Vincent.

CRS Report RS20002, *Federal Land and Resource Management: A Primer*, coordinated by Ross W. Gorte.

CRS Report RL30126, *Federal Land Ownership: Constitutional Authority; the History of Acquisition, Disposal, and Retention; and Current Acquisition and Disposal Authorities*, by Ross W. Gorte and Pamela Baldwin.

CRS Issue Brief IB10093, *National Park Management and Recreation*, coordinated by Carol Hardy Vincent.

U.S. Congress, Committee on Interior and Insular Affairs, *Multiple Use and Sustained Yield: Changing Philosophies for Federal Land Management? The Proceedings and Summary of a Workshop Convened on March 5-6, 1992*, committee print prepared by the Congressional Research Service, No. 11 (Washington, DC: GPO, Dec. 1992).

U.S. Congress, Committee on Energy and Natural Resources, *Outdoor Recreation: A Reader for Congress*, committee print prepared by the Congressional Research Service, S.Prt. 105-53 (Washington, DC: GPO, June 1998).

U.S. Congress, Committee on Environment and Public Works, *Ecosystem Management: Status and Potential. Summary of a Workshop Convened by the Congressional Research Service, March 24-25, 1994*, committee print prepared by the Congressional Research Service, S.Prt. 103-98 (Washington, DC: GPO, Dec. 1994).

Federal Lands Financing [19]

Financial issues are a persistent concern for federal agencies, including the land management agencies. However, the sale or lease of the lands and resources being managed provides these agencies with an opportunity to recover some of their operations and capital costs. This section summarizes the revenues of the four land management agencies and provides a brief overview of annual appropriations, the trust funds and special accounts funded from revenues, and land acquisition funding. It concludes with a discussion of the programs that compensate state and local governments for the tax-exempt status of federal lands.

Table 3. Revenues from the Sale and Use of Agency Lands and Resources for FY2003 (thousands of dollars; excluding deposits to trust funds and special accounts)

Resource	BLM	FWS	NPS	FS
Mineral Leases and Permits	$103,857[a]	n/a[b]	$0	$187,114[c]
Sales of Timber and Other Forest Products	$11,501	n/a[b]	$12	$58,548
Grazing Leases, Licenses, and Permits	$11,828	n/a[b]	—[d]	$4,351
Recreation, Admission, and User Fees	$0[e]	n/a[b]	$0[f]	$44,381
Other	$135,941[g]	n/a[b]	$15	$12,072
Total	**$263,127**	**$6,895**	**$27**	**$306,466**

Sources: For BLM: U.S. Dept. of the Interior, Budget Justifications and Performance Information, Fiscal Year 2005: Bureau of Land Management, p. II-1.

For FWS: U.S. Dept. of the Interior, Budget Justifications and Performance Information, Fiscal Year 2005: U.S. Fish and Wildlife Service, p. 445.

For NPS: U.S. Dept. of the Interior, Budget Justifications and Performance Information, Fiscal Year 2005: National Park Service, p. Overview-26.

For FS: U.S. Dept. of Agriculture, Forest Service, USDA Forest Service FY2005 Budget Justification, pp. A-9 - A-10.

a. Includes mineral leasing on national grasslands, the Naval Oil Shale Reserve, and the National Petroleum Reserve-Alaska, and mining claim and holding fees.

b. n/a: data are not available in published form.

c. Includes estimated $154.5 million collected by Departments of the Interior and Energy for mineral leases and power licenses.

d. Included with revenues for sales of timber and forest products.

e. All BLM recreation fees are now deposited in its Recreation Fee Demonstration Account, totaling $10 million.

f. The NPS is now authorized through several permanently appropriated accounts to retain all such fees in permanently appropriated accounts, totaling $245 million.

g. Includes Treasury deposits from land sales ($13 million), sale of helium ($87 million), other fees, charges, and collections ($33 million), and earnings on investments ($2 million).

Revenues from Activities on Federal Lands

The federal land management agencies are among the relatively few federal agencies that generate revenues for the U.S. Treasury. However, none of these four agencies consistently collects more money than it expends. Revenues are derived from the use or sale of lands and resources. Major revenue sources include timber sales, grazing livestock fees, energy and mineral leases, and fees for recreation uses. The FY2003 revenues collected by these four agencies, excluding deposits to trust funds and special accounts, are shown in Table 3.

Agency Appropriations

Annual Appropriations

Funding for all four of the federal land management agencies is contained in the annual Department of the Interior and Related Agencies appropriations bill. The FS is a USDA agency, but has been included in the Interior bill as a "related agency" since 1955. It receives the largest appropriation of any agency in the Interior bill, with funding of $4.54 billion (including emergency fire funding) in the Interior Appropriations Act for FY2004 (P.L. 108-108). The NPS receives the next largest appropriations of the federal land management agencies, with FY2004 funding of $2.26 billion. For FY2004, the BLM received $1.79 billion (including emergency fire funding). The FWS has the lowest funding of the land management agencies, with FY2004 appropriations at $1.31 billion. For more information on annual funding for these agencies, see CRS Report RL32306, *Appropriations for FY2005: Interior and Related Agencies*, available on the CRS website at [http://www.crs.gov/products/appropriations/apppage.shtml].

Trust Funds and Special Accounts

The federal land management agencies also have a variety of trust funds and special accounts. Some require annual appropriations; most of these are small, but the Land and Water Conservation Fund used for federal land acquisition is relatively large and controversial, and is discussed separately below.

A number of the trust funds and special accounts are permanently appropriated (also known as mandatory spending). This means that the agencies can spend the receipts deposited in the accounts without annual appropriations by Congress. Many of these accounts (15) were established to compensate state and local governments for the tax-exempt status of federal lands; these accounts will be discussed separately below. Others receive funds from particular sources (e.g., excise taxes, timber sales, recreation fees) for grants or for agency operations. The receipts deposited in these accounts are *in addition to* the Treasury receipts shown in Table 3.

The FWS has the largest annual funding in permanently appropriated trust funds and special accounts, with FY2003 budget authority of $661 million. The two largest accounts are the Sport Fish Restoration Trust Fund ($330 million), established by the Federal Aid in Sport Fish Restoration Act; [20] and the Wildlife Restoration Special Account ($235 million), established by the Federal Aid in Wildlife Restoration Act. [21] These accounts are largely funded by excise taxes on equipment related to fishing and hunting, respectively, and the money is distributed to the states mostly to fund fish and wildlife restoration activities by state agencies. The third largest account is the Migratory Bird Conservation Fund ($44 million), which uses the revenues from selling duck stamps to hunters, refuge visitors, stamp collectors, and others to acquire lands for the National Wildlife Refuge System (as noted below, under "Land Acquisition Funding").

The BLM and NPS have numerous permanently appropriated trust funds and special accounts, with total budget authority of $305 million for each in FY2003. Most of the BLM accounts are much smaller than for the other federal land management agencies, but the one largest account — Southern Nevada public land sales — had FY2003 budget authority of $279 million (92% of BLM permanent appropriations for operations).

The NPS permanently appropriated special accounts and trust funds allow the agency to retain 100% of its recreation and admission fees. The largest is the Recreational Fee Demonstration Program, described below. Two funds are unique to the NPS: the concessions improvement account and park concessions franchise fees (a combined total of $54 million in FY2003). Two other funds are common to all four land management agencies, but are significantly larger for the NPS. One is the fund for maintaining employee quarters ($16 million for the NPS, less than $11 million total for the other three agencies) paid by rent from employees. Another consists of contributions and donations from interested individuals and groups ($29 million for the NPS; less than $3 million total for the other three agencies).

The FS has the least annual funding in permanently appropriated trust funds and special accounts. The FS has 20 accounts with FY2003 budget authority of $285 million. Six of the eight largest are directly or substantially related to timber sales, including the Salvage Sale Fund ($58 million), the Knutson-Vandenberg Fund ($48 million), other cooperative deposits ($41 million), the Reforestation Trust Fund ($30 million), National Forest roads and trails ($12 million), [22] and brush disposal ($12 million).

Finally, two programs were established to authorize the four agencies to retain recreation fees. The first, recreation fee collection costs (P.L. 103-66, §10002(b)), allows the agencies to retain up to 15% of recreation fees to cover the costs to collect the fees. The second, much larger program is the Recreational Fee Demonstration Program, created to allow the agencies to test the feasibility and public acceptability of user fees to supplement appropriations for operations and maintenance (P.L. 104-134, §315). This "Fee Demo" program authorized new or increased entrance fees at federal recreation sites from FY1996 through FY1998; it has been extended multiple times, and now is authorized for fee collections through December 31, 2005 (with expenditures through FY2008). FY2003 collections are $124 million for the NPS, $37 million for the FS, $9 million for the BLM, and $4 million for the FWS.

Land Acquisition Funding

The largest source of funding for federal land acquisition is the Land and Water Conservation Fund. LWCF is a special account created in 1964 specifically to fund federal land acquisition and state recreation programs. It can be credited with revenues from federal recreation user fees (other than those collected under the Recreational Fee Demonstration Program and the Fee Collection Cost Program), the federal motorboat fuel tax, and surplus property sales; these are supplemented with revenues from federal offshore oil and gas leases, up to the authorized level of $900 million annually.

LWCF does not operate the way a "true" trust fund would in the private sector. The fund is *credited* with deposits from specified sources, but Congress must enact appropriations annually for the agencies to spend money from the fund. Through FY2004, $27.2 billion has been credited to the LWCF, and $13.8 billion has been appropriated. Unappropriated funds remain in the U.S. Treasury and can be spent for other purposes.

The 105th, 106th, and 107th Congresses considered legislation that would have supplemented or supplanted the LWCF and fully funded it for 15 years. The Clinton Administration successfully pursued another avenue (the Lands Legacy Initiative that led to the creation of the Conservation Spending Category) to increase funding for LWCF federal land acquisition through the annual appropriations process and to use some of the LWCF authorization for other (non-acquisition) federal programs. President Bush has expanded on this latter approach, proposing in FY2005 to fully fund LWCF — requesting $900.2 million

— but use more than half of the total for non-acquisition federal programs, including several Fish and Wildlife Service and Forest Service programs. In FY2003, LWCF appropriations for federal land acquisition alone totaled $313.0 million, and in FY2004 they declined to $169.7 million, both down from the FY1998 peak of $897.1 million. For FY2005, President Bush has requested $220.2 million for LWCF federal land acquisition.

Other federal programs also provide funding for federal land acquisition. The largest is the FWS's Migratory Bird Conservation Fund (MBCF). Receipts from the sale of duck stamps to hunters, refuge visitors, stamp collectors, and others are deposited in this account. The funds are permanently appropriated to the FWS to acquire lands for the National Wildlife Refuge System, and often provide more than half the total FWS land acquisition funding. In FY2003, the FWS used $43.8 million of MBCF for land acquisition.

The BLM has a mandatory spending program for land acquisition and other activities in Nevada, funded from sales of BLM land in that state (Southern Nevada Public Land Management Act, SNPLMA, P.L. 105-623). This program allows money from BLM land sales in Nevada to be used for land acquisition by the federal land management agencies, but also for capital improvements on federal lands and state and local government purposes. Since 2000, this program has generated more than $400 million, and it is projected to generate $338 million in FY2004 and $846 million in FY2005. The portion spent on federal land acquisition varies, and totaled $38.6 million in FY2003. This relatively small amount is attributable in part to the newness of the program and it is expected to increase in coming years. In addition, the FS has a very small program (about $1 million annually) for acquiring lands in certain parts of Utah and California.

Figure 2 shows federal land acquisition funding since FY1995. Total funding rose from a low of $181.5 million in FY1996 to a peak of $936.7 million in FY1998, then declined to $395.4 million in FY2003. Funding for federal land acquisition (excluding SNPLMA) is estimated at $212.0 million for FY2004, and at $263.4 million under President Bush's FY2005 budget request. [23]

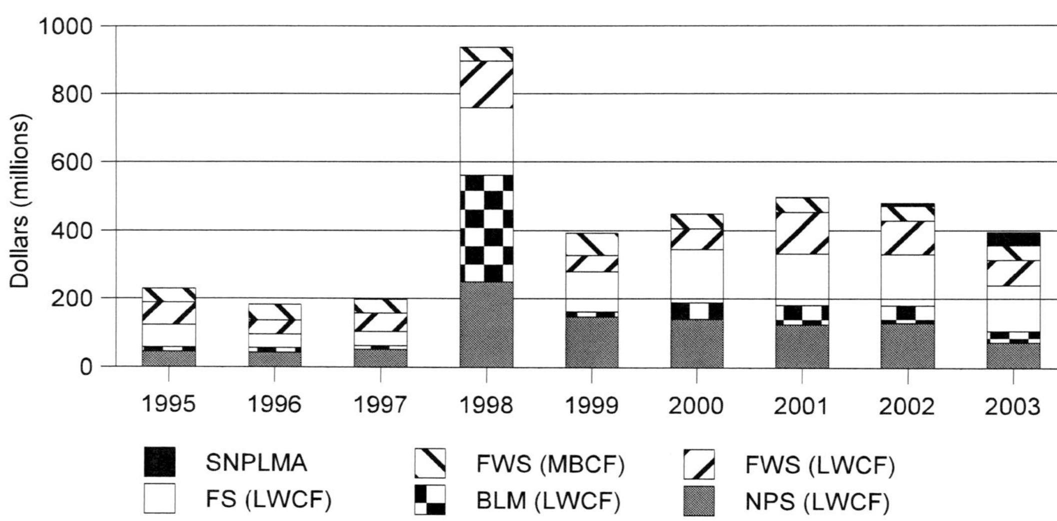

Figure 2. Federal Land Acquisition Funding, FY1995-FY2003.

Compensation to State and Local Governments

Because federal property is exempt from state and local taxation, Congress has enacted mechanisms to compensate state and local governments for tax revenues that would have been collected if the lands were privately owned. Many of the mechanisms provide for sharing revenues from federal lands with state and/or local governments; only the NPS has no agency-specific compensation system. The Payments In Lieu of Taxes (PILT) Program provides additional revenues.

Revenue-Sharing

The amount and percentage of federal revenues that are shared with state and/or local governments depends upon the history of the land and the type of activities generating the revenues. Congress created the simplest system for revenue-sharing for FS lands. Since 1908, the agency has returned 25% of its gross revenues to the states for use on roads and schools in the counties where the national forests are located. The states determine which road and school programs are to be funded, and how much goes to each program, but the amount allocated to each county is determined by the FS and the states cannot retain any of the funds. For the national grasslands, 25% of *net* revenues go directly to the counties. In addition, three counties in Minnesota receive a special payment of 0.75% of the appraised value of the Superior NF lands in the county. Payments for these FS programs are permanently appropriated from any FS revenues; in FY2003, total FS payments were $393 million.

Because of concerns over declining timber revenues in many areas, and the approaching end of the special "spotted owl payments" program, [24] the 106th Congress debated bills to modify the FS revenue-sharing program. In the Secure Rural Schools and Community Self-Determination Act of 2000 (P.L. 106-393), Congress enacted a six-year program allowing counties to supplant the historic 25% payment with the average of the three highest payments to the state between 1986 and 1999. Of these high-3 payments, 15%-20% must be spent on certain county programs or on projects on federal lands recommended by a local advisory committee or chosen by the FS. This program accounted for 72% of the $393 million in FS payments in FY2003.

For BLM lands and revenues, the revenue-sharing system is more complicated. The share going to state and local entities ranges from 0% to 90% of gross program revenues, as specified in individual statutes. For example, states and counties receive 12.5% of revenues from grazing within grazing districts (under §3 of the Taylor Grazing Act of 1934) and 50% of revenues from grazing outside grazing districts (under §15 of the Taylor Grazing Act). Another example is timber sale revenues. The states and counties receive 4% of timber revenues from most BLM lands. However, the counties receive up to 75% from the heavily timbered Oregon and California (OandC) railroad grant lands in Western Oregon. [25] Counties with the Coos Bay Wagon Road (CBWR) grant lands (adjoining and usually identified with the OandC lands) similarly receive up to 75%, but actual payments are limited by county tax assessments. Because the OandC and CBWR payments have been largely from timber sales, which have declined since the late 1980s, they were included with national forest lands (see above) in the spotted owl payments program and the six-year program of payments at the average of the three highest, under P.L. 106-393.

These examples demonstrate the complexity of the legal direction to share BLM revenues with state and local governments. The BLM revenue-sharing payments are permanently appropriated, with 10 separate payment accounts; FY2003 budget authority was $157 million, of which $111 million was for the OandC and CBWR lands and $38 was related to oil leasing in the National Petroleum Reserve-Alaska.

Finally, the FWS has a revenue-sharing program, but payments depend on the history of the land. For refuges reserved from the public domain, the payments are based on 25% of *net* revenues (in contrast to 25% of *gross* revenues from FS lands other than national grasslands). For refuges which have been created on lands acquired from other landowners, payments are based on the *greatest* of: 25% of net revenues, 0.75% of fair market value of the land, or $0.75 per acre. The National Wildlife Refuge Fund is permanently appropriated for making these payments, but net revenues have been insufficient to make the authorized payments. Although payments have been supplemented with annual appropriations, total payments — $14 million in FY2003 — consistently have been less than the authorized level.

Payments in Lieu of Taxes

The most comprehensive federal program for compensating local governments for the tax-exempt status of federal lands was created in the 1976 Payments in Lieu of Taxes (PILT) Act. PILT payments are made in addition to any revenue-sharing payments, although the payments may be reduced by such revenue-sharing payments, as discussed below. Federal lands encompassed by this county-compensation program include lands in the National Forest System, lands in the National Park System, and those administered by the BLM, plus the National Wildlife Refuge System lands reserved from the public domain, and a few other categories of federal lands.

In 1994, Congress amended the PILT Act to more than double the authorized payments over five years, to adjust for inflation between 1976 and 1994, and to build in adjustments for future inflation. The two formulae used to calculate the FY2003 authorized payment level for each county with eligible federal lands are:

1. Which is *less*: (a) the county's eligible acres times $0.27 per acre; or (b) the county's payment ceiling (determined by county population level). Pick the lesser of these two. This option is called the *minimum provision*.
2. Which is *less*: (a) the county's eligible acres times $2.02 per acre; or (b) the county's payment ceiling (determined by county population level). Pick the lesser of these two, and from it subtract the previous year's total payments under other payment or revenue-sharing programs of the agencies that control the eligible land (as reported by each state to the BLM). This option is called the *standard provision*.

The county is authorized to receive whichever of the above calculations (1 or 2) is *greater*. This calculation must be made for all counties individually to determine the national authorization level.

In contrast to most of the revenue-sharing programs, PILT requires annual appropriations from Congress. Those appropriations generally had been sufficient to compensate the counties at the authorized level prior to the 1994 amendments. Those amendments raised the authorization; however, subsequent appropriations have been substantially below the increased authorization. Figure 3 compares the level of authorization and appropriation for each year since FY1993.

Issues

Several financing themes are perennial issues for Congress, involving fees charged (or not charged) and how these revenues relate to agency activities. One issue has been the question of whether prices set administratively (rather than by markets) subsidize some resource users. This issue typically has focused on fees for private livestock grazing on federal lands and for hardrock (locatable) minerals that are currently available for private development under a claims system without royalty payments. Another issue is whether "below-cost" timber sales should continue if the government is losing money on them. In addition, whether to permanently authorize the Recreational Fee Demonstration Program, and which agencies' lands and programs to include, is a continuing congressional focus.

Another persistent issue is determining the annual appropriations for the Department of the Interior and related agencies (including the FS). The budget levels for the agencies often are controversial, especially in today's climate of increasing budget deficits and expenditures for the war on terrorism. Legislative provisions and directions/restrictions on spending contained in appropriations bills, commonly referred to as environmental and resource "riders," often are the most controversial parts of these bills.

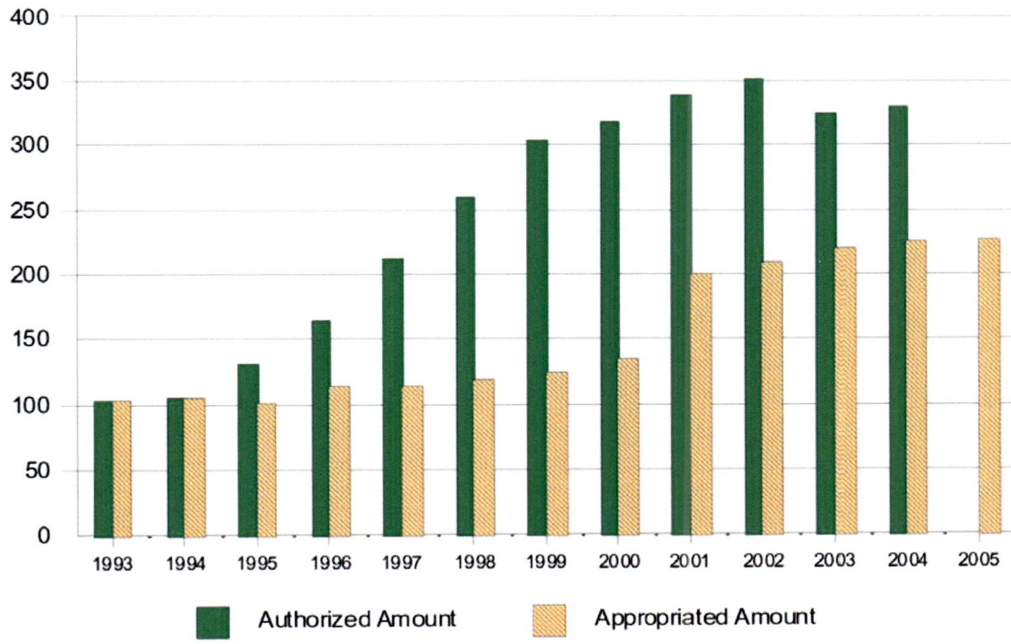

Sources: The authorization levels were calculated by the BLM based on the formula in statute, while the appropriation levels were taken from laws appropriating funds for the Department of the Interior.

Notes: The FY2004 authorized amount is an estimate; the FY2005 authorized amount is not yet estimated. The FY2005 appropriation level reflects the Administration's request. Authorization for a given year depends on receipts from the previous year from the agencies that administer the eligible lands. Consequently, no authorization level can be determined for FY2005.

Figure 3. PILT: Authorized and Appropriated Amounts, FY1993-FY2005 (in millions of $).

Funding for wildfire protection has grown significantly in recent years, following the severe fire seasons of 2000 and 2002. Annual appropriations for fire suppression operations have not been sufficient, and the agencies have used their authority to borrow from other accounts to fund fire suppression. These borrowings typically are repaid in an emergency supplemental appropriation bill or in the subsequent annual appropriations bill. However, the borrowed funds are not always repaid promptly, leading to funding shortfalls in the accounts from which the funds were borrowed (such as land acquisition).

Major Statutes

Department of the Interior and Related Agencies Appropriations Act for FY2004 (the most recent in the annual series of such acts): Act of Nov. 10, 2003; P.L. 108-108.

Forest Service Revenue-Sharing Act: Act of May 23, 1908; ch. 192, 35 Stat. 251. 16 U.S.C. §500.

Land and Water Conservation Fund Act of 1965: Act of Sept. 3, 1964; P.L. 88-578, 78 Stat. 897. 16 U.S.C. §460*l*.

Payments in Lieu of Taxes Act: Act of Oct. 20, 1976; P.L. 94-565, 90 Stat. 2662. 31 U.S.C. §§6901-6907.

Secure Rural Schools and Community Self-Determination Act of 2000: Act of Oct. 19, 2000; P.L. 106-393.

CRS Reports and Committee Prints [26]

CRS Report RL32306, *Appropriations for FY2005: Interior and Related Agencies*, coordinated by Carol Hardy Vincent and Susan Boren. (The most recent in an annual series of such reports.)

CRS Report RL30335, *Federal Land Management Agencies' Permanently Appropriated Accounts*, by Ross W. Gorte, M. Lynne Corn, and Carol Hardy Vincent.

CRS Report 98-980, *Federal Sales of Natural Resources: Pricing and Allocation Mechanisms,* by Ross W. Gorte.

CRS Report 90-192, *Fish and Wildlife Service: Compensation to Local Governments*, by M. Lynne Corn.

CRS Report RL30480, *Forest Service Revenue-Sharing Payments: Legislative Issues*, by Ross W. Gorte.

CRS Report RS21503, *Land and Water Conservation Fund: Current Status and Issues,* by Jeffrey Zinn.

CRS Issue Brief IB10093, *National Park Management and Recreation*, coordinated by Carol Hardy Vincent.

CRS Report RL31392, *PILT (Payments in Lieu of Taxes): Somewhat Simplified*, by M. Lynne Corn.

THE NATIONAL FOREST SYSTEM [27]

The National Forest System (NFS) is administered by the Forest Service (FS) in the U.S. Department of Agriculture. The NFS is comprised of national forests, national grasslands, and various other designations. Although NFS lands are concentrated (87%) in the West, the FS administers more federal land in the East than all other federal agencies combined. NFS lands are administered for sustained yields of multiple uses, including outdoor recreation (camping, hiking, hunting, sightseeing, etc.), livestock grazing, timber harvesting, watershed protection, and fish and wildlife habitats.

Background [28]

In 1891, Congress granted the President the authority (now repealed) to establish forest reserves from the public domain. Six years later, in 1897, Congress stated that the forest reserves were:

> to improve and protect the forest within the reservation, or for the purpose of securing favorable conditions of water flows, and to furnish a continuous supply of timber for the use and necessities of the citizens of the United States.

Initially, the reserves were administered by the Division of Forestry in the General Land Office of the Department of the Interior. In 1905, this division was combined with the USDA Bureau of Forestry, renamed the Forest Service, and the administration of the 56 million acres of forest reserves (renamed *national forests* in 1907) was transferred to the new agency within the Department of Agriculture. NFS management is one of the three principal FS programs. [29]

In 1906 and 1907, President Theodore Roosevelt more than doubled the acreage of the forest reserves. In 1907, Congress limited the authority of the President to add to the system in certain states. [30] Then in 1910, Congress repeated the limitation in the Pickett Act. In 1911, Congress passed the Weeks Law, authorizing additions to the NFS through the purchase of private lands. Under this and other authorities, the system has continued to grow slowly, from 154 million acres in 1919 to 192.5 million acres in 2003. This growth has resulted from purchases and donations of private land and from land transfers, primarily from the BLM.

Organization

The NFS includes 155 national forests with 188 million acres (97.6% of the system); 20 national grasslands with 4 million acres (2.0%); and 121 other areas, such as land utilization projects, purchase units, and research and experimental areas, with 0.8 million acres (0.4%). [31] The NFS units are arranged into nine administrative regions, each headed by a regional forester. The nine regional foresters report to the NFS Deputy Chief, who reports to the Chief of the Forest Service. In contrast to the heads of other federal land management agencies, the

Chief traditionally has been a career employee of the agency. The Chief reports to the Secretary through the Undersecretary for Natural Resources and Environment.

The NFS regions often are referred to by number, rather than by name. Table 4 identifies the number, states encompassed, and acreage for each of the regions. Although the NFS lands are concentrated in the seven western FS regions, including Alaska (87%), the FS manages more than half of all federal land in the East. *Inholdings* shown in Table 4 is land (primarily private) within the designated boundaries of the national forests (and other NFS units) which is not administered by the FS. Inholdings sometimes pose difficulties for FS land management, because the agency generally does not regulate the development and use of the inholdings. The uses of private inholdings may be incompatible with desired uses of the federal lands, and constraints on crossing inholdings may limit access to some federal lands. Many private landowners, however, object to federal restrictions on the use of their lands and to unfettered public access across their lands. This is particularly true in the Southern and Eastern Regions, where nearly half of the land within the NFS boundaries is inholdings.

Table 4. The National Forest System

Forest Service Region		**States containing NFS lands**[a]	**National Forest System Acreage**[b]	
Region Name	**No.**	**States**	**Federal**	**Inholdings**
Northern	1	ID, MT, ND	25,441,585	2,727,271
Rocky Mountain	2	CO, NE, SD, WY	22,069,840	2,380,838
Southwestern	3	AZ, NM	20,805,767	1,668,087
Intermountain	4	ID, NV, UT, WY	32,003,788	2,250,034
Pacific Southwest	5	CA	20,137,345	3,629,680
Pacific Northwest	6	OR, WA	24,737,016	2,660,525
Southern	8	AL, AR, FL, GA, KY, LA, MS, NC, OK, PR, SC, TN, TX, VA	13,273,000	12,324,182
Eastern	9	IL, IN, ME, MI, MN, MO, NH, NY, OH, PA, VT, WI, WV	12,061,766	9,895,489
Alaska	10	AK	21,980,905	2,375,273
National Forest System Total			**192,511,012**	**39,911,379**

Source: U.S. Dept. of Agriculture, Forest Service, *Land Areas of the National Forest System, as of Sept. 30, 2004*, Tables 1 and 2, from [http://www.fs.fed.us/land/staff/lar/LAR03/], visited Feb. 20, 2004.

Notes: In 1966, Region 7, the Lake States Region, was merged with Region 9, the Northeastern Region, to form the current Eastern Region. Although this merger left 9 regions, the numbering sequence skips 7 and ends with 10, as shown in the table.

a. This column lists only states (and territories) that currently contain NFS lands.

b. *Federal* is federally owned land managed by the FS. *Inholdings* are private and other government lands within NFS boundaries that are not administered or regulated by the FS.

MANAGEMENT

The management goals for the national forests were first established in 1897, as described above. Management goals were further articulated in §1 of the Multiple-Use Sustained-Yield Act of 1960 (MUSYA), which states:

> It is the policy of the Congress that the national forests are established and shall be administered for outdoor recreation, range, timber, watershed, and wildlife and fish purposes. The purposes of this Act are declared to be supplemental to, but not in derogation of, the purposes for which the national forests were established as set forth in the Act of June 4, 1897.... The establishment and maintenance of areas as wilderness are consistent with the purposes and provisions of this Act.

MUSYA directs land and resource management of the national forests for the combination of uses that best meets the needs of the American people. Management of the resources is to be coordinated for *multiple use* — considering the relative values of the various resources, but not necessarily maximizing dollar returns, nor requiring that any one particular area be managed for all or even most uses. The act also calls for *sustained yield* — a high level of resource outputs maintained in perpetuity but without impairing the productivity of the land. Other statutes, such as the Endangered Species Act, that apply to all federal agencies also apply.

NFS planning and management is guided primarily by the Forest and Rangeland Renewable Resources Planning Act (RPA) of 1974, as amended by the National Forest Management Act (NFMA) of 1976. Together, these laws encourage foresight in the use of the nation's forest resources, and establish a long-range planning process for the management of the NFS. RPA focuses on the national, long-range direction for forest and range conservation and sustainability. [32] RPA requires the FS to prepare four documents for Congress and the public: an Assessment every 10 years to inventory and monitor the status and trends of the nation's natural resources; a Program every five years to guide FS policies; a Presidential Statement of Policy to accompany the Program and guide budget formulation; and an Annual Report to evaluate implementation of the Program. [33]

NFMA requires the FS to prepare a comprehensive land and resource management plan for each unit of the NFS, coordinated with the national RPA planning process. [34] The plans must use an interdisciplinary approach, including economic analysis and the identification of costs and benefits of all resource uses. Planning regulations (36 C.F.R. §219) were issued in 1979, then revised in 1982. Revision of the 1982 regulations was begun with an advance notice of proposed rulemaking in 1991, and proposed revised regulations were issued in 1995. In 1997, the Secretary of Agriculture chartered a Committee of Scientists to review the planning process, and its March 1999 report, *Sustaining the People's Lands*, made numerous recommendations. [35] On October 5, 1999, the Clinton Administration proposed new regulations (64 *Federal Register* 54073), with final regulations revising the planning process on November 9, 2000 (65 *Federal Register* 67514). These regulations would have increased emphasis on ecological sustainability, and would have been implemented over several years.

On December 6, 2002, in response to concerns about whether the Clinton regulations could be implemented and about the lack of emphasis on economic and social sustainability, the Bush Administration proposed new regulations (67 *Federal Register* 72700) to supplant the Clinton regulations before they were implemented. The proposed Bush regulations seek to balance ecological sustainability with economic and social considerations, and would reduce national direction in FS decision-making. Final regulations have not been issued.

Congress has provided further management direction within the NFS by creating special designations for certain areas. Some of these designations — wilderness areas, wild and scenic rivers, and national trails — are part of larger management systems affecting several federal land management agencies; these special systems are described in later chapters of this article.

In addition to these special systems, the NFS includes several other types of land designations. The NFS contains 21 national game refuges and wildlife preserves (1.2 million acres), 20 national recreation areas (2.9 million acres), 4 national monuments (3.7 million acres), 2 national volcanic monuments (167,427 acres), 6 scenic areas (130,435 acres), a scenic-research area (6,637 acres), a scenic recreation area (12,645 acres), a recreation management area (43,900 acres), 3 special management areas (91,265 acres), 2 national protection areas (27,600 acres), 2 national botanical areas (8,256 acres), a primitive area (173,762 acres) and a national historic area (6,540 acres). [36] Resource development and use is generally more restricted in these specially designated areas than on general NFS lands, and specific guidance typically is provided with each designation.

Land Ownership

Designation

As noted above, in 1891, the President was authorized to reserve lands from the public domain as forest reserves (16 U.S.C. §471, now repealed), but this authority was subsequently limited by Congress, and it appears that no new NFS lands were reserved in the West after 1907. However, many proclamations and executive orders subsequently have modified boundaries and changed names, including establishing new national forests from existing NFS lands. National forests in the East generally were established between 1910 and 1950, with the Hoosier and Wayne Forests (in Indiana and Ohio, respectively) the last proclaimed, in 1951.

Presidential authority to proclaim forest reserves from the public domain was restricted piecemeal. The 1897 Act established management direction by restricting the purposes for the reserves. The 1907 Act that renamed the forest reserves as the national forests also prohibited the establishment of new reserves in six western states, although President Theodore Roosevelt did not sign the law until he had reserved 16 million acres in those states. Presidential authority to withdraw public lands to establish new national forests was not formally repealed until 1976. [37] Today, establishing a new national forest from public domain lands or significantly modifying the boundaries of an existing national forest created from the public domain requires an act of Congress. [38]

Acquisition Authority

The Secretary of Agriculture has numerous authorities to add lands to the NFS. The first and broadest authority was in the Weeks Law of 1911 (as amended by NFMA; 16 U.S.C. §515):

> The Secretary is hereby authorized and directed to examine, locate, and purchase such forested, cut-over, or denuded lands within the watersheds of navigable streams as in his judgment may be necessary to the regulation of the flow of navigable streams or for the production of timber.

Originally, the acquisitions were to be approved by a National Forest Reservation Commission, but the Commission was terminated in 1976 by §17 of NFMA.

Other laws also authorize land acquisition for the national forests, typically in specific areas or for specific purposes. For example, §205 of FLPMA authorizes the acquisition of access corridors to national forests across nonfederal lands (43 U.S.C. §1715(a)). The Southern Nevada Public Land Management Act of 1998 authorizes acquisition of environmentally sensitive lands in Nevada, some of which have been added to the National Forest System. Also, under the Federal Land Transaction Facilitation Act, the Secretary of Agriculture may acquire inholdings and other nonfederal land. (See discussion of BLM "Disposal Authority," below.)

Finally, the Bankhead-Jones Farm Tenant Act of 1937 authorizes and directs the Secretary of Agriculture to establish (7 U.S.C. §1010):

> a program of land conservation and land utilization, in order to correct maladjustments in land use, and thus assist in controlling soil erosion, reforestation, preserving natural resources, protecting fish and wildlife, developing and protecting recreational facilities, mitigating floods, preventing impairment of dams and reservoirs, developing energy resources, conserving surface and subsurface moisture, protecting the watersheds of navigable streams, and protecting public lands, health, safety, and welfare ....

Initially, the act authorized the Secretary to acquire submarginal lands and lands not primarily suitable for cultivation (§1011(a)); this provision was repealed in 1962. This authority allowed the agency to acquire and establish the 20 national grasslands and 6 land utilization projects that account for 2% of the NFS. In addition, millions of acres acquired under this authority have been transferred to the BLM.

Disposal Authority

The Secretary of Agriculture has numerous authorities to dispose of NFS lands, all constrained in various ways and seldom used. In 1897, the President was authorized (16 U.S.C. §473):

> to revoke, modify, or suspend any and all Executive orders and proclamations or any part thereof issued under section 471 of this title, from time to time as he deems best for the public interests. By such modification he may reduce the area or change the boundary lines or may vacate altogether any order creating a national forest.

The 1897 Act also provided for the return to the public domain of lands better suited for agriculture or mining. These provisions have not been repealed, but §9 of NFMA prohibits the return to the public domain of any land reserved or withdrawn from the public domain, except by an act of Congress (16 U.S.C. §1609).

The 1911 Weeks Law authorizes the Secretary to dispose of land "chiefly valuable for agriculture" which was included in lands acquired (inadvertently or otherwise), if agricultural use will not injure the forests or stream flows and the lands are not needed for public purposes (16 U.S.C. §519).

The Bankhead-Jones Farm Tenant Act authorizes the disposal of lands acquired under its authority, with or without consideration, "under such terms and conditions as he [the Secretary of Agriculture] deems will best accomplish the purposes of this" title, but "only to public authorities and only on condition that the property is used for public purposes" (7 U.S.C. §1011(c)). Yet the grasslands were included in the NFS in 1976 and current regulations (36 C.F.R. §213) refer to them as being "permanently held."

The 1958 Townsites Act authorizes the Secretary to transfer up to 640 acres adjacent to communities in Alaska or the 11 western states for townsites, if the "indigenous community objectives ... outweigh the public objectives and values which would be served by maintaining such tract in Federal ownership" (16 U.S.C. §478a). There is to be a public notice of the application for such transfer, and upon a "satisfactory showing of need," the Secretary may offer the land to a local governmental entity at "not less than the fair market value."

The 1983 Small Tracts Act authorizes the Secretary to dispose of three categories of land, by sale or exchange, if valued at no more than $150,000 (16 U.S.C. §521e):

> (1) tracts of up to 40 acres interspersed with or adjacent to lands transferred out of federal ownership under the mining laws *and* which are inefficient to administer because of their size or location; (2) tracts of up to 10 acres encroached upon by improvements based in good faith upon an erroneous survey; or (3) road rights-of-way substantially surrounded by nonfederal land and not needed by the federal government, subject to the right of first refusal for adjoining landowners.

The land can be disposed of for cash, lands, interests in land, or any combination thereof for the value of the land being disposed (16 U.S.C. §521d) plus "all reasonable costs of administration, survey, and appraisal incidental to such conveyance" (16 U.S.C. §521f).

Finally, in Title II (the Education Land Grant Act) of P.L. 106-577, Congress authorized the FS to transfer up to 80 acres of NFS land for a nominal cost upon written application of a public school district. Section 202(e) provides for reversion of title to the federal government if the lands are not used for the educational purposes for which they were acquired.

Issues

In the past few years, the focus of discussions and legislative proposals on FS management of the NFS has been forest health and wildfires, especially in the intermountain West. The 2000 and 2002 fire seasons were, by most standards, among the worst since 1960. Many believe that excessive accumulations of biomass — dead and dying trees, heavy undergrowth, and dense stands of small trees —reflect degraded forest health and make forests vulnerable to conflagrations. These observers advocate rapid action to improve forest health — including prescribed burning, thinning, and salvaging dead and dying trees — and that rapid action is needed to protect NFS forests and nearby private lands and homes. Critics counter that authorities to reduce fuel levels are adequate, treatments that remove commercial timber degrade forest health and waste taxpayer dollars, and expedited processes for treatments are a device to reduce public oversight of commercial timber harvesting.

In September 2000, President Clinton requested an additional $1.6 billion (for the FS and the BLM) for fire protection including funds to pay for the 2000 summer's fire suppression efforts and for fuel treatment to address forest health in the *wildland-urban interface* (i.e., wildlands near communities threatened by potential wildfire conflagrations). Congress included much of this funding in the FY2001 Interior Appropriations Act (P.L. 106-291), and has continued to fund FS and BLM wildfire programs at more than double the level of the 1990s. Nonetheless, fuel treatment funding is still far below the amount that would be needed to reduce fuels on the federal lands many identify as at high risk of significant ecological damage from wildfire. (For further information, see "Current Issues" section of CRS Report RL30755, *Forest Fire/Wildfire Protection*, by Ross W. Gorte.)

In August 2002, President Bush proposed a Healthy Forests Initiative to expedite fuel reduction treatments for federal forests. Because the 107th Congress did not enact legislation on this initiative, portions of it were accomplished through regulatory changes. These include categorically excluding some fuel reduction treatments from NEPA environmental reviews and public involvement (68 *Federal Register* 33814, June 5, 2003); modifying the FS administrative appeal process (68 *Federal Register* 33582, June 4, 2003); categorically excluding small timber sales from NEPA environmental reviews and public involvement (68 *Federal Register* 44598, July 29, 2003); and allowing agencies to consult their own personnel on ESA impacts, known as *counterpart* regulations (68 *Federal Register* 68254, December 8, 2003).

On December 2, 2003, Congress enacted the Healthy Forests Restoration Act of 2003 (P.L. 108-148) containing parts of the President's Healthy Forests Initiative. One title, which garnered most of the attention in debates over the legislation, established an expedited process for fuel reduction activities. Other titles provide research and financial assistance in using forest biomass; direction on surveying and controlling insects and diseases; watershed forestry assistance to states and private landowners; and payments to private landowners for protecting special forestlands.

Another major issue concerns whether, when, and where to build forest roads. Road construction is supported by those who use the roads for access to the national forests for timber harvesting, fire control, recreation (including hunting and fishing), and other purposes. New roads are opposed by others, on the grounds that they can degrade the environment both during and after construction, exacerbate fire risk and spread invasive species, alter areas that some wish to preserve as pristine wilderness, and be expensive to build and maintain. Decisions over road building and protecting roadless areas generally have been made locally, which led to much local litigation.

In October 1999, the Clinton Administration proposed a nationwide rule to provide "appropriate long-term protection for ... 'roadless' areas." Final regulations were to become effective on March 13, 2001, but the Bush Administration delayed the effective date and subsequent court actions have prevented implementation. On July 15, 2003, the Bush Administration issued an advanced notice of proposed rulemaking to gather comments on roadless area management (68 *Federal Register* 41864). On December 30, 2003, the Administration provided a temporary exemption from the roadless rule for the Tongass NF in Alaska (68 *Federal Register* 75136). Final regulations on roadless area protection are still in development. However, interim guidance has returned decisions about roadless area protection to the local or regional level, raising the possibility of litigation over local decisions.

Major Statutes

Cooperative Forestry Assistance Act of 1978: Act of July 1, 1978; P.L. 95-313, as amended, 92 Stat. 365. 16 U.S.C. §§2101, et seq.
Forest and Rangeland Renewable Resources Planning Act of 1974 (RPA): Act of August 17, 1974; P.L. 93-378, 88 Stat. 476. 16 U.S.C. §§1600, et seq.
Forest and Rangeland Renewable Resources Research Act of 1978: Act of June 30, 1978; P.L. 95-307, 92 Stat. 353. 16 U.S.C. §§1641, et seq.
Healthy Forests Restoration Act of 2003: Act of December 3, 2003; P.L. 108-148, 117 Stat. 1887. 16 U.S.C. §§6501-6591.
Multiple-Use Sustained-Yield Act of 1960 (MUSYA): Act of June 12, 1960; P.L. 86-517, 75 Stat. 215. 16 U.S.C. §§528, et seq.
National Forest Management Act of 1976 (NFMA): Act of October 22, 1976; P.L. 94-588, 90 Stat. 2949. 16 U.S.C. §§1601, et al.
Organic Administration Act of 1897: Act of June 4, 1897; ch. 2, 30 Stat. 11. 16 U.S.C. §§473, et seq.
Pickett Act: Act of June 25, 1910; ch. 421, 36 Stat. 847.
Weeks Law of 1911: Act of March 1, 1911; ch. 186, 36 Stat. 961. 16 U.S.C. §§515, et al.

CRS Reports and Committee Prints [39]

CRS Issue Brief IB10076, *Bureau of Land Management (BLM) Lands and National Forests*, coordinated by Ross W. Gorte and Carol Hardy Vincent.
CRS Report 98-917, *Clearcutting in the National Forests: Background and Overview*, by Ross W. Gorte.
CRS Report 98-233, *Federal Timber Harvests: Implications for U.S. Timber Supply*, by Ross W. Gorte.
CRS Report RS20822, *Forest Ecosystem Health: An Overview*, by Ross W. Gorte.
CRS Report RL30755, *Forest Fire/Wildfire Protection*, by Ross W. Gorte.
CRS Report RL30647, *The National Forest System Roadless Areas Initiative*, by Pamela Baldwin.
CRS Report RS21544, *Wildfire Protection Funding*, by Ross W. Gorte.
CRS Issue Brief IB10124, *Wildfire Protection in the 108th Congress*, by Ross W. Gorte.
CRS Report RS21880, *Wildfire Protection in the Wildland-Urban Interface*, by Ross W. Gorte.

BUREAU OF LAND MANAGEMENT [40]

The Bureau of Land Management (BLM) manages 261.5 million acres of land, nearly 12% of the land in the United States. Most of this land is in the West, with about one-third of the total in Alaska. These lands include grasslands, forests, high mountains, arctic tundra, and deserts. They contain diverse resources, including fuels and minerals; timber; forage; wild horses and burros; fish and wildlife habitat; recreation sites; wilderness areas; archaeological, paleontological, and historical sites; and other natural heritage assets. The agency also is responsible for approximately 700 million acres of federal subsurface mineral resources throughout the nation, and supervises the mineral operations on an estimated 56 million acres of Indian Trust lands. Another key BLM function is wildland fire management and suppression on approximately 370 million acres of DOI, other federal, and certain nonfederal lands.

Background

BLM was created in the Department of the Interior in 1946 by merging two agencies — the General Land Office and the U.S. Grazing Service. The General Land Office, created by Congress in 1812, helped convey lands to pioneers settling the western lands. The U.S. Grazing Service was established in 1934 to manage the public lands best suited for livestock grazing, in accordance with the Taylor Grazing Act of 1934. [41] This law sought to remedy the deteriorating condition of public rangelands due to their overuse as well as the drought of the 1920s and depression of the early 1930s.

The Taylor Grazing Act provided for the management of the public lands "pending [their] final disposal." This language expressed the view that the lands might still be transferred to private or state ownership, and that the federal government was serving only as custodian until that time. However, patenting of the more arid western lands had already slowed, and there was growing concern about the condition of resources on these lands. These factors, and a changing general attitude towards the public lands, contributed to their retention by the federal government.

For decades Congress debated whether to retain or dispose of the remaining public lands, and how best to coordinate their management. Studies throughout the 1960s culminated in the 1970 report of the Public Land Law Review Commission entitled *One-Third of the Nation's Land*. Three successive Congresses deliberated, and in 1976 Congress enacted a comprehensive public land law entitled the Federal Land Policy and Management Act of 1976 (FLPMA). [42]

FLPMA sometimes is called the BLM Organic Act because portions of it consolidated and articulated the agency's responsibilities. This law established, amended, or repealed many management authorities dealing with public land withdrawals, land exchanges and acquisitions, rights-of-way, advisory groups, range management, and the general organization and administration of BLM and the *public lands*, which were defined as the lands managed by BLM.

Congress also established in FLPMA the national policy that "the public lands be retained in federal ownership, unless as a result of the land use planning procedures provided for in this act, it is determined that disposal of a particular parcel will serve the national interest...." This retention policy contributed to a "revolt" during the late 1970s and early 1980s among some westerners who continued to hope that the federal presence in their states might be reduced through federal land transfers to private or state ownership. The resultant "Sagebrush Rebellion" —objecting to federal management decisions and in some cases to the federal presence itself — was directed primarily toward the BLM.

Since the 1780s, nearly 1.3 billion acres of federal land have been transferred to individuals, businesses, and states. This total includes approximately 287 million acres for homesteaders; 328 million acres to states for public schools, public transportation systems, and various public improvement projects; and 94 million acres for railroads.

The last large transfer of BLM land occurred in 1980 with passage of the Alaska National Interest Lands Conservation Act (ANILCA). [43] This act transferred approximately 80 million acres from BLM to the other federal land management agencies. BLM also is required by law (ANILCA, the Alaska Native Claims Settlement Act, and the Alaska Statehood Act) to transfer ownership of more than 155 million acres of federal lands to the state of Alaska and Alaska Natives. Approximately 127 million acres have been conveyed (or tentatively approved), and BLM continues to transfer land to Alaska and the Alaska Native corporations.

Organization

BLM headquarters in Washington, DC, is headed by the Director, a political appointee who reports to the Secretary of the Interior through the Assistant Secretary for Land and Minerals Management. There are 12 BLM state offices, each headed by a state director, and each BLM state office administers a geographic area that generally conforms to the boundary of one or more states. Under each state office there are field offices, each headed by a field manager responsible for "on the ground" implementation of BLM programs and policies. Line authority is from the director to state directors, terminating at the field manager level.

In addition, there are six national level support and service centers: the National Office of Fire and Aviation (Boise, ID); the National Training Center (Phoenix, AZ); the National Science and Technology Center (Denver, CO); the National Human Resources Management Center (Denver, CO); the National Business Center (Denver, CO); and the National Information Resources Management Center (Denver, CO). [44]

BLM maintains over 1 billion land and mineral records from the nation's history, including legal land descriptions, land and mineral ownership and entitlement records, and land withdrawal records. The agency conducts cadastral surveys to locate and mark the boundaries of federal and Indian lands. BLM's Public Land Survey System is the foundation of the nation's land tenure system. BLM is making its public lands and mineral records available on the Internet to improve public access to, and the quality of, the information. The survey records and land descriptions are being converted to digital, geospatial format. [45] BLM also is involved in a joint project with the Forest Service, states, counties, and private industry to develop a National Integrated Land System, a geospatial reference for lands throughout the nation regardless of ownership. A goal is to develop a common approach to compiling and making available the documents relating to the status of land so users can obtain all the attributes about a chosen parcel. [46]

Management

Overview

FLPMA set the framework for the current management of BLM lands. Among other important provisions, the law provides that:

- the national interest will be best realized if the public lands and their resources are periodically and systematically inventoried and their present and future use is projected through a land use planning process coordinated with other Federal and State planning efforts ...
- management be on the basis of multiple use and sustained yield unless otherwise specified by law ...
- the United States receive fair market value of the use of the public lands and their resources unless otherwise provided for by statute ...
- the public lands be managed in a manner that will protect the quality of scientific, scenic, historical, ecological, environmental, air and atmospheric, water resource, and archeological values; that, where appropriate, will preserve and protect certain public lands in their natural condition; that will provide food and habitat for fish and wildlife and domestic animals; and that will provide for outdoor recreation and human occupancy and use....

Thus, FLPMA established the BLM as a multiple-use, sustained-yield agency. However, some lands are withdrawn from one or more uses, or managed for a predominant use. The agency inventories its lands and resources and develops land use plans for its land units. All BLM lands (except some lands in Alaska), as well as the 700 million acres of mineral resources managed by BLM, are covered by a land use plan. Although plans are to be amended or revised as new issues arise or conditions change, a large number of land use plans were developed in the 1970s or 1980s and are in need of substantial revision or replacement to take account of changes during recent years. In FY2001, BLM began a multiyear effort to develop new land use plans and update existing ones, driven by such changes as increased demands for energy resources, a rise in use of off-highway vehicles and other types of recreation, additions to the National Landscape Conservation System, new listings of species under the Endangered Species Act, a buildup of biomass fuels on public lands, and a need to mitigate the effects of wildfires.

Rangelands

Livestock grazing is permitted on an estimated 162 million acres of BLM land. In some western states, more than half of all cattle graze on public rangelands during at least part of the year, although the forage consumed on federal lands is a small percentage of all forage consumed by beef cattle nationally. The grazing of cattle and sheep, and range management programs generally, are authorized by the Taylor Grazing Act, FLPMA, and the Public Rangelands Improvement Act of 1978 (PRIA). The Taylor Grazing Act converted the public rangelands from a system of common open grazing to one of exclusive permits to graze allotted lands. FLPMA set out overall public land management and policy objectives. PRIA reflected continuing concern over the condition and productivity of public rangelands and established more specific range management provisions for BLM. An example is a new grazing fee formula that was temporary but essentially has been continued under executive order.

BLM's range programs include management of wild horses and burros under the Wild, Free-Roaming Horses and Burros Act of 1971. [47] Currently there are about 60,000 wild horses and burros under BLM management — 36,000 on public land and 24,000 in long-term holding facilities. The herd size on the range is significantly more than the agency has determined is appropriate (ecologically sustainable) —approximately 26,400. BLM seeks to reduce animals on the range through adoption, fertility control, permanent or temporary holding facilities, and other means. In its FY2005 Budget Justification, BLM cites insufficient funds to remove animals from the range and care for those in holding facilities. For years, management of wild horses and burros has been controversial.

Energy and Minerals

BLM administers onshore federal energy and mineral resources. The agency is responsible for approximately 700 million acres of federal subsurface minerals, and supervises the mineral operations on about 56 million acres of Indian trust lands. An estimated 165 million of the 700 million acres have been withdrawn from mineral entry, leasing, and sale, except for valid existing rights. Lands in the National Park System (except National Recreation Areas), Wilderness System, and the Arctic National Wildlife Refuge (ANWR) are among those withdrawn. Mineral development on 182 million acres is subject to the approval of the surface management agency, and must not be in conflict with the land designation. Wildlife refuges (except ANWR), wilderness study areas, and identified roadless areas, among others, are in this category.

There are three approaches to development of federal mineral resources. One approach is locating and patenting mining claims for hard rock (locatable) minerals. A second approach is competitive and noncompetitive leasing of lands for leaseable minerals (oil, gas, coal, potash, geothermal energy, and certain other minerals). A third approach is the sale or free disposal of common mineral materials (e.g., sand and gravel) not subject to the mining or leasing laws.

In 2003, 42% of the coal, 11% of the natural gas, and 5% of the oil produced in the United States were derived from BLM managed resources. [48] These resources generate large revenues. For FY2003, the total on-shore mineral revenues (including royalties, rents, and bonus bids) were $2.2 billion, a substantial increase over recent years primarily due to higher oil and gas prices. The demand for energy from BLM managed lands continues to increase, and a goal of the Bush Administration is to augment energy supply from federal lands.

National Landscape Conservation System

In 2000, BLM created the National Landscape Conservation System, comprised of different types of units —national monuments, conservation areas, wilderness areas, wilderness study areas, wild and scenic rivers, and scenic and historic trails. Approximately 42 million acres currently are in the system (excluding trails and rivers), to give them greater recognition, management attention, and resources, according to BLM statements. Areas are managed based on their relevant authorities; for instance, the 6.5 million acres of designated wilderness are managed in accordance with FLPMA and the Wilderness Act. Another 15.6 million acres of wilderness study areas are to be managed by BLM to maintain their suitability for wilderness designation until legislation is enacted to determine their final status. (For more information on wilderness, see "The National Wilderness Preservation System," below.)

The agency's 15 national monuments and 17 national conservation areas are a particular focus of the system. BLM management emphasizes resource conservation overall and in general units are to serve outdoor recreationists. Other activities, such as grazing and hunting, may continue if they are compatible with the designation.

The proximity of BLM lands to many areas of population growth in the West has led to an increase in recreation on some agency lands. Recreational activities include hunting, fishing, visiting cultural and natural sites, birdwatching, hiking, picnicking, camping, boating, mountain biking, and off-highway vehicle driving. BLM collects money for permits for recreation on its lands, such as permits issued to hunting and fishing guide outfitters. The agency also charges entrance and use fees on some of its lands under the Recreational Fee Demonstration Program authorized by Congress. The growing and diverse nature of recreation on BLM lands has increased the challenge of balancing different types of recreation, such as hiking and driving off-highway vehicles, and balancing recreation with other land uses.

Fire Management

Recent fire seasons have been among the most severe in decades due to long-term drought, build-up of fuels, and increased population in the wildland-urban interface. BLM carries out fire management on approximately 370 million acres of DOI, and certain other federal and nonfederal lands. [49] The Forest Service provides fire protection of the national forests. A focus of both agencies is implementation of the national fire plan, under a 10-year strategy developed jointly by the agencies and other partners. Goals of the strategy are to improve fire prevention and suppression, reduce fuels, restore fire- adapted ecosystems, and promote community assistance. Another focus of the agencies is implementation of the Healthy Forests Restoration Act of 2003 (P.L. 108-148), which sought to expedite fuel reduction on federal lands and authorized other forest protection programs.

Land Ownership

General

BLM lands often are intermingled with other federal or private lands. Many federal grants consisted of alternating sections of lands, often referred to as "checkerboard," resulting in a mixed ownership grid pattern. FLPMA consolidated procedures and clarified responsibilities regarding problems that arise because of this ownership pattern, including rights-of-way across public lands for roads, trails, pipelines, power lines, canals, reservoirs, etc. FLPMA also provided for land exchanges, acquisitions, disposals, and remedies for certain title problems.

Acquisition Authority [50]

BLM has rather broad, general authority to acquire lands principally under §205 of FLPMA. Specifically, the Secretary is authorized (43 U.S.C. §1715(a)):

> to acquire pursuant to this Act [FLPMA] by purchase, exchange, donation, or eminent domain, lands or interests therein: *Provided,* That with respect to the public lands, the Secretary may exercise the power of eminent domain only if necessary to secure access to public lands, and then only if the lands so acquired are confined to as narrow a corridor as is necessary to serve such purpose.

BLM may acquire land or interests in land, especially inholdings, to protect threatened natural and cultural resources, increase opportunities for public recreation, restore the health of the land, and improve management of these areas. The agency often acquires land by exchange, and completed 132 exchanges in FY2003. Although FLPMA and NFMA were amended in 1988 to "streamline ... and expedite" the process, exchanges may still be time consuming and costly because of problems related to land valuation, cultural and archaeological resources inventories, and other issues. Recent concerns about the BLM exchange program, including regarding the determination of fair market value and the extent of public benefit of exchanges undertaken, prompted BLM to change the requirements and procedures of the program. [51]

Disposal Authority

The BLM can dispose of public lands under several authorities. A primary means of disposal is through exchanges, just as a primary means of acquisition is through exchanges. Disposal authorities include sales under FLPMA, patents under the General Mining Law of 1872, transfers to other governmental units for public purposes, and other statutes. [52]

With regard to sales, §203 of FLPMA authorized the BLM to sell certain tracts of public land that meet specific criteria (43 U.S.C. §1713(a)):

1. such tract because of its location or other characteristics is difficult and uneconomic to manage as part of the public lands, and is not suitable for management by another Federal department or agency; or
2. such tract was acquired for a specific purpose and the tract is no longer required for that or any other Federal purpose; or
3. disposal of such tract will serve important public objectives, including but not limited to, expansion of communities and economic development, which cannot be achieved prudently or feasibly on land other than public land and which outweigh other public objectives and values, including, but not limited to, recreation and scenic values, which would be served by maintaining such tract in Federal ownership.

The size of the tracts for sale is to be determined by "the land use capabilities and development requirements." Proposals to sell tracts of more than 2,500 acres must first be submitted to Congress, and such sales may be made unless disapproved by Congress. [53] Tracts are to be sold at not less than their fair market value, generally through competitive bidding, although modified competition and non-competitive sales are allowed.

The General Mining Law of 1872 [54] allows access to certain minerals on federal lands that have not been withdrawn from entry. Minerals within a valid mining claim can be developed without obtaining full title to the land. However, with evidence of minerals and sufficient developmental effort, mining claims can be patented, with full title transferred to the claimant upon payment of the appropriate fee — \$5.00 per acre for vein or lode claims (30 U.S.C. §29) or \$2.50 per acre for placer claims (30 U.S.C. §37). Non-mineral lands used for associated milling or other processing operations can also be patented (30 U.S.C. §42). Patented lands may be used for purposes other than mineral development.

The Recreation and Public Purposes Act (43 U.S.C. §869) [55] authorizes the Secretary, upon application by a qualified applicant, to:

> dispose of any public lands to a State, Territory, county, municipality, or other State, Territorial, or Federal instrumentality or political subdivision for any public purposes, or to a nonprofit corporation or nonprofit association for any recreational or any public purpose consistent with its articles of incorporation or other creating authority.

The act specifies conditions, qualifications, and acreage limitations for transfer, and provides for restoring the lands to the public domain if conditions are not met.

BLM also conducts land disposals under two recent laws providing for land disposal and establishing funding sources for subsequent land acquisition. First, the Federal Land Transaction Facilitation Act (Title II, P.L. 106-248, 43 U.S.C. §2301) provides for the sale or exchange of land identified for disposal under BLM's land use plans "as in effect" at enactment. Land sales are being conducted under the provisions of FLPMA. The proceeds from the sale or exchange of public land are to be deposited into a separate Treasury account (the Federal Land Disposal Account). Funds in the account are available to both the Secretary of the Interior and the Secretary of Agriculture to acquire inholdings and other nonfederal lands (or interests therein) that are adjacent to federal lands and contain exceptional resources. However, the Secretary of the Interior can use not more than 20% of the funds in the account for administrative and other expenses of the program. Not less than 80% of the funds for acquiring land are to be used to purchase land in the same state in which the funds were generated, while the remaining funds may be used to purchase land in any state. The law's findings state that it would "allow for the reconfiguration of land ownership patterns to better facilitate resource management; contribute to administrative efficiency within Federal land management units; and allow for increased effectiveness of the allocation of fiscal and human resources within the Federal land management agencies..."

Second, the Southern Nevada Public Land Management Act (P.L. 105-623) allows the Secretary of the Interior, through the BLM, to sell or exchange certain land around Las Vegas. The Secretary, through the BLM, and the relevant local government unit jointly choose the lands offered for sale or exchange. State and local governments get priority to acquire lands under the Recreation and Public Purposes Act. Much of the money from the sales is deposited into a special account that may be used for purposes including the acquisition of environmentally sensitive lands in Nevada. Some of the proceeds of land sales are set aside for other purposes, such as the State of Nevada general education program.

Withdrawals [56]

FLPMA also mandated review of public land withdrawals in 11 western states to determine whether, and for how long, existing withdrawals should be continued. A withdrawal is an action that restricts the use or disposition of public lands; for instance, some lands are withdrawn from mining. The agency continues to review approximately 70 million withdrawn acres, giving priority to about 26 million acres that are expected to be returned by another agency to BLM, or, in the case of BLM withdrawals, made available for one or more uses. To date, BLM has completed reviewing approximately 8 million withdrawn acres, mostly BLM and Bureau of Reclamation land; the withdrawals on more than 7 million of these acres have been revoked. The review process is likely to continue over the next several years, in part because the lands must be considered in BLM's planning process and the withdrawals must be supported by documentation under the National Environmental Policy Act (NEPA).

Issues

The public continues to value and use BLM lands for their diverse attributes and opportunities — open spaces, cultural resources, recreational pursuits, energy development, livestock grazing, timber production, etc. Issues and conflicts arise from these diverse and often opposing interests, with energy issues being among the most contentious. The President is promoting an expanded role for federal lands in supplying energy, and Congress is debating the extent, type, and location of development on federal lands. BLM has adopted regulatory changes to increase access to energy resources, such as streamlining the permitting process for oil and gas exploration and development. The emphasis on expanded production has exacerbated old controversies over the balance of uses of federal lands.

The development and patenting of hardrock minerals on public lands continues to receive attention. A focus has been the effect of BLM's revised hardrock mining regulations on the environment and the level of mining activity. A perennial debate is whether to change the 1872 mining law, which allows claimants to develop the minerals within a claim without paying royalties, and to patent the lands and obtain full title to the land and its minerals for a small fee ($2.50 or $5.00 an acre). The amount of land withdrawn from mineral entry or development has long been controversial and the subject of many lawsuits. A recent Legal Opinion of the Solicitor of the Department of the Interior allowed for multiple millsites per mining claim, reversing a 1997 Opinion and continuing concerns over the environmental impact of mining and the availability of lands for mineral development.

Rangeland management presents an array of issues. They include recent proposed changes in grazing regulations that would allow shared title of range improvements and private acquisition of water rights, reduce requirements for public input into grazing decisions, and make other changes. Another issue involves the terms and renewal of expiring grazing permits and leases, with recent law authorizing the automatic renewal of permits and leasing expiring through FY2008. The restriction or elimination of grazing on federal land because of environmental and recreational concerns is being discussed, and the grazing fee that the federal government charges for private livestock grazing on federal lands has been controversial since its inception. Other range issues include the condition of federal rangelands, the spread of invasive plant species, consistency of BLM and FS grazing programs, the role of Resource Advisory Councils, access across private lands, and management of riparian areas. Concerns about the wild horse and burro program relate to the removal, adoption, and treatment of the animals and BLM's administration of the program. A focus is BLM's current efforts to achieve its identified optimal herd size on the range.

Recent, severe wildfires have challenged BLM's fire management program and prompted the adoption of the National Fire Plan and the Healthy Forests Restoration Act. One issue is reducing the risk of wildland fire on federal lands through fuels reductions and other treatments. A second issue is the sufficiency of funds and procedures for suppressing fires, and the effect of borrowing funds from other programs for fire fighting. A third issue is the effect of fire on resource conditions, a compounding factor in areas experiencing drought, invasive species, and other changes.

A number of preservation and recreation matters have come to the fore. These include whether to establish or restrict protective designations; the effect of protective designations on land uses; and the role of Congress, states, and the public in making designations. Congress is examining executive actions designating national monuments on BLM and other federal lands under the Antiquities Act of 1906, [57] and discussing whether to restrict the President's authority to create monuments. Conflicts over different types of recreation, especially high-impact (e.g., OHV use) versus low-impact uses (e.g., backpacking), appear to have become more prevalent. With dramatic population growth in the West in the vicinity of BLM lands, and the public value on federal lands for recreation, these conflicts can be expected to remain prevalent. Another issue is access to public lands, including restrictions such as limits on use of off-highway vehicles. Other issues are the impact minerals within a claim without paying royalties, and to patent the lands and obtain full title to the land and its minerals for a small fee ($2.50 or $5.00 an acre). The amount of land withdrawn from mineral entry or development has long been controversial and the subject of many lawsuits. A recent Legal Opinion of the Solicitor of the Department of the Interior allowed for multiple millsites per mining claim, reversing a 1997 Opinion and continuing concerns over the environmental impact of mining and the availability of lands for mineral development.

Rangeland management presents an array of issues. They include recent proposed changes in grazing regulations that would allow shared title of range improvements and private acquisition of water rights, reduce requirements for public input into grazing decisions, and make other changes. Another issue involves the terms and renewal of expiring grazing permits and leases, with recent law authorizing the automatic renewal of permits and leasing expiring through FY2008. The restriction or elimination of grazing on federal land because of environmental and recreational concerns is being discussed, and the grazing fee that the federal government charges for private livestock grazing on federal lands has been controversial since its inception. Other range issues include the condition of federal rangelands, the spread of invasive plant species, consistency of BLM and FS grazing programs, the role of Resource Advisory Councils, access across private lands, and management of riparian areas. Concerns about the wild horse and burro program relate to the removal, adoption, and treatment of the animals and BLM's administration of the program. A focus is BLM's current efforts to achieve its identified optimal herd size on the range.

Recent, severe wildfires have challenged BLM's fire management program and prompted the adoption of the National Fire Plan and the Healthy Forests Restoration Act. One issue is reducing the risk of wildland fire on federal lands through fuels reductions and other treatments. A second issue is the sufficiency of funds and procedures for suppressing fires, and the effect of borrowing funds from other programs for fire fighting. A third issue is the effect of fire on resource conditions, a compounding factor in areas experiencing drought, invasive species, and other changes.

A number of preservation and recreation matters have come to the fore. These include whether to establish or restrict protective designations; the effect of protective designations on land uses; and the role of Congress, states, and the public in making designations. Congress is examining executive actions designating national monuments on BLM and other federal lands under the Antiquities Act of 1906,[57] and discussing whether to restrict the President's authority to create monuments. Conflicts over different types of recreation, especially high-impact (e.g., OHV use) versus low-impact uses (e.g., backpacking), appear to have become more prevalent. With dramatic population growth in the West in the vicinity of BLM lands, and the public value on federal lands for recreation, these conflicts can be expected to remain prevalent. Another issue is access to public lands, including restrictions such as limits on use of off-highway vehicles. Other issues are the impact of recreation on resources and facilities and the collection of fees for recreation use, for example, under the Recreational Fee Demonstration Program.

Another key topic relates to the amount of land BLM owns and how the land is managed. Contemporary questions have centered on how much land should be acquired versus conveyed to state, local, or private ownership, and under what circumstances. Congress confronts concerns about acquisition of private land, the effectiveness of land exchange programs, and the effect of public ownership on state taxes and authorities. A related issue is whether to expand the non-federal role in managing federal lands.

Major Statutes

Alaska National Interest Lands Conservation Act of 1980: Act of Dec. 2, 1980; P.L. 96-487, 94 Stat. 2371. 16 U.S.C. §§3101, et seq.

Federal Land Exchange Facilitation Act of 1988: Act of Aug. 20, 1988; P.L. 100-409, 102 Stat. 1086. 43 U.S.C. §1716.

Federal Land Policy and Management Act of 1976: Act of Oct. 21, 1976; P.L. 94-579, 90 Stat. 2744. 43 U.S.C. §§1701, et seq.

Federal Land Transaction Facilitation Act: Act of July 25, 2000; P.L. 106-248, 114 Stat. 613. 43 U.S.C. §§2301, et seq.

General Mining Law of 1872: R.S. 2319, derived from Act of May 10, 1872; ch. 152, 17 Stat. 91. 30 U.S.C. §§22, et seq.

Materials Act of 1947: Act of July 31, 1947; ch. 406, 61 Stat. 681. 30 U.S.C. §§601, et seq.

Mineral Leasing Act for Acquired Lands: Act of Aug. 7, 1947; ch. 513, 61 Stat. 913. 30 U.S.C. §§351-359.

Mineral Leasing Act of 1920: Act of Feb. 25, 1920; ch. 85, 41 Stat. 437. 30 U.S.C. §§181, et seq.

Public Rangelands Improvement Act of 1978: Act of Oct. 25, 1978; P.L. 95-514, 92 Stat. 1803. 43 U.S.C. §§1901, et seq.

Southern Nevada Public Land Management Act of 1998: Act of Oct. 19, 1998; P.L. 105-263, 112 Stat. 2343. 31 U.S.C. §6901 note.

Taylor Grazing Act of 1934: Act of June 28, 1934; ch. 865, 48 Stat. 1269. 43 U.S.C. §§315, et seq.

Wild Horses and Burros Act of 1971: Act of Dec. 15, 1971; P.L. 92-195, 85 Stat. 649. 16 U.S.C. §§1331, et seq.

CRS Reports and Committee Prints [58]

CRS Issue Brief IB10076, *Bureau of Land Management (BLM) Lands and National Forests*, coordinated by Ross W. Gorte and Carol Hardy Vincent.

CRS Report RS21402, *Federal Lands, "Disclaimers of Interest," and R.S. 2477*, by Pamela Baldwin.

CRS Report RS21232, *Grazing Fees: An Overview and Current Issues*, by Carol Hardy Vincent.

CRS Report RL32244, *Grazing Regulations and Policies: Changes by the Bureau of Land Management*, by Carol Hardy Vincent.

CRS Report RL32142, *Highway Rights of Way on Public Lands: R.S. 2477 and Disclaimers of Interest*, by Pamela Baldwin.

CRS Issue Brief IB89130, *Mining on Federal Lands*, by Marc Humphries. CRS Report RS20902, *National Monument Issues*, by Carol Hardy Vincent. CRS Report RS21423, *Wild Horse and Burro Issues*, by Carol Hardy Vincent. CRS Report RS21544, *Wildfire Protection Funding*, by Ross W. Gorte.

THE NATIONAL WILDLIFE REFUGE SYSTEM [59]

The National Wildlife Refuge System (NWRS) is dedicated primarily to the conservation of animals and plants. Other uses — hunting, fishing, recreation, timber harvest, grazing, etc. — are permitted only to the extent that they are compatible with the purposes for which the refuge was created. [60] In 1997, Congress established compatible wildlife-dependent recreation as a priority for the NWRS. Some have characterized the NWRS as intermediate in protection between the BLM and FS lands and NPS lands, but this is not entirely accurate. [61] The NWRS resembles the FS or BLM lands in allowing some commercial uses, but in certain cases, uses (e.g., public access) can be substantially more restricted than for NPS lands.

Background

The first national wildlife refuge was established at Pelican Island, FL, by executive order of President Theodore Roosevelt in 1903. By September 30, 2002, there were 540 refuges totaling 92.1 million acres in 50 states, the Pacific Territories, Puerto Rico, and the Virgin Islands (see Figures 4 and 5.) [62] The largest increase in acreage by far occurred with the addition of 53 million acres of refuge land under the Alaska National Interest Lands Conservation Act of 1980. Alaska now has 76.8 million acres of refuge lands — 80.5% of the system. Within 63 of the refuges are 78 designated wilderness areas, ranging from 2 acres at Green Bay National Wildlife Refuge (NWR) in Wisconsin to 8.0 million acres at Arctic NWR in Alaska. [63]

The NWRS includes two other categories of land besides refuges: (1) the 203 Waterfowl Production Area (WPA) districts, private lands managed in accordance with agreements between the farmers and ranchers who own the land and the FWS; and (2) 50 Wildlife Coordination Areas (WCAs), owned primarily by FWS, but also by other parties, including some federal agencies; they generally are managed by state agencies under agreements with the FWS. These bring the NWRS to 793 units. [64] These two additional categories bring the total land in the NWRS (counting refuges, WPAs, and WCAs) to 95.4 million acres. In approximately 1.7 million acres of the NWRS, FWS has secondary jurisdiction: the FWS has some influence over activities on these lands, but the lands are owned or managed principally by some other agency, subject to the mandates of that agency.

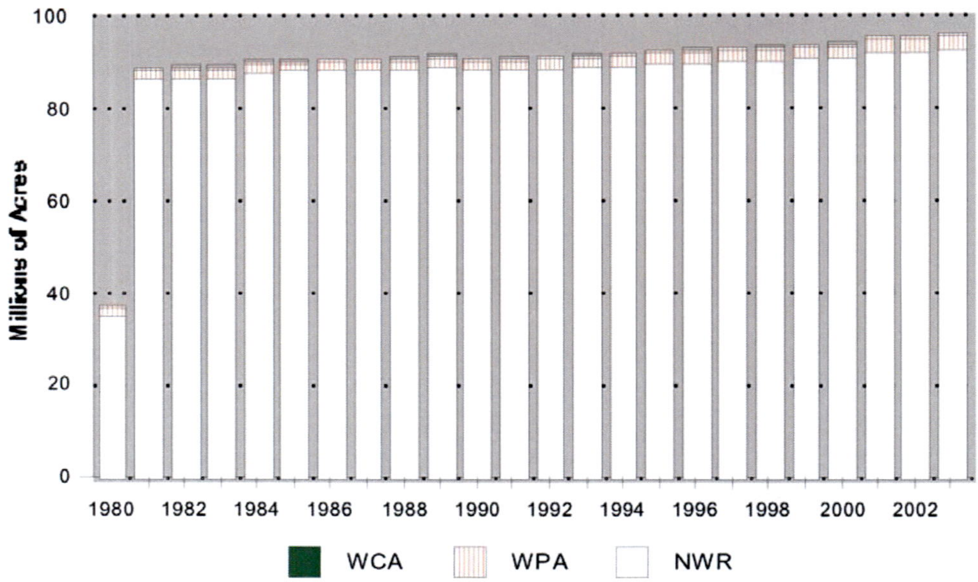

Figure 4. Acreage in the National Wildlife Refuge System (FY1980-FY2003).

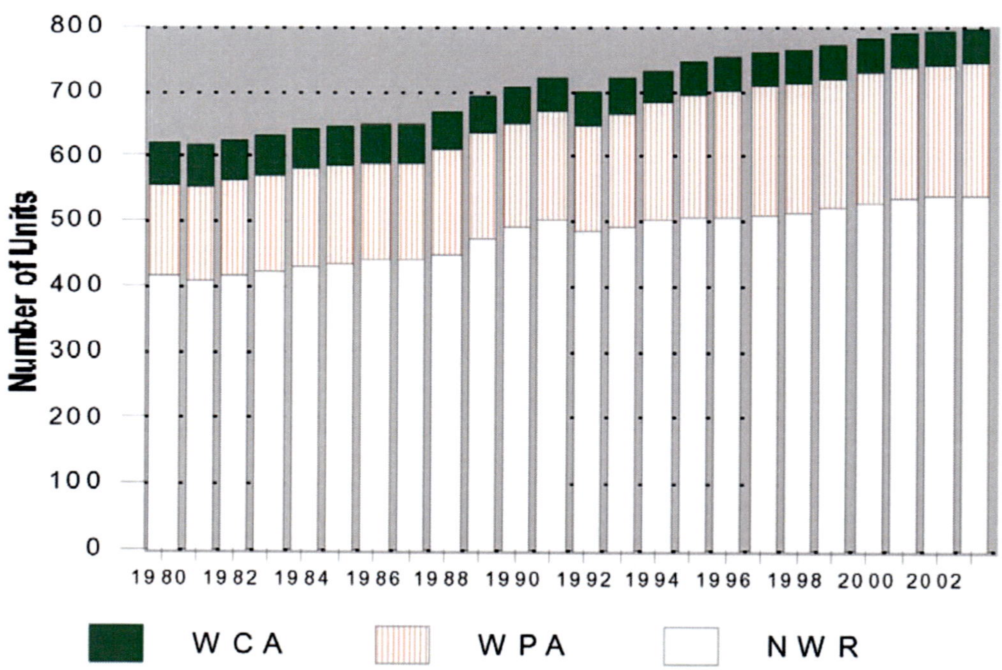

Source: Annual Report of Lands Under Control of the U.S. Fish and Wildlife Service, as of Sept. 30 of each fiscal year.

Notes: Major acreage was added to the system in December 1980 under ANILCA. ANILCA also consolidated a number of existing Alaskan refuges. In 1992, the number of units dropped due to consolidation of various refuges.

Figure 5. Number of Units in the National Wildlife Refuge System (FY1980-FY2003).

Organization and Management

The National Wildlife Refuge System Administration Act of 1966, [65] as amended, stated the purpose for establishing the system as consolidating the several authorities of the Secretary of the Interior over lands administered for the conservation and protection of fish and wildlife. Conservation of wildlife is the primary emphasis in the three types of areas in the NWRS, but the options for alternative resource use within the areas vary.

In the 105th Congress, the National Wildlife Refuge System Improvement Act of 1997 (P.L. 105-57) [66] addressed overarching refuge management controversies facing the FWS. This law clarified that the purpose of the NWRS is the "conservation, management and, where appropriate, restoration of the fish, wildlife and plant resources and their habitats." Another key provision of this law designated "compatible wildlife-dependent recreational uses involving hunting, fishing, wildlife observation and photography, and environmental education and interpretation as priority public uses of the Refuge System." It also required that priority public uses must "receive enhanced consideration over other general public uses in planning and management within the System." At the same time, the law continued the statutory policy that activities that are not wildlife-dependent (e.g., grazing, growing hay, etc.) may be permitted, provided they are compatible with wildlife. Some interest groups argued that the resulting regulations did not allow for sufficient public access for some forms of recreation, such as off-road vehicles or personal watercraft.

Wildlife refuges provide habitat for various plant and animal species, particularly emphasizing habitat for migratory waterfowl and for endangered species. Individual refuges may consist of single contiguous blocks or disjunct parcels scattered over a larger area. Research on wildlife conservation is carried out by the FWS on refuges (as well as on other areas). [67] Energy and mineral activities are permitted in certain refuges and under certain circumstances; any mineral rights owned by the United States are administered by BLM. Hunting, fishing, and other recreational uses frequently are permitted, but only to the extent that these activities are compatible with the major purposes for which a particular refuge was established. In refuges set aside for migratory birds, waterfowl hunting is limited to 40% of the refuge area unless the Secretary determines that hunting in a greater area is beneficial.

WPAs are managed primarily to provide breeding habitat for migratory waterfowl. [68] As of September 30, 2002, these areas totaled 2.9 million acres, of which 0.7 million acres were federally owned and 2.2 million acres were managed by the private landowners under leases, easements, or agreements with FWS. These areas are found mainly in the potholes and interior wetlands of the North Central states, a region sometimes called "North America's Duck Factory." In these areas, there is considerably less conflicting resource use, in part because the areas managed under lease are not subject to the federal mining and mineral leasing laws, and because the size of individual tracts is relatively small. However, the leased lands may be less secure as wildlife habitat because they may be converted later to agricultural use by the private owners. The WCAs (0.3 million acres) are owned primarily by FWS, but also by other parties, including some federal agencies; they are managed by state wildlife agencies under cooperative agreements with FWS.

The management of the NWRS is divided into three tiers: the 793 individual NWRS units under seven regional offices, and the national office in Washington, DC. Each of the seven regional offices is administered by a regional director who has considerable autonomy in operating the refuges within the region. FWS is headed by a director, a deputy director, and

11 assistant directors who head programs not only for the National Wildlife Refuge System, but also for Wildlife and Sport Fish Restoration; Migratory Birds; Fisheries and Habitat Conservation; Endangered Species; Law Enforcement (titled "Chief"); International Affairs; External Affairs; Budget, Planning, and Human Resources; Business Management and Operations; and Information Resources Technology Management.

Land Ownership

Growth of the NWRS may come about in a number of ways. Certain laws provide general authority to expand the NWRS, including primarily the Migratory Bird Treaty Act (MBTA) of 1929, [69] but also the Fish and Wildlife Coordination Act, the Fish and Wildlife Act of 1956, and the Endangered Species Act. [70] These general authorities allow the FWS to add lands to the Refuge System without specific congressional action.

Some units have been created by specific acts of Congress (e.g., Protection Island NWR, WA; Bayou Sauvage NWR, LA; or John Heinz NWR, PA). [71] Other units have been created by executive order. Also, FLPMA authorizes the Secretary of the Interior to withdraw lands from the public domain for additions to the NWRS, although all withdrawals exceeding 5,000 acres are subject to congressional approval procedures (43 U.S.C. §1714(c)). [72]

Acquisition Authority

The primary acquisition authority has been the MBTA. This act authorizes the Secretary to recommend areas "necessary for the conservation of migratory birds" [73] to the Migratory Bird Conservation Commission, after consulting with the relevant governor (or state agency) and appropriate local government officials (16 U.S.C. §715c). The Secretary may then purchase or rent areas approved by the Commission (§715d(1)), and "acquire, by gift or devise, any area or interest therein ..." (§715d(2)). [74]

New acquisitions result from transfers from the public domain or lands acquired from other owners. Nonfederal lands and interests in lands to create or add to specific NWRS units may be accepted as donations or purchased. Purchases may be made on a willing buyer/willing seller basis or under condemnation authorities. Condemnation authority was last used, under congressional direction contained in P.L. 99-333, for Protection Island NWR in 1986. [75] Purchases, regardless of authority or funding source, are rarely large. In FY2002, 68,014 acres were acquired (as opposed to transferred from other federal agencies), while $90.6 million was spent on acquisition. [76] As might be expected, refuges in western states tend to be formed from lands reserved from the public domain, while eastern refuges tend to be acquired lands.

The purchase of refuge lands is financed primarily through two funding sources: the Migratory Bird Conservation Fund (MBCF) and the Land and Water Conservation Fund (LWCF, see "Federal Lands Financing," above). [77] MBCF acquisitions have emphasized wetlands essential for migratory waterfowl, while LWCF acquisitions have encompassed the gamut of NWRS purposes. MBCF is supported from three sources (amounts in parentheses are FY2003 receipts deposited into the MBCF):

- the sale of hunting and conservation stamps (better known as *duck stamps*) purchased by hunters and certain visitors to refuges ($25.1 million); [78]

- import duties on arms and ammunition ($18.5 million); and
- 70% of certain refuge entrance fees ($0.15 million).

MBCF funds are permanently appropriated to the extent of these receipts and (after paying for engraving, printing, and distribution of the stamps) may be used for the "location, ascertainment, and acquisition of suitable areas for migratory bird refuges ... and administrative costs incurred in the acquisition" of the new acquisitions whose number varies from year to year (16 U.S.C. §718d(b)). However, the acquisition must be "approved by the Governor of the State or appropriate State agency" (§715k-5). The predictability of MBCF funding makes it assume special importance in the FWS budget. This contrasts with LWCF funding, which has fluctuated significantly from year to year. In FY2003, the MBCF received $43.8 million from its permanently appropriated sources, and Congress appropriated $72.9 million from the LWCF for FWS land acquisition.

Disposal Authority

With certain exceptions, NWRS lands can be disposed only by an act of Congress (16 U.S.C. §668dd(a)(6)). Also, for refuge lands reserved from the public domain, FLPMA prohibits the Secretary from modifying or revoking any withdrawal which added lands to the NWRS (43 U.S.C. §1714(j)). For acquired lands, disposal is allowed only if: (1) the disposal is part of an authorized land exchange (16 U.S.C. §668dd(a)(6) and (b)(3)); or (2) the Secretary determines the lands are no longer needed and the Migratory Bird Conservation Commission approves (§668dd(a)(5)). In the latter case, the disposal must recover the acquisition cost or be at the fair market value (whichever is higher).

Issues

The most enduring controversy concerning the NWRS has been that of conflicting uses, with some critics arguing that FWS has been too lenient in its decisions about commercial and extractive uses or developed recreation; others criticize its policies as too restrictive. Specific conflicts have arisen between such activities as grazing, energy extraction, power boat recreation, motorized access, and similar activities on the one hand, and the purposes for which refuges were designated on the other. [79]

In recent years, a controversy developed over the propriety of hunting (and, to a lesser extent, fishing) on refuge lands. The pro-hunting position is based largely on two arguments: (1) the purchase of migratory duck stamps by hunters has paid for a substantial portion of refuge land, mainly in areas suitable for waterfowl habitat; and (2) the animal population is the appropriate measure of conservation, and removal of individual animals for human use is not harmful, and may be beneficial as long as the population growth rate is maintained. The anti-hunting argument holds that no place can be considered a "refuge" if its major wildlife residents are regularly hunted. They contend further that since fewer people now hunt [80] and the enjoyment of this sport hinders use of the land by others (by restricting access for safety reasons), then hunting should be eliminated to allow fuller access by non-hunting users. While various bills have been introduced over the years to eliminate or restrict hunting on refuges, others have been introduced to support it.

Over the past several years, the backlog of unmet maintenance needs of the federal land management agencies has been an issue of focus of the Congress and the Administration. Although there is debate over the amount of FWS money that should be spent on the deferred maintenance backlog versus the acquisition of additional federal lands, there is broad consensus that maintenance of the NWRS has lagged. The funding for deferred maintenance projects in the NWRS increased from \$48.1 million in FY2002 to \$66.5 million in FY2004. The maintenance backlog is expected to figure in the debate over appropriations in future years.

One refuge — the Arctic National Wildlife Refuge — remains locked in a decades-long controversy regarding proposals for energy development in the biologically and geologically rich northern part of this refuge. This complex issue is covered extensively in CRS Report RL31278, *Arctic National Wildlife Refuge: Background and Issues*, coordinated by M. Lynne Corn, and in CRS Issue Brief IB10111, *Arctic National Wildlife Refuge (ANWR): Controversies for the 108th Congress*, by M. Lynne Corn, Bernard A. Gelb, and Pamela Baldwin.

Major Statutes

Alaska National Interest Lands Conservation Act of 1980: Act of December 2, 1980; P.L. 96-487, 94 Stat. 2371. 16 U.S.C. §3101, et seq.

Endangered Species Act of 1973: Act of Dec. 28, 1973; P.L. 93-205, 87 Stat. 884. 16 U.S.C. 1531-1544.

Fish and Wildlife Act of 1956: Act of August 8, 1956; ch. 1036, 70 Stat. 1120. 16 U.S.C. §742a, et seq.

Fish and Wildlife Coordination Act of 1934: Act of March 10, 1934; ch. 55, 48 Stat. 401. 16 U.S.C. §661-667e.

Migratory Bird Treaty Act of 1918: Act of July 13, 1918; ch. 128, 40 Stat. 755. 16 U.S.C. §703-712.

National Wildlife Refuge System Administration Act of 1966: Act of October 15, 1966; P.L. 90-404, 80 Stat. 927. 16 U.S.C. §668dd-668ee.

National Wildlife Refuge System Improvement Act of 1997: Act of October 9, 1997; P.L. 105-57. 16 U.S.C. §668dd.

San Francisco Bay National Wildlife Refuge: Act of June 30, 1972; P.L. 92-330, 86 Stat. 399. 16 U.S.C. §668dd note. (A typical statute establishing a refuge.)

CRS Reports and Committee Prints [81]

CRS Report RL31278, *Arctic National Wildlife Refuge: Background and Issues*, M. Lynne Corn, coordinator.

CRS Issue Brief IB10111, *Arctic National Wildlife Refuge (ANWR): Controversies for the 108th Congress*, by M. Lynne Corn, Bernard A. Gelb, and Pamela Baldwin.

CRS Report 90-192, *Fish and Wildlife Service: Compensation to Local Governments*, by M. Lynne Corn.

THE NATIONAL PARK SYSTEM [82]

Perhaps the federal land category best known to the public is the National Park System. The National Park Service (NPS) currently manages 388 system units, including 56 units formally entitled *national parks* (often referred to as the "crown jewels" of the system), as well as national monuments, battlefields, military parks, historical parks, historic sites, lakeshores, seashores, recreation areas, reserves, preserves, scenic rivers and trails, and other designations. The system has grown to a total of 84.4 million acres — 79.0 million acres of federal land, 1.2 million acres of other public land, and 4.2 million acres of private land — in 49 states, the District of Columbia, and U.S. territories. Passage of ANILCA in 1980 roughly doubled the acreage of the National Park System because of the large size of the new parks in Alaska. The acreage has been relatively stable in recent years, as new authorizations and land acquisitions have been modest. The NPS has the often contradictory mission of facilitating access and serving visitors while protecting and preserving the natural, historic, and cultural integrity of the lands and resources it manages.

Background

By the Act of March 1, 1872, Congress established Yellowstone National Park in the then-territories of Idaho, Montana, and Wyoming "as a public park or pleasuring ground for the benefit and enjoyment of the people." [83] The park was placed under the exclusive control of the Secretary of the Interior, who was responsible for developing regulations to "provide for the preservation, from injury or spoliation, of all timber, mineral deposits, natural curiosities, or wonders within said park, and their retention in their natural condition." [84] Other park functions were to include developing visitor accommodations, building roads and trails, removing trespassers (mostly poachers) from the park, and protecting "against wanton destruction of fish and game." [85]

When Yellowstone National Park was authorized, there was no concept or plan for the development of a system of such parks. The concept now firmly established as the National Park System, embracing a diversity of natural and cultural resources nationwide, evolved slowly over the years. This idea of a national park was an American invention of historic proportions, marking the start of a global conservation movement that today accounts for hundreds of national parks (or equivalent conservation preserves) throughout the world. The American National Park System continues to serve as an international model for preservation.

At the same time that interest was growing in preserving the scenic wonders of the American West, efforts were underway to protect the sites and structures associated with early Native American cultures, particularly in the Southwest. In 1906, Congress enacted the Antiquities Act to authorize the President "to declare by public proclamation [as national monuments] historic and prehistoric structures and other objects of historic or scientific interest." [86] In the years following the establishment of Yellowstone, national parks and monuments were authorized or proclaimed, principally from the public domain lands in the West, and were administered by the Department of the Interior (initially with help from the U.S. Army). However, no single agency provided unified management of the varied federal parklands.

On August 25, 1916, President Woodrow Wilson signed the act creating the National Park Service, a new federal agency in the Department of the Interior with the responsibility for protecting the national parks and many of the monuments then in existence and those yet to be established. This action reflected a developing national concern for preserving the nation's heritage. This "Organic Act" states that the National Park "Service then established shall promote and regulate the use of Federal areas known as national parks, monuments and reservations ... to conserve the scenery and the natural and historic objects and the wildlife therein and to provide for the enjoyment of the same in such manner and by such means as will leave them unimpaired for the enjoyment of future generations." [87] By executive order in 1933, President Franklin D. Roosevelt transferred 63 national monuments and military sites from the Forest Service and War Department to the National Park Service. This action was a major step in the development of a truly national system of parks. [88]

Of the four federal land management agencies, the NPS manages the most diverse collection of units. More than 20 different designations are used for park sites or areas, ranging from the traditional national park designation to scenic rivers and trails, memorials, battlefields, historic sites, historic parks, seashores, lakeshores, recreation areas, and monuments. Because of this variety of park unit designations and the public perception of lesser status for units lacking the *national park* designation, Congress sought to establish that all units in the system are to be considered of equal value. A 1970 law stated that all NPS units are part of "one national park system preserved and managed for the benefit and inspiration of all people of the United States...." [89] In 1978, Congress amended that law to reassert the system-wide standard of protection for all areas administered by the NPS. [90]

Organization and Management

The National Park Service manages the 388 units of the National Park System. The Director of the National Park Service, headquartered in Washington, DC, is the chief administrative officer of the Service, with an immediate staff of two deputy directors, five associate directors, and a number of policy and program office managers. Directly overseeing NPS operations is the Interior Department's Assistant Secretary for Fish, Wildlife, and Parks. In addition, the National Park Service Advisory Board, composed of private citizens with requisite experience and expertise, advises on management policies and on potential additions to the system. In 2001, the Advisory Board issued a report with recommendations on the future of the National Park System. [91]

The individual park units are arranged in seven regional offices, each headed by a regional director. The NPS had traditionally operated with 10 regional offices but eliminated three, while also forming a system of "park clusters." The reorganization, a part of the Clinton Administration's "reinvention" of government that involved downsizing and streamlining, was primarily designed to shift resources and personnel from central offices to field units. Regional offices and cluster support offices provide certain administrative functions and specialized staff services and expertise which were not believed to be practicable to have in each park unit. This shared assistance is particularly important to the smaller units. The individual units are overseen by a park superintendent, with staff generally commensurate with the size, public use, and significance of the unit. The park units in Alaska are an exception to this, with relatively few personnel in comparison to the large size of the holdings.

As stated, the basic NPS mission is twofold: (1) to conserve, preserve, protect, and interpret the natural, cultural, and historic resources of the nation for the public and (2) to provide for their enjoyment by the public. To a considerable extent, the NPS contributes to meeting the public demand for certain types of outdoor recreation. Scientific research is another activity encouraged in units of the Park System. Management direction is provided in the general statutes and in those that create and govern individual units. In general, activities which harvest or remove the resources within units of the system are not allowed. Mining, for instance, is generally prohibited, although in a limited number of national parks and monuments some mining is allowed, in accordance with the Mining in the Parks Act of 1976 (P.L. 94-429). Also, in authorizing certain additions to the system, Congress has specified that certain natural resource uses, such as oil and gas development or hunting, may — or shall — be permitted in specific units; examples include national preserves such as Big Cypress and national recreation areas such as Glen Canyon. Other uses are dealt with in specific enactments, such as the 1911 law dealing with rights-of-way through Park System units.

Land Ownership

Designation and Acquisition Authority

Most units of the National Park System have been created by Acts of Congress. In 1998, Congress amended existing law pertaining to the creation of new units to standardize procedures, improve information about potential additions, prioritize areas, focus attention on outstanding areas, and ensure congressional support for studies of possible additions. [92] The Secretary of the Interior is to investigate, study, and monitor nationally significant areas with potential for inclusion in the system. The Secretary is to submit annually to Congress a list of areas recommended for study for potential inclusion in the National Park System. The Secretary also is required to submit to Congress each year a list of previously studied areas that contain primarily historical resources, and a similar list of areas with natural resources, with areas ranked in order of priority for possible inclusion in the system. In practice, NPS performs these functions assigned to the Secretary.

In assessing whether to recommend a particular area, the NPS is required by law to consider: whether an area is nationally significant, and would be a suitable and feasible addition to the National Park System; whether an area represents or includes themes, sites, or resources "not adequately represented" in the system; and requests for studies in the form of public petitions and congressional resolutions. An actual study requires authorization by Congress, although the NPS may conduct certain preliminary assessment activities. In preparing studies, NPS must consider certain factors also established in law. After funds are made available, NPS must complete a study within three fiscal years.

Under the Antiquities Act of 1906, the President is authorized to proclaim national monuments on federal land, and to date about 120 monuments have been created by presidential proclamations. Many areas initially designated as national monuments were later converted into national parks by acts of Congress. Before 1940, Presidents used this authority frequently (for proclaiming 87 national monuments), but in 1978 President Carter set aside more land as national monuments (56 million acres in Alaska) than any other President. [93]

President Clinton used his authority under the Antiquities Act 22 times to proclaim 19 new monuments and enlarge 3 others. Other agencies also manage some national monuments, with the BLM managing many of the monuments created by President Clinton.

In addition to establishing a unit of the National Park System, an act of Congress may set the boundaries of the unit and authorize the NPS to acquire the nonfederal lands within those boundaries. The major funding source for such land acquisition has been the Land and Water Conservation Fund, described above in the section entitled "Federal Lands Financing." The Secretary is to include, in a report to Congress at least every three years, a "comprehensive listing of all authorized but unacquired lands within the exterior boundaries of each unit" (16 U.S.C. §1a-11(a)) and a "priority listing of all such unacquired parcels" (16 U.S.C. §1a-11(b)). Further, the general management plan for each unit is to include "indications of potential modifications to the external boundaries of the unit, and the reasons therefor" (16 U.S.C. §1a-7). The Secretary is to identify criteria to evaluate proposed boundary changes (16 U.S.C. §1a-12). Further, the Secretary is authorized to make minor boundary adjustments for "proper preservation, protection, interpretation, or management" and to acquire the nonfederal lands within the adjusted boundary (16 U.S.C. §460*l*-9(c)).

Disposal Authority

Units (and lands) of the National Park System established by acts of Congress can be disposed of only by acts of Congress. Non-NPS lands encompassed by minor boundary adjustments can be acquired through land exchanges, but, unlike for some of the other federal land management agencies, the Secretary may not convey property administered as part of the National Park System to acquire lands by exchange. [94] Finally, the Secretary cannot modify or revoke any withdrawal creating a national monument. [95] Thus, with minor exceptions, National Park System lands can be changed from that status or disposed of only by an act of Congress.

Issues

Striking a balance between appropriate public use of National Park System lands for recreation and protecting the integrity of park resources is a continuing challenge to the NPS and the congressional committees providing agency oversight. Motorized recreation in NPS units presents particular challenges, with debates over the economic and environmental impacts of, safety of, and level of access for such types of recreation and the adequacy of existing laws and regulations governing motorized use. Manufacturers and user groups fear that NPS limits would be economically damaging to communities and industries serving users, unfairly restrict access, and set a precedent for other federal land managers. Others, including environmentalists, fear that failure to adequately manage motorized use will damage resources and other park users, and increase pressure for additional forms of motorized access.

One focus of the motorized recreation debate is commercial air tours over NPS units. Currently, the NPS and the Federal Aviation Administration (FAA) are developing air tour management plans for park units to implement a law regulating commercial air tours over park units, and the FAA has proposed a rule providing safety standards for commercial air tours including over park units. Other issues relate to NPS regulation of the use of personal watercraft (PWC), such as jet skis, and snowmobiles in national parks. The NPS is developing regulations governing PWC for 16 park units to settle a successful lawsuit over unrestricted PWC use. Litigation and appeals continue over different versions of snowmobile regulations that would either restrict or allow snowmobile use in Yellowstone and Grand Teton National Parks and the John D. Rockefeller Jr. Memorial Parkway.

Over the years, Congress has added new units to the Park System as well as expanded the management responsibilities of the NPS. These new obligations, together with increased numbers of visitors, have stretched the Park System's operational capabilities and contributed to a multibillion dollar backlog of deferred maintenance. While overall NPS appropriations have increased annually in recent years, they have not kept pace with operational and maintenance needs. Increased priorities on security and protection also have affected park funding. The NPS claims to be implementing President Bush's initiative, begun in FY2002, to eliminate a then-estimated $4.9 billion maintenance backlog over five years; there is disagreement about whether the Administration is on track to eliminate the maintenance backlog. By the end of FY2004, the NPS expects to have completed a computerized inventory and assessment of every facility in the Park System, and by FY2006, estimated costs of repairing facilities and a list of maintenance priorities.

Congress authorized a Recreational Fee Demonstration Program to supplement NPS and other land management agency appropriations with higher entrance and recreation user fees (described above under "Federal Lands Financing"). There is controversy over whether to make the program permanent and if so in what form and for which agencies — for the NPS only, all four land management agencies currently participating in the program, or additional federal agencies (such as the federal water project agencies — the Bureau of Reclamation and the Corps of Engineers). The temporary program was initiated in the FY1996 Omnibus Consolidated Rescissions and Appropriations Act (P.L. 104-134, §315), and allows most of the higher fees charged by participating agencies to be retained at the sites where the money is collected, rather than returned to the U.S. Treasury. It continues to be tested by the agencies and has been extended in appropriations laws, most recently through December 2005 for fee collection to give the authorizing committees time to consider establishing a permanent program. Many citizens have objected to paying additional fees for previously free or low-cost recreation in the national forests, but have expressed few objections to higher fees for the National Park System. The Administration has asked Congress to make the program permanent for the four major federal land management agencies.

Over the last two decades, Congress has created two dozen National Heritage Areas (NHAs) to conserve, commemorate, and promote areas and their resources. There is disagreement over whether to enact generic legislation for the creation and management of NHAs, to continue allowing variety in their creation and operation, or to cease creating and funding these areas. For NHAs, the NPS assists communities in attaining the designation, and supports state and community efforts through seed money, recognition, and technical assistance. Proponents claim that heritage areas protect important resources and traditions; promote tourism and community revitalization; and help prevent new, and perhaps costly or inappropriate, additions to the Park System. Opponents fear that the heritage program is potentially costly and could be used to extend federal control over nonfederal lands.

Congressional leaders have at times packaged a large number of diverse park, public land, and recreation related bills into omnibus measures to expedite passage in the closing days of a Congress. Neither the 106th nor the 107th Congress enacted an omnibus parks bill.

Because of the growing number of park and recreation related bills that have passed in one chamber or been reported by an authorizing committee, some observers feel that prospects are favorable for development of an omnibus measure late in the 108th Congress.

Major Statutes [96]

Mining in National Parks: Act of Sept. 28, 1976; P.L. 94-429, 90 Stat. 1342. 16 U.S.C. §§1901-1912.

National Park Service General Authorities Act of 1970: Act of Aug. 18, 1970; P.L. 91-383, 84 Stat. 825. 16 U.S.C. §1a-1, §1c.

National Park Service Organic Act of 1916: Act of Aug. 25, 1916; ch. 408, 39 Stat. 535. 16 U.S.C. §§1-4.

National Parks Omnibus Management Act of 1998: Act of Nov. 13, 1998; P.L. 105-391, 112 Stat. 3497. 16 U.S.C. §5901, et seq.

Omnibus Parks and Public Lands Management Act of 1996: Act of Nov. 12, 1996; P.L. 104-333, 110 Stat. 4093. 16 U.S.C. §1, et seq.

Preservation of American Antiquities: Act of June 8, 1906; ch. 3060, 34 Stat. 225. 16 U.S.C. §§431-433.

Recreational Fee Demonstration Program: §315 of the Interior and Related Agencies Appropriations Act, 1996, §101(c) of the Omnibus Consolidated Rescissions and Appropriations Act, 1996, Act of Apr. 26, 1996; P.L. 104-134, 110 Stat. 1321-200. 16 U.S.C. §460*l* — 6a Note.

Yellowstone National Park Act: R.S. 2474, derived from Act of March 1, 1872; ch. 24, 17 Stat. 32. 16 U.S.C. §21, et seq.

CRS Reports and Committee Prints [97]

CRS Issue Brief IB10126, *Heritage Areas: Background, Proposals, and Current Issues*, by Carol Hardy Vincent and David Whiteman.

CRS Issue Brief IB10093, *National Park Management and Recreation*, coordinated by Carol Hardy Vincent.

CRS Report RS20158, *National Park System: Establishing New Units*, by Carol Hardy Vincent.

CRS Report RL31149, *Snowmobiles: Environmental Standards and Access to National Parks*, by James E. McCarthy.

Special Systems on Federal Lands

There are currently three special management systems that include lands from more than one federal land management agency: the National Wilderness Preservation System, the National Wild and Scenic Rivers System, and the National Trails System. These systems were established by Congress to protect special features or characteristics on lands managed by the various agencies. Rather than establish new agencies for these systems, Congress directed the existing agencies to administer the designated lands within parameters set in statute.

THE NATIONAL WILDERNESS PRESERVATION SYSTEM [98]

The Wilderness Act defines wilderness as "undeveloped federal land ... without permanent improvements." Further, wilderness generally consists of *federal* land that is primarily affected by the forces of nature, relatively untouched by human activity, and primarily valued for solitude and primitive recreation. Lands eligible for inclusion in the system are areas that generally contain more than 5,000 acres or that can be managed to maintain their pristine character.

Background

The National Wilderness Preservation System was established in 1964 by the Wilderness Act. It was based on a FS system that was established administratively in 1924, but reserves to Congress the authority to include areas in the system. The Wilderness Act designated 9.1 million acres of national forest lands as wilderness, and required the FS, NPS, and FWS to review the wilderness potential of lands under their jurisdiction. These reviews were completed within the required 10 years, with wilderness recommendations presented to Congress. The FS also chose to expand its review to all NFS roadless areas (the first and second Roadless Area Review and Evaluation, RARE and RARE II), and presented wilderness recommendations in 1979. A comparable review of BLM lands was required by FLPMA in 1976, and the BLM finalized wilderness recommendations in 1991.

Organization and Management

Wilderness areas generally are managed to protect and preserve their natural conditions. Permanent improvements, such as buildings and roads, and activities which significantly alter existing natural conditions, such as timber harvesting, generally are prohibited. The Wilderness Act allowed mineral exploration and leasing for 20 years (through December 31, 1983), and directed that valid existing mineral rights be permitted to be developed under "reasonable regulations" to attempt to preserve the wilderness characteristics of the area. The Wilderness Act also specified that existing livestock grazing and motorboat or airstrip uses be allowed to continue. In addition, Congress has included exceptions to the act's management limitations in subsequent laws designating specific areas.

The National Wilderness Preservation System contains more than 105 million acres in 44 states, as shown in Table 5 (data column 1). This amounts to nearly one-sixth (16%) of all federal land. More than half of all wilderness acres are in Alaska (57 million, 55%); this accounts for about a quarter of the federal land in the state. Another 42 million acres of wilderness (41%) are in the 11 western states. In total, this wilderness acreage represents 12%

of the federal land in those states, ranging from 1% in Nevada to 38% in Washington. The remaining 4 million acres (4%) are in the other states (the Atlantic Coast through the Great Plains, plus Hawaii). This is 8% of the federal land in other states, ranging from 0% in six states to 52% in Florida.

No one agency manages the system. Rather, all four agencies currently manage wilderness areas. (See Table 5.) The FS manages nearly 35 million acres of designated wilderness. This comprises 18% of all NFS lands. Nearly 6 million acres of NFS wilderness land (16%) are in Alaska, and another 27 million acres (78%) are in the 11 western states. The FS also manages 2 million acres of wilderness in the other states (6%), and 26 (of those other 38) states have wilderness areas.

More than half of the NPS lands are designated wilderness (43 million acres, 56%). Approximately three-quarters of all NPS wilderness land is in Alaska (33 million acres, 76%), and significant NPS wilderness areas also are in California, Florida, and Washington.

The FWS manages nearly 21 million acres of wilderness. This represents 22% of FWS lands. Nearly 19 million acres of FWS wilderness areas (90%) are in Alaska, and significant FWS wilderness areas also are in Arizona. Overall, about half of the states have wilderness areas within the purview of the FWS.

The BLM currently manages more than 6 million acres of wilderness (as shown in Table 5), a small fraction of all BLM lands (2%). Approximately two-thirds of BLM wilderness is in the California desert, and another quarter is in Arizona. BLM also manages relatively small amounts of wilderness in several other states.

Designation

The Wilderness Act reserves to Congress the authority to designate wilderness areas as part of the National Wilderness System. Congress has designated many particular wilderness study areas, in addition to the broader agency reviews required under the Wilderness Act and FLPMA. How long study areas must be administered to preserve their wilderness character depends on the language of the law requiring the study; some areas are available for other uses when the agency recommends against designation, but others must be protected until Congress releases them.

Congress began expanding the system in 1968, four years after it was established. The most significant expansion was included in the Alaska National Interest Lands Conservation Act of 1980, which established 35 new wilderness areas in Alaska with more than 56 million acres. This action more than tripled the system at that time.

For the decade following the FS recommendations in 1979, Congress generally addressed possible wilderness designations for all FS lands within a state. Many statewide FS wilderness bills were introduced, but their enactment was held up in the early 1980s until a compromise over *release language [99]* broke the legislative stalemate. This compromise — which allowed but did not compel the FS to maintain wilderness attributes of released lands — led Congress to enact 21 wilderness laws designating 8.6 million acres of predominately NFS wilderness in 21 states. The 103rd Congress (1993-1994) also substantially expanded the system, with NFS wilderness areas in Colorado and BLM and NPS wilderness areas in the California Desert.

Congress continues to consider further expansion of the National Wilderness Preservation System. More than 29 million acres, mostly NPS lands in Alaska, have been recommended by the agencies to Congress for inclusion in the system. Numerous areas continue to be reviewed for their wilderness potential by the federal land management agencies.

Table 5. Federally Designated Wilderness Acreage, by State and Agency

State	Total Acreage	Forest Service	National Park Service	Fish and Wildlife Service	Bureau of Land Management
Alabama	41,367	41,367	0	0	0
Alaska	57,522,408	5,753,448	33,079,611	18,689,349	0
Arizona	4,528,973	1,345,008	444,055	1,343,444	1,396,466
Arkansas	153,655	116,578	34,933	2,144	0
California	14,154,062	4,430,849	6,122,045	9,172	3,591,996
Colorado	3,345,091	3,142,035	60,466	3,066	139,524
Connecticut	0	0	0	0	0
Delaware	0	0	0	0	0
Florida	1,426,327	74,495	1,300,580	51,252	0
Georgia	485,484	114,537	8,840	362,107	0
Hawaii	155,590	0	155,590	0	0
Idaho	4,005,712	3,961,667	43,243	0	802
Illinois	32,782	28,732	0	4,050	0
Indiana	12,945	12,945	0	0	0
Iowa	0	0	0	0	0
Kansas	0	0	0	0	0
Kentucky	18,097	18,097	0	0	0
Louisiana	17,025	8,679	0	8,346	0
Maine	19,392	12,000	0	7,392	0
Maryland	0	0	0	0	0
Massachusetts	2,420	0	0	2,420	0
Michigan	249,219	91,891	132,018	25,310	0
Minnesota	815,952	809,772	0	6,180	0
Mississippi	6,046	6,046	0	0	0
Missouri	71,113	63,383	0	7,730	0
Montana	3,443,038	3,372,503	0	64,535	6,000
Nebraska	12,429	7,794	0	4,635	0
Nevada	1,581,871	823,585	0	0	758,286
New Hampshire	102,932	102,932	0	0	0
New Jersey	10,341	0	0	10,341	0
New Mexico	1,625,117	1,388,262	56,392	39,908	140,555
New York	1,363	0	1,363	0	0
North Carolina	111,419	102,634	0	8,785	0
North Dakota	39,652	0	29,920	9,732	0
Ohio	77	0	0	77	0

Table 5. (Continued)

State	Total Acreage	Forest Service	National Park Service	Fish and Wildlife Service	Bureau of Land Management
Oklahoma	23,113	14,543	0	8,570	0
Oregon	2,274,152	2,086,504	0	925	186,723
Pennsylvania	9,031	9,031	0	0	0
Rhode Island	0	0	0	0	0
South Carolina	60,681	16,671	15,010	29,000	0
South Dakota	77,570	13,426	64,144	0	0
Tennessee	66,349	66,349	0	0	0
Texas	85,333	38,483	46,850	0	0
Utah	800,614	772,894	0	0	27,720
Vermont	59,421	59,421	0	0	0
Virginia	177,214	97,635	79,579	0	0
Washington	4,317,133	2,569,391	1,739,763	839	7,140
West Virginia	80,852	80,852	0	0	0
Wisconsin	42,323	42,294	0	29	0
Wyoming	3,111,232	3,111,232	0	0	0
Territories	0	0	0	0	0
Total	**105,176,917**	**34,807,965**	**43,414,402**	**20,699,338**	**6,255,212**

Sources: The sources for this table were generally the same as for Table 2, except NPS data are from their website at [http://wilderness.nps.gov/maplocator.cfm], visited February 24, 2004. Data in the table are updated by CRS to reflect laws enacted after the publication dates.

Issues

Wilderness designations continue to be controversial. Restrictions on the use and development of designated wilderness areas often conflict with the desires of some groups, while providing the values sought by others. In an attempt to find a balance between development and protection, Congress has enacted general standards and prohibitions for wilderness protection (e.g., no motorized access), and general and specific exemptions to those standards and prohibitions (e.g., *continued* motorboat use where such use was occurring prior to the designation). Exceptions often reflect agreements for specific areas, but widespread compromise between development and preservation interests generally remains elusive.

Several current issues surround the possible protection of the remaining FS and BLM roadless areas. One issue focuses on BLM lands in Utah, but has national relevance. Central to the controversy is whether BLM may currently designate *wilderness study areas* (WSAs) — areas that are statutorily entitled to automatic and continuing protections. Section 603 of FLPMA required the BLM to review the wilderness potential of its lands, and, by 1991, to recommend areas to the President, who then could recommend areas to the Congress for possible inclusion in the National Wilderness Preservation System. In response, BLM first inventoried its lands to determine which lands met the basic size criteria and might have wilderness characteristics, then conducted a more in-depth review of these lands to determine which among them possessed wilderness characteristics. Lands found to have wilderness character were designated as WSAs and studied further. Many WSA lands were then recommended to Congress in the early 1990s for inclusion in the National Wilderness Preservation System. These wilderness recommendations are still pending for Utah and many other western states. Approximately 1.9 million of 2.5 million acres of WSAs in Utah were recommended; some Utah wilderness bills before Congress have recommended more acreage, some less.

Section 603 also requires BLM to protect the wilderness characteristics of "such areas" until Congress directs otherwise. This *non-impairment* standard prevents most development, and BLM has applied it to all WSAs, including those that BLM did not recommend for wilderness designation. Therefore, whether BLM can designate new WSAs and whether the non-impairment standard can be applied to these or other lands are important issues both for those seeking to protect the lands and those seeking to develop them — either the automatic and continuing protections of the non-impairment standard apply, or protections may only be provided through the slower, less certain, and more changeable land use planning process under §202 of FLPMA.

Following debate over additional wilderness areas proposed in legislation, Secretary Babbitt in 1996 used the §201 FLPMA inventory authority to identify an additional 2.6 million acres in Utah as having wilderness qualities. Although the stated purpose of the inventory was only to ascertain which lands had wilderness characteristics and report on those, Utah filed suit alleging various flaws in this process, and alleging that the inventory was illegal, even under §201. The district court enjoined the inventory preliminarily, but the 10th Circuit remanded to the district court to dismiss (on various grounds) all but the claim that related to de facto wilderness management of the inventoried lands. (*Utah v. Babbitt* 137 F. 3d 1193 (10th Cir. 1998)). The Department of the Interior subsequently settled the case, and on September 29, 2003, issued new wilderness guidance (Instruction Memoranda No. 2003-274 and 2003-275). These directives apply to BLM lands nationwide, except for Alaska and certain categories of lands, and take the position that the §603 authority terminated in 1993, that BLM cannot administratively create more WSAs under §603 or other authority, and that the non-impairment standard cannot be applied to non-WSA lands. Rather, protective management of the remaining BLM roadless areas can occur only through the relevant land management plans. Others disagree with this interpretation, and the issues are currently in litigation. The importance of these issues is accentuated by the emphasis of the Bush Administration on energy development of the federal lands, and by the promulgation of new regulations on *disclaimers of interest* that may facilitate the validation of highway rights-of-ways in roadless areas, thereby disqualifying additional lands from further consideration.

Another Utah wilderness controversy has widespread implications for management of WSAs generally. A suit was filed to compel BLM to protect WSAs from impairment by increased off-road vehicle use. The Supreme Court ruled in

Norton v. Southern Utah Wilderness Alliance that although the protection of WSAs was mandatory, it was a programmatic duty and not the type of discrete agency obligation that could be enforced under the APA. Also, the Court concluded that language contained in relevant FLPMA land use plans indicating that WSAs would be monitored constituted management goals that might be modified by agency priorities and available funding, and was not a basis for enforcement under the APA (5 U.S.C. §706(1)).

The management of the remaining FS roadless areas has also seen recent changes. FS roadless areas nationwide were administratively protected from most timber cutting and most roads under a Clinton Administration rule (66 Fed. Reg. 3244 (January 12, 2001)) that was subsequently enjoined, and would be replaced by a Bush Administration proposed rule (69 Fed. Reg. 42636 (July 16, 2004)). The proposed rule would provide interim management for the FS roadless areas and allow a period of time during which a state governor may petition for a special rule governing the management of roadless areas in a particular state. After this petition period, management of roadless areas would be governed by any special rules that are developed, or by the relevant forest plan.

Major Statutes

Alaska National Interest Lands Conservation Act of 1980: Act of Dec. 2, 1980; P.L. 96-487, 94 Stat. 2371.

California Desert Protection Act of 1994: Act of Oct. 31, 1994; P.L. 103-433, 108 Stat. 4471.

Wilderness Act: Act of Sept. 3, 1964; P.L. 88-577, 78 Stat. 890. 16 U.S.C. §§1131, et seq.

CRS Reports and Committee Prints [100]

CRS Report RL30647, *The National Forest System Roadless Areas Initiative*, by Pamela Baldwin.

CRS Report 98-848, Wilderness *Laws: Prohibited and Permitted Uses*, by Ross W. Gorte.

CRS Report RL31447, *Wilderness: Overview and Statistics*, by Ross W. Gorte.

CRS Report RS21917, *Bureau of Land Management (BLM) Wilderness Review Issues*, by Ross W. Gorte.

CRS Report RS21290, *Wilderness Water Rights: Language in Laws from the 103rd Congress to Date*, by Pamela Baldwin and Ross Gorte.

The National Wild and Scenic Rivers System [101]

Background

The National Wild and Scenic Rivers System was established in 1968 by the Wild and Scenic Rivers Act (P.L. 90-542, 16 U.S.C. §§1271-1287). The act established a policy of preserving selected free-flowing rivers for the benefit and enjoyment of present and future generations, to complement the then-current national policy of constructing dams and other structures (such as flood control works) along many rivers. Three classes of wild and scenic rivers were established under the act, reflecting the characteristics of the rivers at the time of designation, and affecting the type and amount of development that may be allowed thereafter. The classes of rivers are:

- *Wild* rivers are free from impoundments (dams, diversions, etc.) and generally inaccessible except by trail, where the watersheds (area surrounding the rivers and tributaries) are primitive and the shorelines are essentially undeveloped;
- *Scenic* rivers are free from impoundments in generally undeveloped areas but are accessible in places by roads;
- *Recreational* rivers are readily accessible by road, with some shoreline development, and possibly may have undergone some impoundment or diversion in the past.

Rivers may come into the system either by congressional designation or state nomination to the Secretary of the Interior. Congress initially designated 789 miles in 8 rivers as part of the National Wild and Scenic Rivers System. Congress began expanding the system in 1972, and made substantial additions in 1976 and in 1978 (413 miles in 3 rivers, and 688 miles in 8 rivers, respectively). The National Wild and Scenic Rivers System was more than doubled by designation of rivers in Alaska in ANILCA in 1980. In January 1981, Interior Secretary Cecil Andrus approved 5 rivers designated by the state of California, increasing the system mileage by another 20% (1,235 miles). The first additions under the Reagan Administration were enacted into law in 1984, with the addition of 5 rivers including more than 300 miles. The next large addition came in 1988, with the designation of more than 40 river segments in Oregon, adding 1,400 miles. In 1992, 14 Michigan river segments totaling 535 miles were added. The 106th and 107th Congresses added new designations to the system which now includes 163 river units with 11,302.9 miles in 38 states and Puerto Rico. [102] (See Table 6.)

Organization and Management

Land areas along rivers designated by Congress generally are managed by one of the four federal land management agencies, where federal land is dominant. However, land use restrictions and zoning decisions affecting private land in wild and scenic corridors generally are made by local jurisdictions (e.g., the relevant county, township, city, etc.) where appropriate. The boundaries of the areas along wild and scenic rivers are identified by either the Interior or Agriculture Secretary, depending on land ownership within the corridor. The area included may not exceed an average of 320 acres per mile of river designated (640 acres per mile in Alaska), an average of 1/4 mile width of land on each side of the river.

Where wild and scenic river corridor boundaries include state, county, or other public land, or private land, federal agencies have limited authority to purchase, condemn, exchange, or accept donations of state and private lands within the corridor boundaries. Additionally, federal agencies are directed to cooperate with state and local governments in developing corridor management plans.

In response to controversies associated with management of lands within wild and scenic river corridors, several recent designations have included language calling for creation of citizen advisory boards or other mechanisms to ensure local participation in developing management plans. Even without such direction, management plans for river corridors involving predominantly private lands usually are developed with input from local jurisdictions, prior to designation.

Table 6. Mileage of Rivers Classified as Wild, Scenic, and Recreational, by State and Territory, 2003

State	Wild	Scenic	Recreational	Total
Alabama	36.40	25.00	0.00	61.40
Alaska	2,955.00	227.00	28.00	3,210.00
Arizona	18.50	22.00	0.00	40.50
Arkansas	21.50	147.70	40.80	210.00
California	685.80	199.60	986.85	1,872.25
Colorado	30.00	0.00	46.00	76.00
Connecticut	0.00	0.00	14.00	14.00
Delaware[a]	0.00	15.60	79.00	94.60
Florida	32.65	7.85	8.60	49.10
Georgia[a]	39.80	2.50	14.60	56.90
Idaho[a]	321.90	34.40	217.70	574.00
Illinois	0.00	17.10	0.00	17.10
Kentucky	9.10	0.00	10.30	19.40
Louisiana	0.00	19.00	0.00	19.00
Maine	92.50	0.00	0.00	92.50
Massachusetts	0.00	33.80	38.50	72.30
Michigan	79.00	277.90	267.90	624.80
Minnesota[a]	0.00	193.00	59.00	252.00
Mississippi	0.00	21.00	0.00	21.00
Missouri	0.00	44.40	0.00	44.40
Montana	161.90	66.70	139.40	368.00
Nebraska[a]	0.00	76.00	126.00	202.00
New Hampshire	0.00	13.50	24.50	38.00
New Jersey[a]	0.00	119.90	146.80	266.70
New Mexico	90.75	20.10	10.00	120.85
New York[a]	0.00	25.10	50.30	75.40
North Carolina[a]	44.40	95.50	52.00	191.90
Ohio	0.00	136.90	76.00	212.90
Oregon[a]	635.65	381.40	798.05	1,815.10
Pennsylvania[a]	0.00	111.00	298.80	409.80
South Carolina[a]	39.80	2.50	14.60	56.90
South Dakota[a]	0.00	0.00	98.00	98.00
Tennessee	44.25	0.00	0.95	45.20
Texas	95.20	96.00	0.00	191.20
Washington	0.00	108.00	68.50	176.50
West Virginia	0.00	10.00	0.00	10.00
Wisconsin[a]	0.00	217.00	59.00	276.00
Wyoming	20.50	0.00	0.00	20.50
Puerto Rico	2.10	4.90	1.90	8.9
U.S. Total[b]	**5,350.60**	**2,457.20**	**3,495.10**	**11,302.90**

Source: U.S. Dept. of the Interior, National Park Service. River Mileage Classifications for Components of the National Wild and Scenic Rivers, Washington, DC: Jan. 2002, available on the NPS website at [http://www.nps.gov/rivers/wildriverstable.html], visited May 7, 2004.

Also, personal communication with John Haubert, Division of Park Planning and Special Studies, NPS, U.S. Dept. of the Interior, Washington, DC, on February 12, 2004.

a. This state shares mileage with some bordering states, where designated river segments are also state boundaries. Figures for each state reflect the total shared mileage, resulting in duplicate counting.
b. Figure totals represent the actual totals of classified mileage in the United States and do not reflect duplicate counting of mileage of rivers running between state borders. Because the figures for individual states do reflect the shared mileage, the sum of the figures in each column exceeds the indicated column total.

Management of lands within wild and scenic corridors generally is less restricted than in some protected areas, such as wilderness areas, although management varies with the class of the designated river and the values for which it was included in the system. Administration is intended to protect and enhance the values which led to the designation, but Congress also directed that other land uses not be limited unless they "substantially interfere with public use and enjoyment of these values" (§10(a) of the 1968 Act). Primary emphasis for management is directed toward protecting aesthetic, scenic, historic, archaeologic, and scientific features of the area. Road construction, hunting and fishing, and mining and mineral leasing may be permitted in some instances, as long as the activities are consistent with the values of the area being protected and with other state and federal laws.

Designation

Rivers may be added to the system either by an act of Congress, usually after a study by a federal agency, or by state nomination with the approval of the Secretary of the Interior. Congress has identified numerous rivers as potential additions to the system. The Secretaries of the Interior and Agriculture are required to report to the President on the suitability of these rivers for wild and scenic designation, who in turn submits recommendations to Congress.

State-nominated rivers may be added to the National Wild and Scenic Rivers System only if the river is designated for protection under state law, is approved by the Secretary of the Interior, and is permanently administered by a state agency (§2(a)(ii) of the 1968 Act). Management of these state-nominated rivers may be more complicated because of the diversity of land ownership in these areas. Fewer than 10% of the federal wild and scenic river designations have been made in this manner.

Issues

Concern over land management issues and private property rights have been the predominant issues associated with designation of wild and scenic rivers since the inception of the 1968 Act. Initially, the river designations involved land owned and managed primarily by the federal agencies; however, over the years, more and more segments have been designated that include private lands within the river corridors. The potential use of condemnation authority in particular has been quite controversial. Congress has addressed these issues in part by encouraging development of management plans during the wild and scenic river study phase, prior to designation, and by avoiding condemnation. According to the National Park Service, condemnation has "almost ceased to be used [since] the early 1980s." [103] Another issue that arises from time to time is the nature of state or federal projects allowed within a wild and scenic corridor, such as construction of major highway crossings, bridges, or other activities that might affect the flow or character of the designated river segment.

Major Statutes

Wild and Scenic Rivers Act: Act of Oct. 2, 1968; P.L. 90-542, 82 Stat. 906. 16 U.S.C. §1271, et seq.

CRS Reports and Committee Prints [104]

CRS Report RL30809, *The Wild and Scenic Rivers Act and Federal Water Rights*, by Pamela Baldwin.

National Trails System [105]

The National Trails System (NTS) was created in 1968 by the National Trails System Act (P.L. 90-543, 16 U.S.C. §§1241-1251). This act established the Appalachian and Pacific Crest National Scenic Trails, and authorized a national system of trails to provide additional outdoor recreation opportunities and to promote the preservation of access to the outdoor areas and historic resources of the nation. The system includes four classes of national trails:

- *National Scenic Trails (NST)* provide outdoor recreation and the conservation and enjoyment of significant scenic, historic, natural, or cultural qualities;
- *National Historic Trails (NHT)* follow travel routes of national historic significance;
- *National Recreation Trails (NRT)* are in, or reasonably accessible to, urban areas on federal, state, or private lands; and
- *Connecting or Side Trails* provide access to or among the other classes of trails.

Background

During the early history of the United States, trails served as routes for commerce and migration. Since the early 20th Century, trails have been constructed to provide access to scenic terrain. In 1921, the concept of the first interstate recreational trail, now known as the Appalachian National Scenic Trail, was introduced. In 1945, legislation to establish a "national system of foot trails" as an amendment to a highway funding bill, was considered but not reported by committee. [106]

As population expanded in the 1950s, the nation sought better opportunities to enjoy the outdoors. [107] In 1958, Congress established the Outdoor Recreation Resources Review Commission (ORRRC) to make a nationwide study of outdoor national recreation needs. A 1960 survey conducted for the ORRRC indicated that 90% of all Americans participated in some form of outdoor recreation and that walking for pleasure ranked second among all recreation activities. [108] On February 8, 1965, in his message to Congress on "Natural Beauty," President Lyndon B. Johnson called for the nation "to copy the great Appalachian Trail in all parts of our country, and make full use of rights-of-way and other public paths." [109] Just three years later, Congress heeded the message by enacting the National Trail System Act. [110]

The National Trails System began in 1968 with only two scenic trails. One was the Appalachian National Scenic Trail, stretching 2,160 miles from Mount Katahdin, ME, to Springer Mountain, GA. The other was the Pacific Crest National Scenic Trail, covering 2,665 miles from Canada to Mexico along the mountains of Washington, Oregon, and California. The system was expanded a decade later when the National Parks and Recreation Act of 1978 designated four NHTs with more than 9,000 miles, and another NST, along the Continental Divide, with 3,100 miles. Today, the federal portion of the system consists of 23 national trails (8 scenic trails and 15 historic trails) covering almost 40,000 miles, more than 800 recreation trails, and 2 connecting and side trails. In addition, the act has authorized more than 1,100 rails-to-trails [111] conversions.

Organization and Management

Each of the 23 national trails is administered by either the Secretary of the Interior or the Secretary of Agriculture under the authority of the National Trails System Act. The NPS administers 16 of the 23 trails, the FS administers 4 trails, the BLM administers 1 trail, and the NPS and BLM jointly administer 2 NHTs. The Secretaries are to administer the federal lands, working cooperatively with agencies managing lands not under their jurisdiction. Management responsibilities vary depending on the type of trail.

National Scenic Trails

NSTs provide recreation, conservation, and enjoyment of significant scenic, historic, natural, or cultural qualities. The use of motorized vehicles on these long-distance trails is generally prohibited, except for the Continental Divide National Scenic Trail which allows: (1) access for emergencies; (2) reasonable access for adjacent landowners (including timber rights); and (3) landowner use on private lands in the right of way, in accordance with regulations established by the administering Secretary.

National Historic Trails

These trails follow travel routes of national historical significance. To qualify for designation as a NHT, the proposed trail must meet the following criteria: (1) the route must have historical significance as a result of its use and documented location; (2) there must be evidence of a trail's national significance with respect to American history; and (3) the trail must have significant potential for public recreational use or historical interest. These trails do not have to be continuous, and can include land and water segments, marked highways paralleling the route, and sites that together form a chain or network along the historic route. Examples include the Mormon Trail and the Oregon Pioneer Trail.

National Recreation Trails

The Park Service is responsible for the overall administration of the national recreation trails program, including coordination of nonfederal trails, although the FS administers NRTs within the national forests. NRTs are existing trails in, or reasonably accessible to, urban areas, and are managed by public and private agencies at the local, state, and national levels. Various NRTs provide recreation opportunities for the handicapped, hikers, bicyclists, cross country skiers, and horseback riders.

Connecting and Side Trails

These trails provide public access to nationally designated trails or connections between such trails. In 1990, the Secretary of the Interior designated: 1) the 18-mile Timm's Hill Trail, WI, which connects Timm's Hill to the Ice Age NST, and 2) the 186-mile Anvik Connector, AK, a spur of the Iditarod NHT which joins that trail to the village of Anvik on the Yukon River. Connecting and side trails are administered by the Secretary of the Interior, except that the Secretary of Agriculture administers trails on national forest lands.

Designation

As defined in the National Trails System Act, NSTs and NHTs are long distance trails and are designated by acts of Congress. NRTs and connecting and side trails may be designated by the Secretaries of the Interior and Agriculture with the consent of the federal agency, state, or political subdivision with jurisdiction over the lands involved. Of the 39 completed feasibility studies requested by Congress since 1968, 5 NSTs and 15 NHTs have been designated.

The Secretaries are permitted to acquire lands or interest in lands for the Trails System by written cooperative agreements, through donations, by purchase with donated or appropriated funds, by exchange, and, within limits, by condemnation. The Secretaries are directed to cooperate with and encourage states to administer the nonfederal lands through cooperative agreements with landowners and private organizations for the rights-of-way or through states or local governments acquiring such lands or interests.

Issues [112]

The level of funding continues to be a major issue. With the exception of the Appalachian and the Pacific Crest NSTs, the National Trails System Act does not provide for sustained funding of designated trails operations, maintenance, and development, nor does it authorize dedicated funds for land acquisition. The Federal Surface Transportation Program is a major funding source for trails, shared use paths, and related projects in the United States. Prior to 1991, highway funds were to be used only for highway projects and selected bicycle transportation facilities. With the passage of the Intermodal Surface Transportation Efficiency Act of 1991 (ISTEA, P.L. 102-240) and subsequently reauthorized as the Transportation Equity Act for the 21st Century (TEA-21, P.L. 105-178), many trail projects paths became eligible to receive federal highway program funds. Program funding increases are being considered in the reauthorization of TEA-21. [113]

One of the weaknesses of the system, according to critics, is that "a poor definition exists of which kinds of trails should be part of the system (except for NHT criteria)." [114] While it is relatively easy to add new trails, it has proven more difficult to provide them with adequate staffing and partnership resources.

Another issue is whether the federal government should be given authority to acquire land for existing trails, and the extent of any such authority. Between 1978 and 1986, Congress authorized nine national scenic and historic trails but prohibited federal authority for land acquisition. The trails are the Oregon, Mormon Pioneer, Lewis and Clark, Iditarod, and Nez Perce National Historic Trails, and the Continental Divide, Ice Age, North Country, and Potomac Heritage National Scenic Trails. Legislation to authorize federal land management agencies to purchase land from willing sellers was considered, but not enacted, by the 106th and 107th Congresses. Willing seller legislation has been reintroduced in the 108th Congress. Trails authorized since 1986 typically have included land acquisition authority.

Finally, some trails supporters have advocated a nationwide promotion to inform the public about the National Trails System. They assert that most Americans are unaware of the system and the breathtaking scenes and journeys into the past which can be experienced along the national scenic and historic trails. However, there is concern that a significant increase in the number of trails users could overwhelm present staffing and resources.

Major Statutes [115]

National Parks and Recreation Act of 1978: Act of Nov. 10, 1978; P.L. 95-625, 92 Stat. 3467.

National Trails System Act: Act of Oct. 2, 1968; P.L. 90-543, 82 Stat. 919. 16 U.S.C. §1241, et seq.

Outdoor Recreation Act of 1963: Act of May 28, 1968; P.L. 88-29. 16 U.S.C. §4601.

Appendix 1. Major Acronyms Used in this Article

ACEC:	Area of Critical Environmental Concern
ANILCA:	Alaska National Interest Lands Conservation Act
ANWR:	Alaska National Wildlife Refuge
BLM:	Bureau of Land Management
DOD:	Department of Defense
DOI:	Department of the Interior
EIS:	Environmental Impact Statement
FAA:	Federal Aviation Administration
FLPMA:	Federal Land Policy and Management Act of 1976
FS:	Forest Service
FWS:	Fish and Wildlife Service
ISTEA:	Intermodal Surface Transportation Efficiency Act of 1991
LWCF:	Land and Water Conservation Fund
MBCF:	Migratory Bird Conservation Fund
MUSYA:	Multiple-Use Sustained-Yield Act of 1960
NEPA:	National Environmental Policy Act of 1969
NFMA:	National Forest Management Act of 1976
NFS:	National Forest System
NHA:	National Heritage Area
NHT:	National Historic Trails
NPS:	National Park Service
NRT:	National Recreation Trails
NST:	National Scenic Trails
NWR/NWRS:	National Wildlife Refuge/National Wildlife Refuge System
O and C:	Oregon and California (grant lands)
OCS:	Outer Continental Shelf
ORRRC:	Outdoor Recreation Resources Review Commission
PILT:	Payments in Lieu of Taxes (Act and Program)
PRIA:	Public Rangelands Improvement Act of 1978
PWC:	Personal Watercraft
RPA:	Forest and Rangeland Renewable Resources Planning Act of 1974
RTP:	Recreational Trails Program
TEA-21:	Transportation Equity Act for the 21st Century
USDA:	United States Department of Agriculture
WCAs:	Wildlife Coordination Areas
WPAs:	Waterfowl Production Areas

Appendix 2. Definition of Selected Terms

Acquired lands: land obtained by the federal government from a state or individual, by exchange, or through purchase (with or without condemnation) or gift. One category of federal lands.

Entry: occupation of public land as first step to acquiring title; can also mean application to acquire title.

Federal land: any land owned or managed by the federal government, regardless of its mode of acquisition or managing agency.

Homesteading: the process of occupying and improving public lands to obtain title. Almost all homesteading laws were repealed in 1976 (extended to 1986 in Alaska).

Impoundment: man-made impediment to the free flow of rivers or streams, such as a dam or diversion.

Inholdings: state or private land inside the designated boundaries of lands owned by the federal government, such as national forests or national parks.

Land and Water Conservation Fund: the primary source of federal funds to acquire new lands for recreation and wildlife purposes to be administered by federal land management agencies. The fund is derived largely from receipts from the sale of offshore oil and gas (16 U.S.C. 460*l*), but funds must be appropriated annually.

Land withdrawal: an action that restricts the use or disposition of public lands, e.g., for mineral leasing.

Leaseable minerals: minerals that can be developed under federal leasing systems, including oil, gas, coal, potash, phosphates, and geothermal energy.

Lease: contractual authorization of possession and use of public land for a period of time.

Mining claim: a mineral entry and appropriation of public land that authorizes possession and the development of the minerals and may lead to title.

Multiple use land: federal lands which Congress has directed be used for a variety of purposes.

Patent: a document that provides evidence of a grant from the government —usually conveying legal title to public lands.

Payments in Lieu of Taxes: a program administered by BLM which provides payments to local governments which have eligible federal lands within their boundaries.

Public domain land: One category of federal lands consisting of lands ceded by the original states or obtained from a foreign sovereign, through purchase, treaty, or other means. By contrast, "acquired lands" are obtained from an individual or state.

Public land: various meanings. Traditionally has meant the public domain lands subject to the public land disposal laws. Defined in FLPMA to refer to the lands and interests in land owned by the United States that are managed by the BLM, whether public domain or acquired lands. Also, commonly used to mean all federal, state, and local government-owned land.

Rangeland: land with a plant cover primarily of grasses, forbs, grasslike plants, and shrubs. Most federal rangeland is managed by the BLM and the FS and is leased (or used under permit) for private grazing use.

Release language: congressional direction on the timing and extent of future wilderness considerations, and on the management of roadless areas pending future wilderness reviews, if any.

Reservation: public land withdrawn from general access for a specific public purpose or program.

Right-of-way: a permit or easement that authorizes the use of lands for specific purposes, such as construction of a forest access road, installation of a pipeline, or placement of a reservoir.

Subsurface mineral estate: typically refers to a property interest in mineral resources below ground.

Surface estate: typically refers to a property interest in surface lands and the above-ground resources.

Sustained yield: a high level of resource outputs maintained in perpetuity, but without impairing the productivity of the land.

Water right: right to use or control water. Such rights typically are granted by the states, although the United States may have federal water rights as well.

Wetlands: areas predominantly of soils that are situated in water-saturated conditions during part or all of the year, and support water-loving plants, called hydrophytic vegetation. They are transitional between terrestrial and aquatic systems, and are found where the water table generally is at or near the surface.

Wilderness: undeveloped federal land, usually 5,000 acres or more and without permanent improvements, that is managed (either administratively or by statute) to protect and preserve natural conditions.

Wildlife refuge: land administered by the FWS for the conservation and protection of fish and wildlife. (Hunting, fishing, and other forms of wildlife-related recreation typically are allowed, consistent with the purposes of the refuge.)

ENDNONTES

[1] This section was prepared by Carol Hardy Vincent.

[2] U.S. General Services Administration, *Overview of the United States Government's Owned and Leased Real Property: Federal Real Property Profile as of September 30, 2003*. See Table 16 of the report on the agency's website at *[http://www.gsa.gov/gsa/cm_attachments/ GSA_DOCUMENT/Annual%20Report%20%20FY2003-R4_R2M-n11_0Z5RDZ-i34K-pR. pdf]*, visited March 8, 2004.

[3] In this article, the term *federal land* refers to any land owned or managed by the federal government, regardless of its mode of acquisition or managing agency. *Public domain land* is used when the historical distinction regarding mode of land acquisition is relevant, i.e., when a law specifically applies to those lands that originally were ceded by the original states or obtained from foreign sovereigns (including Indian tribes) as opposed to being acquired from individuals or states. *Public land* refers to lands managed by the Bureau of Land Management, consistent with §103(e) of the Federal Land Policy and Management Act of 1976 (FLPMA, P.L. 94-579; 43 U.S.C. §§1701, et seq.).

[4] Several other agencies manage some of the remaining 43.4 million acres (6.5%) of federal land. The Department of Defense (DOD), including the Army Corps of Engineers, is the fifth largest federal land manager. Because land management is not DOD's primary mission, these lands are not discussed in this article. Nonetheless, military lands often are noteworthy for their size, which can provide important open space, and for their historic, cultural, and biological resources. Moreover, because access is sometimes severely restricted, these lands may contain ecological resources in nearly pristine condition. In addition, the General Services Administration owns or

rents lands and buildings to house federal agencies and also administers the excess/surplus system of property disposal.

[5] For the text of the law and other information, see the Indiana Historical Bureau, *Land Ordinance of 1785*, at *[http://www.statelib .lib.in.us/www/ihb/resources/docldord. html]*, visited April 1, 2004.

[6] For the text of the law and other information, see: *[http://www.ourdocuments.gov/ doc.php?doc=8]*, visited April 1, 2004.

[7] These major land acquisitions gave rise to a distinction in the laws between *public domain lands*, which essentially are those ceded by the original states or obtained from a foreign sovereign (via purchase, treaty, or other means), and *acquired lands*, which are those obtained from a state or individual by exchange, purchase, or gift. (Some 601.5 million acres, 89.5% of all federal lands, are public domain lands, while the other 70.3 million acres, 10.5% of federal lands, are acquired lands.) Many laws were passed that related only to the vast new public domain lands. Even though the distinction has lost most of its underlying significance today, different laws may still apply depending on the original nature of the lands involved. The lessening of the historical significance of land designations was recognized in the FLPMA, which defines *public lands* as those managed by BLM, regardless of whether they were derived from the public domain or were acquired. For more information on the Louisiana Purchase, see [http://www.ourdocuments.gov/ doc.php?doc=18], and on the 1848 Treaty with Mexico see [http://www.ourdocuments.gov/ doc.php?doc=26], both visited April 1, 2004. For more information on the Oregon Compromise, see the Center for Columbia River History, *The Oregon Treaty, 1846*, at *[http://www.ccrh.org/comm/ river/docs/ ortreaty.htm]*, visited April 1, 2004.

[8] For more information, see the Act of May 20, 1862; ch. 75, 12 Stat. 392 and *[http:// www.ourdocuments.gov/doc.php?doc=31]*, visited April 1, 2004.

[9] U.S. Dept. of the Interior, Bureau of Land Management, *Public Land Statistics, 2002,* Table 1-2 (Washington, DC: GPO, April, 2003). Available on the BLM website at *[http://www.blm.gov/natacq/pls02/]*, visited April 1, 2004.

[10] U.S. Dept. of Commerce, Bureau of the Census, *Historical Statistics of the United States, Colonial Times to 1970* (Washington, DC: GPO, 1976), H. Doc. No. 93-78 (93rd Congress, 1st Session), pp. 428-429. FLPMA, enacted in 1976, repealed the Homestead Laws; however, homesteading was allowed to continue in Alaska for 10 years. For the text of FLPMA and other information on the law, see the BLM website at *[http://www.blm.gov/ flpma]*, visited April 1, 2004.

[11] For more information, see *[http://www.ourdocuments.gov/ doc.php?doc=45]*, visited April 1, 2004.

[12] "Yo-Semite" was established by an act of Congress in 1864, to protect Yosemite Valley from development, and was transferred to the State of California to administer. In 1890, surrounding lands were designated as Yosemite National Park, and in 1905, Yosemite Valley was returned to federal jurisdiction and incorporated into the park. For the text of the law, see the NPS website at *[http://www.cr.nps.gov/ history/online_ books/anps/anps_1a.htm]*, visited April 1, 2004. Still earlier is the 1832 establishment in Arkansas of Hot Springs Reservation, which was dedicated to public use in 1880 and as Hot Springs National Park in 1921.

[13] For the text of the law establishing the system, see the National Park Service website at *[http://www.cr.nps.gov/history/online_books/anps/ anps_1i.htm]*, visited April 1, 2004.

[14] For more information, see the BLM website at *[http://www.blm.gov/ flpma/organic. htm]*, visited April 1, 2004.

[15] For more information, see 30 U.S.C. §§ 181, et seq. and the BLM website at *[http://www.ca.blm.gov/caso/1920act.html]*, visited February 12, 2004.

[16] 43 U.S.C. §§ 315, et seq.

[17] FLPMA also established a comprehensive system of management for the remainder of the western public lands, and a definitive mission and policy statement for the BLM.

[18] The most current copies of CRS products are available at *[http://www.crs.gov/]*.

[19] This section was prepared by Ross W. Gorte.

[20] This is also known as the Dingell-Johnson Act and the Wallop-Breaux Act.

[21] This is also known as the Pittman-Robertson Act.

[22] Since FY1998, this account has been available for forest health improvement activities, as well as for building and repairing roads and trails.

[23] Funding for land acquisition under SNPLMA is excluded from FY2004 and FY2005 figures because funds are released after (1) monies from federal lands sales have been collected, and (2) lands have been nominated for acquisition. For FY2004, the SNPLMA budget for lands nominated for acquisition is $110.6 million, but not all nominated lands will be acquired. Nominations for FY2005 will not be completed until after the end of FY2004.

[24] For national forests that contain northern spotted owl habitat, which led to lower timber sale levels, payments were set at 85% of the FY1986-FY1990 average for FY1994, and declining by 3 percentage points annually, to 58% in FY2003.

[25] A third of the county payment (i.e., 25% of the total) is returned to the General Treasury to cover appropriations for access roads and reforestation; thus, the counties actually receive 50% of the revenues.

[26] The most current copies of CRS products are available at *[http://www.crs.gov/]*.

[27] This section was prepared by Ross W. Gorte.

[28] For more information, see the Forest History Society, *U.S. Forest Service History*, at *[http://www.lib.duke.edu/forest/usfscoll/]*, visited February 20, 2004.

[29] The second principal FS program continues the original role of the Bureau of Forestry: to provide forestry assistance to states and to nonindustrial private forest owners. The authorities for assistance programs were consolidated and clarified in the Cooperative Forestry Assistance Act of 1978. Forestry research is the third principal FS program. Congress first authorized forestry research in 1928 "to insure adequate supplies of timber and other forest products"; the research authorities were streamlined by the Forest and Rangeland Renewable Resources Research Act of 1978.

[30] Congress enacted the limitation in response to Roosevelt's 1906 reservations. Roosevelt needed the funds provided in the 1907 act, but proclaimed additional reserves after it was enacted, but before he signed it into law.

[31] U.S. Dept. of Agriculture, Forest Service, *Land Areas of the National Forest System, as of September 30, 2004*, Table 1 at *[http://www.fs.fed.us/land/staff/lar/LAR03/]*, visited Feb. 20, 2004.

[32] See U.S. Congress, Office of Technology Assessment, *Forest Service Planning: Setting Strategic Direction Under RPA*, OTA-F-441 (Washington, DC: U.S. Govt. Print. Off.,

July 1990). Available on the Princeton University website, at *[http://www.wws.princeton.edu/~ota/ disk2/1990/9019_n.html]*, visited February 12, 2004.

[33] Since 1997, provisions in the Interior Appropriations Acts have prohibited the FS from completing the overdue 1995 and 2000 RPA Programs, because, it has been asserted, the Government Performance and Results Act (GPRA) planning and reporting requirements have replaced the RPA Program. A Presidential Statement of Policy accompanied the first (1976) RPA Program, and Congress enacted a second Statement of Policy (1980), but no subsequent Statements of Policy have been issued. The *Report of the Forest Service* is printed annually, although no report was published for FY1999 or FY2000, and the reports typically are published several months later than required by law. They are required to be presented to Congress with the annual budget justifications. The Assessments continue to be prepared.

[34] See U.S. Congress, Office of Technology Assessment, *Forest Service Planning: Accommodating Uses, Producing Outputs and Sustaining Ecosystems*, OTA-F-505 (Washington, DC: U.S. Govt. Print. Off., Feb. 1992). Available on the Princeton University website, at *[http://www.wws.princeton.edu/~ota/disk1/1992/9216_n.html]*, visited February 12, 2004.

[35] Available on the Forest Service website at *[http://www.fs.fed.us/emc/ nfma/includes/ cosreport/Committee%20of%20Scientists%20 Report.htm]*, visited February 12, 2004.

[36] U.S. Dept. of Agriculture, Forest Service, *Land Areas of the National Forest System, as of September 30, 2003*, Tables 10-12 and 15-26, at *[http://www.fs.fed.us/land/ staff/lar/LAR03/]*, visited February 20, 2004.

[37] The 1891 authority was repealed by §704(a) of FLPMA. The following day, in §9 of NFMA, Congress also prohibited the return of any NFS lands to the public domain without an act of Congress.

[38] The President can still create new national forests from lands acquired under the Weeks Law of 1911 (16 U.S.C. §521).

[39] The most current copies of CRS products are available at [http://www.crs.gov/]. Also, for further information on the Forest Service, see its website at *[http://www.fs.fed.us]*, visited February 12, 2004.

[40] This section was prepared by Carol Hardy Vincent.

[41] For more information, see 43 U.S.C. §§315, et seq. and the website of the University of New Mexico School of Law at [*http://ipl.unm.edu/cwl/fedbook/taylorgr.html]*, visited April 1, 2004.

[42] P.L. 94-579; 90 Stat. 2744, 43 U.S.C. §§ 1701, *et seq*.

[43] For the text of the law, see the FWS website at *[http://www.r7.fws.gov/asm/anilca/ toc.html]*, visited April 1, 2004.

[44] For information on the six support and service centers, see the BLM website at *[http://www.blm.gov/nhp/directory/index.htm]*, visited April 1, 2004.

[45] The system, the Geographic Coordinate Data Base, is available on the BLM website at *[http://www.blm.gov/gcdb/]*, visited March 16, 2004.

[46] More information on the National Integrated Land System is available on the BLM website at *[http://www.blm.gov/nils/]*, visited March 16, 2004.

[47] For more information, see 16 U.S.C. §§1331, et seq. and the BLM website at *[http:// www.wildhorseandburro.blm.gov/theact.htm]*, visited April 1, 2004.

[48] Fifty percent of the revenues collected from on-shore leasing are returned to the states (except Alaska which receives 90%) in which the lands are located (30 U.S.C. §191).

[49] For BLM wildland fire statistics, see the agency's website at *[http://www.fire.blm.gov/stats/]*, visited April 1, 2004.

[50] Under Title II of P.L. 106-248, the Federal Land Transaction Facilitation Act (43 U.S.C. §2301), the Secretary of the Interior and the Secretary of Agriculture may use funds from the disposal of certain BLM lands to acquire inholdings and other nonfederal lands. Also, the Southern Nevada Public Land Management Act of 1998 (P.L. 105-263) provides for the disposal, by sale or exchange, of lands in Nevada. The proceeds are used to acquire environmentally sensitive lands in Nevada, among other purposes. A description of these funding sources is provided under "disposal authority." The Land and Water Conservation Fund, addressed in the chapter on "Federal Lands Financing," is a primary means of funding BLM land acquisition.

[51] Other authorities provide for acquisitions in particular areas.

[52] Desert lands can be disposed under other laws. The Carey Act (43 U.S.C. §641) authorizes transfers to a state, upon application and meeting certain requirements, while the Desert Land Entry Act (43 U.S.C. §321) allows citizens to reclaim and patent 320 acres of desert public land. These latter provisions are seldom used, however, because the lands must be classified as available and sufficient water rights must be obtained. Other authorities provide for land sales in particular areas. The Homestead Act and many other authorities for disposing of the public lands were repealed by FLPMA in 1976, with a 10-year extension in Alaska. The General Services Administration has the authority to dispose of surplus federal property under the Federal Property and Administrative Services Act of 1949; however, that act generally excludes the public domain, mineral lands, and lands previously withdrawn or reserved from the public domain (40 U.S.C. §472(d)(1)).

[53] 43 U.S.C. §1713 (c). This procedure and certain other provisions of FLPMA may be unconstitutional under *Immigration and Naturalization Service (INS)* v. *Chadha*, 462 U.S. 919 (1983).

[54] For a description of the law, see the BLM website at *[http://www.blm.gov/nhp/300/wo320/minlaw.htm]*, visited April 1, 2004.

[55] For a description of the law, see the BLM website at *[http://www.blm.gov/nhp/what/lands/realty/rppa.htm]*, visited April 1, 2004.

[56] For a table identifying public land withdrawals 1942-2003, see the BLM website at *[http://www.blm.gov/nhp/what/plo/plo7394.htm]*, visited April 1, 2004.

[57] For the text of the law, see the NPS website at *[http://www.cr.nps.gov/local-law/anti1906.htm]*, visited April 1, 2004.

[58] The most current copies of CRS products are available at [http://www.crs.gov/]. Also, for further information on BLM, including on many of the programs and responsibilities addressed in this section, see the agency's website at *[http://www.blm.gov]*, visited April 1, 2004.

[59] This section was prepared by M. Lynne Corn.

[60] Distinct pre-existing rights (e.g., to develop minerals, easements, etc.) are rarely acquired along with the land. Where they exist and their ownership is considered essential, these rights must be purchased from the landowners, who are otherwise able to exercise them.

[61] For example, some refuges (especially island refuges for nesting seabirds) may be closed to the public — an unlikely restriction for an NPS area, given the NPS mandate to provide for public enjoyment of park resources.

[62] In FY1992, there was a consolidation of units of the Refuge System. The drop in numbers of units shown in Figure 5 in that year is due to this change.

[63] There is also one wilderness area at an FWS National Fish Hatchery in Colorado.

[64] The 482 administrative sites and 69 fish hatcheries administered by FWS are not part of the system, and total only 22,671 acres.

[65] For the text of the law and other information, see the FWS website at *[http://refuges.fws.gov/policyMakers/mandates/index.html]*, visited Feb. 13, 2004.

[66] For the text of the law and other information, see the FWS website at *[http://refuges.fws.gov/policyMakers/mandates/HR1420/index.html]*, visited Feb. 13, 2004.

[67] Most of the research function was administratively transferred to the U.S. Geological Survey (in the Department of the Interior) in FY1996.

[68] This program is distinct from USDA programs to conserve wetlands.

[69] For the text of the law and other information, see the FWS website at *[http://migratorybirds.fws.gov/intrnltr/treatlaw.html]*, visited Feb. 13, 2004.

[70] For the text of the law and other information, see the FWS website at *[http://migratorybirds.fws.gov/intrnltr/treatlaw.html]*, visited Feb. 13, 2004.

[71] Of the 540 refuges, 34 (6.3%) were created under specific laws naming those particular refuges.

[72] These procedures result in congressional termination of executive actions other than by statute, and thus may be unconstitutional in light of *INS* v. *Chadha*, 462 U.S. 919 (1983).

[73] While the MBTA definition of "migratory bird" includes, potentially, almost all species of birds, in practice, the focus of acquisition has been on game birds (e.g., certain ducks, geese, etc.). Non-game species tend to benefit secondarily, though areas without game birds are rarely acquired with MBTA funds.

[74] This authority (and its related funding mechanism) is so commonly used that the distribution of refuges is a good approximation of the four major flyways for migratory waterfowl.

[75] Personal communication from FWS Realty Office, Feb. 9, 2004. Not counted are 11 instances of so-called "friendly condemnations," in which FWS, in cooperation with a willing seller, used the courts to achieve favorable tax treatment, or to settle questions of fair market value, clouded title, or similar problems. Some critics of condemnation authority have suggested that the existence of so-called "hostile" condemnation authority has affected some land sales, to the extent that some sellers feel intimidated — that they have little real choice in the decision to sell, even if condemnation authority was not formally used. If such intimidation exists, its extent is unclear, but legislation was introduced in the 105th Congress to restrict FWS land acquisitions without specific congressional approval. Ultimately, a provision was added in P.L. 105-277 forbidding the use of "any of the funds appropriated in this Act for the purchase of lands or interests in lands to be used in the establishment of any new unit of the National Wildlife Refuge System unless the purchase is approved in advance by the House and Senate Committees on Appropriations in compliance with the reprogramming procedures contained in Senate Report 105-56." This or a similar

provision has been incorporated in subsequent appropriations acts. Because the Migratory Bird Conservation Fund and the Southern Nevada Public Lands Management Act funds are not appropriated in annual appropriations acts, purchases from those funds are unaffected by such provisions.

[76] The dollars spent were not necessarily spent on those particular 68,014 acres, due to a lag between payments and transfers of title, completion of paperwork, and other factors.

[77] See "Land Ownership" in BLM chapter, above, for information on a funding source created under the Southern Nevada Public Land Management Act. Funds obtained under this act from federal land sales may be used to acquire environmentally sensitive lands in Nevada, among other purposes. Some of these Nevada acquisitions have become additions to the National Wildlife Refuge System.

[78] For information on how "duck stamp" money is spent, see the FWS website at *[http://duckstamps.fws.gov/Conservation/conservation.htm]* visited February 13, 2004.

[79] U.S. General Accounting Office, *National Wildlife Refuges: Continuing Problems with Incompatible Uses Call for Bold Action*, GAO/RCED 89-196 (Washington, DC: GPO, Sept. 1989), 84 p.

[80] U.S. Dept. of the Interior, Fish and Wildlife Service, *2001 National Survey of Fishing, Hunting, and Wildlife-Associated Recreation* (Washington, DC: 2001). The survey is available on the FWS website at *[http://fa.r9.fws.gov/surveys/surveys.html]*, visited Feb. 13, 2004. The number of hunters did not decline significantly from the previous surveys, but as a percent of the total U.S. population, there has been a general downward trend over approximately 30 years.

[81] The most current copies of CRS products are available at *[http://www.crs.gov/]*. Also, for further information on the National Wildlife Refuge System, including on many of the programs and responsibilities addressed in this chapter, see the FWS website at *[http://www.fws.gov]*, visited February 13, 2004.

[82] This section was prepared by David Whiteman.

[83] 16 U.S.C. §21.

[84] 16 U.S.C. §22. In the early years, the Interior Department relied on the U.S. Army for enforcement of the regulations and protection of the park units.

[85] For more information on the establishment of Yellowstone National Park, see Aubrey L. Haines, *Yellowstone National Park: Its Exploration and Establishment* (Washington, DC: 1974), available on the NPS website at *[http://www.cr.nps.gov/history/online_books/ haines1/]*, visited Mar. 8, 2004.

[86] 16 U.S.C. §431.

[87] 16 U.S.C. §1.

[88] For more information, see U.S. Dept. of the Interior, *History of the National Park Service*, available on the NPS website at *[http://www.cr.nps.gov/history/hisnps/NPShistory.htm]*, visited Mar. 8, 2004.

[89] National Park System General Authorities Act of 1970, P.L. 91-383; 16 U.S.C. §1a-1, §1c.

[90] Redwood National Park Expansion Act, P.L. 95-250; 16 U.S.C. §1a-1.

[91] *Rethinking the National Parks for the 21st Century*, National Park Service Advisory Board Report 2001, available on the NPS website at *[http://www.nps.gov/policy/futurereport.htm]*, visited Mar. 8, 2004.

[92] National Parks Omnibus Management Act of 1998, P.L. 105-391; 16 U.S.C. §1a-5.

[93] Congress rescinded these withdrawals and reestablished most of the lands as national monuments, national parks, or national preserves in ANILCA.

[94] 16 U.S.C. §460*l*-9(c).

[95] 43 U.S.C. §1714(j). While Presidents may modify monument boundaries, it is not certain that a President can revoke a national monument. (See CRS Report RS20647, *Authority of a President to Modify or Eliminate a National Monument*, by Pamela Baldwin.)

[96] There are hundreds of laws establishing or modifying specific units of the National Park System, in addition to the few general laws listed here.

[97] The most current copies of CRS products are available at *[http://www.crs.gov/]*. Also, for further information on the National Park System, see the NPS website at *[http://www.nps.gov]*, visited Mar. 8, 2004.

[98] This section was prepared by Ross W. Gorte.

[99] Release language provides congressional direction on the timing and extent of future wilderness considerations (i.e., when the land would be reviewed for possible wilderness), and on the interim management of roadless areas, pending any future wilderness reviews. See CRS Report RS21917, *Bureau of Land Management (BLM) Wilderness Review Issues*, by Ross W. Gorte.

[100] The most current copies of CRS products are available at *[http://www.crs.gov/]*.

[101] This section was prepared by Sandra L. Johnson.

[102] U.S. Dept. of the Interior, National Park Service, *River Mileage Classifications for Components of the National Wild and Scenic Rivers System* (Washington, DC: Jan. 2002). Available on the NPS website at *[http://www.nps.gov/rivers/wildriverstable.html]*, visited May 7, 2004.

[103] U.S. Dept. of the Interior, National Park Service, *Wild and Scenic Rivers and the Use of Eminent Domain* (Washington, DC: Nov. 1998). Available on the NPS website at *[http://www.nps.gov/rivers/ publications/eminent-domain.pdf]*, visited Feb. 13, 2004. Condemnation and subsequent acquisition of land by the federal government (in fee title, or fee-simple) has been used along 4 rivers since 1968: the Rio Grande, the Eleven Point River, the St. Croix, and the Obed, resulting in the acquisition of 1,413 acres. Condemnation of land for easements has occurred on 8 rivers amounting to 6,339.7 acres. The FWS is the only agency that has never used condemnation to acquire land or an easement for a wild and scenic river corridor.

[104] The most current copies of CRS products are available at [*http://www.crs.gov/]*. Also, for more information on the National Wild and Scenic Rivers System, see the NPS website at [*http://www.nps.gov/rivers]*, visited Feb. 13, 2004.

[105] This section was prepared by Sandra L. Johnson.

[106] Donald D. Jackson, "The Long Way 'Round," *Wilderness*, vol. 51, no. 181 (summer, 1998): 19-20.

[107] Outdoor Recreation Resources Review Commission, *Outdoor Recreation for America* (Washington, DC: Jan. 1962), p. 34.

[108] Ibid., p. 1.

[109] *Congressional Record*, vol. 111 (Feb. 8, 1965): 2087.

[110] The act is available on the NPS website at *[http://www.nps.gov/ncrc/ programs/nts/legislation.html]*, visited Feb.13, 2004.

[111] 16 U.S.C. §1247(d); 49 C.F.R. §1152.29.

[112] For information on current legislation related to trails, see CRS Issue Brief IB10093, *National Park Management and Recreation*, coordinated by Carol Hardy Vincent.

[113] ISTEA also established the National Recreational Trails Funding Program, renamed the Recreational Trails Program (RTP) under TEA-21. RTP is not part of the National Trails System. Rather, RTP is a state-administered, federal-aid grant program which provides funds to local governments. The fund is administered by the Department of Transportation in consultation with the Department of the Interior. RTP provides funds to the states to develop and maintain recreational trails and trail-related facilities for both nonmotorized and motorized recreational trail uses. Trail uses include bicycling, hiking, in-line skating, crosscountry skiing, snowmobiling, off-road motorcycling, all-terrain vehicle riding, four-wheel driving, or using other off-road motorized vehicles.

[114] Steven Elkinton, "How the National Trails System Has Changed Since 1968," *Pathways Across America*, (Spring 1998): 10.

[115] For further information on the National Trails System, see the NPS website at *[http://www.nps.gov/ncrc/programs/nts/index.html]*, visited Feb. 13, 2004.

In: Natural Resources
Editor: Jeanette B. Pauling

ISBN 978-1-60456-982-7

Chapter 3

CONSERVATION, NATURAL RESOURCE MANAGEMENT AND DEVELOPMENT CHALLENGES IN RURAL AFRICA: EVIDENCE FROM EAST AFRICA

Miyuki Iiyama[1], Patti Kristjanson[2], Joseph Ogutu[2], Joseph Maitima[2], Patrick Kariuki[2], Yasuyuki Morimoto[3], and Henning Baur[1]

[1]World Agroforestry Centre, Nairobi, Kenya
[2]International Livestock Research Institute, Nairobi, Kenya
[3]Bioversity International, Nairobi, Kenya

ABSTRACT

There is consensus in the international community that development and poverty alleviation in rural Africa are among the most urgent global agendas for the 21st century. Many rural Africans have traditionally depended on natural resources. Land use patterns are highly heterogeneous across diverse agro-ecological/farming systems and even within the systems, some being more extensive, while others being more intensive. These days a range of factors, including increasing population pressure and global climate change, has made it impossible for development through conventional extensive technologies or degradational pathways to be sustainable as a viable strategy. To achieve both development and environmental goals, sound agricultural intensification technologies through more intensive and efficient use of inputs internal to systems, or conservation pathways, must be identified and tailored to specific local needs and conditions to be adopted by rural households, while enabling policy and infrastructure should be availed by government and development agencies.

This chapter investigates the challenges that Africa has faced in rural development and natural resource management and seeks guidance for policies and research. Firstly, the chapter gives an overview of the current state of heterogeneous agro-ecological and farming systems and the development challenges posed by population growth and climate change in rural Africa. We propose a conceptual framework to guide empirical research in effectively examining the multi-dimensional aspects of the evolution of farming systems/resource management and review how the framework is applied at meso-level in the recent literature. Secondly, a case study from a Rift Valley community in western Kenya is presented to show micro-level evidence of diverse portfolios of technology options in a semi-arid environment.

It turns out that some conservation pathways may exist to promote more sustainable development in rural Africa, possibly through the better integration of system components, i.e., crop and livestock, and the inclusion of agroforestry into the farming systems. Concurrently, there are also degradational pathways entailing substantial trade-offs between promoting economic development vs. conserving natural resources. To promote conservation development pathways, policies not only need to identify optimal technology portfolios best suited to local conditions and exploit the complementarities among system components but also to provide education with farmers to augment their human capital assets and to promote stable non-farm/off-farm income opportunities to enable investment in resource management. The chapter concludes by synthesising the findings for policy implications and by presenting another emerging challenge of rising food/fuel prices and a subsequent future research agenda.

1. Introduction

While globally the percentage of people who live in absolute poverty declined from 40% to 18% between 1981 and 2004, in Africa it has stayed almost constant at 42% to 41% with the number of extremely poor almost doubling from 168 million to 298 million (Chen & Ravallion 2007; Collier 2007; Kates and Dasgupta 2007). An African exceptionalism dominates the development needs of today and contributing to its reduction through identifying different strategies from those used elsewhere is one of the grand challenges of sustainable science (Kates and Dasgupta 2007).

Within sub-Saharan Africa (SSA), we focus on rural areas where more than 70% of the population live, a majority of whom are poor. As most rural Africans are critically dependent on natural resources for their livelihoods (Barrett et al. 2002; Williams et al. 2004; Ellis & Freeman 2005; Dar and Twomlow 2007; Frost et al. 2007), agriculture, including crops, livestock and agroforestry, does play a major role in poverty alleviation and sustainable development as an economic activity and as a provider of environmental services. In achieving economic development and poverty alleviation through agricultural development, rural African populations need sustainable technologies that increase the productivity and resilience of production systems even under fragile biophysical conditions (Dar and Twomlow 2007).

One estimate suggests that a 4% annual sustained growth rate of agricultural production in SSA is an absolute requirement (Sanchez and Leakey 1997). Yet, the region has long failed to achieve increased agricultural productivity (Bullock 1997), missing out on the Green Revolution (Sanchez and Leakey 1997; Dorward et al. 2004). Indeed, SSA lags behind the rest of the world, with an overall net decline in agricultural productivity (Dar and Twomlow 2007). Between 1980 and 2000, food production per capita declined by 0.01% per year in Africa, while in Asia and Latin America it grew by 2.3% and 0.9% respectively (Kates and

Dasgupta 2007). In what aspects are rural sectors in SSA exceptional from those of other developing regions in not benefiting from advanced agricultural technologies?

SSA countries consist of diverse agro-ecosystems and farming systems accordingly, ranging from commercial agriculture in high potential zones, subsistence crop–livestock mixed farming in semi-arid zones, and pastoral activities in arid-zones (Thornton et al. 2002; Kristjanson et al. 2005; Okwi et al. 2007). Indeed, the heterogeneous and risky rainfed farming systems of SSA—the broader mix of crops grown in the region; the agro-ecological complexities and heterogeneity of the region; and the lack of infrastructure, markets and supporting institutions—have so far all contributed to limiting the scope of the Green Revolution in the region (World Bank 2007). Furthermore, two-thirds of the rural population in SSA live in less-favoured areas defined as arid and semi-arid or with poor market access (World Bank 2007). Given this pervasive heterogeneity in agriculture and rural society in SSA, it is critical to pursue and formulate strategies tailored to local needs/contexts and to integrate agricultural intensification with sustainable management of local resources within small/medium-scale farming sectors (Dar and Twomlow 2007; Frost et al. 2007).

While heterogeneity in agro-ecological and farming systems in SSA has already made agricultural productivity growth difficult, there are emerging factors, both internal social dynamics of population growth and exogenous shocks of global climate change, which have made African sustainable development even more challenging (Sanchez 2000; Beg et al. 2002). SSA has recently been experiencing faster population growth than other developing regions (Thornton et al. 2002). Increasing population pressure has been held primarily responsible for the increasing conversion of indigenous forests into agricultural land and for the expansion of agricultural/pastoral activities on marginal lands, thus leading to depletion and degradation of the inherently fragile soil and resource bases (Zhang et al. 2000; Amissah-Arthur and Miller 2002). Concurrently, global climate change, e.g. changes in annual rainfall, has also negatively affected agricultural output. Persistent rural poverty has accelerated rapid urbanisation without productivity and employment growth, as falls in agricultural output and the resulting poverty have forced rural residents to migrate to urban areas (Ndiaye and Sofranko 1994; Barrios et al. 2006; Dar and Twomlow 2007).

While rural poverty alleviation needs growth in agriculture, increasing population pressure and subsequent decreasing resource bases have made it impossible for development through conventional extensive agricultural technologies to be sustainable as a viable growth strategy. Furthermore, global climate change could expose rural populations to ever more uncertain climatic risks. To achieve both poverty alleviation and environmental goals, sound agricultural intensification technologies and better resource management practices must be adopted by rural households, while enabling policy and infrastructural environments need to be provided by government and development agencies. Otherwise, there would be a vicious cycle of stagnant agricultural growth, persistent poverty, soil depletion, resource degradation, deforestation, loss of biodiversity, and more vulnerability to climate change.

Agricultural intensification through better utilisation of locally available resources through integration of system components, i.e. crop, livestock and agroforestry, without depending much on expensive external inputs, is especially desirable considering the poverty of rural populations. Therefore, the major research agenda for researchers and scientists would be to identify various agricultural development and resource management pathways across different agro-ecological zones/farming systems and to examine factors affecting respective pathways so as to better formulate policies to promote sustainable development pathways with optimal resource utilisation practices.

Yet, analyses can be quite complicated since agro-ecological and farming systems consist of diverse system components (crop, livestock, agroforestry, nutrients, natural resources) that interact dynamically in response to changing environment, such as increasing population pressure and climate change, aside from the extensive heterogeneity of agro-ecological and farming systems in SSA. Furthermore, interactions of diverse system components can take diverse pathways, in a complementary way or with trade-offs, not only across different agro-ecological and farming systems but also between heterogeneous plots/farms within particular systems. In other words, in research, we have to deal with (a) multi-dimensional aspects of agro-ecological and farming systems, i.e. interactions, complementarities or trade-offs, of multiple system components (among crop, livestock, agroforestry, nutrients, natural resources, etc.), at (b) certain layers of analytical scales (at farm-level, meso-level). A substantial number of empirical studies and surveys have been conducted for separate models on particular crop/animal types or technologies in rural Africa and there have been more frameworks to analyse multi-dimensional aspects of poverty such as livelihoods approach. On the other hand, unfortunately, there have been few established conceptual frameworks for guiding research and analysis of multi-dimensional aspects of agricultural intensification, making it rather difficult to convert distinctive case studies into comparable interpretations and synthesise them into policy formulations for integrated natural resource management.

The major objective of this chapter is to investigate the challenges that Africa has faced in rural development and natural resource management. In order to facilitate such investigation, we attempt to provide the conceptual framework for guiding research to allow the examination of multi-dimensional aspects of diverse system components and their interactions, especially complementarities/trade-offs, at various analytical scales. Then we present how to apply the guidance to the analysis to identify critical factors promoting optimal development and resource management pathways for policy formulation. Accordingly, Section 2 gives an overview of the development challenges in rural Africa, proposes key criteria and parameters included in conceptual frameworks for guiding research and analysis, and reviews the recent literature on empirical studies. In Section 3, some of the criteria are applied to guiding research and analysis of the micro-level data on rural development and natural resource management in the mixed crop–livestock-agroforestry system of a Rift Valley community in western Kenya. The case study attempted to identify and interpret diverse agricultural development and resource management pathways in the study area, to examine socio-economic, physical and institutional factors determining the households' choices of technology portfolios with incentives for sustainable natural resource management, and to discuss policy options. Section 4 concludes by synthesising the findings for policy implications and future research agendas that advocate for a holistic system analysis approach to assess and evaluate viable technology options in rural Africa.

2. Farming Systems, Natural Resources, and Development Needs

2.1. Status and Challenges

As mentioned in the Introduction, there are two dimensions in Africa's stagnant agricultural growth: the inherent heterogeneity in agro-ecological/farming systems which has prevented agricultural technological breakthroughs, and emerging factors such as population growth and climate change which have further burdened an inherently fragile soil and resource base. This sub-section outlines the status of the systems in SSA and emerging challenges.

Heterogeneous Agro-ecological and Farming Systems

Understanding heterogeneity in agro-ecological and farming systems and the local potential is critical in the search for alternative strategies to increase agricultural productivity and sustainable resource management in SSA. In economic perspective, productivity increases in agriculture have come from specialization/intensification. Yet, African severe biophysical and climate conditions often limit the scope of specialization and risk-averse farmers often opt for diversification (Ellis 2000; Ellis and Francis 2005). Indeed, from ecological perspective diversification may be better than highly specialized, even mono-cropping, systems which may destabilize the fragile balance of local biodiversity and ecosystems. Since soils and climatic conditions of a region largely determine the suitability of different crops and their yield potential along with the potential of integration with livestock and agroforestry, mapping agro-ecological regions may facilitate the identification of optimal farming patterns, i.e. cropping, livestock keeping and agroforestry, for increasing agricultural production sustainably (Bullock 1997). While we do not discuss the significance of mapping in development policy making here, we review the methodology of mapping to deal with the inter-regional heterogeneity and the intra-system diversification in agro-ecological and farming systems in Africa.

For example, FAO has worked on refining the agro-ecological zone approach for crop systems. A set of information assembled for the agro-ecological zone delimitation included choice of crops (wheat, paddy rice, maize, pearl millet, sorghum, soybean, cotton, phaseolus bean, white potato, sweet potato and cassava) and identification of their climatic and soil requirements, assemblies of agro-climatic data (with emphasis on temperature and water availability whose combination is expressed in the length of the growing period) and of soil data. The information was then combined to produce a land inventory map. Such a map enables calculation of the maximum potential yield of each crop in each zone, taking into consideration how ideal the soil conditions were and problems of soil management where climatic conditions were less than ideal, and to produce a land suitability assessment for each particular crop (Bullock 1997). In summary, the FAO agro-ecological zone definition was mainly concerned with crops. Of course, crop types in SSA are far more diverse, and for a reasonably generic agricultural system classification to be applied to the region, refinements would be required to handle diverse cropping (and probably agroforestry) systems more adequately (Kruska et al. 2003). However, a certain focus will be inevitable to simplify the classification.

The small-scale farming sector in SSA rarely lacks a livestock component (Mortimore 1991; Thorne 1998). In mixed farming systems, livestock can contribute either to sustainable development by providing organic inputs into crop/agroforestry through better integration of system components or to resource degradation if managed extensively without integration under high population pressure (Iiyama et al. 2007a; 2007b). Agro-climatic and demography are both important factors in the definition of the farming systems including livestock components, as population density determines the available area of land for livestock farming (McIntire et al. 2002). To develop future scenarios of possible system changes in response to climate change and population growth in the future as discussed later, it may be convenient to develop the classification defined not only by climate but also by land cover and human population density for crop–livestock systems rather than for crops only to assess the development challenges and the status of natural resource management in SSA. What follows deals with (crop–) livestock production systems.

Thornton et al. (2002) and Kruska et al. (2003) proposed the development of a global livestock production system classification put forward by Seré and Steinfeld (1996) who disaggregated the systems by agro-ecological conditions and population density. The livestock systems are divided into: livestock only; rangeland based systems (areas with minimum cropping); mixed rainfed systems (mostly rainfed cropping combined with livestock); mixed irrigated systems (where a significant portion of cropping uses irrigation and is interspersed with livestock); and others (areas with the population density over 450 square km). Each sub-system is further disaggregated by agro-ecological potential as defined by the length of growing period (LGP); i.e. arid/semiarid zone (with LGP <180), humid/semi-humid zone (with LGP >180 and <270), and temperate /tropical highland zone (average temperature in growing season >5°C and <20°C or a month or more with an average >5°C) (Thornton et al. 2002; Kruska et al. 2003).

Diversity in crop–livestock systems in SSA is illustrated in Table 1. In 2000, 70% of the total population of SSA depended on mixed rainfed crop–livestock systems which account for 27% of the total land area, while 10% depended on livestock only systems and 1% on irrigated systems. Mixed rainfed systems are geographically widely distributed across SSA, depending on agro-ecological conditions and population density. For example, in West Africa, mixed rainfed systems are observed between zones neither too arid for crop cultivation nor too humid to allow diseases for livestock (Manyong et al. 2006). In East Africa, mixed farming systems are common in the highlands, and also in some semi-arid/sub-humid zones (Thornton et al. 2002).

Challenges

While principally defined by population density and agro-climatic conditions, agricultural settings in the farming systems in SSA are continuously evolving in response to changing conditions such as population growth and climate change (Pell 1999).

Table 1. Geographical and Demographic Distribution of Livelihood Production System

	% of land area	% of human population 2000	population density 2000	population density 2050	times population in 2000
livestock production system					
Livestock only	**37**	**10**	**7**	**17**	**2.41**
rangeland arid/ semi-arid	26.18	6.70	7	17	2.49
rangeland humid/ semi-humid	10.20	2.66	7	18	2.68
rangeland temperate & highlands	0.87	0.52	15	0	0
Mixed Rainfed	**27**	**70**	**67**	**158**	**2.35**
mixed rainfed arid/ semi-arid	14.17	25.06	46	105	2.28
mixed rainfed humid/ semi-humid	9.67	30.16	81	199	2.45
mixed rainfed temperate & highlands	3.30	14.59	115	263	2.29
Irrigated	**1**	**1**	**53**	**96**	**1.80**
mixed irrigated arid/ semi-arid	0.46	0.66	38	64	1.71
mixed irrigated humid/ semi-humid	0.00	0.02	155	422	2.72
mixed irrigated temperate & highlands	0.04	0.35	219	420	1.91
Others (landless city & others)	**35**	**19**	**14**	**35**	**2.47**
Total	**100**	**100**	**26**	**61**	**2.36**
Total (square km, population)	(24,066,355 square km)	(626,972, 000 persons)			

Note: calculated from the data from Thornton et al. (2002) and Kruska et al. (2003).

Population Growth

Both livestock rangeland systems and mixed rainfed systems in SSA (from arid/semi-arid, sub-humid/humid, to temperate/highland zones) will see population density more than double by the year 2050 (Table 1). This expected population growth will require an expansion in food production and increase competition between crops and livestock. McIntire et al. (1992) claim that in the short term, conflicts would occur over the use of high quality land, while in the long term, population growth will intensify competition of crop and livestock enterprises for both land and labour. Rising population would also necessitate the expansion of cultivated areas, replacing pastures and thereby reducing the grazing area for animals. This indicates that unless farmers introduce intensive technologies such as high-yielding crop varieties or improved livestock breeds, it would be difficult to meet expected rising demand for animal products by the growing population (Delgado et al. 1999; Pell 1999; Steinfeld et al 2006).

Climate Change

In addition, recent climate change further affects agricultural outputs negatively (Barrios et al. 2006). The African continent is particularly vulnerable to the impacts of climate change because of factors such as widespread poverty and overdependence on rain-fed agriculture (IPCC 1998). Changes in climate will further add stresses to a deteriorating situation. A sustained increase in mean ambient temperatures beyond 1°C would cause significant changes in forest and rangeland cover; species distribution, composition, and migration patterns; and biome distribution. Many countries on the continent are prone to recurrent droughts, which could seriously impact the availability of food. African populations may also face challenges that will emanate from extreme climate events such as floods (and resulting landslides in some areas), strong winds, droughts, and tidal waves. High population growth rates, and lack of significant investment - coupled with a highly variable climate - have made it difficult for several countries to develop adaptation capabilities and patterns of livelihood that would reduce pressure on the natural resource base.

Nutrient Depletion and Soil Degradation

Sanchez and Leakey (1997) claim that static or decreasing crop yields in Africa are already occurring in the inherently less fertile, sandy soils of the savannahs and the Sahel, because of population increases in these more marginal areas and due to nutrient depletion. They have been indicative of a vicious cycle of population pressure, expansion of extensive agriculture on marginal soils, soil depletion, resource degradation, deforestation of indigenous forests, loss of biodiversity and watersheds, stagnant agricultural growth, persistent rural poverty and accelerated urban migration.

"In addition to marked reductions in crop productivity, nutrient depletion triggers several negative side effects on farm such as less fodder for cattle, less fuelwood for cooking, smaller amounts of crop residues, and less manure from the cattle. These in turn further increase runoff and erosion losses because there is less plant cover to protect the soils from wind and water erosion.... deforestation in search of the few remaining pockets of fertile land in densely populated areas often results in an almost total removal of trees from the landscape. Lack of tree protection at the upper parts of watersheds severely affects their functioning. Increasing soil erosion from unproductive cropland, communal grazing lands and denuded watersheds leads to silting of reservoirs, lakes and coastal areas and can lead to the eutrophication of fresh waters. Food shortages and famines become more acute during drought years. Lack of opportunities for cash income pushes people off the land and into urban areas where many cannot find productive jobs, further taxing the limited urban infrastructure" (Sanchez and Leakey 1997).

Urbanisation

Individuals living in marginal areas may be forced to migrate to urban areas if the marginal lands become less productive under increased population pressures new climate conditions (IPCC 1998). The growth of urban areas may boost the demand for non-traditional food products, such as rice, fruits and vegetables, thus creating new reliable domestic markets for rural farmers, if they have capitals to undertake new technologies and ventures. In turn, as infrastructure is already approaching its limits in urban areas, rapid urbanisation prompted by persistent rural poverty and agricultural stagnation should substantially increase the demand for modern energy (Wolde-Rufael 2006). As electricity provision is very limited in SSA (Karekezi & Kithyma 2002), most countries are predominantly dependent on traditional biomass fuels for their energy; 70–90% of primary energy supply and up to 95% of the total consumption (Karekezi 2002). Charcoal is especially popular for household use but its production process is very inefficient, thus the increased demand in urban areas has led to accelerated deforestation in rural areas (Morgan and Moss 1985; Cline-Cole 1990; Mwampamba 2007). The rural poor without capital assets to undertake productive farming increasingly find charcoal making by exploiting natural resources an easy means to earn ready cash (Iiyama et al. 2008). Accelerated deforestation has led to land degradation by exhausting soil organic contents (Ndiaye and Sofranko 1994; Chidumayo and Kwibisa 2003), further escalating the vicious cycle through aggravating the adverse impact of global climatic change on farm productivity.

Degradational vs Conservation Pathways

To feed a growing population, rural smallholders in African will need to accelerate the expansion of their production activities from subsistence to commercial farming and diversification into off-farm income generating activities. Much of the past expansion in commercial crop and livestock production has been managed by increased use of land at low inputs of capital and labour. As unoccupied land diminishes, increasing areas of natural vegetation have been transferred to arable areas with shorter fallow cycles. Concurrently, competition between grazing and cultivating systems for available land has more than intensified. Hence, soil fertility is expected to decline unless some measures are taken to improve soil management (Iiyama et al. 2007a; 2007b).

Yet, the long-term relationship between land resource degradation and demographic pressure should not be necessarily negative and linear. A cycle of poverty and environmental degradation can be reversed with land intensification through better crop–livestock integration and incorporation of trees within farms as well as through re-investment of capitals/income from off-farm/non-farm activities into external input use. This has indeed happened in the semi-arid Machakos District of Kenya, where despite increasing population pressure since the 1930s farmers were able to reverse land degradation through an indigenous soil conservation technology and agroforestry adoption that improved both crop and livestock productivity (Tiffen et al. 1994; Sanchez and Leakey 1997).

Therefore as Mortimore (1991) suggested, the farming systems in SSA are confronted with a choice between: (1) a degradational pathway—increasing the frequency of use without additional inputs, failing to replenish soil chemical properties or to conserve physical properties; and (2) a conservation pathway—increasing inputs, especially of labour, to maintain or raise productivity per hectare. Since most African smallholders are poor, it is unlikely that a conservation pathway can be achieved solely through an increased use of expensive external inputs, such as inorganic fertilisers. Therefore a conservation pathway should rather make efficient use of inputs internal to the systems and complementarities through interactions/integration of system components, i.e. crop, livestock, trees, as much as possible.

For example, in mixed crop–livestock systems, under demographic pressure, there is increased demand for integration in order not only to ease competition over resource use between components but also to exploit their complementarities (McIntire et al. 1992; Christiaensen et al. 1995). Crop–livestock integration, defined as a process by which farmers intensify their activities by integrating components of crop and livestock activities, is expected to be an economically feasible and environmentally sound conservation pathway for poor agropastoralists (Mortimore 1998; McIntire et al. 1992; Christiaensen et al. 1995; Iiyama et al. 2007b). The benefits of crop–livestock interactions are several. Animal traction could improve the quality and timeliness of farming operations now done by hand, thus raising crop yields and farm household incomes. Farm animals provide manure to improve soils. Livestock sales would generate cash to buy inputs. Keeping animals on the farm could also provide a use for other resources such as crop residue, which might be wasted in the absence of animals (Mortimore 1998; McIntire et al. 1992; Christiaensen et al. 1995; Thorne et al. 2002; Bationo et al. 2004; Manyong et al. 2006).

Agroforestry practices also have considerable potential for helping solve some of Africa's development and resource management challenges, as agroforestry is defined as a dynamic, ecologically-based, natural resource management system that, through the integration of trees in farms and rangeland, diversifies and sustains smallholder production for increased social, economic and environmental benefits (Sanchez and Leakey 1997; Ong et al. 2007). Agroforestry trees can supply farm households with a wide range of products for domestic use or sale, including food, medicine, livestock feed and timber, and environmental and social services such as soil fertility, moisture conservation and boundary markers. For example, high-value trees can fit in specific niches on farms while leaving more open land to staple food crops or other profitable crops such as vegetables. Trees for timber and fuelwood trees can also be grown on farm boundaries with leguminous fodder trees under them or as contour hedges on sloping land. In such farms, income is increased and diversified, providing resilience against weather or price disruptions. Soil erosion is minimized, nutrient cycling maximized and above- and below-ground biodiversity enhanced (Erskine 1991; Sanchez and Leakey 1997; Franzel et al.2001; Thangata and Alavalapati 2003).

The potential for integrated crop, animal and tree production is perceived to be high while further population growth is expected in the next few decades (Mortimore 1991; Kristjanson and Thornton 2004). Of course, the realities are not always ideal and the optimal pathways are rarely evolving themselves spontaneously. Yet, if productivity is to increase because of increasing demand and increasing land pressure, then there are real research needs to enhance the complementarities between the existing system components (Thornton and Herrero 2001).

2.2. Concepts and Models

This sub-section proposes a conceptual framework for integrated system analyses and key parameters examined in the analysis of development and natural resource management.

General Conceptual Framework

Researchers and policy makers are urgently required to identify development and resource management pathways within particular local/institutional contexts, to examine the limiting factors/enabling environment for development and resource management practices, and to provide technological/institutional support for poor African smallholders to adopt optimal pathways that contribute to poverty alleviation, food security and sustainable resource use.

Yet, what makes research challenging is that agro-ecological and farming systems in SSA consist of distinctive but tightly interdependent components or sub-systems which are highly heterogeneous across regions depending on agro-climatic and demographic conditions. Furthermore, these systems have been dynamically evolving in response to changing circumstances, such as population growth and climate change as well as market conditions, while farmers may pursue multiple objectives (e.g. food security and income maximisation) with multiple system components (e.g. crops, animals, trees and natural resources) and through livelihood diversification (into various farm and off-farm activities).

While a wide variety of models exist for separate crop and livestock to assess the adoption potential of independent technologies, few models are available on the interaction of various crop and animal types, and integration with agroforestry or other 'natural resource management' and 'sustainable agriculture' practices (Franzel et al. 2001; Ong et al. 2007). A new integrated model is required to analyse interactions of diverse system components with a larger agro-ecosystem composed of non-agricultural systems, market systems and other biophysical conditions, to incorporate quantitative relations between system components, and to model optimal pathways of system component integration in terms of efficient nutrient cycling, in order to estimate the long-term impact of existing strategies on the sustainability of the system (Thornton and Herrero 2001; Herrero et al. 2007).

In other words, analytical methodologies for empirical research to identify the limiting factors/enabling environment for sustainable development and resource management are, at a minimum, required simultaneously to deal with multi-dimensional aspects of the systems, i.e. interactions (either complementarities or trade-offs) among crops, animals, trees and natural resources and the circumstances/factors affecting the evolution of agro-ecological/farming systems at particular analytical scale (meso-, farm-, or sector-level). A set of logical methodological steps is required to adequately represent the components of and transactions within and between the systems to be modelled. These steps include characterizing production systems, i.e. biophysical scales, management and interaction intensity, farm household objectives, temporal scales, and modelling the key components and processes.

In guiding empirical studies, we propose a conceptual framework that will reduce the complexity, consisting of three analytical steps (Box 1). The first step starts by identifying (a) distinctive development/resource management pathways observed at (b) a particular scale, either at (b-1) meso-level (regional or across different development/land use domains across regions) or at (b-2) farm-level (farms/household types with different land use/resource management patterns even within a region). Interactions of system components (crops, animals, trees and natural resources) of each development/resource management pathway are then examined to determine whether their interactions are more of trade-offs or of complementarities. These pathways are then evaluated as degradational or conservation pathways. The second step examines potential circumstances or factors affecting the adoption of (a) respective degradational/conservation pathways at a particular analytical scale, i.e. agro-ecological, demographic and market conditions at (b-1) meso-level, and capital asset endowments and livelihood strategies at (b-2) farm-level. The following paragraphs explain the assumptions/methodologies concerning (a) complex interactions of system components for the development/resource management pathways and (b) the factors affecting the evolution of pathways at diverse analytical scales.

Box 1. A Conceptual Framework/Analytical Steps

(1) identification of (a) development/resource management pathways at (b) a particular scale
  (a) identification of diverse development/resource management pathways
  - look at multi-dimensional system components (crop, animals, trees and natural resources)
  - examine the interactions (complementarities/trade-offs) between system components
  - interpret as degradational (trade-off) or as conservation (complementary) pathways
  (b) determination of the analytical scale
  - (b-1) meso-level: development domains reflecting heterogeneity in the pathways
  - (b-2) farm -level: farm types reflecting heterogeneity in the pathways

(2) examination of factors affecting each of (a) the pathways at (b) a particular analytical scale
  (b-1) meso-level...agro-ecological, demographic, market access and conditions
  (b-2) farm -level...capital assets, livelihood strategies (especially off-farm income)

(3) policy recommendation

System Components of Development/Resource Management Pathways

The initial stage of the research requires the identification of (a) development/resource management pathways at (b) a particular analytical scale by examining the interactions (complementarities/trade-offs) between system components (crop, animals, trees, natural resource) and interpreting them as degradational (trade-off) or as conservation (complementary) pathways.

Using an integrated model or the concept of system analysis approach is often advocated when dealing with multiple dimensions of particular farming systems. The systems analysis approach attempts to analyse interactions of system components with a larger agro-ecosystem composed of non-agricultural systems, market systems and other biophysical conditions, to incorporate quantitative relations between crop and animal production, and to model optimal pathways of system component integration in terms of efficient nutrient cycling, in order to estimate the long-term impact of existing strategies on the sustainability of the system (Thornton and Herrero 2001; Herrero et al. 2007). As the farming systems in SSA are facing tremendous challenges due to population growth and climate change, modelling systems can help identify and quantify significant interactions that occur between the various components of smallholder systems through simulation exercises of existing land use patterns or interventions.

Thornton and Herrero (2001) propose that a conceptual framework for modelling crop–livestock systems should meet several requirements if the resulting models are to be used reliably in a variety of systems analysis and impact assessment studies. Among the requirements they list are: to describe and quantify the interactions between the system's components; to represent the farmer's management practices; to determine the impact of management strategies on use of land and other resources; and to allow the possibility of studying both the medium- and the long-term effects of the strategies investigated. Still, empirical application of a modelling framework is quite challenging if dealing with all the interactions occurring in the system.

One way to tackle the complexity in modelling is to develop relatively simple models based on either experimental or empirical farm types with site-specific parameters, by integrating information in a rational way to address specific research priorities. On-station research with the simulation of whole farm systems allows maximum biological and economic responses to the farm models under optimal conditions to be closely monitored.

However, the simulation model approach often does not replicate treatments in space, while environmental factors, including agro-ecological, demographic and market conditions, significantly vary across regions and these local modifiers substantially affect localised system evolution which does not necessarily follow optimal pathways. Furthermore, though incorporating the basic elements of local farming systems as system components, i.e. crops, animals, trees and natural resources, the on-station model farm approach fails to simulate the behaviour and management of farms which face highly risky environments and thus manage them through livelihood diversification.

In the analyses of the interactions of diverse system components, relative effects of the local modifiers at meso-level and of engagement in off-farm income activities on development/resource management pathways at farm-level should be explicitly treated and empirically investigated. It is thus important to determine at which analytical scale the analysis is conducted to identify development/resource management pathways at the initial analytical step.

Analytical Layers/Scales

African farming systems are characterised by heterogeneity and diversity both at meso- and farm-level whose understanding is critical in formulating effective intervention (World Bank 2007). Most empirical studies using econometric models attempt to examine diverse factors promoting the evolution of the development/resource management pathways and especially in identifying the factors affecting the adoption of optimal pathways (conservation pathways) with incentives of better resource management, against degradational pathways.

These models are roughly divided into two groups; one group which emphasizes meso-level parameters, assuming whether a farm adopts a particular technology or not is a function of location specific factors, and the other which focuses on farm-level parameters or household-specific factors on the development/resource management pathways. Even in the discussion on targeting of interventions for sustainable agricultural development and resource management in SSA, there is an ongoing debate on the usefulness of geographic targeting (i.e. meso-level) versus targeting of specific household types (i.e. farm-level) (Kruseman et al. 2006). We review the assumptions on key factors either at meso-level or farm-level that are likely to affect the diverse evolutional pathways/heterogeneous land use patterns in rural SSA.

Mixed farming systems in SSA at a given place and time are largely defined by agro-ecological potential and population density, therefore land use/resource management pathways show certain spatial patterns with some areas observing more farms adopting intensification technologies than others (Iiyama et al. 2007b). Furthermore, access to markets/infrastructure is also among the important factors that drive land use change. For example, in general, the levels of agricultural intensification and crop–livestock interactions are low in arid, sparsely populated zones, but relatively higher in cooler more densely populated zones. Opportunities for development of high-value perishable commodities, such as horticultural crops or dairy, are likely to be greatest in areas with relatively high market access and agricultural potential (Staal et al. 2002; Pender et al. 2004a; Kristjanson et al. 2005; Place et al. 2006; Kruseman et al. 2006; Manyong et al. 2006; Okwi et al.2007).

The underlying theme of the meso-level analysis is that agricultural/soil and demographic conditions and market/infrastructural access are key factors that determine land use/livelihood options available to households (Pender et al. 2004a; Kruseman et al. 2006). Agricultural potential largely influences the absolute advantage (productivity) of a location in production of particular agricultural commodities, while access to markets and infrastructure, and population pressure help to determine the comparative advantage (profitability) of particular livelihoods, given the absolute advantages. Yet, improved access to markets and infrastructure has more ambiguous theoretical impacts on land use, land management practices and resource conditions, because of the ambiguous effects of output prices on incentives to conserve land (Pender et al. 2004a). It is suggested that if diversity between villages is more important than heterogeneity amongst households, geographical targeting can be considered as an effective strategy for selectively enhancing a process of agricultural intensification (Pender et al. 2004a; Kruseman et al. 2006). In efficiently capturing the dimension of locational factors, more recent studies incorporate GIS (geographical information system)-derived measures into their econometric models (Kristjanson et al. 2002; Staal et al. 2002; Manyong et al. 2006; Okwi et al. 2007).

However, there also exist heterogeneities in land use/resource management patterns among households sharing similar biophysical, demographic and market conditions (Evans and Ngau 1991; Tittonell et al. 2005; Iiyama et al. 2008).Farm-level analytical models then tend to assume that levels of capital asset endowments of particular livelihood diversification patterns adopted by households along with physical and institutional characteristics of plots affect the adoption of agricultural intensification and resource management technologies, in empirically examining the factors affecting heterogeneous land use patterns at community-level.

Agricultural intensification is a dynamic process involving the decision making process of individual farms to adopt new technologies in response to challenges posed to their systems by population growth, climatic changes and market opportunities (McIntire et al. 1992; Pender et al. 2004a). Yet, incentives to pursue environmentally sustainable practices are commonly lower than incentives to simply extract natural resources in an arid/semi-arid environment where the majority of Africa's poorest and most food-insecure households live (Dar and Twomlow 2007). To survive in a harsh and variable environment, rural households often pursue a range of livelihood strategies to diversify their income sources into various farm and off-farm activities as a means to reduce risk from specialisation and, if possible, respond to rapidly changing market conditions (Ellis 2000; Barrett et al. 2001; Dar and Twomlow 2007). As households are different in capital asset endowments and capability to pursue different development paths or livelihood diversification portfolios with different incentives for resource management (Ellis 2000; Barrett et al. 2002; Williams et al. 2004), the rate at which technologies are adopted can be heterogeneous among households even within a small community (Tittonell et al. 2005; Iiyama et al. 2008).

In deriving meso-/sector-/macro-level policy implications, meso-level analyses may provide more straightforward recommendations than farm-level analyses. Nevertheless, detailed community-level case studies are also needed in order to more adequately address policy concerns for understanding what the effects of a household's capital asset endowments are with respect to the adoption of relatively high-return, sustainable agricultural activities. A few micro-level studies on rural livelihoods have revealed that households pursuing highly diverse income diversification strategies, usually including off-farm options, are more likely to adopt new farming technologies. These households are relatively well endowed with respect to education and skills (Evans and Ngau 1991; Iiyama et al. 2008). This implies that for poverty alleviation, meso-/macro-level development policies need to be multi-sectoral, encompassing education, and both farm and off-farm activities.

2.3. Methodologies and Application

Analytical methodologies for empirical studies on agricultural development and natural resource management in SSA are, at a minimum, required to identify dominant development/natural resource management pathways in particular locations, by simultaneously dealing with multi-dimensional aspects of the systems, i.e. interactions between multiple system components of crops, animals, trees, and natural resources. Then the analysis should include an examination of the factors affecting the evolution of the development/resource management pathways at a particular analytical scale, i.e. locational factors such as agro-ecological, demographic and market conditions at meso-level, and household-specific factors such as capital asset endowments and livelihood diversification strategies.

In empirical application, it is often difficult to capture multi-dimensional aspects of development/resource management pathways, the interactions and dynamics of system components, in the analysis. For example, the multi-dimensionality of crop–livestock integration includes the use of manure, animal traction, crop residue, and agricultural by-products as feed within the same farm enterprise (Manyong et al. 2006). However, most literature on crop–livestock integration deals with selected technologies as proxies to some dimensions of agricultural intensification rather than holistically treating all the technologies. For example, Staal et al. (2002) focus on the three technologies—keeping of dairy cattle, planting of specialised fodder, and use of concentrate feed—as proxies of crop–livestock integration in mixed smallholder farming systems in central and western Kenya, and investigate the effects of locational factors on technology adoption. Kristjanson et al. (2002) select the adoption of genetically improved double-purpose cowpea varieties as a proxy of crop–livestock integration in West Africa, and examine the ability of village-level factors to potentially influence spatial patterns in crop–livestock evolution pathways.

The typology of crop–livestock integration pathways or development/natural resource management pathways has long been challenging. Earlier attempts tried to disaggregate multi-dimensional features of farming and integrated natural resource management and to classify farming systems into domains/zones with particular features (Mortimore 1991). There are also new attempts to derive integrated, location/farm-specific indices of agricultural intensification by summarizing and reducing the multiple dimensionality of the interaction of system components. There are still only a few empirical studies at meso-level that have attempted to invent integrated indices to capture multi-dimensional aspects of farming system evolution (Pender et al. 2004a; Kruseman et al. 2006; Manyong et al. 2006), while there are even fewer case studies at micro-level (Iiyama et al. 2007b). The methodology used and implications of the work of Pender et al. (2004) are reviewed below.

Pender et al. (2004a) propose the concept of development domains and development pathways to investigate spatial patterns and factors affecting evolution in land use/income strategies across different locations in Uganda, and to test the hypothesis that the opportunities and constraints for sustainable development depend upon the comparative advantages that exist in a particular location. They define a "development domain" as a geographical region having similar comparative advantages, based upon similar agro-climatic conditions, access to markets and population density. In turn, a "development pathway" is defined as a common pattern of change in income strategy. This concept is more general than farming systems since it incorporates non-farm as well as on-farm activities, and is dynamic since it refers to changes and not merely income strategies pursued at a particular point in time. Their key research questions include: (i) what are the dominant development pathways occurring in different development domains in Uganda since 1990, and their relationship to land use and land management; (ii) what factors determine the development of particular development pathways and changes in land use and land management; and (iii) what are the implications of different development pathways, policies, programmes and other causes of change for natural resource and human welfare conditions.

While the high quality time-series and cross-sectional data on changes in land use and income strategies have virtually not been available in Uganda, Pender et al. (2004) collected some of the information on income strategies, perceptions of change in human welfare and natural resource conditions, land use, and land management using the following survey method. A community-level survey was conducted in 107 communities across different development domains in Uganda between 1999 and 2000 by interviewing with a group of 10–20 individuals representing the community to collect information. Where information about changes was sought, the focus was on changes during 1990–99. They used a common method of ranking perceptions of change in all cases: +2.major increase (or improvement), +1.minor increase, 0.no change, -1.minor decrease, -2.major decrease. As they acknowledged, given the qualitative and subjective nature of the data used, the findings of the study should be regarded as suggestive rather than definitive and should be confirmed by further study using more objective and quantitative (though more costly) methods. Even so, this approach is useful to estimate the overall evolution of land use and income strategies in Uganda, where it is extremely expensive to collect high-quality data at national scale.

Several steps were used to analyse the data. Firstly, different development domains in Uganda were classified based upon available secondary information related to agricultural potential (based on six agro-climatic zones), market access and population density (at the second lowest administrative unit). There are 24 possible domains, though only 18 are represented to any significant extent in the study region. Secondly, the factor analysis used data on the primary activities of men in 1999 and changes in the three main activities since 1990 to identify the development pathways. The first six factors have a clear interpretation as development pathways. Thirdly, the econometric analysis focused on determinants of the development pathways (as measured by the factor scores from the factor analysis) and changes in land use, land management practices, purchased input use, and various indicators of change in natural resource conditions and human welfare. The fixed explanatory variables included in the regression models include dummy variables for the agro-climatic zones, market access class, population density class, and whether there is irrigation in the village.

As a result of the factor analysis, six dominant development pathways were identified. These were: [1] expansion of cereals production; [2] expansion of banana and coffee production; [3] non-farm development; [4] expansion of horticulture; [5] expansion of cotton; and [6] stable coffee production. It is interpreted that the general pattern of agricultural development occurring in Uganda during the 1990s involved increasing specialization and commercialization of economic activities in different locations, based upon differences in comparative advantage.

In general, the econometric analysis found that the factors hypothesized to determine the comparative advantage of different development pathways—including agricultural potential, access to markets and infrastructure, and population density—are significantly associated with the development pathways, though different factors are important for different pathways. Agro-climatic conditions are particularly important for distinguishing areas of [1] cereal expansion from [2]/[4] perennials areas. Higher population density favours [1] intensified production of cereals, [4] horticulture and [3] non-farm activities, while closer access to rural markets favours [3] non-farm development and, moderately, [2] expansion of banana and coffee production. Access to irrigation is critical for [4] horticultural development, and improved access to roads is important for [3] non-farm development. Non-governmental organisations (NGOs) appear to foster [3] non-farm development, while CBOs are associated with [1] expanded cereal production.

The econometric analyses also revealed the association between respective development pathways, and the adoption of natural resource management as well as the changes in natural resource and human welfare conditions, controlling the impact of agro-ecological conditions, population growth and market access. Among the six development pathways, [2] expansion of banana and coffee was most strongly associated with adoption of soil and water conservation practices, including mulch, compost, manure and recycling of plant residues, and improvements in resource conditions, such as quality of forests, natural water, and human welfare. In contrast, while associated with improved nutrition in children, [1] expansion of cereals production was associated with decreased availability of grazing land and forests and decreased quality of forests, without use of external inputs and investment in improved land management. [3] Non-farm development was associated with the adoption of some resource conservation measures, such as mulching and recycling of crop residues, and some improvement in woodlots and natural water.

Based on the results, the dominant development pathways in Uganda are interpreted. Promotion of [2] expansion of banana and coffee production pathway may be a potential ''win-win-win'' development strategy, or 'conservation pathway', benefiting the environment while contributing to economic growth and poverty reduction, where this pathway is suited. [1] Expansion of cereals production without use of external inputs and investment in improved land management, as is common in Uganda, may not be sustainable because most cereals have a poor ground cover, exposing the soil to erosion and because a significant proportion of cereals is usually marketed, exporting soil nutrients from the farm. Increased efforts to protect remaining forest and woodland areas, and promotion of improved technology adoption through agricultural technical assistance programmes and development of markets, will be key to agricultural modernization and assuring sustainable land use where cereals expansion is occurring. Promotion of [3] non-farm development offers both environmental and economic benefits. By reducing dependence on crop production and promoting tree planting, non-farm activities appear to reduce soil erosion and improve water availability and quality.

In summary, Pender et al. (2004a) show that the development pattern in Uganda has been associated with changes in land use and agricultural practices, including expansion of cultivated areas, settlements and woodlots at the expense of fallow, forest and wetlands; increased adoption of purchased inputs; and resource conservation practices. They also reveal that the extent to which economic development is consistent with sustainable use of natural resource bases depends upon, among other things, the development pathways being pursued in different locations. These results imply that some ''win-win-win'' opportunities, or conservation pathway, may exist to promote more sustainable development in Uganda, for example, by promoting [3] the banana–coffee development pathway. Concurrently, there are also trade-offs between conserving forests and wetlands vs. promoting economic development through pursuing [1] expansion of cereal production which apparently lacks the incentives for sustainable resource management. Such trade-offs should be adequately considered as development strategies in Uganda and elsewhere.

There are few integrated models in existence to analyse development/natural resource management pathways at farm-level analysis, while a few case studies attempt to deal with the association between heterogeneous farm-livelihood strategy clusters and the adoption of natural resource management (Tittonell et al. 2005; Iiyama et al. 2008). In Section 3, we present a farm-level case study to apply the conceptual framework and to employ an integrated index to identify heterogeneous development/resource management pathways observed in a Rift Valley community in western Kenya. The aim is to examine the interaction between system components of each pathway, i.e. crop, livestock, trees and natural resources, and to investigate key factors affecting the adoption of these pathways by households.

3. Case Study from a Rift Valley Community

3.1. Introduction to a Case Study

Most rural populations in SSA are dependent on mixed systems for survival (Thornton et al. 2002; Kristjanson and Thornton 2004). Within mixed rainfed farming systems, semi-arid zones are considered marginal for farming and are characterised by low population density. However, as higher potential zones become overpopulated, agropastoralists have gradually migrated to more arid zones in search of unoccupied land. Once settled, they have expanded cultivated and grazing areas with shorter fallow cycles, exhausting nutrients in inherently organic-deficient soils (Pell 1999; Place et al. 2003). As the population increases, semi-arid zones must accommodate more people on fragile soils. As Mortimore (1991) suggested, mixed farming systems in semi-arid zones in Africa are confronted with a choice between a degradational pathway—increasing the frequency of use without additional inputs, failing to replenish soil chemical properties or to conserve physical properties—and a conservation pathway (increasing inputs, especially labour, to maintain or raise productivity per hectare).

To sustain soils, conservation crop–livestock intensification pathways must be urgently identified and promoted and the role of livestock needs to be investigated. This is because, while animals are often blamed for degradation, they may be an essential component of intensification, which in turn creates the economic conditions for conservation land management (Mortimore 1991; McIntire et al.1992). While a number of studies have already been implemented in high potential zones (Shepherd and Soule 1998; Clay et al. 2002; Tittonell et al. 2005; Place et al. 2006), fewer studies have been conducted in semi-arid zones on the impact of diverse crop–livestock pathways on land degradation such as some monographs, for example, by Tiffen et al. (1994). In-depth case studies are urgently needed.

This Section presents empirical evidence of diverse crop–livestock (and horticulture/agroforestry) evolution pathways in a semi-arid community. The Kerio River Basin is located at the foot of the Great Rift Valley escarpment in western Kenya. The valley floor is hotter and drier than the escarpment and highlands and used to be considered neither habitable nor arable. When people first settled there in the 1970s, the lower parts of the valley became severely degraded with the formation of gullies and loss of natural vegetation due to expansion of grain production and grazing of indigenous animals. For the past two decades, however, some households have introduced horticulture and semi-zero grazing of exotic animal breeds on homestead plots in the upper parts of the valley. Residents claim that soils in the upper valley have been healing due to manure application, terracing and mulching in contrast to the degraded soils in the lower valley.

Our research question is to investigate factors affecting a household's decisions to adopt either conservation or degradational pathways. Perceived heterogeneity in land use patterns and associated soil quality in the study area indicate the significant correlation at plot level between types of crops planted and degree of crop–animal integration. This suggests that land use pattern is determined by plot characteristics (i.e. location and tenure forms). At the same time, it is households that ultimately decide to adopt particular portfolios of crop and animal types (defined as crop–livestock diversification [CLD] patterns) and allocate their resources accordingly. Therefore, our hypothesis is whether a degradational pathway (CLD with low levels of soil management) or a conservation pathway (CLD with high levels of soil management) is adopted dependent on plot characteristics or on household characteristics.

The next sub-section describes the hypothesis, the study area and analytical methods used in this study. In the analytical process, land use patterns of the 177 households in the study area are first examined for 386 plots at plot level. Secondly, a new set of variables to represent the CLD patterns of the households is derived using principal component analysis. Thirdly, the effects of household and plot characteristics on the choices of the CLD patterns are tested using regression analysis. Sections 3.3 and 3.4 present and discuss the results. Brief policy implications are provided in Section 3.5.

3.2. Methods

Hypotheses

The major factors determining spatial patterns of crop–livestock pathways are agro-ecological, demographic and market conditions (Mortimore 1991; McIntire et al. 1992; Kristjanson et al. 2002; Staal et al. 2002; Thornton et al. 2002; Pender et al. 2004a; Manyong et al. 2006; Iiyama et al. 2007b). However, even within a small area, crop–livestock pathways have been highly heterogeneous among households (Shepherd and Soule 1998; Tittonell et al. 2005). Observation of heterogeneous pathways at farm scales indicates that causes of the variability are not only biophysical but also socio-economic. In-depth case studies are necessary to understand crop–livestock pathways from a perspective of the livelihood strategies of households.

The adoption of crops and livestock has been commonly analysed as independent components (Benin et al. 2004; Pender et al. 2004b; Kristjanson et al. 2005; Lacy et al. 2006). But, investment in resource management is not made in isolation from the preceding investment in crop and livestock activities. Farmers who have invested in valuable perennials (e.g. fruits) may find adoption of soil conservation practices more attractive than in the absence of such prior investments (Barrett et al. 2002). Improved breeds of animals are more likely to be stall-fed within farms and more integrated with crop production (Staal et al. 2002; Bationo et al. 2004). If synergies exist between components, giving incentives for better management, then it is important to adopt a system approach to analyse these synergies.

We assume that if a household is engaged in a CLD pattern involving crop [A] and livestock of type [B], then the household allocates proportionately more land to crop [A] and holds more livestock of type [B] than other types within its portfolio. Different CLD patterns have different levels of interactions between components (Kristjanson and Thornton 2004). CLD patterns associated with more intensive input use are interpreted as conservation pathways while those with less input use are interpreted as degradational pathways. Our main hypothesis is that households select CLD patterns to maximise utility under their constraints, i.e. resource endowments, access to off-farm income, availability of farming tools or characteristics of plots. Particular CLD patterns give households incentives to allocate land, labour and capital to resource management.[1]

More conservation CLD patterns may require labour, skills or capital intensive technologies, and thus are constrained by a household's human capital asset endowments[2] (Reardon and Vosti 1995; Benin et al. 2004; Pender et al. 2004b). Effects of off-farm income activities such as regular (e.g. formal employment and business) or casual income activities (e.g. charcoal making or day labour) and remittances are, however, ambiguous as they provide capital to invest in technologies while constraining labour availability (de Jager et al. 2001; Barrett et al. 2002; Tittonell et al. 2005; Perz et al. 2006; Morera and Gladwin 2006).

Degradational CLD patterns may be more constrained by the tenure or physical characteristics of land that households can access. Tenure characteristics refer to how land was acquired (Pender et al. 2004b). Households with large tracts of inherited land may not necessarily use all of it if they are not engaged in extensive cultivation. However, even under customary tenure systems where no plots are formally registered, households may purchase, hire or borrow plots to cultivate particular varieties of crops when they need more land than what they inherited. Physical characteristics of plots, i.e. slope, soil types and distance from

[1] For more detail on the concept of CLD patterns see Iiyama et al. (2007a) who identified an optimal pathway with higher income and more manure application among five CLD patterns and examined household/homestead characteristics adopting the optimal CLD pattern. Our study examines plot-level resource management and inputs for all the plots and the relative effects of human capital asset endowments, off-farm income access and tenure/physical characteristics of plots for all the potential CLD patterns.

[2] The education of the household head should also be an important component of human capital assets for households. However, in the statistical analysis in Section 3.3, we did not include this variable in the regression models for investigating the determinants of CLD patterns to avoid multi-collinearity, because this is highly correlated with other key variables hypothesised to affect the choices of CLD patterns by households, such as the age of the household head (correlation ratio: –0.68) and access to regular off-farm income generating activities (correlation ratio: 0.40).

homesteads, also affect the choices households make in adopting particular crop and livestock varieties (Benin et al. 2004; Morera and Gladwin 2006; Herrero et al. 2007).

Given that theory does not tell us much about the relative weight of a household's capital asset endowments and plot characteristics in determining the choice of crop–livestock pathways, we take an empirical approach and examine the factors that help explain the variation seen in CLD patterns across a somewhat typical, semi-arid agropastoral district in East Africa.

Study Area

Keiyo District is located along the basin of Kerio River, which flows northwards to Lake Turkana, in the Rift Valley Province of western Kenya. Keiyo District can be roughly subdivided into three agro-ecological zones: the highlands (altitude 2,500–3,000 m) to the west, the escarpment (1,300–2,500 m) in the centre, and the valley floor (1,000–1,300 m) to the east (SARDEP 2002). This study focuses on households representing part of the valley floor community.

There are 16 sub-locations in Keiyo District, each occupied by a different clan. One of these, Rokocho Sub-location, consisting of 177 households, was randomly selected for this study to represent typical agropastoral communities in semi-arid regions in East Africa. The valley floor is hot for most of the year, with temperatures varying between 22°C and 31°C. Average annual rainfall ranges between 700 and 1,000 mm but high evaporation limits the LGP (Thornton et al. 2002; SARDEP 2002). A major tarmac road traverses the sub-location from north to south. Other infrastructural developments in Rokocho include a Christian mission with a training centre. The household survey was carried out between July and September 2006 using a structured questionnaire and field visits.

Before the early 1960s it was considered unviable to farm in the basin as there were no permanent sources of water. During the 1970s, in search of land, people slowly started to settle in the valley. Initially, expansion of grain production and extensive grazing in the lower valley led to serious soil degradation, with loss of natural vegetation and formation of gullies. Since 1985, the construction of the tarmac road has greatly transformed the livelihoods of people in the valley. Institutions such as churches and NGOs have also stimulated development initiatives by providing villagers with management training and capital for investing in horticulture and exotic livestock breeds. Some households have introduced horticulture and semi-zero grazing of exotic animal breeds on homestead plots in the upper parts of the valley. Furthermore, the development of water projects has allowed more people to adopt intensive farming on homesteads. Residents claim that soils in the upper valley have been healing due to manure application, terracing and mulching in contrast to the degraded soils in the lower valley.

These developments have also led to changes in land use and transactions. The land tenure system is primarily customary. Land from the valley floor up to the highlands mostly belongs to one clan. Even households located on the valley floor sometimes have plots on the escarpment and in the highlands. Clan land is subdivided among extended families and the family land is further subdivided into parcels owned by nuclear families through inheritance. However, some family plots are currently too small to be further subdivided. In such cases, one is encouraged to acquire land elsewhere by purchasing, hiring or borrowing it. While individual rights to land are well recognized, land is often used as an open access resource for grazing by clan members, unless it is properly fenced. Currently, some households that practise horticulture have started fencing their homestead plots for exclusive use.

Today, the households plant various types of crops either on single plots or on several plots spread over different agro-ecological zones and keep various kinds of livestock. We classified crops into four categories: (1) drought-resistant crops: sorghum, millet and cassava; (2) staple crops: maize, beans, cowpeas, green grams and groundnuts; (3) fruits: mangoes, pawpaws, citrus fruits, bananas and avocadoes; and (4) commercial crops: wheat, potatoes and carrots. We similarly classified livestock into four categories: (1) improved breeds of cattle (exotic and crossbred cattle); (2) dairy goats; (3) indigenous cattle; and (4) sheep and goats.

Analytical Methods

The first analytical step is to examine resource management at plot level. The total number of plots claimed by the 177 households was 386. These plots were either owned (inherited, purchased or given), rented (at a fee) or borrowed (at no fee). Most plots were located either on the lower or upper parts of the valley, while some were on the escarpment or highlands (Figure 1). The location proxies indicate the physical characteristics of farms. For example, the lower valley is flat and dry and contains sandy soils. Dominant crops include staple (maize and beans) and drought-resistant (sorghum and millet) crops, while livestock graze freely in open areas. The upper valley, where homesteads are located, is relatively flat to moderately sloped, with sandy and clayey soils, horticulture is currently practised here. Although the escarpment is very steep, drought-resistant crops or staple crops are cultivated there. The highlands are moderately sloped, cool and receive sufficient precipitation, and are ideal for commercial crops (see SARDEP 2002).

Secondly, we attempt to derive household-specific composite variables representing CLD patterns, from variables representing household shares of particular crop and livestock activities. Accurate calculation of areas cultivated to particular crops was difficult because households often had access to more than one plot, and planted different crops on the same plots, as is the practice in other parts of rural Africa (Benin et al. 2004; Pender et al. 2004b; Waithaka et al. 2006). In order to circumvent this difficulty, households were asked to approximate the percentages of plots used for each crop type. Then, principal component analysis was used to derive new sets of composite variables representing 'CLD patterns' from those variables describing shares of crop and livestock activities. The principal components can reveal complementary (positively correlated) or substitute (negatively correlated) crop and livestock activities (Iiyama et al. 2007a).

Thirdly, ordinary least squares (OLS) regressions were used to evaluate putative determinants of the CLD patterns. The dependent variables in these regressions were the principal component scores while the independent variables included household characteristics, access to various off-farm income streams, tenure and physical characteristics of the land which households had access to, and possession of specific farm implements. For tenure and physical characteristics of the land, we calculated shares of land owned by households by mode of acquisition and by location.

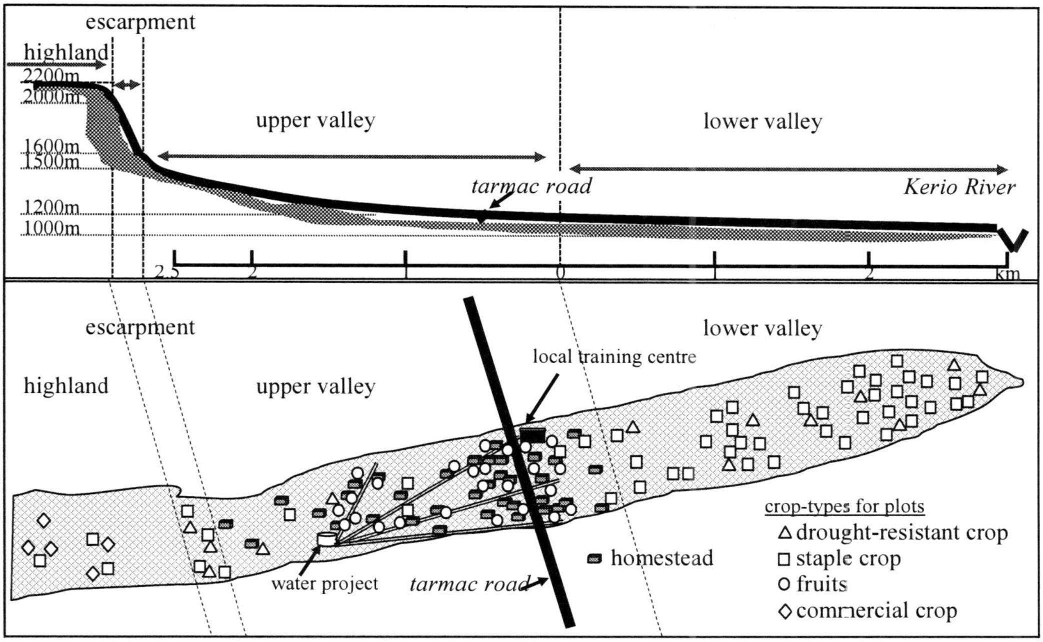

Figure 1. Land Use Patterns in the Study Area.

3.3. Results

Soil Management at Plot Level

At the time of the survey, the 177 households in the study area had access to 386 plots. Most of the plots were acquired through inheritance. Even before the 1970s, when only a few people had settled in the valley, the clan land in the upper valley, escarpment and highlands had already been subdivided into family plots, while the lower valley land remained communal. After the 1970s, the clan elders demarcated the lower valley for clan members resident in the valley, as demand for exclusive individual arable plots increased. Currently, there has been some transaction in plots through purchase or rental contracts between those who inherited large tracts of land and those who inherited little but are willing to expand cultivation.

Spatial distribution of the plots across the different agro-ecological sections is shown in Table 2. Among the 386 plots (the last row), more than half (57%) of the plots were in the upper valley (including 177 homestead plots) while the fewest (4%) were in the highlands, although the size of individual plots varied across/within a particular section. Across the sections (the last column), the most commonly crops planted were the staples, followed by fruits; 37% of the plots were not planted. Over 60% of plots in the lower valley or the escarpment were planted with staple crops. In the upper valley, 36% of plots were planted with fruits, mostly on the homestead plots, while 45% of plots were not planted. The highland plots were planted with commercial crops (wheat, tomatoes and vegetables), staple crops or an intercrop of these two categories. These spatial patterns indicate that choices of which crop types to plant is largely determined by the location of the plots, reflecting factors such as distance from homesteads, slope, soil type, temperature and water availability.

Table 2. Locations of 386 Plots by Crop-Type

	lower valley no. (%)	upper valley no. (%)	escarpment no. (%)	highland no. (%)	all sections no. (%)
CROP-TYPE					
drought-resistant	1(1)	13(6)			14(4)
Staple	77(68)	6(3)	20(61)	3(18)	106(27)
Fruits	2(2)	80(36)			82(21)
commercial				6(35)	6(2)
drought-resistant+staple	8(7)	9(4)			17(4)
with fruits and/or commercial		12(5)		4(24)	16(4)
nappier grass		2(1)			2(1)
not planted	26(23)	100(45)	13(39)	4(24)	143(37)
Total	114(100)	222(100)	33(100)	17(100)	386(100)

Table 3. Soil Fertility Management and Labour Inputs by Plot Level

	no. plots	terraced (yes=1, no=0)	manure (kg/acre)	fertiliser (ksh/acre)	family labor (mhrs/year)	hired labour (mhrs/year)
Crop-type						
drought-resistant	14	0.29	14	0	1 830	9
Staple	106	0.08	0	0	598	65
Fruits	82	0.74	522	0	1 245	101
commercial	6	0.17	5	1 167	150	1 051
drought-resistant+staple	17	0.18	0	0	1 098	31
with fruits and/or commercial	16	0.63	281	216	1 656	190
nappier grass	2	0	0	0	0	0
not planted	143	0.06	0	0	0	0
Total	386	0.25	123	27	614	65
F-value		38.92***	10.4***	41.6***	20.0***	11.9***

Plot-level applications of conservation measures (terracing and manure/fertiliser applied) and labour input (family and hired labour input) are presented in Table 3. Plots planted with fruits were more likely to be associated with intensive management (74% terraced, 522 kg/acre manure, 1,245 family man-hours/year [mhr]/year), followed by plots intercropped with fruits and/or commercial crops. Plots planted with commercial crops received little manure but a relatively large value of chemical fertilisers and hired labour (1,167 KSh/acre, 1,051 hired mhr/year). More family labour was used in plots planted with drought-resistant crops (1,830 mhr/year) than in other plots, probably because plots planted with millet and sorghum require supervision to keep wild animals away. In contrast, plots planted with staple crops were less associated with intensive management (8% terraced, no manure/fertiliser application and less labour). In general, crop types seem to affect levels of soil management, degrees of manure integration and labour input. Fruits can be associated with the conservation pathway, characterised by better soil management and higher manure and labour input, and staple crops with the degradational pathway where these factors are not applied.

Identification of Conservatory and Degradational Pathways

Household-level portfolios of crop–livestock activities are summarized in Table 4. The mean area of land used per household was 2.28 acres, of which 1.27 acres (55%) was used for cultivating staple crops, 0.80 acres (35%) was planted with fruits, while the remaining land was under drought-resistant and commercial crops. Households owned an average of 5.14 tropical livestock units (TLUs),[3] of which 2.69 TLUs (52%) comprised indigenous cattle, 1.64 TLUs (32%) consisted of sheep and goats and 0.79 TLUs (15%) were exotic and crossbred cattle. Dairy goats accounted for 1% of the total livestock holding. The averages, however, tend to mask heterogeneities in the adoption of certain crop/livestock types among households, in complementarities between crops and livestock (see Iiyama et al. 2007a) or the existence of certain patterns in crop–livestock combinations that we have explored further below.

Table 4. Household-Level Portfolios for Crop–Livestock Activities

Variables of crop-livestock activities	N	mean	Std.D	min	max	share
Proportion of land allocated to particular crop by households						
land with staple crop (acres/ratio)	177	1.27	2.59	0	21	0.55
land with fruits (acres/ratio)	177	0.80	1.29	0	10	0.35
land with drought-resistant crop (acres/ratio)	177	0.14	0.40	0	2	0.06
land with commercial (acres/ratio)	177	0.07	0.39	0	4	0.03
total acres used (acres)	177	2.28	2.99	0	24	
Proportion of particular animals kept by households						
no. of indigenous cattle (TLU/ratio)	177	2.69	5.31	0	38	0.52
no. of sheep/goats (TLU/ratio)	177	1.64	4.36	0	44	0.32
no. of improved cattle (TLU/ratio)	177	0.79	1.88	0	10	0.15
no. of dairy goats (TLU/ratio)	177	0.03	0.11	0	1	0.01
total animals owned (TLU)	177	5.14	7.45	0	44	

Table 5. Dominant CLD Patterns (Principal Components)

	Component

[3] The TLU is calculated as follows: a bull is equivalent to 1.29 TLU; a cow to 1 TLU; a calf to 0.7 TLU; and sheep and goat to 0.11 TLU (Kristjanson et al. 2002).

	CLD I maize+ind cattle	**CLD II imp cattle +fruits**	**CLD III extensive crop**	**CLD IV sheep/goats**	**CLD V dairy goats**
	+staple crop +indigenous cattle -fruits	+improved cattle +fruits, +land use -drought-resistant crop	-indigenous cattle -fruits +land use	+sheep& goats	+dairy goats -commercial crop
Land Allocated to					
drought-resistant crop(%)	-0.04	**-0.66**	0.22	-0.34	-0.21
staple crop(%)	**0.80**	0.18	0.35	-0.06	0.20
fruits(%)	**-0.70**	**0.35**	**-0.48**	0.24	0.08
commercial crop(%)	-0.14	0.24	0.11	-0.40	**-0.50**
total acre used(acres)	0.15	**0.57**	**0.46**	0.11	-0.06
Animals Held in					
improved cattle(%)	-0.35	**0.66**	0.28	-0.14	-0.10
dairy goats(%)	-0.10	0.07	0.04	-0.30	**0.83**
Indigenous cattle(%)	**0.60**	0.07	**-0.67**	-0.06	-0.12
sheep/goats(%)	-0.16	-0.34	0.38	**0.74**	0.00
total animals(TLU)	**0.54**	0.30	-0.17	0.37	-0.11

To extract a new set of variables representing CLD patterns from the original large number of crop–livestock activities, principal component analysis was used. In choosing the number of components, we used two criteria: (1) we retained components sufficient to explain a high percentage (70% to 90%) of the total variation in the original variables; and (2) we excluded principal components whose eigenvalues were less than 1 (Everitt and Dunn 2001). We then attempted to interpret each principal component with factor weights exceeding 0.5 in absolute values, or less, if deemed necessary. Five principal components extracted from the original crop–livestock portfolio variables explained 71.5% of the total variation in the data in Table 5.

The five principal components are explained as follows. Staple crop (mainly maize) and indigenous cattle were positively associated with the first principal component, while growing fruits was negatively correlated with this component. Thus this principal component is interpreted as *CLD I [maize and indigenous cattle]*. The second component was strongly associated with the proportion of improved cattle and total land used and negatively associated with the proportion of land sown to drought-resistant crops. Although it was less than 0.5, the weight for fruits was higher than that for the other components (*CLD II [improved cattle and fruits]*). The third component was negatively associated with indigenous cattle and fruits while positively associated with total land used (*CLD III [extensive crop production]*). Proportion of sheep and goats in the total TLU was strongly associated with the fourth component (*CLD IV [sheep and goats]*). Finally, the fifth component was strongly associated with the proportion of dairy goats in the total TLU (*CLD V [dairy goats]*).

Determinants of Conservatory/Degradational Pathways

We examined the determinants of the different CLD patterns using econometric analysis. For the dependent variables, we used the principal component factor scores derived from the principal component analysis. Independent variables include capital asset variables, access to off-farm income, share in acres of land by mode of acquisition (tenure), share in acres of land by location and implements (Appendix 1). Share of land by mode of acquisition summed up to one. Therefore, we excluded the share of land acquired through inheritance, because this type of land may have been acquired by chance, e.g. your father happens to own large tracts of land to bequeath or you were his only male heir. Similarly, the sum of shares of land by location was one. We excluded shares of land on the escarpment, as the dominant crops are staple crops, similar to those in the lower valley. The results are presented in Table 6.

CLD pattern I (maize + indigenous cattle) was negatively associated with access to regular and casual off-farm income generating activities and share of land in the upper valley. CLD pattern II (improved cattle + fruits) was significantly associated with gender of the household head, family labour, participative years in a farmers' group, access to regular off-farm income, share of land in the highlands and plough ownership. CLD pattern III (extensive crop production) was strongly associated with age of the household head, share of land hired, share of land in the lower valley and highlands, and a plough. In CLD pattern IV (sheep and goats), gender of the household head, share of land purchased and share of land in the lower valley had positive effects, while experience of having stayed outside (due to temporal labour migration or permanent immigration), distance to training centre, share of land in the highlands and availability of tap water at the homestead had negative effects. Distance to a training centre, share of land in the highlands and availability of tap water were negatively associated with CLD pattern V (dairy goats).

3.4. Discussions

The second principal component, CLD pattern II (improved cattle and fruits), can be interpreted as a conservation pathway as plots cropped with fruits were more associated with terracing and application of manure/labour. In contrast, CLD patterns I (maize and indigenous cattle) and III (extensive crop production) are degradational pathways, as they are more associated with a higher share of plots devoted to staple crops and negatively associated with plots with fruits. However, we could not readily determine whether CLD patterns IV (sheep and goats) and V (dairy goats) are conservation or degradational pathways, as they are less associated with total land cropped. Dairy goats are more likely to be integrated with crops as they are managed intensively with more stall-feeding than free-range indigenous small ruminants.

Let us first compare the two contrasting crop–livestock pathways, CLD pattern I (maize + indigenous cattle) and CLD pattern II (improved cattle + fruits). CLD pattern I was a degradational crop–livestock pathway, where maize and indigenous animal production are rarely integrated. This pattern was associated with lack of access to off-farm income activities. Conversely, CLD pattern II, a combination of improved cattle and fruits, was a conservation pathway. Fruits are mostly planted on homestead plots, while improved cattle are kept within or near the plots. This pattern was more strongly associated with human capital assets, e.g. labour and skills through experience in a farmers' group, and engagement in formal employment or business.

Table 6. Determinants of the CLD Patterns (OLS results)

	CLD I maize+ind cattle		CLD II impr cattle+fruits		CLD III extensive crop		CLD IV sheep/goats		CLD V dairy goats	
	B	standard error	B	standard error	B	standard error	B	standard error	B	standard error
(Constant)	1.39	0.81 *	-1,19	0.74	-0.52	0.81	0.60	0.79	1.53	0.70 **
hh characteristics										
age	0.00	0.00	0.00	0.00	0.01	0.00 **	0.00	0.00	-0.01	0.00
gender(male1,female0)	0.07	0.21	0.48	0.19 **	0.21	0.21	0.38	0.20 *	-0.25	0.18
family labour(AE)	0.00	0.04	0.10	0.04 **	-0.03	0.04	0.05	0.04	0.02	0.04
years in group	0.01	0.02	0.03	0.01 **	-0.01	0.02	-0.01	0.01	0.00	0.01
experience outside	0.10	0.17	-0.17	0.16	-0.11	0.17	-0.32	0.16 *	-0.11	0.15
min to training centre	0.00	0.00	-0.01	0.00	0.00	0.00	-0.01	0.00 ***	-0.01	0.00 **
off-farm income access										
off-farm regular	-0.84	0.27 ***	0.45	0.25 *	-0.20	0.27	0.14	0.27	-0.11	0.24
off-farm casual	-0.55	0.25 **	-0.07	0.23	-0.22	0.25	-0.05	0.24	0.05	0.21
remittance	-0.03	0.32	0.30	0.30	-0.21	0.33	0.51	0.32	0.07	0.28
tenure characteristics(acquisition)										
share purchased	0.02	0.26	0.11	0.24	0.32	0.26	0.64	0.25 **	-0.10	0.23
share given	2.24	1.61	-1.02	1.49	-1.25	1.62	-2.10	1.57	0.79	1.41
share hired	0.46	0.40	-0.49	0.37	1.17	0.40 ***	0.42	0.39	0.30	0.35
share borrowed	-0.16	0.43	-0.19	0.39	0.68	0.43	0.62	0.42	-0.19	0.37
physical characteristics(location)										
share upper valley	-1.16	0.51 **	0.23	0.47	0.33	0.51	0.79	0.50	-0.26	0.46
share lower valley	0.34	0.53	0.56	0.49	1.17	0.53 **	0.89	0.52 *	-0.13	0.45
share highland	-0.98	0.66	1.33	0.61 **	1.89	0.66 ***	-1.23	0.64 *	-2.15	0.58 ***
farming equipments										
a plough	-0.62	0.97	2.59	0.89 ***	3.27	0.97 ***	-0.15	0.95	-0.75	0.84
tap domestic	-0.28	0.36	0.29	0.33	-0.57	0.36	-1.81	0.35 ***	-0.61	0.31 *
R Square	0.32		0.42		0.30		0.31		0.22	
Adjusted R Square	0.24		0.35		0.22		0.23		0.14	
F	4.03 ***		6.26 ***		3.81 ***		3.89 ***		2.52 ***	

(note) total observation: 177 households. ***: statistically significant at <.01, **:<.05, *:<.1.

Higher income from dairy products and fruits and regular off-farm activities allow households to invest in not only assets but also resource management, such as terracing. This implies that access to human capital assets and off-farm income are important factors making the role of livestock either negative or positive in the adoption of pathways.

Tenure characteristics of plots appear not to much affect the choices between CLD patterns I (maize + indigenous cattle) and II (improved cattle + fruits), although they do influence choices of crop–livestock patterns III (extensive crop; associated with more hired land) and IV (sheep and goats; associated with more purchased land). Households engaged in pattern III may need to hire land for extensive cultivation, while those engaged in CLD pattern IV purchase land if they initially have little. With respect to land access by location, households in CLD patterns III and IV have more access to land in the lower valley, ideal for staple crops, but this effect is not significant for CLD pattern I (maize + indigenous cattle) although households in pattern I allocated more land to staple crops. Maize is more extensively grown on plots in the lower valley, far away from homesteads, while indigenous cattle and small ruminants are extensively grazed on open plots. These cultivation and grazing patterns may lead to fewer incentives to invest in soil conservation measures.

Factors influencing the adoption of soil conservation measures by poor agropastoralists in fragile ecosystems have also attracted the attention of other researchers. However, these researchers pay little attention to complementary relationships between crops and livestock. As a result, their findings are often contradictory to ours. For example, Clay et al. (2002) found that in Rwanda terracing was associated with physical characteristics of land and smaller landholdings. In contrast, our results indicated that adoption of soil conservation measures had to do with particular combinations of crops and animals (CLD patterns II [improved cattle + fruits; more adoption] vs. CLD III [extensive crop; less adoption]; both are associated with larger areas under use and share of land in the highlands). Freeman and Coe (2002) suggested that in eastern Kenya farmers with larger livestock holdings were more likely to adopt soil fertility measures. Our study showed that it was not the number of animals but types of animals and their levels of integration with crops (CLD pattern I [maize + indigenous cattle; less adoption] vs. CLD pattern II [improved cattle + fruits; more adoption]) that were associated with the use of soil fertility measures.

Our findings confirm what Barrett et al. (2002) suggested about investment in soil conservation not being made in isolation with the preceding investment in portfolio of crop and livestock activities (Barrett et al. 2002; Place et al. 2002; Tittonell et al. 2005). Our results suggest that livestock can be a cause of degradation or an opportunity for sustainable management in semi-arid regions, and that this depends on the overriding importance of household capital asset endowments and reliable off-farm income over physical/tenure characteristics of plots.

In the study area, the CLD patterns of staple crops with indigenous animals turned out to be degradational pathways. These CLD pathways may contribute to food security and higher income in the short term, thus providing households with incentives to undertake these pathways. However, these pathways, without proper soil management, have economic–environment trade-offs that lead to degraded resource bases. In fact, these pathways were similar to the scenario predicted by McIntire et al. (1992) for semi-arid agropastoral communities in Africa in response to the growing population. Conversely, CLD pattern II (improved cattle + fruits) was identified as a conservation crop–livestock pathway. This pathway has embedded incentives to integrate components through providing fodder and manure reciprocally within the farms, and their high economic return ensures that households invest in maintaining the fertility and sustainability of the resource bases they depend on.

This case study from a small area indicates that the cause of degradation is not only biophysical but also socio-economic, and could be reversible through better incorporation of livestock with human wisdom. Inferred policy suggestions are to provide proper extension services for technology dissemination and to ensure educational and better return diversification opportunities for households to invest in better soil management.

4. Conclusion

This chapter has reviewed the challenges that Africa has faced in rural development and natural resource management. As describing African exceptionalism and understanding its causes are prerequisites to policies and solutions for reducing African poverty, we highlighted two dimensions of Africa's rural poverty and stagnant agricultural growth. The inherent heterogeneity in agro-ecological/farming systems has prevented agricultural technological breakthroughs. In turn, emerging factors such as population growth and climate change have further burdened inherently fragile soil and resource bases and can exacerbate the vicious cycle of stagnant agricultural growth, persistent rural poverty, soil depletion, resource degradation, and accelerated deforestation, unless some urgent measures to halt and reverse this cycle are taken. The heterogeneity in agro-ecological/ farming systems in SSA requires researchers, policy makers and all those concerned to search for policies and solutions which reflect the different causes, problems, and opportunities for specific contexts and places.

Agricultural intensification through better utilisation of locally available resources through integration of system components, i.e. crop, livestock and agroforestry, is especially desirable considering the poverty of rural populations. Therefore the major research agenda for researchers and scientists is to identify diverse agricultural development and resource management pathways in particular agro-ecological zones/farming systems and to examine factors affecting respective pathways so as to better formulate policies to promote sustainable development pathways with optimal resource management practices. We propose a conceptual framework to guide the examination of (a) multi-dimensional aspects of agro-ecological and farming systems, i.e. interactions, complementarities or trade-offs, of multiple system components (among crop, livestock, agroforestry, nutrients, natural resources, etc.); and (b) certain layers of analytical scales (at farm-level, meso-level).

We also reviewed the meso-level study from Uganda by Pender et al. (2004) in Section 2.3 and presented the farm-level empirical case study from a Kenyan Rift Valley community in Section 3, to see how to apply the conceptual framework and to implement empirical case studies by employing the concept of "development pathways" in an integrated framework. The meso-level analysis showed that the extent to which economic development is consistent with sustainable use of natural resource bases depends upon, among other things, the development pathways being pursued in different locations, which are then affected by agro-ecological, demographic and market conditions. In turn, the micro-level study showed that there exists extensive heterogeneity even within a small community, in the patterns of the technology portfolios with different levels of incentives for sustainable resource use, and that households' capital asset endowments as well as off-farm income diversification affect the patterns.

Both the meso-level and farm-level case studies imply that some "win-win-win" opportunities, or conservation pathway, may exist to promote more sustainable development; for example, by promoting [3] the banana–coffee development pathway in Uganda and [CLD pattern II: improved cattle and fruits] in the Kenyan Rift Valley. Interestingly, both pathways are associated with the inclusion of agroforestry into the farming systems. To promote such conservation development pathways, policies not only need to identify optimal technology portfolios best suited to local conditions and exploit the complementarities but also to provide education and training with farmers to augment their human capital assets and to promote stable non-farm/off-farm income opportunities in order to encourage investment in resource management. Concurrently, there are degradational pathways entailing substantial trade-offs between promoting economic development vs. conserving natural resources. Both [1] expansion of cereal production in Uganda and [CLD pattern I: maize and indigenous cattle]/[CLD pattern III: extensive crop production] in the Kenyan Rift Valley apparently lack the embedded incentives for sustainable resource management. Such trade-offs should be adequately considered as development strategies.

Newly Emerging Challenge and Future Research Agenda

Along with population pressure and climate change, another factor has recently emerged—rising food prices—which might exacerbate the hardship that SSA countries and rural populations face (Von Braun 2007; Ghambari 2008). The price of corn has more than doubled in the last two years along with that of other staple food crops and prices for basic staples will remain high for an extended period of time due to multiple factors. The soaring cost of food and fuel has already led to riots in Haiti and Egypt and a general strike in Burkina Faso in mid-April 2008.Various factors have been blamed for raising the food prices, including droughts in Australia and Europe, financial market speculators, and increased demand for food and a changing diet in large developing countries such as China and India. Yet increasing demand for biofuels and expansion of ethanol production in USA, Europe and Brazil is referred to among the most significant causes. There are some predictions that the planned biofuel expansion would increase international prices 26-72 percent for maize and by 19-44 percent for oilseeds by the year 2020 and that the increase in crop prices is accompanied by a net decrease in availability and access to food by the poor (Von Braun 2007).

Considering that many poor households in rural SSA are deficient in food, the rising prices of basic staple food crops will aggravate the poverty and increase the risk of hunger and starvation. Poverty might drive the poor rural population to seek for alternative sources of income to obtain food at markets by exploiting natural resources, further accelerating resource degradation and deforestation. Furthermore, searching for vast land and cheap labour for the stable supply of imported feedstocks, private companies and capitals from developed countries have recently rushed into SSA countries to invest in plantation for biofuel feedstocks, not only for bioethanol such as maize and sugarcane but also for biodiesel from non-edible oilseed plants such as Jatropha curcas. The trade-offs between food and fuel will actually be accelerated when biofuels become more competitive under the circumstances of skyrocketing petroleum prices in relative to food and when consequently land, water, and capital are diverted to them. It is even not certain what consequences biofuel production would have on environment, soil, resource bases, and biodiversity. To soften the trade-off and mitigate the growing price burden for the poor in SSA, it is necessary to accelerate investment in food and agricultural technologies as well as in research to assess the socio-economic and environmental impacts of biofuel provisions.

We conclude this chapter by proposing a future agenda for the research contributing to development and poverty alleviation in Africa. This paper has proposed a conceptual framework for guiding integrated research and analysis on agricultural development and natural resource management at meso-level and at farm-level. Yet, there is also a significant need to facilitate the analyses at sector-/macro-level. Most countries in SSA are poor and have severe resource constraints. Therefore balancing attention between favoured and less-favoured sub-sectors, regions and households is one of the toughest policy dilemmas and requires guidance based on sound scientific data/analyses on sector linkages, growth, employment and environmental effects of agricultural development and sustainable resource management (World Bank 2007). Sector-level/macro-level analyses will be especially important to predict/assess the socio-economic and environmental impacts of rising food/fuel prices, to act promptly to identify the most vulnerable/affected, and to formulate policy interventions to the poor to adapt themselves to ever more challenging circumstances.

APPENDIX 1: EXPLANATORY VARIABLES FOR THE CLD PATTERNS

	N	Mean	Std.D	Min	Max
Household characteristics					
age of the head	177	46.85	17.63	20	102
gender of the head(male=1,female=0)	177	0.78	0.42	0	1
family labour(Adult Equivalent)	177	3.30	1.76	1	8.14
participation in farmers group(years)	177	2.50	5.03	0	26
minute distance to training centre(min)	177	28.06	24.08	1	195
experience of having stayed outside(yes=1, no=0)	177	0.28	0.45	0	1
Access to off-farm income					
regular off-farm income(yes=1, no=0)	177	0.30	0.46	0	1
casual off-farm income(yes=1, no=0)	177	0.50	0.50	0	1
remittance (yes=1, no=0)	177	0.12	0.33	0	1
Total land owned(acres)	177	7.55	18.12	0.50	201
Share of land access by mode of acquition(tenure characteristics)					
land inherited(share)	177	0.75	0.39	0	1
land purchased(share)	177	0.13	0.30	0	1
land given(share)	177	0.00	0.04	0	0.50
land hired(share)	177	0.07	0.19	0	0.92

land borrowed(share)	177	0.04	0.18	0	1
Share of land access by location(physical characteristics)					
land in lower valley/Endo[flat, dry, hot](share)	177	0.28	0.30	0	1
land in upper valley[moderate slope, hot](share)	177	0.63	0.31	0	1
land in escarpment[steep,warm](share)	177	0.05	0.14	0	1
land in highland[moderate slope, wet, cool](share)	177	0.04	0.15	0	1
Farming implements					
a plough	177	0.01	0.08	0	1
tap domestic	177	0.94	0.24	0	1

REFERENCES

Amissah-Arthur, A.,. & Miller, R.B. (2002). Remote Sensing Applications in African Agriculture and Natural Resources: Highlighting and Managing the Stress of Increasing Population Pressure. *Advances in Space Research, Vol. 30(11)*, 2411-2421.

Barrett, C.B., Reardon, T., & Webb, P. (2001). Nonfarm Income Diversification and Household Livelihood Strategies in Rural Africa: Concepts, Dynamics and Policy Implications, *Food Policy, Vol.26,* 315-331.

Barrett, C.B., Place, F., & Aboud, A.A. (2002). *Natural Resources Management in African Agriculture: Understanding and Improving Current Practices*. Oxon and New York: CABI publishing.

Barrios, S., Bertinelli, L., & Strobl, E. (2006). Climatic Change and Rural–urban Migration: The Case of Sub-Saharan Africa. *Journal of Urban Economics, Vol.60(3),*357-371.

Bationo, A., Nandwa, S.M., Kimetu, J.M., Kinyangi, J.M., Bado, B.V., Lompo, F., Kimani, S., Kihanda, F., & Koala, S. (2004). Sustainable Interaction of Crop-Livestock Systems through Manure Management in Eastern and Western Africa: Lessons Learned and Emerging Research Opportunities. In T.O. Williams, S. Tarawali, P. Hiernaux, & S. Fernández-Rivera. (Eds.), *Sustainable Crop-Livestock Production for Improved Livelihoods and Natural Resource Management in West Africa* (pp.173-198). Nairobi: International Livestock Research Institute.

Beg, N., Morlot, J.C., Davidson, O., Afrane-Okesse, Y., Tyani, L., Denton, F., Sokona, Y., & Thomas, J.P. (2002). Linkages between Climate Change and Sustainable Development. *Climate Policy, Vol.2*, 129–144.

Benin, S., Smale, M., Pender, J., Gebremedhin, B., & Ehui, S. (2004). The Economic Determinants of Cereal Crop Diversity on Farms in the Ethiopian Highlands. *Agricultural Economics, Vol.31*, 197-208.

Bullock, P. (1997). Agro-ecological Characterisation, Food Production and Security. *Perspectives for Agronomy, Vol. 25*, 29-37.

Chen, S., & Ravallion, M (2007). Poverty and Hunger Special Feature: Absolute Poverty Measures for the Developing World, 1981–2004. *PNAS (Proceedings of the National Academy of Sciences of the United States of America), Vol.104 (43)*, 16757–16762.

Chidumayo, E.N., & Kwibisa, L. (2003). Effects of Deforestation on Grass Biomass and Soil Nutrient Status in Miombo Woodland, Zambia. *Agriculture, Ecosystems & Environment , Vol.96(1-3)*, 97-105.

Christiaensen, L., Tollens, E., & Ezedinma, C. (1995). Development Patterns under Population Pressure: Agricultural Development and the Cassava-Livestock Interaction in Smallholder Farming Systems in Sub-Saharan Africa. *Agricultural Systems, Vol. 48(1)*, 51-72.

Clay, D.C., Kelly, V., Mpyisi, E., & Reardon, T. (2002). Input Use and Conservation Investments among Farm Households in Rwanda: Patterns and Determinants. In C.B.Barrett, F. Place, & A.A.Aboud. (Eds.), *Natural Resources Management in African Agriculture: Understanding and Improving Current Practices* (pp.103-114). Oxon and New York: CABI publishing.

Cline-Cole, R.A., Main, H.A.C., & Nichol, J.E. (1990). On Fuelwood Consumption, Population Dynamics and Deforestation in Africa. *World Development ,Vol.18(4)*, 513-527.

Collier, P. (2007). Poverty Reduction in Africa. *PNAS (Proceedings of the National Academy of Sciences of the United States of America), Vol.104 (43)*, 16763–16768.

Dar ,W.D., & Twomlow, S.J. (2007). Managing Agricultural Intensification: The Role of International Research. *Crop Protection, Vol.26(3)*, 399-407.

De Jager, A.., Onduru, D., van Wijk, M.S., Vlaming, J., & Gachini, G.N. (2001). Assessing Sustainability of

Low-External-Input Farm Management Systems with the Nutrient Monitoring Approach: A Case Study in Kenya. *Agricultural Systems,Vol.69*, 99-118.

Delgado, C., Rosegrant, M., Steinfeld, H., Ehui, S., & Courbois, C. (1999). *Livestock to 2020: The Next Food Revolution*. Food Agriculture, and Environment Discussion Paper 28. Washington D.C.: International Food Policy Research Institute.

Dorward, A., Kydd, J., Morrison, J., & Urey, I. (2004). A Policy Agenda for Pro-Poor Agricultural Growth. *World Development, Vol.32(1)*, 3-89.

Ellis, F. (2000). *Rural Livelihoods and Diversity in Developing Countries*. Oxford: Oxford University Press.

Ellis, F., & Freeman, H.A. (2005). *Rural Livelihoods and Poverty Reduction Policies*. London and New York: Routledge.

Erskine, J.M. (1991). Agroforestry: Its Development as a Sustainable, Productive Land-use System for Low-resource Farmers in Southern Africa. *Forest Ecology and Management. Vol.45(1-4)*, 281-291.

Evans, H.E., & Ngau, P. (1991). Rural-Urban Relations, household Income Diversification and Agricultural Productivity. *Development and Change, Vol.22*, 519-545.

Everitt, B.S., & Dunn, G. (2001). *Applied Multivariate Data Analysis: Second Edition*. London: Arnold.

Franzel, S., Coe, R., Cooper, P., Place, F., & Scherr, S.J. (2001). Assessing the Adoption Potential of Agroforestry Practices in Sub-Saharan Africa. *Agricultural Systems, Vol. 69(1-2)*, 37-62.

Freeman, A.H., & Coe, R. (2002). Smallholder Farmers' Use of Integrated Nutrient-Management Strategies: Patterns and Possibilities in Machakos District of Eastern Kenya. In C.B.Barrett, F. Place, & A.A.Aboud. (Eds.), *Natural Resources Management in African Agriculture: Understanding and Improving Current Practices* (pp.143-154). Oxon and New York: CABI publishing.

Frost, P., Campbell, B., Luckert, M., Mutamba, M., Mandondo, A., & Kozanayi, W. (2007). In Search of Improved Rural Livelihoods in Semi-Arid Regions through Local Management of Natural Resources: Lessons from Case Studies in Zimbabwe. *World Development, Vol. 35(11)*, 1961-1974.

Ghanbari, H.N. (2008). World Bank Chief Biofuels Boosting Food Prices. NPR News April 11, 2008. http://www.npr.org/templates/story/story.php?storyId=89545855.

Herrero, M., González-Estrada, E., Thornton, P.K., Quirós, C., Waithaka, M.M., Ruiz, R., & Hoogenboom, G. (2007). IMPACT: Generic Household-Level Databases and Diagnostics Tool for Integrated Crop- Livestock System Analysis. *Agricultural Systems, Vol.92,* 240-265.

Iiyama, M., Maitima, J., & Kariuki, P. (2007a). Crop-Livestock Diversification Patterns in Relation to Income and Manure Use: A Case Study from a Rift Valley Community, Kenya. *African Journal of Agricultural Research, Vol. 2(3)*, 58-66.

Iiyama, M., Kaitibie, S., Kariuki, P., & Morimoto, Y. (2007b). The Status of Crop-Livestock Systems and Evolution toward Integration: A Review Paper. *Annals of Arid Zones, Vol.46 (3&4)*, 301-323.

Iiyama, M., Kariuki, P., Kristjanson, P., Kaitibie, S., & Maitima, J. (2008). Livelihood Diversification Strategies, Incomes and Soil Management Strategies: A Case Study from Kerio Valley, Kenya. *Journal of International Development, Vol.20*, 380-397.

IPCC (Intergovernmental Panel on Climate Change). (1988). *The Regional Impacts of Climate Change: An Assessment of Vulnerability*. Cambridge: Cambridge University Press.

Karekezi, S. (2002). Poverty and Energy in Africa- A Brief Review. *Energy Policy, Vol.30(11-12)*, 915-919.

Karekezi, S., & Kithyoma, W. (2002). Renewable Energy Strategies for Rural Africa: Is a PV-led Renewable Energy Strategy the Right Approach for Providing Modern Energy to the Rural Poor of Sub-Saharan Africa? *Energy Policy, Vol. 30(11-12)*, 1071-1086.

Kates, R W., & Dasgupta, P. (2007). African Poverty: A Grand Challenge for Sustainability Science. *PNAS (Proceedings of the National Academy of Sciences of the United States of America), Vol. 104 (43),* 16747–16750.

Kristjanson, P., Okike, I., Shirley, A., Tarawali, R., Kruska, V.M., & Singh, B.B. (2002). Evaluating Adoption of New Crop-Livestock-Soil-Management Technologies using Georeferenced Village-Level Data: The Case of Cowpea in the Dry Savannahs of West Africa. In C.B.Barrett, F. Place, & A.A.Aboud. (Eds.), *Natural Resources Management in African Agriculture: Understanding and Improving Current Practices* (pp.169-180). Oxon and New York: CABI publishing.

Kristjanson, P.M., & Thorton, P.K. (2004). Methodological Challenges in Evaluating Impact of Crop-Livestock Interventions. In T.O. Williams, S. Tarawali, P. Hiernaux, & S. Fernández-Rivera. (Eds.), *Sustainable Crop-Livestock Production for Improved Livelihoods and Natural Resource Management in West Africa* (pp.160-172). Nairobi: International Livestock Research Institute.

Kristjanson, P., Radney, M., Baltenweck, I., Ogutu, J., & Notenbaert, A. (2005). Livelihood Mapping and Poverty Correlates at a Meso-Level in Kenya. *Food Policy, Vol.30*, 568-583.

Kruseman, G., Ruben, R., & Tesfay, G. (2006). Diversity and Development Domains in the Ethiopian Highlands. *Agricultural Systems, Vol.88*, 75-91.

Kruska, R.L., Reid, R.S., Thornton, P.K., Henninger, N., & Kristjanson, P.M. (2003). Mapping Livestock- oriented Agricultural Production Systems for the Developing World. *Agricultural Systems, Vol. 77(1)*, 39-63.

Lacy, S.M., Cleveland, D.A., & Soleri, D. (2006). Farmer Choice of Sorghum Varieties in Southern Mali, *Human Ecology, Vol.34(3)*, 331-353.

Manyong, V.M., Okike, I., & Williams, T.O. (2006). Effective Dimensionality and Factors Affecting Crop-livestock Integration in West African Savannas: a Combination of Principal Component Analysis and Tobit Approaches. *Agricultural Economics, Vol.35 (2)*, 145–155.

McIntire, J., Bourzat, D., & Pingali, P. (1992). *Crop-Livestock Interaction in Sub-Saharan Africa.* World Bank Regional and Sectoral Studies). Washington D.C.: The World Bank.

Morera, M.C., & Gladwin, C.H. (2006). Does Off-Farm Work Discourage Soil Conservation? Incentives and Disincentives Throughout Two Honduran Hillside Communities. *Human Ecology,Vol.34(3)*, 355-378.

Morgan, W.B., & Moss, P.A. (1985). Biomass Energy and Urbanisation: Commercial Factors in the Production and Use of Biomass Fuels in Tropical Africa. *Biomass, Vol.6(4)*, 285-299.

Mortimore, M. (1991). *A Review of Mixed Farming Systems in the Semi-Arid Zone of Sub-Saharan Africa.* Working Document No.17. International Livestock Centre for Africa, Addis Ababa.

Mwampamba, T.H. (2007). Has the Woodfuel Crisis Returned? Urban Charcoal Consumption in Tanzania and its Implications to Present and Future Forest Availability. *Energy Policy,Vol.35*, 4221-4234.

Ndiaye, S.M., Sofranko, A.J. (1994). Farmers' Perceptions of Resource Problems and Adoption of Conservation Practices in a Densely Populated area. *Agriculture, Ecosystems & Environment, Vol. 48(1)*, 35-47.

Okwi, P., Ndeng'e, G., Kristjanson, P., Arunga, M., Notenbaert, A., Omoloa, A., Henninger, N., Benson, T., Kariuki, P., & Owuor, J. (2007). Spatial Determinants of Poverty in Rural Kenya. *PNAS (Proceedings of the National Academy of Sciences of the United States of America), Vol.104 (43)*, 16769–16774.

Ong, C.K., Anyango, S., Muthuri, C.W., & Black, C.R. (2007). Water Use and Water Productivity of Agroforestry Systems in the Semi-arid Tropics. *Annals of Arid Zone. 46(3&4)* in press.

Pell, A.N. (1999). Integrated Crop–livestock Management Systems in Sub-saharan Africa. *Environment, Development and Sustainability, Vol.1*, 337-248.

Pender, J., Jagger, P., Nkonya, E., & Sserunkuuma, D. (2004a). Development Pathways and Land Management in Uganda. *World Development, Vol.32(5)*, 762-792.

Pender, J., Nkonya, E., Jagger, P., Sserunkuuma, D., & Ssali, H. (2004b). Strategies to Increase Agricultural Productivity and Reduce Land Degradation: Evidence from Uganda. *Agricultural Economics, Vol.31,* 181-195.

Perz, S.G., Walker, R.T., & Caldas, M.M. (2006). Beyond Population and Environment: Household Demographic Life Cycles and Land Use Allocation Among Small Farms in the Amazon. *Human Ecology, Vol.34(4)*, 829-849.

Place, F., Franzel, S., DeWolf, J., Rommelse, R., Kwesiga, F., Niang, A., & Jama, B. (2002). Agroforestry for Soil-Fertility Replenishment: Evidence on Adoption Processes in Kenya and Zambia. In C.B.Barrett, F. Place, & A.A.Aboud. (Eds.), *Natural Resources Management in African Agriculture: Understanding and Improving Current Practices* (pp.155-168). Oxon and New York: CABI publishing.

Place, F., Barrett, C.B., Freeman, H.A., Ramisch, J.J., & Vanlauwe, B. (2003). Prospects for Integrated Soil Fertility Management Using Organic and Inorganic Inputs: Evidence from Smallholder African Agricultural Systems. *Food Policy, Vol.28,* 365-378.

Place, F., Kristjanson, P., Staal, S., Kruska, R.L., deWolff, T., Zomer, R., & Njuguna, E.C. (2006). Development Pathways in Medium-high Potential Kenya: A Meso-level Analysis of Agricultural Patterns and Determinants. In J. Pender, F. Place, & S. Ehui. (Eds.), *Strategies for Sustainable Land Management in the East Africa Highlands.*Washington D.C.: International Food Policy Institute.

Reardon, T., & Vosti, S.A. (1995). Links between Rural Poverty and the Environment in Developing Countries: Asset Categories and Investment Poverty. *World Development, Vol.23(9),*1495-1506.

Sanchez, P.A., & Leakey, R.R.B. (1997). Land Use Transformation in Africa: Three Determinants for Balancing Food Security with Natural Resource Utilization. *Perspectives for Agronomy, Vol. 25,* 19-27.

Sanchez, P.A. (2000). Linking Climate Change Research with Food Security and Poverty Reduction in the Tropics. *Agriculture, Ecosystems and Environment, Vol.82 (1-3),* 371-383.

SARDEP. (2002). *SARDEP Keiyo/Marakwet, Participatory Land Use Plans for Community-based Natural Resource Management, Transect E.* Iten: The Semi-Arid Development Programme.

Seré, C., & Steinfeld, H. (1996). *World Livestock Production Systems: Current Status, Issues and Trends.* FAO Animal Production and Health Paper 127. Rome: FAO.

Shepherd, K.D., & Soule, M.J. (1998). Soil Fertility Management in West Kenya: Dynamic Simulation of Productivity, Profitability and Sustainability at Different Resource Endowment Levels. *Agriculture, Ecosystems and Environment, Vol.71,* 131-145.

Staal, S.J., Baltenweck, I., Waithaka, M.M., deWolff, T., & Njoroge, L. (2002). Location and Uptake: Integrated Household and GIS Analysis of Technology Adoption and Land Use, with Application to Smallholder Dairy Farms in Kenya. *Agricultural Economics, Vol.27,* 295-315.

Steinfeld, H., Wassenaar, T., & Jutzi, S. (2006). Livestock Production Systems in Developing Countries: Status, Drivers, Trends. *Rev.sci.tech.Off.int.Epiz. Vol.25(2),* 505-156.

Thangata, P.H., & Alavalapati, J.R.R. (2003). Agroforestry Adoption in Southern Malawi: the Case of Mixed Intercropping of Gliricidia Sepium and Maize.*Agricultural Systems, Vol.78(1),* 57-71.

Tiffen, M., Mortimore, M., & Gichuki, F. (1994). *More People, Less Erosion: Environmental Recovery in Kenya.* Chichester: John Wiley & Sons.

Thorne, P.J. (1998). Crop Livestock Interactions. A Review of Opportunities for Developing Integrated Models. (Unpublished Consultants Report to the ILRI-SLP). Llangefni, UK: Stirling Thorne Associates.

Thornton, P.K., & Herrero,] M. (2001). Integrated Crop-Livestock Simulation Models for Scenario Analysis and Impact Assessment. *Agricultural Systems, Vol.70,* 581-602.

Thornton, P.K., Kruska, R.L., Henninger, N., Krisjanson, P.M., Reid, R.S., Atieno, F., Odero, A.N, & Ndegwa, T. (2002). *Mapping Poverty and Livestock in the Developing World.* Nairobi: ILRI (International Livestock Research Institute).

Tittonell, P., Vanlauwe, B., Leffelaar, P.A., Rowe, E.C., & Giller, K.E. (2005). Exploring Diversity in Soil Fertility Management of Smallholder Farms in Western Kenya I. Heterogeneity at Region and Farm Scale. *Agriculture, Ecosystems & Environment, Vol.110*, 149-165.

Von Braun, J. (2007). *The World Food Situation: New Driving Forces and Required Actions.* IFPRI's Bi-Annual Overview of the World Food Situation presented to the CGIAR Annual General Meeting, Beijing December 3, 2007.

Waithaka, M.M., Thornton, P.K., Herrero, M., & Shepherd, K.D. (2006). Bio-economic Evaluation of Farmers' Perceptions of Viable Farms in Western Kenya. *Agricultural Systems, Vol.90*, 243-271.

Williams, T.O., Tarawali, S., Hiernaux, P., & Fernández-Rivera, S. (2004). *Sustainable Crop-Livestock Production for Improved Livelihoods and Natural Resource Management in West Africa.* Nairobi: International Livestock Research Institute.

Wolde-Rufael, Y. (2006).Electricity Consumption and Economic Growth: a Time Series Experience for 17 African Countries. *Energy Policy, Vol. 34(10)*, 1106-1114.

World Bank (2007). *World Development Report 2008: Agriculture for Development.* Washington DC: The World Bank.

Zhang, Q., Justice, C.O., & Desanker, P.V. (2002). Impacts of Simulated Shifting Cultivation on Deforestation and the Carbon Stocks of the Forests of Central Africa. *Agriculture, Ecosystems &Environment, Vol.90(2)*, 203- 209.

In: Natural Resources
Editor: Jeanette B. Pauling

ISBN 978-1-60456-982-7

Chapter 4

PROTECTION OF RIPARIAN LANDSCAPES IN ISRAEL

Tseira Maruani and Irit Amit-Cohen
Department of Geography and Environment, Bar-Ilan University, Ramat-Gan, Isral

ABSTRACT

Riparian landscapes are natural habitats of unique ecological and scenic values, which are highly sensitive to human intervention and impact. Yet, due to their qualities, and especially the presence of water, they are also usually attractive for recreation purposes. This is more so in arid and semi-arid zones like Israel. Nevertheless, in the past, the importance of riparian landscapes in Israel did not receive adequate attention in policy and planning. As a result, over the years they were exposed to various negative impacts, including pollution by industrial and agricultural effluents, exploitation of water for agricultural and other purposes, and land use conflicts. Although in recent years with the growing awareness of their ecological and recreational potential, considerable efforts are being invested in the rehabilitation of deteriorated riparian landscapes, their protection is still deficient.

This chapter reviews and examines policy tools used for the protection of riparian landscapes in Israel, based mainly on regulations, reports and existing literature. It concludes by offering some lessons for policy-making in general and suggestions for improving the protection of riparian landscapes in Israel in particular.

Keywords: environmental policy, river corridors, conservation, open spaces

INTRODUCTION

Riparian landscapes are natural habitats of unique ecological and scenic values, which are highly sensitive to human intervention and impact (Goren, 2000). Yet, due to their qualities, and especially the presence of water, they are also usually attractive for development as well as for recreation purposes. This is more so in arid and semi-arid zones like Israel (Burmil,

1999; Patten, 1998). Nevertheless, in the past, the values of riparian landscapes in Israel did not receive adequate attention in policy and physical planning. As a result, they were exposed over the years to various negative impacts, including pollution by industrial and agricultural effluents and household sewage, exploitation of water for agricultural and other purposes, political disputes and land use conflicts (Amir-Shapira and Feldman, 1999; Gabbay, 1998). In recent years, mainly since the year 2000, with the growing awareness of their ecological and recreational potential, considerable efforts are being invested in the rehabilitation of deteriorated riparian landscapes. Nonetheless, according to a recent report most of the rivers in Israel and their surroundings still suffer from pollution and other negative impacts (Amir-Shapira, 2007).

This chapter reviews the protection of riparian landscapes in Israel. It presents the policy tools used for protection of riparian landscapes up to the year 2000, examines their effectivity and reveals embedded deficiencies. The methodology is based on the review and content analysis of various sources, mainly laws, reports and literature. The first part of the chapter introduces the importance of riparian landscapes in general, covering among others ecological, environmental and scenic aspects. It than presents the subject of riparian landscapes in Israel and the factors that affected policy and priorities concerning the use of water in general and protection of riparian landscapes in particular. The second part reviews and examines protection tools, focusing on legislation, institutional structure and physical planning. The third and last part of the chapter discusses the deficiencies and weaknesses that were revealed and proposes improvements to the existing state.

The Importance of Riparian Landscapes

According to Naiman & Décamps (1997) a riparian zone encompasses the stream channel and that adjacent portion of the terrestrial landscape from the high water mark toward the uplands, where vegetation might be influenced by elevated water tables or flooding. The width of a riparian zone and the diversity of its functional attributes are related to the size of the stream, its position within the drainage network, the hydrologic regime and the local geomorphology (Gregory et al., 1991; Naiman & Décamps, 1997). In other words, a riparian zone may be regarded as a linear physical landscape entity composed of aquatic and terrestrial components and the interface between them. Riparian landscapes are unique ecosystems, highly important ecologically and environmentally, and they constitute a visually and functionally outstanding component of the open space system. They form complex habitats, richer than the average with species of plants, animals and microorganisms, thus contributing to overall biodiversity (Gregory et al., 1991; Naiman et al., 1993). These habitats and the richness of species they sustain are especially sensitive to various impacts and interferences, including seasonal or other changes in water physical qualities (like temperature, salinity or electric mobility) or quantities (Allan, 2004; Goren, 2000; Karr, 1994; Naiman & Décamps, 1997; Pollock et al., 1998; Shandas, 2007; Stauffer & Best, 1980). They are considered the most diverse, dynamic and complex habitats (Goren, 2000; Gregory et al., 1991; Naiman & Décamps, 1997).

Riparian ecosystems perform a variety of environmental and ecological services (Allan, 2004; Brauman et al., 2007; Hale & Adams, 2007; Naiman & Décamps, 1997; Patten, 1998).

Many of these are considered life-supporting systems (De Groot, 1992; Naveh, 1997), although they are difficult to evaluate in economic terms (Chavas, 2000; Constanza, 2000). Due to their linear nature, riparian landscapes are natural ecological corridors, allowing connectivity between habitats and patches in the landscape (Beier & Noss, 1998; Bentrup & Kellerman, 2004; Jongman, 1995; Machtans et al., 1996; Naiman et al., 1993; Ndubisi et al., 1995; Shkedi & Sadot, 2000; Taylor et al., 1995; Walmsley, 2006; Weber et al., 2006). This is especially important in populated areas, where riparian landscapes may be the last remnants of an open natural space within a built-up area. Another function that is especially important in populated areas is their potential as catchement basins for floods, thus avoiding damage to property and lives (Brody et al., 2007; McHarg, 1969; State Comptroller, 1993). They are also attractive for recreation and leisure activities, and due to their linear form are natural candidates for greenway planning, combining opportunities for recreation with conservation of nature, landscape and heritage values (Ahern, 1995; Baschak & Brown, 1995; Bryant, 2006; Fábos, 2004, 1995; Jim & Chen, 2003; Lewis, 1964; Li et al., 2005; Little, 1990). Open lands along rivers and streams are also often used for agriculture, because of their fertility, due to embedded sediments, and relatively level plains (Bentrup & Kellerman, 2004; Karr, 1994).

Riparian landscapes are extremely vulnerable to human impact. Surface water from all over the drainage basin might carry with it soil particles and various pollutants, including pesticides, fertilizers and agricultural wastes into the stream. Their potential for conservation, recreation or agriculture is diminished by conflicts and liabilities from various sources. Pollution by industrial and agricultural effluents and overflow of sewage from treatment plans harms the landscape, disqualifies water for irrigation, prevents recreational water-related activities (e.g. swimming and boating) and repels potential users in general. Exploiting river water for irrigation decreases the availability of water for natural system functions. Though riparian landscapes are attractive for development and recreation, they may be contradictory to certain types of agricultural uses. Moreover, floods may cause damage to agriculture and other uses within the flooded area.

Nevertheless, the presence of water is a potentially dominant factor that attracts development. Unfortunately, often the resulting development ends up with the construction of buildings and infrastructure too close to the water line, thus interfering with the ecological functions of the riparian system.

Considering their uniqueness and attractiveness on the one hand and their vulnerability to various impacts on the other, riparian landscapes are in need of effective protection from inappropriate uses. In Israel, a hot and dry land, such landscapes are especially important. The next section describes the factors that affect rivers and riparian landscapes in Israel.

THE RIVERS IN ISRAEL

The priorities concerning water and riparian landscapes in Israel stem from physical conditions – mainly geomorphology and climate – combined with ideological and geopolitical factors.

Israel is situated on the eastern side of the Mediterranean basin, with geomorphology and climate changing both along the north-south axis and the east-west one. The north and center of the country lie within the Mediterranean climate zone, characterized by a short rainy winter and a long, hot and dry summer while the south of the country is more desert-like. The mountainous northern areas are the rainiest with an average of 800-1000 millimeters per year, decreasing in the central zone the a yearly average of 500-600 millimeters. Eastward and southward the average decreases to 100 millimeters and less. These quantities may fluctuate from year to year, and, in addition, there is high occurrence of droughts. All these factors add up to a continual condition of water shortage (Menahem, 1999).

The area of the State of Israel is intersected longitudinally by a series of mountain ranges that divide it into an eastern basin, where rivers flow towards the Jordan River, the Sea of Galilee and the Dead Sea, along the natural eastern borders, and a western basin, where rivers flow into the Mediterranean Sea. The western basin's climate is milder and relatively rainy, while the eastern basin's is hot and dry. Due to the limited rain quantities, many river sections are in fact seasonal streams, flowing during winter and spring, and drying out in the summer until the next rainy season. In the dry south, the streams are characterized by short strong flows following rain events, which dry out quickly. Only a few rivers that are fed by year-round springs have water flowing in all seasons.

Seasonal streams are exceptionally sensitive because of the fluctuations in water availability for habitat performance in addition to the fact that some of them do not enjoy a strong flow even in the rainy season. These characteristics affect their public conceptual image as landscapes fit for conservation or suitable for recreation purposes. River sections that run through areas declared as nature reserves or national parks are protected, along with the whole area, under the National Parks and Nature Reserves Law of 1963. However, a river or stream crossing an area that is not characterized by special scenic or nature values were usually not grasped as deserving protection. Consequently, they are under pressures for development, especially in areas of level topography, such as the inner and the coastal plains.

The most important rivers, considering water discharge amounts and landscape impact are in Israel's western basin, crossing the coastal plain where the majority of the population (about 80%) is concentrated. These also have the highest potential for recreation. However, their proximity to densely settled areas has resulted in their deterioration due to various negative impacts, such as: trapping riparian waters for agricultural use and other purposes, pollution by agricultural and industrial effluents, overflow of sewage from treatment facilities, construction or agricultural cultivation close to the water line, neglect and garbage disposal (Amir-Shapira & Feldman, 1999).

In addition to this, because of the scarcity of water resources and frequent droughts, the national water policy focused on keeping control over all water sources and prioritizing the use of water for agriculture and other uses. For example, since the mid 1950s, most of the water from the Yarkon springs was captured and transported to agricultural fields in the Negev (the southern region of the land) through the Yarkon-Negev pipeline; as a result, the Yarkon River, the main river in the core, densely-populated area of Israel - once a wide deep stream that the British soldiers had to cross by boats when conquering the land from the Turks in the year 1917 – deteriorated into a narrow and shallow stream, where most of the flow consisted of industrial effluents and initially-treated sewage. The negative impacts on riparian landscapes call for examination of existing protection and management tools and their effectivity.

Protection of Riparian Landscapes in Israeli Legislation

The protection of landscapes by legislation is a universally accepted model for the conservation of outstanding scenic or natural values (Maruani and Amit-Cohen, 2007). Legislation is a source of authority and constitutes a strongly effective policy tool. Yet this tool has its drawbacks, among them low flexibility, requiring a long, complicated bureaucratic process whenever a change in legislation is desired. This is also a source of conflict between conservationists and developers and landowners. On the other hand, protection based on a statutory declaration is stronger than any other protection tool, and provides the relevant authorities with enforcement measures.

In Israel, legislation concerning water resources, including rivers, is complex, involving a multitude of laws and regulations as well as a multitude of authorities and organizations that are meant to enforce them (Kaplan, 2004). This section presents three laws that are the most relevant to the protection of riparian landscapes, as follows: the Water Law, the Drainage Law and the Rivers Authorities Law.

The Water Law

The Water Law, enacted in 1959, should be understood in the context of the general scarcity of water resources in Israel, the relative average low rainfall and the frequent droughts, on the one hand, and the centralistic governance style and intensive involvement of the State, on the other (Menahem, 1999). The main objectives of the law were to secure the State's sovereignty over all water sources and ensure their utilization for the benefit of Israeli society. The law determines that "... the water sources in the State are owned by the public, controlled by the State and designated for its population and development needs. The water sources for that matter are the springs, the streams, the rivers..." etc. (Water Law, sec.1-2). The law regulates the management of water sources, including allocation for users and preservation of water quality. For these purposes, the law created several institutions, among them a National Water Board, headed by the Water Commissioner. The law gave priority to the agricultural sector, which at the time was regarded not only as a leading sector in the national economy but also as the ideological and political elite of Israeli society (Menahem, 1999; Schiffman, 1999). This was reflected in various attributes of the law, among them its subordination to the Minister of Agriculture, including the power to appoint the Water Commissioner, who was to lead the design and implementation of water policy in Israel. Thus, it is no wonder that the first seven elected commissioners were from the agricultural sector, as were also most of the National Water Board members (Menahem, 1999). Only forty years later, in the 1990s, following ideological, political and social change processes in Israeli society, including the decrease in the economic and ideological importance of agriculture and the acceleration of development (Maruani, 2005; Schiffman, 1999), the Water Law was transferred to the authority of the Minister of National Infrastructures and some of its powers were split among several other institutional structures. Laster (2004) claims that this split in authorities is the reason for the decrease in water quality, in contrast to Western Europe where a centralistic approach was adopted.

The Water Commissioner, among others, used his powers collect water from springs and rivers, and allocate it to consumers, thus reducing the natural flow, ignoring the ecological consequences, which, in turn, also had a negative impact on the attractiveness and availability of the surrounding area for recreation (Laster, 1995).

The only reference in the Water Law to the protection of land near water sources is the available option to define buffer strips for purposes such as "...protection of water, of water source ...", that are wide "... no more than is necessary for the purpose of the buffer strip..." (sec.14-15). No references are made to purposes involved in the protection of landscape or other values embedded in the terrestrial area outside the water itself.

The Water Law reflects a utilitarian approach towards water resources, and almost completely ignores other values. Some years ago the law was amended, and to the list of uses for water allocation was added the "...protection and rehabilitation of nature and landscape values, including springs, rivers and wetland habitats" (sec.6). However, there is no other reference to such a goal anywhere else in the law, and its implementation is totally dependent on the awareness and the good will on the part of the decision makers. It should also be noted that the interests of the Head of the Water Authority (who replaced the original Water Commissioner, following an amendment in 2006) and the Ministry of National Infrastructures do not coincide with the interests of landscape conservation. This was even truer in the past, when the main interest of the Water Commissioner and the Ministry of Agriculture was the supply of water to the agricultural sector.

The Drainage Law

The Drainage Law (or in its full name: the Drainage and Flood Protection Law) was legislated in 1957, after floods in the mid 1950s covered vast areas, mainly agricultural fields, causing severe economic damage. The objective of the law was to prevent the recurrence of floods by forming suitable institutions to manage drainage. This law, too, was subordinated to the Minister of Agriculture – and still is - since agricultural lands were conceived as being most threatened by potential floods. The priority given to agriculture is expressed in the first section of the law, which defines "drainage" as "...any operation intended to concentrate, to store, to carry or to remove surface or any other water which harm or may harm agriculture, public health..." etc.

The Drainage Law states that the "...Minister of Agriculture may... establish a drainage authority..." (Drainage Law, sec.11), but the establishment of such an authority is not obligatory. The law also specifies the duties and powers of such an authority, including regulating drainage and initiating drainage projects within its jurisdiction. The roles of a drainage authority as they are specified and defined in the law do not refer to the protection of the relevant riparian landscapes in any other way. In addition to drainage authorities, the law determines the establishment of a National Drainage Board to advise the Minister on matters of drainage, such as the declaration of drainage zones or the approval of drainage projects (sec.2). This is an obligatory body, complementing the relevant institutional structure for regulating drainage and preventing floods.

The Drainage Law defines some relevant terms for its purposes including "channel" and "buffer strip." A Channel is defined as "...river, stream... and any other water route... where water is flowing or standing always or occasionally." A buffer strip is defined as "strips of land along both sides of a channel (sec.1). The law prohibits agricultural cultivation or construction within a buffer strip. However, according to the law, the overall width of buffer strips on both sides should not exceed half the channel's width, and no more than 5 meters each (sec.5-6). It is needless to say that the potential protection of the riparian habitat is very limited given such conditions.

The Drainage Law, like the Water Law, expresses the priority given to agriculture. Most drainage projects during the 1960s and 1970s were intended to solve drainage problems in agricultural and open areas, although in populated areas potential damage from floods to property and persons is much higher. Moreover, since the legislation of the Drainage Law in 1957, the scope of development for residential, occupational and infrastructure uses increased greatly, much of it was at the expense of open and agricultural lands where rains could have previously penetrated the soil. As a result, the amounts and intensity of surface flow towards rivers increased considerably, and with them the risk of floods. In spite of that, the Drainage Law was not updated to include instructions regarding measures for the control of drainage in new development plans. This neglect resulted in recurrent flood events in various areas, causing millions dollars worth of damage (Laster, 2004; State Comptroller, 1993, 1999b).

The Rivers Authorities Law

The Rivers Authorities Law (RA Law: the full name being "Rivers and Springs Authorities Law") from 1965 complements the Water Law and the Drainage Law by referring not only to the protection of the water but also to the land adjacent to it, thus expressing the values of riparian landscapes for the first time in Israeli legislation. This expression is also reflected in the ministerial subordination; when legislated, the RA Law was subordinated to both the Ministry of Interior and the Ministry of Agriculture; however, it was transferred to the Ministry of Environment after it was created in 1989.

The RA Law states that the "...Minister may... establish an authority for a certain river or part of it... or impose on a drainage authority powers of a river authority..." (RA Law, sec.2). That is to say, a river authority – like a drainage authority – is not obligatory. Among the duties of a river authority, the law counts "protection of the landscape and nature values along the river on both sides..." but also regulation of the river's water flow and drainage within its jurisdiction (sec.3). This means that there is an overlap between the duties of a Drainage Authority and that of a River Authority, albeit they are related to different ministries. Laster (2004) claims that the law was intended to manage the rivers on a watershed approach basis, but actually it did not enable that, since it demanded subordination to the Water Law and the Water Commissioner. Moreover, the jurisdiction of a River Authority does not necessarily cover a whole watershed. For example, the jurisdiction of the Yarkon River Authority was limited to 20 meters on each side of the river.

The RA Law was implemented for the first time in the year 1988 – 23 years after its legislation – with the establishment of the Yarkon River Authority. It took six more years to establish the Kishon River Authority, in 1994, which was the second, and, up–to-now the latest authority based on this law. Laster (2004) comments that the reason it took so long to implement the law was the original subordination to two ministers. Another criticism of the law relates to the absence of a national body, something like the National Drainage Board. In other words, the RA Law represents a particularistic approach, referring to each river separately and lacking a broad vision on a national scale.

INSTITUTIONAL STRUCTURE

While legislation is a source of regulative powers, there is a need for institutions to use these powers and enforce the regulations. In Israel, there are several institutions that have to do with management and protection of riparian landscapes, the most important of them being the Drainage Authorities, the River Authorities and the Rivers Administration. They differ by their status, composition, main objectives, powers and budgeting.

Drainage Authorities

Drainage Authorities (DAs) may be established by the Minister of Agriculture, as already mentioned, subject to the consent of the Minister of Interior and the relevant local municipalities, which are also represented in its composition. The DA is responsible for managing drainage zones within its jurisdiction, including initiating, developing and maintaining drainage projects. The powers of a DA may contribute greatly to the protection of the relevant riparian landscapes, since managing drainage requires, among other things, restrictions on development along the water route.

Following the legislation of the Drainage Law, the Minister of Agriculture issued an ordinance in 1960 establishing 26 DAs. The ordinance specified the jurisdiction allocated for each DA, generally consisting of low-elevated plains, mainly agricultural lands (State Comptroller, 1993). Laster (1995, 2004) comments that the large number of DAs was due to political pressures rather than hydrological needs. Most of them actually operated as organs of the relevant Regional Councils - which are the local municipalities in the rural zones – and were dominated by representatives of the agricultural sector, thus reinforcing its control over water sources.

The recurrence of severe flood events implies the existence of shortcomings and deficiencies in the Drainage Law's implementation in general and in DAs' operation in particular. Especially memorable are the floods of winter 1991-2, when river overflows flooded large areas all around Israel, disrupting the course of everyday life: people had to be temporarily evacuated from their homes, roads became impassable, large agricultural areas were under water and there were even some fatal casualties. The overall direct and indirect damage to households, businesses, public property and agriculture amounted to tens of millions of dollars. Following those events, the State Comptroller (1993) issued a report that pointed out various faults in the DAs' functioning, stating among others that the drainage infrastructure had been neglected over the years and the sums required for proper planning, regulating and maintenance of many rivers were not allocated and invested as should have been done.

In 1996, after studying the State Comptroller's report, the Minister of Agriculture issued an ordinance reorganizing the DA system. Their number was decreased from 26 to 11, each covering a jurisdiction overlapping a natural drainage basin, and together covering the whole country. Each DA is directed independently of the Regional Council system, intended to apply a whole watershed approach rather than serve local interests (Laster, 2004). Although since this reorganization floods have reccurred, it seems that - especially since 2000 - DAs are taking more active measures to prevent flooding, revealing a more environmentally-oriented approach, including the conservation of landscape and ecological values in the riparian zones, in collaboration with other institutions and organizations, such as the Ministry of Environment, the Nature and Parks Authority and the Society for the Protection of Nature (Carmel Drainage Authority 2004).

Rivers Authorities

A River Authority (RA), with powers to limit and control development along the river, is a potentially effective tool in the protection of riparian landscapes. However, this potential cannot be fully realized, partly due to constraints imposed by the RA Law, such as the limited size of the area under the RA's jurisdiction. The RA's effectivity is also limited by its obligation to comply with the Water Authority (RA Law, sec.4), even in cases when their interests are contradictory. An RA's composition is more complex than a DA's, including several government officials. Thus, conflicts between government officials and local municipalities' representatives may also hamper the RA's functioning. Another potential source of conflict is the existence of a DA in the same jurisdiction since the duties and responsibilities according to the Drainage Law and the RA Law partly overlap.

The RA Law states that an RA is appointed to manage a particular river and is supposed to operate independently, following its management's objectives and policies. However, there is lack of a master organization on a national scale to design and lead a comprehensive policy towards the protection of riparian zones. With the absence of national policy, the influence of local interests increases, thus allowing development and infrastructure on or adjacent to riverbanks that should have been preserved.

Nevertheless, an RA is still the only institutional structure that is essentially specified for riparian nature and landscape protection in Israel. This may be exemplified by the Yarkon River Authority (YRA), which since its establishment in 1988 has initiated a master plan for the Yarkon River, seeking, among other goals, to restore the riparian ecosystem and contribute to environmental quality, aesthetic values and climate amelioration (Rachmimov 1996). The YRA develops bicycle trails and areas for recreation along the river and is currently monitoring water quality etc. The YRA was, in fact, a pioneer and a model in river restoration in Israel. Regretfully, however, only one more RA was established till now: the Kishon River Authority (in 1994). Both the Yarkon and the Kishon are large rivers, passing through densely populated areas - the Yarkon in the Tel Aviv metropolis, in the center of the State, and the Kishon in the northern Haifa metropolis - that were in a severely deteriorated state due to pollution from multiple sources, water trapping, etc. However, several other large rivers in a similar condition could have profited from a similar specified institutional structure to manage and restore them.

The Rivers Administration

The Rivers Administration (RAD) was established in 1993 as a mutual initiative of the Ministry of Environment and the Jewish National Fund (JNF), the latter being a historical non-governmental organization that is currently intensively involved in forestry and outdoor recreation. Other institutions and organizations that take part in the RAD are the Nature and Parks Authority, the Ministry of Interior, the Ministry of Agriculture, the Water Authority, the Israel Government Tourist Corporation and the Society for the Protection of Nature which is a non-governmental organization (Amir-Shapira and Feldman, 1999; Gabbay 1998). The declared goals of RAD include: conservation of high-quality open spaces along river channels, controlled development of recreation and tourism foci within riparian zones and rehabilitation of rivers to a state enabling sustainability of unique habitats and landscape values (Amir-Shapira and Feldman, 1999). RAD initiates and promotes plans for the restoration of rivers, issues guidelines for existing and future River Authorities, supports the establishment of local river administrations and is actually involved in many restoration projects that are in progress, especially since 2000. For instance, the RAD takes part in the steering committee of the successful restoration project for the Alexander River – a large coastal river in the Sharon region, and one of the first to enter a restoration program along with the Yarkon River. This is done in collaboration with many other bodies, including the Alexander Drainage Authority, the Emek Hefer Regional Council, the Emek Hefer Streams Society, the Water Authority, the JNF, the Israel Government Tourist Corporation, the Nature Conservation Research Institute, the Ministry of Environment, the Hadera Environmental Association, the Nature and Parks Authority, the Society for the Protection of Nature, the District Planning Commission, the Ministry of Interior and the Israel Lands Administration (Cohen-Shoel 2003). It is clear that when so many organizations are involved, conflicts and clashes of interest are unavoidable and may hamper conservation efforts. For example, the Israel Lands Administration is supposed to manage all public lands, which in Israel amount to 93% of the area of the State. However, since the 1990s, it actually acts as the State's main developer, initiating large intensive development plans wherever possible, driven by economic interests (Maruani, 2005). Such a development-oriented organization is bound to confront conservation-oriented bodies like the Nature and Parks Authority and the Society for Protection of Nature. The RAD, which is guided by a statewide vision regarding rivers and riparian landscapes, can bridge such controversies and promote restoration and conservation efforts.

Nevertheless, the protection offered by the RAD is limited since this is not a statutory body, and consequently lacks regulative and enforcement powers. Whenever action against polluters or other offenders of the riparian landscape is needed, it is the Ministry of Environment that is supposed to interfere and take steps towards enforcement. Also, due to lack of obligatory organizational procedures, RAD's operations are spatially and temporally not consistent in essence, scope and timing. Therefore, in many cases, riparian landscapes in Israel are still subject to the arbitrariness of local authorities, and are not consistently regarded as worthy of protection. In addition, the RAD's potential effectiveness is reduced by budget limitations, since budget allocated for riparian management is divided among too many organizations, including DAs and RAs (Laster, 2004).

The lack of a statutory basis is a source of instability for the RAD, since it may be dismantled by a ministerial decision as quickly as it was established. Nonetheless, since its establishment in 1993, the RAD is a dominant factor in river restoration in Israel.

PHYSICAL PLANNING AS A PROTECTION TOOL

Riparian landscapes are integral parts of the land. As such, physical planning of land uses at national, regional and local levels is a potentially strong tool for their protection. In Israel, land uses are determined by a statutory planning system, according to the Planning and Building Law (PBL) of 1965 (which replaced former British mandatory legislation from 1936). The system is three-tiered, with Planning and Building Commissions at national, district and local levels, each having the power to control lower-tier decisions. All planning commissions may initiate outline plans within their jurisdiction.

National Planning

The Sharon Plan

The Sharon Plan was the first comprehensive national master plan prepared after the declaration of statehood in 1948. The plan was initiated and prepared within the (then) Planning Department of the Ministry of Labor and Construction, by a team headed by architect Arie Sharon, and published in 1951. This plan was not statutory; nevertheless it had significant long-range effects on spatial planning in Israel. The plan refers to five main facets of planning: agriculture, industry, transportation, parks and new cities. The agricultural plan is based on a national water policy that wishes to divert water out of relatively rich sources – among them rivers in the north and the Yarkon in the center of the State – and carry them to the dry south, thus enabling agricultural settlements that are regarded in the plan as a key factor in development and economic independence (Sharon, 1951). In other words, the Sharon Plan again reflects the economic and ideological values attached to agriculture, and grasps the water of the rivers as input for agriculture and not as a landscape component to be protected.

The plan for the parks in the Sharon Plan proposed conservation of certain areas of outstanding nature and landscape values. Four out of those were to be established immediately as national parks, among them two mountainous landscapes: Mount Carmel and Mount Jarmak in the Upper Galilee, and two riparian ones: the Falik Park proposed around the Yarkon and Ayalon rivers in the Tel Aviv metropolis, and a park west of Jerusalem based on the Sorek River (Sharon, 1951). However, although the Sharon Plan as well as the actual implementation of the Carmel and the Jarmak parks significantly affected spatial planning for years to come, the parks proposed around the rivers were ignored as was also the call for using river corridors as buffers between built-up areas. The Sorek corridor area, for example, was reduced over the years due to development (Amit-Cohen et al. 2005).

NOP 31

Statutory planning in Israel at the national level is delineated in the National Outline Plans (NOPs). Out of almost 40 NOPs prepared up to date, only two represent comprehensive national planning. The first of the two was NOP 31, the Combined National Outline Plan for Construction, Development and Immigration Absorption. NOP 31 was prepared and approved in the early 1990s, when Israel was facing a crisis stemming from a sudden unanticipated increase in population due to mass immigration waves from the former USSR (Alterman, 1995). This was the first comprehensive national statutory plan to incorporate environmental considerations on a large scale, stating objectives like: conservation of nature and landscape resources, preservation of surface water quality, nurturing open spaces – among them riparian landscapes - for recreation, and balancing between development and conservation (Feitelson, 1993). The plan enhanced intensification of metropolitan regions in order to preserve open spaces in the rural zone. Despite these good intentions, it has been claimed that they triggered heavy development pressures in the metropolitan core of Israel, even in areas designated for conservation (Maruani, 2005).

NOP 35

The Combined National Outline Plan for Construction, Development and Conservation NOP 35 was approved in 2005, substituting NOP 31, which became obsolete in 1998. This plan, too, aspires to balance between development and conservation, taking this a step further by dividing the whole country into zones defined as development-oriented or conservation-oriented in varying degrees. Theplan specifically refers to river strips – including the water route and the banks 100 meters on each side – and requires every statutory plan to issue instructions concerning conservation of the river and its habitats, protection of its drainage functions, bank stabilization and free access to the public. This seems promising indeed, but it will take a number of years before its achievements can be assessed. However, past experience teaches us that NOP's instructions are not always kept. One example is the National Outline Plan for the Mediterranean coast, NOP 13, which prohibited construction within 100 meters of the water line. That instruction did not always stand up development pressures (State Comptroller, 1999a).

Sectorial NOPs

Most national outline plans are sectorial, each dedicated to a specific subject (e.g. roads, power plants, landfills, etc.). None of the plans that have been prepared until now is designated for the protection of rivers and riparian landscapes, although in some cases, there may be a reference to rivers where this is relevant to the main plan's design. Such is the case of the National Outline Plan for Nature Reserves and National Parks, NOP 8, which offers protection to sections of riparian landscapes that are found within areas designated and declared as a nature reserve or a national park. Yet, the plan does not ensure protection along the whole water route. The National Outline Plan for Forests and Afforestation proposes plantings along riverbanks (Kaplan, 1993), but only in small limited areas, most of them outside of metropolitan zones where demand for recreation is especially high. The National Outline Plan for Tourism, NOP 12, offers another example. It designates some rivers as recreational spaces, among them the Sorek River (Amit-Cohen et al. 2005). Yet, development attractive for tourism is usually intensive and could harm existing riparian ecological and environmental values.

Regional Planning

District Outline Plans (DOPs), like NOPs, are essentially guiding plans, relating to the district under the jurisdiction of a relevant District Commission or part of it. Israel is divided into six administrational districts. Almost all of them had valid DOPs that by the early 1990s were mostly out-of-date, and none of them conceived riparian landscapes as objectives for conservation. An example for the disregard of riparian functions is the Ayalon Highway, crossing Tel Aviv through the route that once was the Ayalon River, leaving a rather narrow channel for winter water flow. Planning of this highway started in the early 1970s and it was opened for use at the beginning of the 1990s. In the winter of 1991/2, parts of it flooded, more than 140 cars were trapped in the flood, and transportation along the highway had to be stopped for some time (State Comptroller, 1993). This has since recurred several times, also causing some casualties.

The Planning Administration in the Ministry of Interior promoted preparation of new DOPs, some of which have already been approved since 2000. The new plans are much more environmentally oriented than the old ones, including special references and instructions for protection and conservation of rivers and riparian landscapes. For example, the new DOP 3/21 for the Central Area District designates "river and its surroundings" for conservation. Still, there are considerable variations between DOPs in their definitions and conservation instructions; some are guiding while others are obligatory, etc. (Maruani, 2005). In other words, the protection offered by DOPs is not consistent in scope and intensity. Moreover, since most current DOPs are relatively new, it will be some more time before their effectiveness in riparian protection can be evaluated.

Local Planning

While national and district outline plans offer general guidelines, Local Outline Plans (LOPs) are more detailed and serve as platform for issuing building permits. The permits are approved and issued by Local Commissions, which are in fact organs of the relevant local municipality, composed of the elected political representatives who constitute the municipal board. Thus, Local Commissions are interested in the promotion of local economic development, even when it is contradictory to conservation needs, and they tend to ignore a broader regional vision. District Commission's control is supposed to minimize the influence of local economic and political interests on land use decisions. However, since riparian landscapes are attractive for housing, it is no wonder that initiatives for development within riparian areas recur, assisted by interested Local Commissions which regardless of their negative impact and potential flood risk (see for instance: Shechori, 1999; Shmul, 2000; Vaserman-Amir, 1999). Development decisions are a major causal factor where floods are concerned (Brody et al., 2007; State Comptroller, 1993). The recurrent flood events in Israel, and their negative impacts and costs indicate that local development interests were not restricted by the District Commissions.

Table 1. Comparison of protection tools

Protection tool		**Designation**	**Relevance**	Power	**Scale**	Implementation
Legislation	Water Law	Low	Medium	High	National	Low
	Drainage Law	High	High	High	National	Low to medium
	River Authorities Law	High	High	High	National	Low to medium
Institutional structure	Drainage Authorities	Medium	High	Medium	Regional	Low
	River Authorities	High	High	Low to medium	Regional	Low to medium
	Rivers Administration	Very high	Very high	Low	National	Medium
Physical planning	Sharon plan	Low	Low	Low	National	Low
	NOP 31	Low	Low	Medium to high	National	Low
	NOP 35	Low	Low	Medium to high	National	?
	Sectorial NOPs	Low	Low to medium	Medium to high	National	Low
	DOPs	Low	Low	Medium to high	Regional	Low
	LOPs	Varies with plan	Varies with plan	High	Local	Varies with plan

DISCUSSION

The examination of legislative, organizational and planning tools used for protection of riparian landscapes in Israel revealed various faults and deficiencies that may explain the still distressing state of these landscapes. Despite restoration efforts undertaken, mainly since 2000, almost all rivers are still polluted and ecologically deteriorated with only limited sections available and accessible for recreational uses.

Table 1 that presents a comparative assessment of protection tools shows that no one tool can be highly rated on all parameters. In addition, no parameter shows a consistently high rating for all tools. One fundamental problem is that no tool – with the possible exception of RAD - is dedicated to the objective of protecting ecological, environmental and scenic values embedded in riparian landscapes. For example, each of the laws examined makes a partial contribution to this objective although they differ in aims and scope. However, none of them regards the protection of riparian landscapes as its main aim. In addition, none of these laws reflects a watershed approach, theoretically or practically, albeit activities taking place anywhere in the watershed area, especially development and various pollution generators, eventually affect the river and the landscape along it. Moreover, partial overlap between the aims and directives of the Drainage law and those of RA Law are a constant source of ambiguity and fuzziness as to duties and responsibilities, on one hand, and inter-organizational and inter-personal frictions and conflicts, on the other. This situation stands in the way of the conservation interest.

The different tools are interconnected. Legislation determines the structure, responsibilities and operational procedures of the organization intended to implement it. Subjects not covered by the law are left to the discretion of organizational decision makers. Hence, awareness of riparian values on the part of decision makers is an important factor in effective protection. Statutory physical planning, too, relies on legislative power, and therefore inter-relations between laws may affect organizational actions. For example, the Drainage Law does not refer to statutory physical planning, while on the other hand the Planning and Building Law does not require a preliminary examination of possible impacts on drainage before the approval of a new development plan. The State Comptroller (1993) pointed out that the planning system allowed development too close to water routes and approved plans on large areas without ensuring suitable measures for infiltration of rains within their boundaries. He argues that the severe floods that were the cause for his report could have been prevented, had suitable instructions been embedded in the Planning and Building Law, thus preventing construction within flood retention areas and conditioning plan approval with proper infiltration and drainage solutions.

The protection of riparian landscapes as was formulated and implemented in Israel expresses a particularistic approach, where each river is conceived as a discrete entity, with a separate DA or RA. For comparison, nature and landscape values within areas that have been declared as nature reserves or national parks all over the state are protected centrally and managed by the Nature and Parks Authority, which is a national statutory institution, established by the National Parks and Nature Reserves Law. It seems that centralistic approach was efficient even when development pressures in Israel increased considerably towards the end of the 20th century. The establishment of the RAD indicates a conceptual change towards rivers as well but its lack of statutory position and the multitude of other relevant organizations reduce its effectivity.

The protection of riparian landscapes also reflects the evolution of environmental awareness in Israel (see also: Fletcher, 2000; Vogel, 1999). For example, the Water Law from 1959 almost completely ignores the environmental functions of water sources, including rivers, while the RA Law from 1965 already regards the protection of riparian environmental values as one of its main aims. The legislation also reflects the prevailing priorities in Israeli society at the time, affected greatly by ideological and national security considerations. In the past, agriculture and development were given priority; agriculture was conceived as a main economic basis and development of spatially dispersed small agricultural settlements also grasped as a tool for dominating national space while environmental needs were overlooked (Hershcovich, 2006; Schiffman 1999). It should be noted that all three laws examined were enacted before the global environmental revolution of the late 1960s. Moreover, as a consequence of the Stockholm Convention in 1972 Israel was one of the first nations to establish an environmentally designated institution in the form of the Environmental Service that was established in 1973 within the Prime Minister's office, and later on as part of the Ministry of Interior. However, the assimilation of environmental awareness was slow, especially among decision makers, until the 1990s when development pressures increased considerably, following a sudden increase of population due to large immigration waves, threatening nature and landscape values, especially in the coastal area and in vicinity of water bodies. This also was one of the triggers for initiation of RAD.

It should also be noted that split authoritative powers, multiplicities and deficiencies that characterize the protection of riparian landscapes in Israel, tend to be typically characteristic of environmental issues, which are naturally complex, interdisciplinary and bound up with economic and social conflicts. In addition, since its independence in 1948, Israel has been facing enormous challenges more than any other developed state, including an unstable geopolitical situation and recurrent wars, absorption of mass immigration waves and serious social conflicts (Alterman, 1995; Fletcher, 2000; Vogel, 1999). Nevertheless, all this still does not explain why former protection frameworks have not been reconstructed in spite of the advances in environmental management and administration in general. For instance, the Drainage Law that was mainly intended to prevent floods is still under the authority of the Ministry of Agriculture although severe damage caused by floods in recent years was mainly in urban areas and not in agricultural fields (State Comptroller, 1993). There is no doubt that the present state of affairs calls for improvement.

Conclusion

Riparian landscapes constitute extremely vulnerable ecosystems. They need protection to preserve the unique aquatic habitats with their biodiversity richness and ecological processes as well as their value for scenic and recreational purposes. In spite of that, their protection in Israel is defective, lacking comprehensive suitable legislation, a statutory institutional structure on a national scale and a sectorially designated NOP. The existing state of affairs is characterized by a complex array of authoritative powers, some split and others overlap, and by deficiencies in formulation and implementation of policies. Only limited segments of specific riparian landscapes may, in fact, be regarded as functional healthy ecosystems.

Several lessons can be drawn from the above discussion. We wish to focus here on those that seem the most important and practical for the State of Israel in the immediate future. First, there is need for a revision of present legislation, integrating together existing laws – mainly Drainage Law and RA Law – rephrasing their aims and directives, and rearranging the institutional structure and its powers according to updated environmental and other needs. This should be done considering a whole watershed approach as has already been suggested by Laster (1995).

Second, the prevailing, rather particularistic, approach should be replaced by a comprehensive centralized one, based on a vision and needs on a national scale. This ought to be reflected in all types of protection tools but especially in the institutional structure, as by establishing a national statutory designated organization (similar to the Nature and Parks Authority) or, alternatively, empowering the existing RAD by adequate legislation, including broader definition of its powers and duties.

Third, increasing environmental awareness in general, and awareness of riparian landscapes' ecological, environmental and scenic aspects in particular, are a key element in promoting protection and conservation of such landscapes. This is true for the general public, as has already been claimed by Lowry (1998), but is even more important where decision makers are concerned. Therefore, educational activities, formal and informal, carry great significance for improving and intensifying riparian protection efforts.

Finally, there is hope for riparian landscapes, even when severely deteriorated, providing suitable protection, restoration tools and a plan of action (see for instance: Harnik 2007, Kirk 2005, Tjallingii 2000). This is especially important in a small, densely populated and dry land like Israel.

REFERENCES

Ahern, J. (1995). Greenways as a Planning Strategy. *Landscape and Urban Planning, 33,* 131-155.

Allan, J.D. (2004). Landscapes and riverscapes: the influence of land use on stream ecosystems. *Annual review of Ecology, Evolution and Systematics, 35*, 257-284.

Alterman, R. (1995). Can planning help in time of crisis? Planners' responses to Israel's recent wave of mass immigration. *Journal of the American Planning Association, 61* (2), 156-177.

Amir-Shapira, D. (2007). *Ranking of polluted rivers.* Ministry of the Environment, www.sviva.gov.il/Environment/Static/Binaries/News/rivers_2006-7-tavla_1.pdf

Amir-Shapira, D. & Feldman, D. (1999). Fresh blood into river veins. *Yarok-Cahol-Lavan, 26,* 4-7 (In Hebrew).

Amit-Cohen I., Cohen, Y., & Cohen, A. (2008). From historical processes to current formation of ecological corridors: Stability and instability of Green Corridors at the margins of Israel's metropolis. *Applied Geography* (forthcoming).

Baschak, L. A. & Brown, R. D. (1995). An ecological framework for the planning, design and management of urban river greenways. *Landscape and Urban Planning, 23* (3-4), 211-225.

Beier, P. & Noss, R. F. (1998). Do habitat corridors provide connectivity? *Conservation Biology*, *12*, 1241-1252.

Bentrup, G. & Kellerman, T. (2004). Where should buffers go? Modeling riparian habitat connectivity in northeast Kansas. *Journal of Soil and Water Conservation, 59* (5) 209-215.

Brauman, K. A., Daily, G. C., Duarte, T. K. & Mooney, H. A. (2007). The nature and value of ecosystem services: an overview highlighting hydrologic services. *Annual Review of Environment and Resources, 32*, 67-98.

Brody, S. D., Zahran, S., Maghelal, P., Grover, H. & Highfield W. E. (2007). The rising costs of floods: examining the impact of planning and development decisions on property damage in Florida. *Journal of the American Planning Association, 73* (3). 330-345.

Bryant, M. M. (2006). Urban landscape conservation and the role of ecological greenways at local and metropolitan scales. *Landscape and Urban Planning, 76* (1-4), 23-44.

Burmil, S., Daniel, T. C. & Hetherington, J. D. (1999). Human values and perceptions of water in arid landscapes. *Landscape and Urban Planning, 44*, 99-109.

Carmel Drainage Authority, (2004). *Drainage and Environment: regularizing rivers with relation to nature, heritage and landscape values*. In collaboration with the Ministry of Environment (In Hebrew).

Chavas, J.P. (2000). Ecosystem valuation under uncertainty and irreversibility. *Ecosystems 3* (1), 11-15.

Cohen-Shoel, N. (2003). *The Alexander River*. The Hadera environmental Association (In Hebrew).

Constanza, R. (2000). Social goals and the valuation of ecosystem services. *Ecosystems 3* (1), 4-10.

De Groot, R.S. (1992). *Functions of Nature: Evaluation of Nature in Environmental Planning Management and Decision-Making*. Wolters-Noordhoff, Amsterdam.

Fábos J.G. (2004). Greenway planning in the United States: its origins and recent case studies. *Landscape and Urban Planning, 68* (2-3), 321-342.

Fábos, J. G. (1995). Introduction and overview: the greenway movement, uses and potentials of greenways. *Landscape and Urban Planning, 33*, 1-13.

Feitelson, E. (1993). Open space conservation and immigration absorption in NOP 31. *The Biosphere, 22* (1), 1-5 (In Hebrew).

Feitelson, E. (1995). Open space conservation in Israel at a turning point. *Horizons in Geography, 42-43,* 7-22 (In Hebrew).

Fletcher, S. (2000). The evolution of coastal management policy in the state of Israel. *Marine Policy, 24,* 395-405.

Frumkin, R. & Kleinhouse, S. (1997). Vegetation changes in Taninim River and the Cabara swamp in the 21st century. *Ecology and Environment,* 4 (2), 65-72 (In Hebrew).

Gabbay, S. (1998). *The Environment in Israel*. Jerusalem: Ministry of the Environment (In Hebrew).

Goren, M. (2000). Human impact on riparian biodiversity and ways for its preservation and restoration. *Agamit, 143,* 17-21 (In Hebrew).

Gregory, S. V., Swanson, F. J., McKee, W. A. & Cummins, K. W. (1991). An ecosystem perspective of riparian zones. *BioScience, 41* (8), 540-551.

Hale, B. W. & Adams, M. S. (2007). Ecosystem management and the conservation of river-floodplain systems. *Landscape and Urban Planning, 80*, 23-33.

Harnik, P. (2007). Nine-Mile RE-Run. www.tpl.org/content_documents/Article_Nine_Mile_ReRun.pdf

Hershcovich, A. (2006). From the "Sharon Plan" to NOP 35 – the ideology of three national outline plans. *Horizons in Geography, 67,* 31-40 (In Hebrew).

Jim, C. Y. & Chen, S. S. (2003). Comprehensive greenspace planning based on landscape ecology principles in compact Nanjing city, China. *Landscape and Urban Planning, 65* (3), 95-116.

Jongman, R. H.G. (2001). Ecological *networks and greenways in Europe: The twentieth century and beyond. Development of European Landscapes*. Conference proceedings, Tartu 2001,1, 18-24.

Jongman, R. H. G. (1995). Nature conservation planning in Europe: developing ecological networks. *Landscape and Urban Planning, 32*, 169-183.

Kaplan, M. (2004). *The Rivers of Israel: Policy and Planning Principles*. Jerusalem: Ministry of the Environment (In Hebrew).

Kaplan, M. (1993). The forest in the 2000s: a national outline plan for forests and forestation - NOP 22. *Ecology and Environment, 1* (1), 25-31 (In Hebrew).

Karr, J. R. (1994). Landscapes and management for ecological integrity. In Kim, K. C. & Weaver, R. D. (eds.), *Biodiversity and Landscapes (pp. 229-251).* Cambridge university press.

Kirk, D. (2005). Seoul peels back concrete to let a river run freely once again. www.csmonitor.com/2005/1013/p07s01-woap.html

Laster, R. (2004). Law, organization and administration. In Kaplan, M. *The Rivers of Israel: Policy and Planning Principles*. Jerusalem: Ministry of the Environment (In Hebrew).

Laster, R. (1995). The Yarkon River Authority: the legal framework for its establishment. In Pergament, D. (Ed.) *The Yarkon (pp. 33-37)*. Yarkon River Authority (In Hebrew).

Lewis, P. (1964). Quality corridors for Wisconsin. *Landscape Architecture 54* (2), 100-107.

Li, F., Wang, R. Paulussen, J. & Liu, X. (2005). Comprehensive concept planning of urban greening based on ecological principles: a case study in Beijing, China. *Landscape and Urban Planning, 72* (4), 325-336.

Little C. E. (1990). *Greenways for America*. Baltimore: The Johns Hopkins University Press.

Lowry, W. R. (1998). *Preserving Public Lands for the Future: The Politics of Intergenerational Goods*. Washington D.C.: Georgetown University Press.

Machtans, C. S., Villard, M.-A. & Hannon, S. J. (1996). Use of riparian buffer strip as movement corridors by forest birds. *Conservation Biology, 10* (5), 1366-1379.

Maruani, T. (2005). *Relations between development entrepreneurship characteristics and open space conservation in metropolitan regions*. Ph.D. thesis, Bar-Ilan University (In Hebrew).

Maruani, T. & Amit-Cohen, I. (2007). Open space planning models: a review of approaches and methods. *Landscape and Urban Planning, 81*, 1-13.

McHarg I.L.1969. *Design with Nature*. New York: John Wiley & Sons, Inc.

Menahem, G. (1999). Water policy in Israel: policy paradigms, policy networks and public policy (pp. 35-68). In Nachmias, D. & Menahem, G. (eds.). *Public policy in Israel.* Jerusalem: The Israel Democracy Institute. (In Hebrew).

Naiman, R. J. & Décamps , H. (1997). The ecology of interfaces: riparian zones. *Annual Review of Ecology Evolution and Systematics,* 28, 621-658.

Naiman, R. J., Décamps , H. & Pollock, M. (1993). The role of riparian corridors in maintaining regional biodiversity. *Ecological Applications, 3* (2), 209-212.

Naveh Z. (1997). The value of open landscape as life supporting systems. *Israel Environment Bulletin, 20* (4), 21-24.

Ndubisi, F., DeMeo, T. & Ditto, N.D. (1995). Environmentally sensitive areas: a template for developing greenway corridors. *Landscape and Urban Planning 33,* 159-177.

Patten, D. T. (1998). Riparian ecosystems of semi-arid North America: diversity and human impacts. *Wetlands, 18* (4), 498-512.

Pollock, M., Naiman, R. J. & Hanley, T. A. (1998). Plant species richness in riparian wetlands – a test of biodiversity theory. *Ecology, 79* (1), 94-105.

Rachmimov, A. (1996). *A Master Plan for the Yarkon River*. The Yarkon River Authority (In Hebrew).

Schiffman, I. (1999). The Limits of Ideology: The Fight for Open Space in Israel (pp. 559-577). In Soden D.L. & Steel, B.S. (eds.), *Handbook of Global Environmental Policy and Administration*. New York: Marcel Decker.

Shandas, V. (2007). An empirical study of streamside landowners' interest in riparian conservation. *Journal of the American Planning Association, 73* (2), 173-184.

Sharon, A. (1951). *Physical Planning in Israel.* Jerusalem: Government Printing office. (In Hebrew).

Shkedi, Y. & Sadot, E. (2000). *Ecological corridors – a practical conservation tool.* Jerusalem: Science Section of the Israel Nature and Parks Authority. (In Hebrew).

SPNI, (2001). The court accepted SPNI's appeal and canceled a permit for high-tech building amidst open landscape. *Bama, 23* (In Hebrew).

State Comptroller, (1999a). Planning land uses on the Mediterranean coast. *Annual report 49,* 361-371 (In Hebrew).

State Comptroller, (1999b). The state drainage infrastructure. *Annual report 49,* 242-248 (In Hebrew).

State Comptroller, (1993). *Reports on the state drainage infrastructures and the Ayalon Highways planning, management and maintenance of the Ayalon Channel.* Jerusalem (In Hebrew).

Stauffer, D. F. & Best, L. B. (1980). Habitat selection by birds of riparian communities: evaluating effects of habitat alterations. *The Journal of Wildlife Management, 44* (1), 1-15.

Taylor J., C. Paine & FitzGibbon, J. (1995). From greenbelts to greenways: four Canadian case studies. *Landscape and Urban Planning, 33,* 47-64.

Tjallingii, S.P. (2000). Ecology on the edge: landscape and ecology between town and country. *Landscape and Urban Planning, 48* (3-4), 103-119.

Vogel, D. (1999), Israeli environmental policy in comparative perspective. *Israel Affairs, 5* (2), 246-264.

Walmsley, A. (2006). Greenways: multiplying and diversifying in the 21st century. *Landscape and Urban Planning, 76* (1-4), 252-290.

Weber, T., Sloan, A. & Wolf, J. (2006). Maryland's green infrastructure assessment: development of a comprehensive approach to land conservation. *Landscape and Urban Planning, 77,* 94-110.

In: Natural Resources
Editor: Jeanette B. Pauling

ISBN 978-1-60456-982-7

Chapter 5

COSTS AND BENEFITS OF FOREST CERTIFICATION IN THE AMERICAS

Frederick Cubbage, Susan Moore
Department of Forestry and Environmental Resources
North Carolina State University, Raleigh, North Carolina
Thresa Henderson
The Forestland Group, Chapel Hill, North Carolina
Michelle M. F. C. Araujo
Faculty of Forestry, University of Toronto, Ontario, Canada

ABSTRACT

Forest certification provides a means to ensure that forests are managed to achieve economic, environmental, and social goals that are the foundation of sustainable forest management and sustainable development. We collected data on forest certification for the major systems in the Americas, including the Forest Stewardship Council (FSC) in Argentina, Brazil, Chile, and the United States, and the Sustainable Forestry Initiative (SFI) in the United States and Canada, Sistema Brasileiro de Certificação Florestal (Cerflor) in Brazil, and Sistema Chileno de Certificación Forestal (Certfor) in Chile. Repoorted average total costs varied considerably depending on forest ownership size, certification system, and country. Median average total costs ranged from $6.45 to $39.31 per ha per year for small tracts of less than 4,000 hectares. The large ownerships of 400,000 ha or more had median costs of $0.07 to $0.49 per ha per year. Mean costs were greater than median costs, due to large expenses for a few firms. Regression results indicated that average total costs for certification were a function of ownership size, but did not vary significantly among certification systems or country, although the sample of reporting firms was small for finding statistical differences. Opinions about benefits of forest certification generally classed firm strategic or management reasons highest, organizational learning factors second, signaling stewardship to external groups third, and improved prices or markets last, but all broad groups were considered important benefits of certification. The largest perceived disadvantages of forest certification were its time and audit costs, and no other disadvantage was rated more than somewhat important. Certified forest firms had relatively evenly mixed opinions about whether certification benefits exceeded costs, but a large majority stated that they would continue forest certification in the future.

INTRODUCTION

Forest certification provides a means to ensure that forests are managed to achieve the tripartite economic, environmental, and social goals that are the foundation of sustainable development. This approach provides a set of standards that certified forests must meet, and which are audited by independent third party auditors. Forest certification has been heralded as a promising new nongovernmental means to ensure sustainable forest management (Ramesteiner and Simula 2002, Cashore et al. 2003, 2004, 2005) that is based on markets and private sector initiative. As such, forest certification may be viewed as a non-state form of law making by global civil society (Meidinger 2003).

In fact, forest certification is one of the most significant changes in forest management and practice in this generation, prompting discussion, standards, implementation, and expansion throughout the world. This book chapter briefly reviews the genesis and extent of forest certification to provide a basis for understanding, and then examines the costs and benefits of forest certification based on some of the first empirical surveys of certified organizations that have provided information regarding this issue.

GENESIS OF FOREST CERTIFICATION

By the early 1990s, there was considerable discussion in the world about sustainable forest management and how to promote it in the marketplace. Much of the development of forest certification systems stemmed from the subsequent efforts by environmental nongovernment organizations (ENGOs) after the United Nations Conference on Environment and Development (UNCED) in Rio de Janeiro in 1992. While UNCED developed world Conventions on Biodiversity and on Climate, agreement on a forest convention was lacking. Eventually, various international protocols for temperate and European forest have developed, but they are not normative or standard setting efforts, but rather monitoring and tracking initiatives. The lack of an international forestry agreement did lead several environmental groups to begin to develop forest certification as a nongovernment response to forestry issues such as deforestation and poor forest management, particularly in the tropics. Certification of forest management practices was developed as the principal nongovernment means to prescribe and reward sustainable forest management.

Many forest certification systems have been developed in the last 15 years, beginning with the Forest Stewardship Council (FSC), which began in 1993. FSC was followed shortly by the Sustainable Forestry Initiative (SFI) in 1995 in the United States and then Canada. The Pan-European Forest Certification Programme began in Europe in 1996. It was renamed the Programme for Endorsement of Forest Certification Schemes—keeping the same PEFC initials—and now reviews and endorses individual certification systems that have been developed at the country level.

In 2001, The Meridian Institute published an analysis that compared the philosophy and standards of the FSC and the U.S. SFI systems. The report executive summary noted that FSC:

> "...began with a strong NGO focus on environmental and social values of natural forest ecosystems to which it adds an economic viability dimension." FSC was "...founded in 1993...to encourage the consuming public to reward exemplary forest management of industrial, private, government, and community-owned forests." Furthermore, FSC has a "...desire to provide market rewards through the labeling of forest products with a logo designed to distinguish products derived from lands certified as complying with a global set of Principles and Criteria of exemplary forest stewardship and management."

The Meridian Institute (2001) report executive summary wrote that SFI:

> "...began with a strong industry focus on forest lands that were acquired or owned for the production of forest products, to which it adds an important environmental dimension." SFI was "...launched by the American Forest & Paper Association in response to sagging public attitudes about the management of the nation's forests...It has evolved into a program that promotes third party certification for forestry practices of member companies and licensees." Furthermore, SFI has "...a philosophy of a 'rising tide' that lifts all boats. It consists of a set of standards aimed at all aspects of the forest industry from landowner to producer and it establishes a baseline for performance that builds on the concepts of sustainable forestry."

The Meridian Institute (2001) noted other programmatic differences. FSC is international in scope and governance, while SFI was a U.S.-oriented program with a major extension to Canada. FSC is a membership organization with a General Assembly and a Board of Directors. SFI was created by the forest industry, and then developed a separate Sustainable Forestry Board. In 2001, FSC International received 85% of its funding from private foundations, and 15% from membership and accreditation fees. During the same period, all the funding for FSC-U.S. came from private foundations. In 2001, SFI received 82% of its funds from member dues and contributions to the State Implementation Committees and 18% from grants and revenue from meetings, publications, and the licensee program.

Both FSC and SFI have evolved substantially since their inception. FSC has expanded throughout the world, with about 31% of its certified forest lands in North America, 10% in South America, and 53% in Europe. SFI has become independent from the American Forest & Paper Association and has its own governance, standards, and financial support. In addition, SFI is now a member of the Programme for Endorsement of Forest Certification Schemes (PEFC). PEFC currently endorses SFI, CSA, CertFor, and CerFlor in the Americas. PEFC began with much of its organization as a response by private landowners in separate countries to develop standards that were more acceptable than the international FSC efforts, and has since evolved into the largest collective body of certification standards.

Sasser et al. (2003) found that environmental nongovernment organizations (ENGOs) generally drove development of forest certification, partially as a means to encourage corporate social responsibility. These ENGOs favored the FSC program, providing technical and administrative contributions and related financial support. ENGOs also instigate direct action campaigns that favor FSC certification, including organized and high profile protests against retailers in order to force them to use certified products, as well as sharp attacks on SFI in the United States (e.g., Dogwood Alliance 2005). However, U.S. firms have preferred SFI in order to maintain more control over certification implementation (Sasser et al. 2006), and one can surmise that many European firms have made a similar decision in their support of PEFC.

Klooster (2005) noted that forest certification spread rapidly due to its focus on wood products retailers. He concluded that this focus, however, limits the spread of forest certification among small and medium size firms as well as community forest management operations. This also raises questions of fairness because it imposes costs on forest managers without providing compensation through higher prices. Klooster (2005) stated that the dominance of big retailers in commodity networks provides an attractive route to rapidly mainstream certification schemes, but it also limits their reach and compromises their equity.

The costs and benefits of forest certification systems are one of the principal issues affecting their adoption. For example, Perera et al. (2007) found that many nonindustrial private forest landowners in Mississippi and Louisiana were familiar with forest certification and up to half supported its merits for promoting sustainable forestry. However, 77% were not willing to pay anything extra for forest certification, and only 4% were willing to pay more than $2.00 per acre per year.

Indeed, Laband (2004) criticized the social burden of forest certification, stating it foists substantial costs and regulatory interference on small landowners without any benefits. Anderson et al. (2006) found that while forest certification was widely promoted, students were likely to pay only slightly more for certified pencils in two university bookstores. On the other hand, many studies have found that consumers and businesses favor certification, and many express a willingness to pay some premium (e.g., Stevens 1998, Jensen 2003, Aguilar and Vlosky 2007).

RESEARCH OBJECTIVES

Despite the considerable literature about forest certification as a governance system and the issues related to its spread, little empirical research has actually addressed its costs and benefits for certified forest landowners. In addition, most studies that have addressed forest certification costs have been general analyses based on economic theory and assumptions about possible levels of costs, or general economic models that examine relative costs among regions based on cost assumptions. Very few studies have actually measured and reported the costs of forest certification based on actual organizational data. Similarly, presumed forest certification benefits are often discussed, but not assessed based on practical experience. Thus the primary objective of this chapter is to provide empirical estimates of forest certification costs and benefits from private firms and public organizations.

We performed a series of personal interviews and surveys with forestry organizations throughout North America and the Southern Cone countries in South America, including the United States, Canada, Brazil, Argentina, and Chile. These have consisted of different studies in 2006 and 2007, but all share common key questions. This chapter summarizes our research to date on the costs and benefits of forest certification. The systems analyzed include FSC in the U.S., Brazil, Argentina, and Chile; SFI in the U.S. and Canada; Sistema Brasileiro de Certificação Florestal (Cerflor) in Brazil, and Sistema Chileno de Certificación Forestal (Certfor) in Chile.

The research summarized here should provide much better data and analysis of forest certification costs and benefits. Data garnered from five principal countries in the Americas provide a valuable picture of forest certification costs and benefits, which can help inform forest management decision-making, as well as policy discussions by private companies, forest certification organizations, and the government.

EXTENT OF FOREST CERTIFICATION

Forest certification has developed rapidly since 1993, and more than 300 million ha, or 8% of the world's 3.9 billion ha of forests were certified as of the end of 2007 (Table 1). The total forest area in the world includes a large amount of dry savannahs with little stocking, so the certified share of well stocked forests is somewhat greater. Approximately 12% of all of the Americas forests are certified. Canada has about 69% of the certified forests in the Americas, which accounts for about 43% of those certified in the world, although this total could include some multiple systems on the same lands.

The largest forest certification system in the world is the Programme for Endorsement of Forest Certification, which has recognized 201 million ha as certified, including 58 million ha in Europe and 135 million ha in the Americas. The Forest Stewardship Council has certified about 93 million ha worldwide. Major forest certification systems in the Americas include FSC with 38 million ha, SFI with 58 million ha; with about 22 million ha in the USA and 36 in Canada, and the Canadian Standards Association (CSA), with 74 million ha. Certfor in Chile and Cerflor in Brazil, which are recognized by PEFC, have 1.68 million ha and 1.0 million ha enrolled, respectively.

Forest certification was largely developed as a means to encourage sustainable forestry in the tropics. However, about 95% of currently certified forest area is in the northern hemisphere of the world. Similarly, only about 5% of certified forests in the Americas are in Central and South America. Forest certification in Latin America was only provided by FSC until 2002, when Cerflor in Brazil and Certfor in Chile were developed by the forest industry and other partners in each country. Those systems have a total of 2.7 million ha in both countries.

As of January 2008, the Forest Stewardship Council (FSC) had provided almost 900 certificates covering 93 million ha in 76 countries. This included 247 certificates and 9,903,558 ha in the Latin American countries from Mexico to Argentina and Chile (Forest Stewardship Council 2008). Brazil and Bolivia have the largest FSC certified areas in Latin America, followed by Mexico and Chile (Table 2).

Table 1. Major Forest Certification Systems in the World, November 2007

System	Area (million ha)
Programme for Endorsement of Forest Certification (PEFC)[1]	200.9[1]
Sustainable Forestry Initiative (SFI)	58.1
Forest Stewardship Council (FSC)	92.9
American Tree Farm System (ATFS)	12.1
Canadian Standards Association (CSA)	73.6
Sistema Chileno de Certificación Forestal (Certfor)	1.7
Sistema Brasileiro de Certificação Florestal (Cerflor)	1.0
Malaysian Timber Certification Council	4.7
Australian Forestry Standard	8.7
Total, All Systems	310.6

[1] Includes 73.6 million ha of CSA in Canada, 58.1 million ha of SFI in U.S and Canada, 1.682 million ha of CertFor in Chile, 0.996 million ha CerFlor in Brazil, 8.7 million ha in Australia, 57.6 million ha in Europe.

Sources: www.fsc.org, www.pefc.org, www.mtcc.com.my, Sustainable Forestry Initiative 2008, www.inmetro.gov.br

Table 2. FSC Forest Certification in the Americas, January 2008

Country	Area (Ha)	Certificates (no.)
Argentina	227 786	11
Belize	104 888	1
Bolivia	1 875 867	18
Brazil	4 885 066	68
Chile	321 004	15
Colombia	58 749	3
Ecuador	48 530	5
Paraguay	2 705	3
Peru	402 478	10
Uruguay	391 578	24
Venezuela	139 650	1
South America	8 458 301	159
Belize	104 888	1
Costa Rica	58 002	19
Guatemala	510 318	13
Honduras	52 886	4
Nicaragua	15 047	4
Panama	10 218	8
Central America	751 359	49
Mexico	693 898	39
U.S.A.	8 978 655	101
Canada	20 181 930	39
North America	29 854 483	179
Total of Above	39 064 143	376

Source: Forest Stewardship Council, January 2008.

CERTIFICATION EVALUATION LITERATURE

A moderate number of studies have assessed the impacts of forest certification in the last few years. These include mainly evaluations of the forest management and social impacts, and a few economic analyses. Most of the focus has been on assessing impacts of FSC, which has readily accessible public certification audit reports. However, a few studies have examined both FSC and SFI, or FSC and PEFC at the same time.

Most studies have been general impact analyses, focusing on the effects of certification on forest practice, environmental, social, or economic components of forest management. We briefly review this literature here, and the certification cost references that exist.

Nussbaum and Simula (2005) discussed the general principles regarding costs and benefits of forest certification, as shown in Table 3. Forest management and economic benefits, social benefits, and environmental benefits may exist. This list closely tracks the objectives intended to be achieved by FSC initially, and subsequent certification systems since.

Nussbaum and Simula (2005) divided costs of forest certification into direct costs and indirect costs. The main direct costs were the costs of changes in forest management and chain-of-custody tracking of certified forest production. Indirect costs were those related to compliance with the forest certification standard, including upgrading forest management and/or wood processing systems.

Table 3. Potential Benefits from Forest Certification

Economic Benefits
Improved performance standards
Enhanced control of resources
Improved management systems, including internal mechanisms of planning, monitoring, evaluation, and reporting.
Reduced regulatory control
Permanent economic viability and opening of new markets
Improved market access and occasional higher prices
Improved enterprise image and business practice
Social Benefits
Addressing the public's environmental and social concerns about forest management
Balancing the objectives of forest owners, other stakeholders, and society
Empowering the poor and less favored
Poverty alleviation
Community participation
Improved workers' rights and living conditions
Environmental Benefits
Environmental conservation
Maintenance and enhancement of biodiversity
Maintenance and enhancement of high conservation value forests

Source: Nussbaum and Simula 2005.

Conversely, Cubbage et al. (2002, 2003, 2008) assessed forest certification implementation on state and university lands in North Carolina, and divided direct and indirect costs somewhat differently. Direct costs included preparation and payment for the forest certification audits, while indirect costs accounted for changes in forest management and future effects on forest investment returns.

Certification Impact Evaluations

Two surveys of certified forest lands in the United States found that environmental practices were generally improved under forest certification schemes. The Texas Forest Service (Simpson et al. 2005) found that implementation of best management practices (BMPs) was statistically higher when the timber was delivered to a Sustainable Forestry Initiative (SFI) certified mill. A study from the Manomet Center for Conservation Sciences (Hagan et al. 2005) found that lands certified under either SFI or FSC had significantly stronger biodiversity practices than non-certified lands. Furthermore, they concluded that there was no difference between FSC and SFI in terms of the overall biodiversity practice scores.

Lemoine et al. (2006) applied a hypothetical GIS analysis to examine whether timber harvest operations in the Cumberland Plateau of Tennessee would meet the current SFI/state Best Management Practice (BMP) and FSC standards for streamside management zones (SMZs). Using a 90% of the entire SMZ in compliance threshold, 76% of the harvest sites would meet the SFI minimum-width standards, but only 15% of those same sites would meet the stricter FSC standards.

Several international studies have examined the effectiveness of forest certification by FSC and PEFC. This includes a series of World Wildlife Fund European Forest Programme studies in Latvia, Estonia, Germany, Russia, Sweden, and the UK. These include individual country reports, and were summarized in a newsletter (WWF 2005). In total, these studies analyzed 2,817 Corrective Action Requests (CARs) made by FSC in those countries, covering 18 million ha of forests.

The WWF (2005) summary concluded that FSC certification improved the conservation status and enhanced biodiversity levels in those forests. This included consistent implementation of Environmental Impact Statements (EISs); identification, mapping and management or protection of natural areas and biotypes; increased deadwood levels; more natural regeneration to favor species diversity; and restoration of threatened forest types. Economic outcomes included better game management; better planning and long-term sustainability; better monitoring of objectives; improved marketing and product tracking; and improved recreational, cultural, and historical benefits. Social benefits included better implementation of health and safety legislation; better equipment training; and public safety improvements.

Newsom and Hewitt (2005) analyzed global FSC/SmartWood impacts and found that certification required operations to make significant changes, and did "...not simply give a rubber stamp of approval to the good players and industry leaders. On average, certified operations were required to make changes affecting fifteen different forestry issues as a result of the forestry assessment." The ten most important categories of required changes included some in social issues–worker training, safety, and communication with stakeholders;

environmental issues–aquatic and riparian areas, sensitive sites, and high conservation value forests; and systems issues–management plans, monitoring, chain of custody, and inventory.

An extensive study by the Federation of Nordic Forest Owner's Organisations (2005) examined the effectiveness and efficiency of FSC and PEFC in Finland, Sweden, and Norway. According to their findings, forest certification has improved sustainable forest management, with the greatest contributions being in the area of environmental protection. This improvement process has required greater environmental investments by forest landowners, but has not yet brought significant economic benefits to forest owners. However, the report does note that the better environmental image may enhance market access in the long term for Nordic timber and wood products.

A speech by Daniels and Caulfield (2008) from the RMK Timberland Group presented several advantages of forest certification for timberland investors in Latin America. In the countries where the laws or the enforcement are weak, certification provides investors certainty that their timberlands are managed to high standards. Forest certification does have costs, but can provide access to international financing and bank loans for developing countries. And in some cases, the only way RMK was allowed to sell wood at all was if it was certified.

Aggregate Economic Impacts

There are likely to be broader impacts of forest certification on forest and timber markets, which can be considered aggregate economic impacts. Many studies focused on these potential impacts based on economic theory, but not based on direct cost estimation of forest certification. This section reviews the economic studies first, and then summarizes some references about direct and indirect costs of forest certification at the forest / organizational level.

Gullison (2003) found that the process of FSC certification improved forest management related to biodiversity. However, he stated that current economic incentives were not sufficient to attract the majority of producers to seek certification, particularly in tropical countries where the costs of improving management to meet FSC guidelines are significantly greater than any market benefits they may receive. Available incentives were even less capable of convincing forest owners to retain forest cover and produce certified timber on a sustainable basis, rather than deforesting their lands for timber and agriculture.

Brown and Zhang (2005) examined the economic welfare impacts of SFI certification on stumpage markets, using assumptions of forest certification costs with economic welfare theory, the measurement of changes in supply and demand curves, and the associated changes in producer and consumer surplus. They found that with predicted changes in producer and consumer surplus, SFI would cost the U.S. economy about $36 million annually. SFI stumpage sellers (industry or large timber investment management organizations as producers) would lose $33 million each year in producer surplus; and consumers would lose $12 million with the higher prices caused by forest certification. These theoretical losses would be offset somewhat by $10 million in gains by nonindustrial private forest landowners, non-SFI industry producers, and public timber owners.

The estimate by Brown and Zhang does not include any nonmarket benefits provided by certified forests, so would be only a partial welfare analysis. Our estimate of the annual harvest stumpage value of $5 billion in the U.S. South (10 billion cubic feet harvested at approximately $0.50 per cubic foot) indicates that the costs from Brown and Zhang would amount to about a 0.7% loss of the total market value of stumpage prices annually, which would be a much smaller share of the total consumer and producer surplus.

Gan (2005) estimated the impacts of forest certification costs on the output, price, and trade of forest products via computable general equilibrium modeling under various scenarios representing tropical, temperate, and global forest certification. Despite causing more severe and extensive impacts, global certification seemed more economically acceptable than regional certification to major timber-producing countries. The regions that would suffer the most from global certification would not be major timber-producing regions, but major net importers of forest products like East Asia.

Gan (2005) assumed a substantial 5%, 15%, and 25% increase in forestry production costs with certification. At that level, the world's forestry output would decline by 0.3% to 5.1%, while the world price would increase by 1.6% to 34.6%. Impacts on global lumber and pulp and paper markets would be much more moderate. In general, forest certification would have larger impacts on trade and price than on output. It would cause trade diversion and substitutions between tropical and temperate forest products and affect regional forest product markets. Because of the possible leakages (deforestation elsewhere) associated with regional certification and the land use shifts resulting from sectoral production shifts at the regional level, forest certification would not necessarily curb tropical deforestation.

Note that each of the preceding economic analyses assessed the impacts of relatively large assumed added costs of forest certification on equilibrium prices, output, and trade using economic theory, and found that those certification costs had adverse social welfare impacts compared to the outcome with free markets. We might note, however, that any public or private interference with free markets will normally lead to decreased benefits per welfare economics analyses, in the absence of externalities. And the theoretical losses found by the analyses were small, even with fairly large costs.

More recently, Busby et al. (2007) examined the impacts that increased timber prices for certified logs would have in encouraging enrollment in forest certification on private land in western Oregon. With an assumed certification bonus of 5% and 10% more than current log prices and a 100-year time horizon, 20% and 60% of the total eligible acres were projected to certify. The impact on improved ecological components of old age stands, however, was minimal. Certification of groups of landowners with a common manager could help prompt more owners to become certified.

Direct and Indirect Organizational Costs

Bass et al. (2001) noted that the largest direct costs of forest management certification vary according to the type of certification–forest management or chain of custody–size of the enterprise, and the distance that certifiers have to travel. Indirect costs of changes in practices depend primarily on the existing quality of management. In tropical natural forests, the costs of certifying natural forest management were comparatively large unless the area is very large.

Bass et al. (2001) reported that one study in Latin America recorded costs of $0.26 to $1.1 per m^3 and up to $4 for small areas. In contrast, Polish state forests had costs of about

$0.02 to $0.03 per m^3. A South African company reported costs of $0.19 per m^3 or 0.03% of the logging cost. U.S. cost of $0.20 to $0.75 per ha were reported for the initial assessment and about $0.03 to $0.15 per ha for the annual surveillance—the same order as the per m^3 cost in Poland. Simula et al. (2004) also examined costs of forest certification, and suggested implementing phased approaches where certification could be achieved in steps over time.

The study by Gan (2005) stated that forest certification would include direct costs of assessing forest certification and monitoring the chain of custody. He classed indirect costs as those for implementing higher forest management standards. Based on various proceedings and organizational reports, and on Carter and Merry (1998), Gan estimated that direct costs are generally between $0.50 and $1.00 per ha, and the cost of monitoring the chain of custody was 0.6% to 1.0% of the product value. He stated that implementing a higher forest management standard could increase forest management costs by 5% to 40%, with an average of 5% to 25%.

In North Carolina, state and university lands were certified by FSC and SFI in 2001. This was a cooperative effort by the Southern Center for Sustainable Forests, comprised of North Carolina State University (NCSU), Duke University, and the North Carolina DENR Division of Forest Resources (DFR). The time and costs for that certification were kept at each institution, and summarized below as reported by Cubbage et al. (2007). In the North Carolina study, certification costs were divided into direct costs for external audits and preparation for the initial certification, indirect costs for the time and expenses required to change forest management or other practices, and for the effects of certification on timber investment returns.

The total direct costs for receiving certification initially for those institutions ranged from $1.24 per ha per year for the DFR to $19.08 per ha per year for NCSU (Table 4). The direct costs to maintain SFI certification ranged from $0.96 per ha per year (NC DFR) to $9.56 per ha per year (Duke). For FSC, the costs ranged from $1.04 (DFR) to $7.19 (NCSU) per ha per year (Table 5).

Table 4. Direct initial costs of obtaining forest certification, North Carolina, 2001 ($)

Practice / System	**NCSU**	**Duke**	**DFR**	**All**
Ha	1 800	3 000	10 900	15 700
	-- cost in dollars per ha --			
Inspections				
FSC ($70,000)	-	-	-	4.38
SFI ($37,000)	9.32	2.72	0.89	2.32
Preparation				
FSC ($15,000)	4.62	1.48	0.15	0.94
SFI ($33,000)	9.76	3.81	0.35	2.08
Total Direct				
FSC ($85,000)	-	-	-	5.31
SFI ($70,000)	19.08	6.52	1.24	4.37

Notes: Initial total costs in parentheses. FSC costs were received as one price for all organizations, so are not separable. NCSU cost includes payment for a second remedy audit.

Table 5. Direct costs of maintaining forest certification per ha per year, North Carolina, 2002-2005 ($/ha)

Practice	Preparation		Audits		Total	
System	*SFI*	*FSC*	*SFI*	*FSC*	*SFI*	*FSC*
NCSU	2.79	4.35	1.93	2.87	4.72	7.19
Duke	8.33	4.40	1.24	1.83	9.56	6.23
NC DFR	0.64	0.57	0.32	0.47	0.96	1.04
Average / Ha / Yr for All	2.27	1.70	0.67	1.01	2.94	2.72

Last, Goetzl (2006) surveyed SFI firms regarding their forest certification costs. He found that much greater costs occurred when the SFI standard was first implemented by an organization. In most organizations that were certified, one or two additional full time equivalent employees could be attributed to adopting the standard, not including SFI standard-related activities that were integrated into other functions. When spread over a firm's total certified area, the external audit costs were relatively small. But they had a wide range from just a few cents to as much as $5.00 per acre. For firms that were dual-certified with FSC, the opportunity costs for forest reserves and set-asides seemed to be greater, but FSC program participation costs appeared to be much lower than for SFI.

Benefits

As noted previously, Nussbam and Simula (2005) classed benefits of forest certification into the traditional economic, social, and environmental components of sustainable development. Rickenbach and Overdevest (2006) and Overdevest and Rickenbach (2006) surveyed expectations and satisfaction of FSC certificate holders in the U.S. and categorized benefits into three classes based on possible social and business motivations of certified organizations. They found that "signaling" benefits of getting better recognition for one's forest practices and public relations were ranked as having the highest satisfaction, exceeding expectations. Participants had the greatest expectations for market benefits, but received less satisfaction with those. The category of "learning" about new forest management practices ranked third in expectations and satisfaction, but satisfaction did exceed expectations.

The numerical differences among these categories developed by Rickenbach and Overdevest (2006) were moderate. Most large landowners were satisfied with forest certification, and small landowners had neutral opinions. Most owners stated that they would maintain their FSC certification. These categories of expectations about forest certification are germane for both cost and benefit considerations, and we draw from them in the analysis of our survey results as described subsequently.

Research Methods

The research that collected cost and benefit information for this chapter was performed from 2006 to 2007 in Argentina, Brazil, the United States and Canada, and Chile, in that order. We performed a series of related studies using mixed methods of personal interviews and email surveys in order to collect the data. Personal interviews were conducted in Argentina and Chile and email surveys were sent in Brazil, the United States, and Canada. This covered the systems of FSC in Brazil, the U.S., Argentina, and Chile, in order of the number of responses. The PEFC systems included SFI in the U.S. and Canada, Certificación Forestal in Chile, and Certificacão Florestal in Brazil. Cubbage performed most of the interviews in Argentina and Chile; Moore and Cubbage administered the email questionnaire in the U.S. and Canada; and Araujo (2007) conducted the email survey in Brazil. We did not survey the American Tree Farm System (ATFS), which provides complimentary forest certification to its members once they meet the standards.

Similar, but not identical, surveys were sent to or discussed with certified firms in each country and each system. The relevant questions discussed in this chapter address certification benefits and costs specifically. Personal interviews were used in Argentina and Chile because it was the only means to get responses to a long survey by a foreign researcher. Those interviews included only 10 firms in total for both countries due to the large expense and time required to conduct the interviews, but more than half the area certified was included in the interview responses. Most firms provided some cost data in the personal interviews.

The questionnaires in the U.S., Canada, and Brazil were comprised of similar questions. The lists of eligible entities were provided by the respective certification organizations in each country. The Dillman (2000) tailored design method was used with the internet survey. For the North American surveys, this included a pre-notice sent one week prior to the questionnaire. The questionnaire was sent with a personalized letter from the researchers, as an attached MS Word file which respondents were asked to fill out, save, and then email it back. Those without working email addresses were sent a hard copy by regular mail. Non-respondents received a second email letter with the survey 11 days later. Remaining non-respondents were sent a third email letter and survey two weeks later. A final letter and survey were emailed two weeks after that to remaining non-respondents. Respondents were offered and sent a summary of the results once compiled. All the questionnaires except the one in Brazil were similar; the one for Brazil included most of the same questions as well as others, and also employed more detailed contact methods.

The relevant survey questions asked respondents to list any costs they could related to; (1) total certification expenses, (2) internal audit preparation fees or consultants, (3) external audit fees, (4) ongoing certification preparation costs, (5) community education and support programs, (5) management changes required to get/maintain certification, or (6) participation in implementation committees or FSC promotion activities.

Respondents completed the survey questions on the costs of forest certification less than any other component of the survey. Costs are of course sensitive and proprietary. Also, several organizations simply did not keep separate cost data for certification as a distinct line item. Others had some costs data, but included all environmental management systems including ISO 14000 and more than one certification system.

The responses received were converted to current U.S. dollars per ha per year based on 2007 exchange rates. Then simple summary statistics were calculated to convert those amounts to average costs by ownership class size. The average total costs were the primary focus of the cost estimates, and are summarized in the results. Last, the average costs for the individual components of costs listed above were summarized.

In addition to the specific questions about monetary costs of forest certification, we asked about the benefits and disadvantages of forest certification, and the likelihood of the firms maintaining certification. Other questions about forest certification impacts and environmental philosophies were included as well, but are not covered in this chapter.

RESULTS

Table 6 summarizes the cost results from our research of certified forest organizations in the Americas. The table summarizes the data by forest certification system, number of total responses and forest ownership size, number of cost responses and ownership size, and country or region. The total number of responses and area were calculated for all organizations that replied to survey.

We had 45 organizations respond from FSC in the U.S., 36 land-owning SFI organizations in the U.S. and Canada, 48 in Brazil, 7 in Argentina, and 3 in Chile. This corresponds to a response rate of more than 60% for the FSC-U.S., SFI, and Brazil email surveys. About half the organizations in Argentina were interviewed, and only about 20% in Chile, although those firms accounted for most of the certified forest land area in the country.

As noted, there were only a few responses for some systems in Argentina and Chile. Those responses appeared to be similar in general, and the sample was too small to find statistically significant differences in the three Southern Cone countries. Thus in order to obtain reasonable results by ownership size and provide data confidentiality, the responses for all the systems and all the countries in the Southern Cone of America were combined.

There were 56 organizations in the five countries that reported total average costs for certification, either as a total amount or as an average cost per hectare. Both responses were converted to total costs per firm and divided by the area certified to estimate average total costs. This provided the sample for most of our cost analyses. This included 14 responding land management firms for FSC; 17 for SFI; and 25 in South America. Thirteen of those firms were dual certified to FSC and one of the other PEFC systems of SFI, Cerflor, or Certfor. In almost all cases, dual certified firms reported the same costs for both systems—they just split the total costs among systems equally.

Table 6. Summary of Forest Ownership Size Class and Average Total Costs per Hectare by Region and Certification System in the Americas, 2007

System/ Size Class	N	Median	Mean	Standard Deviation	Minimum	Maximum
All Responses						
FSC – U.S.						
Area (Ha)	45	22 258	251 392	560 515	405	2 373 599
Cost ($/Ha)	14	0.91	3.24	4.37	0.02	14.11
SFI – N. Amer.						
Area (Ha)	36	133 727	992 675	2 359 951	1 740	11 612 303
Cost ($/Ha)	17	0.37	4.92	13.96	0.01	57.20
South America						
Area (Ha)	58	23 469	95 832	183 941	69	998 596
Cost ($/Ha)	25	1.56	6.89	11.66	0.05	46.16

< 4 000 Ha						
FSC – U.S.						
Area (Ha)	9	2 543	2 112	998	405	3 035
Cost ($/Ha)	3	6.45	8.43	4.99	4.72	14.11
SFI – N. Amer.						
Area (Ha)	3	1 974	1 967	223	1 741	2 185
Cost ($/Ha)	2	39.31	39.31	25.28	21.45	57.20
South America						
Area (Ha)	9	1 811	1 883	1 535	69	3 898
Cost ($/Ha)	5	23.75	17.52	12.23	0.96	30.27
4 001- 40 000 Ha						
FSC – U.S.						
Area (Ha)	16	13 557	14 663	8 466	4 205	38 041
Cost ($/Ha)	7	0.54	2.05	3.78	0.27	10.60
SFI – N. Amer.						
Area (Ha)	5	30 479	25 797	12 677	4 856	37 058
Cost ($/Ha)	3	0.91	1.06	0.64	0.52	1.75
South America						
Area (Ha)	27	13 409	16 011	9 400	4 358	39 072
Cost ($/Ha)	10	2.00	2.97	3.19	0.22	10.82
40 001 – 400 000 Ha						
FSC – U.S.						
Area (Ha)	14	107 244	152 098	103 163	41 125	377 175
Cost ($/Ha)	2	2.40	2.40	2.17	0.86	3.95
SFI – N. Amer.						
Area (Ha)	15	79 725	144 465	110 851	47 754	362 280
Cost ($/Ha)	6	0.27	0.89	1.53	0	3.95
South America						
Area (Ha)	18	90 531	137 583	107 598	42 752	395 678
Cost ($/Ha)	9	1.21	6.08	15.05	0.05	46.16
> 400 000 ha						
FSC – U.S.						
Area (Ha)	6	1 416 431	1 488 275	763 037	607 042	2 373 599
Cost ($/Ha)	2	0.42	0.42	0.57	0.02	0.82
SFI – N. Amer.						
Area (Ha)	12	1 395 682	2 785 867	3 526 274	493 664	11 612 303
Cost ($/Ha)	7	0.07	0.22	0.30	0.02	0.82
South America						
Area (Ha)	4	603 183	658 131	246 212	427 563	998 596
Cost ($/Ha)	1	0.49	0.49	0.49	0.49	0.49

Notes: FSC responses include only U.S.A.; SFI includes U.S.A. and Canada; South America includes FSC in Argentina, Brazil and Chile, combined FSC, Cerflor, and Certfor. Total number of replies and statistics are indicated in the area rows; total number of cost responses and statistics are indicated in the cost rows.

Average Total Costs

Table 6 includes summary statistics for the number of responses, median, mean, standard deviation, minimum, and maximum *total area* and *average total costs (ATC)* reported. *Total area* is simply the total area of the certified forest ownership for all responding organizations in the surveys and interviews. *Average total costs* is the economic term for the total costs divided by the total unit of production, which is hectares in this case. ATC should not be confused with the mean of those average total costs. Note the mean of the average total costs is generally much greater than the median of the average total costs. This is due to the fact that there are several organizations that reported large costs, while a greater number of organizations reported moderate costs. The median may be a more representative gauge of typical average total costs of forest certification given this result, so we use it most in the discussion here.

The data indicated that costs varied greatly depending on ownership size, with larger ownerships having lesser average total costs per area certified. This seems reasonable, since the external audit costs for large ownerships were only moderately more than for small ownerships, so were less per hectare. Similarly, the costs of preparing the environmental management systems and implementing certification were proportionately less for large firms, which probably already had much of these management procedures and controls in place, and could spread any additional costs over more area. Thus the cost per area was divided into logical classes based on the data. These classes were areas of less than 4,000 ha (10,000 ac), 4,001 ha to 40,000 ha, 40,001 to 400,000 ha, and larger than 400,000 ha.

There was a large variation in the results of the average costs of forest certification per area, with the standard deviation actually being larger than the mean for all ownerships. The reported average total costs of forest certification ranged from almost no added costs for one organization to $57.20 per ha per year for the organization with the greatest costs. The median average total costs by system for all responses were $0.91 per ha per year for FSC, $0.37 per ha per year for SFI, and $1.56 per ha in South America. The mean average total costs for all responses were $3.24 per ha per year for FSC, $4.92 per ha for SFI, and $6.89 for South America. Much of this difference probably could be attributed to the differences in ownership size. The median tract size of SFI certified organizations was almost four times larger than the FSC and South America organizations, and the SFI mean ownership size was about four times larger than the FSC respondents and ten times larger that the respondents in South America.

These differences in medians and means among systems, and their large variability, indicates that an analysis by ownership size is more useful. For small ownerships of less than 4,000 ha, median and mean costs were much less for FSC certification. The median average total costs in this case were $6.45 per ha per year; it was $23.75 in South America for all systems, and $39.31 for SFI, although this was for a sample of only two.

Average total costs decreased dramatically for ownership sizes of more than 4,000 ha. For 4,001 to 40,000 ha, the FSC median average total cost was $0.54 per ha per year, for SFI it was $0.91 per ha per year, and in South America it was $2.00 per ha per year. The responding organizations with large tracts of between 40,001 to 400,000 ha had median average total costs of $0.27 per ha per year for SFI, $1.21 for South America, and $2.40 for FSC. The FSC costs were actually greater than for smaller tracts, but this probably was just a random result of the small sample from the two organizations that responded. Only a few responding firms had more than 400,000 ha. The median average total costs for those organizations were \$0.42 per ha per year for FSC, \$0.07 for SFI, and \$0.49 in South America. The forest certification costs appeared to be more in South America for all classes according to the summary statistics.

Regression Analysis

A regression analysis of the average total costs by tract size, system, and country was performed to identify a few selected components that could affect average total costs. In particular, this allowed us to statistically examine the effects of ownership size, system, and country. One extreme outlier was excluded from that regression. The specific form of regression analyzed was:

Average Total Cost (\$/Ha) = f(ownership size, certification system, country)

where:

ownership size	=	the area of the certified forest by each organization
certification system	=	FSC or PEFC-endorsed system – as dummy variables
country	=	U.S.A., Canada, or South America – as dummy variables

Average total costs for regression decreased markedly with increasing average tract size as noted above in Table 6. Thus several transformations of the data were examined to model the L-shaped function of the data. Of those, the best was a log-log function, with a R^2=0.5178 and adjusted R^2=0.5089. The best model was:

$\log_{10}$(average total costs) = f($\log_{10}$(ha), certification system, country).

The resulting summary statistics are shown in Table 7.

The results from this model were significant for the average total cost as a function of the log of hectares, but none of the dummy variables for systems or for country were even close to statistically significant. Thus while Table 6 indicates that average costs by classes differed somewhat among systems and countries, when the ownership size effects by system were considered, these were not statistically significant. This might be attributed to the fact that the ownership size classes still had much different median size classes even within those classes. The sample size for the regressions was small, at only 55 cases in total, so it might not be possible to determine differences among countries or systems with this sample. Also, since 13 of the organizations were dual certified and had the same costs, it might mask system differences as well.

Table 7. Least Squares Linear Regression Results of Log(ATC ($/ha))

Variable	**Coefficient**	**Standard Error**	**T**	**P**	
Constant	2.72131	0.35980	7.56	0.0000	
Log(ha)	-0.58691	0.07708	-7.61	0.0000	
Source	**DF**	**SS**	**MS**	**F**	**P**
Regression	1	19.7854	19.784	57.99	0.000
Residual	54	18.426	0.3412		
Total	55	38.2110			

Individual Cost Components

The respondents also were asked to provide estimates of the cost components for certification. Only those reported from the SFI and FSC surveys in North America are shown below (Table 8). Some individuals provided costs for components, but not total costs, and vice versa. Thus the number of responses for each cost category differs as noted below. Only the median costs per component are reported here because the sample was so small.

The median average total costs remain the same as in Table 6, at $0.91 and $0.37 per ha per year for FSC and SFI, respectively. Audit preparation fees, external audit fees, and ongoing certification preparation costs were somewhat similar, at about $0.38 to $0.48 per ha per year for FSC and $0.11 to $0.19 for SFI. SFI average costs were somewhat less again, but recall that their average tract sizes were much greater. Only a few people reported the amounts spent for community education grants, changes to obtain certification, or program promotion activities. As noted by Goetzil (2006), program participation costs seemed greater for SFI program aparticpants. These costs were generally small, at less than $.06 per ha, but the number of responses limits conclusions about this.

Table 8. Individual Cost Components

Certification Cost Component	**FSC**		**SFI**	
	N	**Median Cost ($/Ha)**	**N**	**Median Cost ($/Ha)**
Total certification expenses	14	0.905	18	0.365
Internal audit and preparation fees	7	0.476	11	0.105
External audit fees	16	0.356	15	0.185
Ongoing certification preparation costs	12	0.456	9	0.152
Community education and support grants	4	0.039	4	0.014
Changes required to get/maintain certification	4	0.059	2	0.151
Activities of SIC membership / FSC promotion	1	0.021	10	0.023

Perceived Benefits

The surveys also asked respondents about their perceived benefits of forest certification. Drawing from the Rickenbach and Overdevest (2006) framework, these can be classed as market, signaling, or learning components, to which we added a fourth category, strategic reasons. As noted, we asked respondents to rank a list of various benefits of forest certification from 1 (not important) to 5 (important) using a Likert scale. The list was purposefully not categorized to avoid biasing any responses. The results were then summarized individually, and classed into the four categories. Results are summarized in Table 9, and notable observations follow.

The first observation is that the organizational strategic reasons were considered the most important, ranging from 3.6 to 4.3 by system and region. However, there were few strategic questions, which might allow a more narrowly focused response. The means for the other three groupings or categories differed little. There was more difference among the rankings between systems than between category of benefits, with the benefits perceived for FSC-US ranking slightly below SFI, which ranked slightly below South America. The means for all groups ranged between 2.8 to 4.3. FSC-US ranged from 2.9 to 3.6 for the four groups; SFI from 3.0 to 3.8; and all systems in South America from 3.3 to 4.3.

Some of the individual factors received much greater or lesser ranks for their perceived benefits, and these were fairly consistent across systems. The strategic position of the firm, corporate social responsibility, better organizational or professional image, and retaining or gaining market access, better management systems and performance, better records, and fostering continuous improvement ranked high as benefits for all systems, with all being assigned a mean score of 3.0 or better. The activities that rated lowest for benefits of certification all had mean scores of 3.2 or less for all systems, with the Argentina scores being the greatest in each case. These included less regulation, a pilot study or project, attract investors and increase stock prices, prevent direct action campaigns or citizen challenges, improve profitability, better morale among employees, better use of science in management.

Certification was perceived to offer somewhat more benefits to SFI firms and to firms in the Southern Cone of South America. The Likert scores in South America for strategic position of the organization, corporate social responsibility, firm image, market access and market capture, better management systems, better worker training, better records, and foster continuous improvement were a half to full point greater than in the other two systems. The firms in Latin America seemed more enthusiastic about forest certification, whether in personal interviews or in responses to the email survey. While certification is not as pervasive in South America, individuals at certified firms really did express their belief in the merits of better environmental and social practices for the situation for their firms and their countries. Corporate social responsibility, value of public relations, better professional image, market access, better records, and foster continuous improvement ranked high in all systems in all countries in the Americas.

Table 9. Likert Score Ranking of the Perceived Benefits of Forest Certification

Characteristic	FSC – U.S.	SFI – U.S. & Canada	All – South America
Firm Strategic or Management Factors			
strategic position of organization	3.6	3.8	4.3
satisfy senior management decision	3.3	3.8	4.2
right thing to do/corporate social responsibility	3.8	3.8	4.3
Mean for Category	3.1	3.3	4.3
Signaling to External Interest Groups			
prevent direct action campaigns/citizen challenges	2.4	2.9	3.2*
credibility with regulatory agencies	2.6	3.0	3.8
less regulation	2.3	2.9	3.2
value of public relations	3.8	4.1	4.0
better organizational/professional image	3.6	3.5	4.4
better public, landowner, supplier communications	2.8	3.2	3.9
Mean for Category	3.0	3.3	3.8
Improved Markets or Prices			
improve profitability	2.8	2.8	3.4
retain / gain market access	3.4	3.8	4.4
capture new market/marketing /sales tool	3.1	3.4	4.1
attract investors and increase stock prices	1.7	2.3	3.0*
better timber and product prices	2.8	2.5	3.3
Mean for Category	2.8	3.0	3.6
Improved Organizational Learning			
better management systems and performance	3.2	3.4	4.2
better working training and safety	2.7	3.1	4.3
better records	3.1	3.3	3.9
better internal communications and discussions	2.9	3.3	3.8
better morale among employees	2.7	2.6	3.1
employee empowerment	2.5	2.7	2.8*
better use of science in management	2.8	2.8	3.3
improve management efficiencies	2.8	2.8	3.9
better forest management and practices	3.1	3.1	4.4
better planning and implementation	3.2	3.2	3.9
obtain useful dialogue with external auditors	2.7	3.1	3.9
improve upper management knowledge or practices	2.6	3.3	3.4
foster continuous improvement	3.2	3.5	4.3
self-discovery of nonconformance	3.0	3.5	3.8
pilot study or project	2.1	2.2	2.1
Mean for Category	2.9	3.2	3.7

1=not important; 2=somewhat important; 3=neutral; 4=important; 5=very important.

* indicates data only for Argentina and Chile.

Perceived Disadvantages

The perceived disadvantages of forest certification represent another opinion-based means of assessing its costs (Table 10). These disadvantages were also asked separately without grouping them by class to avoid a bias in the responses. Then for this analysis, they were classed according to the broad categories of signaling, markets, and organizational learning. In this case, the group means were somewhat more discriminating. By country, disadvantages related to too much public interaction and openness ranged from 1.8 to 2.1; those related to adverse impacts of forest management, records, and analysis ranged from 1.9 to 2.4, and those related to audit cost and time ranged from 3.2 to 3.5.

In general, public interaction, adverse impacts of forest management, and record keeping were seen as somewhat of a disadvantage, but not as major problems. In this case, there was not a lot of difference among certification systems. Organizations certified by FSC perceived fewer problems with external communication requirements with certification, but more problems with lack of price or market advantages. Firms in South America seemed to have fewer issues with organizational management and learning than in North America.

Table 10. Likert Score Ranking of the Perceived Disadvantages of Forest Certification

Characteristic	FSC – U.S.	SFI – U.S. & Canada	All – South America
Signaling to External Interest Groups			
too much public interaction	1.9	2.2	2.1
public disclosure of audit results	1.7	2.0	2.3
too much openness	1.5	2.1	2.2
capitulation to green groups / lobby	2.0	2.4	2.0
Mean for Category	1.8	2.2	2.2
Markets or Prices			
audit costs	4.1	3.7	3.2
time and preparation costs	4.1	4.0	3.1
added costs for forest management	3.4	3.4	3.2
decreased returns on investments	2.4	2.6	1.7*
Mean for Category	3.5	2.4	2.8
Improved Organizational Learning			
negative changes in forest management	2.6	2.3	2.5
limits professional discretion and flexibility	2.6	2.4	3.1
adversarial auditing process	2.2	2.3	2.2
too much record keeping, too little action	3.3	3.2	3.3
poor morale among workers	2.0	2.2	1.9*
too much science / consultations	1.8	1.9	1.8*
too much planning / paralysis by analysis	2.3	2.4	1.5*
more discussion than management	2.2	2.4	1.6*
Mean for Category	2.4	2.4	2.2

1=not important; 2=somewhat important; 3=neutral; 4=important; 5=very important.

* indicates data only for Argentina and Chile.

Time, audit, and forest management costs and reduced professional flexibility were the only factors rated as more than a 3.0 on average in all countries/systems. For all systems, too much openness, too much science, too much public interaction, or poor morale due to certification were seen as the least significant disadvantages. Overall, these responses indicate that some of the often criticized components of certification, public interaction and forest management impacts did not seem very important, but the audit and preparation costs did.

Perceived Achievement of Benefits and Costs

In addition to the benefits and costs ranking, respondents in North America were asked to provide a broad ranking of their achievement of their objectives by broad category of strategic, signaling, markets, or learning (Table 11). Before certification, expectations for signaling improved stewardship to external groups ranked highest, improved market share and strategic position/corporate responsibility were about the same as the second of the objectives, and better internal management, records, training, morale, and science ranked least important. However there were moderately important or better scores (3.4+) for these for all systems.

After certification, the mean rankings for three of the categories—strategic position, signaling stewardship, and better records and management—remained greater than 3.4 for all systems. However, the achievement of improved markets or prices was most disappointing in both systems, with a 1.91 and 1.97 ranking for FSC and SFI, respectively. In addition, there was some shortfall of achieved benefits versus expected for three of the four categories—markets, strategic position, and signaling stewardship, with markets being the most disappointing. Mean ranks for better management, records, training, morale, and science improved substantially.

Table 11. Expected and Realized Benefits of Certification, FSC and SFI, North America

Possible Benefit / System	Expected Benefit Before Certification – Ranking		Actual Certification Benefit – Ranking	
	FSC	SFI	FSC	SFI
strategic position, corporate responsibility	3.73	3.89	3.45	3.46
signaling stewardship commitment to external groups	4.13	4.19	3.80	3.62
improved market share or prices	3.78	3.24	1.91	1.97
better internal management, records, training, morale, and science	3.00	3.32	3.40	3.76

1=not important; 2=somewhat important; 3=neutral; 4=important; 5=very important.

Retention of Forest Certification

Last, the respondents were asked about their perceptions of the overall costs and benefits of forest certification and whether they planned to retain forest certification (Table 12). In a question about the relative benefits and costs of forest certification, the respondents for both FSC-U.S. and SFI had a fairly evenly mixed distribution of responses. SFI had more respondents who felt that the benefits exceeded the costs (17 vs. 10), and FSC had more who felt that the costs exceeded the benefits (20 vs. 18).

In North America, a majority of respondents in both systems felt that certification had achieved their objectives, although FSC had more negative responses. Despite some mixed responses on the overall benefits and costs, almost everyone in SFI felt that they would maintain certification. The responses from procurement organizations were equally positive about the benefits of SFI certification. These responses are not entirely consistent, but the intent to retain certification seemed clear, while perhaps the benefit and cost assessment was more subjective. A large majority of FSC landowners responded similarly, but there was a greater share of respondents who were uncertain or probably would not maintain certification. We did not have a sample of all the South American countries, but those in Argentina and Chile all felt that certification had achieved their objectives and seven of nine responses said that they would definitely continue certification, and two were uncertain.

Table 12. Costs vs. Benefits and Retention of Forest Certification

Characteristic	**FSC – U.S.**	**SFI – U.S. &**
	-- number of responses --	
Costs and Benefits of Forest Certification		
benefits greatly exceed costs	8	7
benefits exceed costs	10	10
benefits equal costs	7	10
costs exceed benefits	12	8
costs greatly exceed benefits	8	2
Has Forest Certification Achieved Objectives?		
definitely yes	13	11
probably yes	15	20
uncertain	4	4
probably not	6	2
definitely not	6	0
Will Firm Maintain Forest Certification?		
definitely yes	10	17
probably yes	19	17
uncertain	12	2
probably not	3	1
definitely not	1	0

CONCLUSIONS

This research reported here has summarized the first comprehensive empirical study of the costs and benefits of forest certification. The literature on forest certification has consistently identified costs and benefits as important variables, and many other components of these factors are closely linked as well. The results reported here are our first overview of this subject, and do bear more scrutiny and statistical analysis, yet provide many insights already.

The forest certification impact evaluation studies have generally found that forest certification does prompt changes in forest management (e.g., WWF 2005, Federation of Nordic Forest Owners' Organisations 2005) and a few studies have been able to document improved forest management practices on the ground (e.g., Hagan et al. 2005, Simpson et al. 2005). The literature on economic modeling of forest certification has made various assumptions about costs to assess (the adverse) market equilibrium impacts (e.g., Brown and Zhang 2005, Gan 2005, Busby et al. 2007), but has been lacking empirical cost data. Similarly, various articles have demonstrated some consumer willingness to pay for certified forest products (e.g., Anderson et al. 2006, Aquilar and Vlosky 2007) or criticized the social agendas and adverse impacts of forest certification (Laband 2004). But most of this literature does not provide empirical information on producer benefits. Additionally, many authors have examined the role of certification as a non-state policy instrument, corporate social responsibility, and the role of interest groups in expansion of this system (Gulison 2003, Cashore et al 2004, Sasser et al. 2007).

Our results provide useful new empirical evidence that relates to many of the research questions addressed in these prior studies. First, it is apparent that forest certification costs and benefits are crucial in the practice, perceptions, and adoption by forest landowners. This is demonstrated by the magnitude of the costs reported by forest landowners in our surveys, and in particular in the distribution of those costs by forest ownership size. Similarly, many benefits were identified in the surveys.

Costs

The median and mean reported average total costs for small forest tracts of less than 4000 hectares were expensive, at $6.45 per ha per year for FSC-US to $39.31 per ha per year for SFI, which surely would deter adoption for small ownerships. Costs decreased significantly with increasing tract size, becoming as little as $0.27 per ha per year for SFI in the 40,001 ha to 400,000 ha size class, and $2.40 for FSC-US, and less than $0.50 per ha per year for ownerships greater than 400,000 ha. Reported costs for the FSC system were less for small ownerships than SFI, and vice versa. Costs in the Southern Cone countries in South America were generally greater than in North America. However, these median costs by ownership size class proved not to be statistically significant with regression analysis. Thus average total costs among systems and countries were a statistically significant function only of ownership size. Some of this could be due to the small sample size, which would make it difficult to find statistically significant differences, and the fact that 13 organizations were dual certified and had the same reported costs for a FSC and PEFC system.

These cost results do confirm and quantify the perceptions that forest certification costs are significant, but also indicate that they decrease rapidly with increasing tract size. Some of this could be attributed to the fact that relatively fixed auditing and preparation costs are spread over more area. Some also could be attributed to the fact that most large organizations and firms already have significant environmental management systems and staff, and can integrate forest certification systems into their ongoing operations at little additional effort or expense. Thus the assumptions used in much of the literature of costs of up to 25% more for certified lands (e.g., Gan 2005) are very expensive. Most landowners with reasonably large tracts would have much lower direct costs, perhaps less than 1% of current costs. This would suggest that aggregate economic welfare impacts are likely to be small also.

These costs by tract size results indicate why low cost approaches such as the FSC group certification and small low impact managed forests, or the American Tree Farm System individual or group certification are important for small forest landowners. They also indicate that issues with equity in the distribution of costs and benefits of forest certification for small owners exist, as posited by previous theoretical literature.

Benefits

While we were not able to measure it, cost differences also might be attributable to how far a firm was from complying with the certification standards. Firms that already have excellent practices and perhaps an environmental management system (EMS) in place would probably incur little added costs. Newly certified firms without an EMS would need to spend more. Similarly, there may be cost differences between plantation and natural forests, which we were unable to determine.

The perceptions of benefits of forest certification also provide insight to previous research. Forest certification is perceived to have a wide range of benefits, including firm strategic factors, signaling to external interest groups, improved markets or prices, and improved organizational learning. In general, for all forest certification systems in all countries, respondents rated the value of these broad categories at some level of importance. Some individual components of these categories—strategic position of the organization, corporate social responsibility, better image, retaining market access, and continuous improvement—were notably important. These results agree with those of Rickenbach and Overdevest (2006) for FSC-US, and extend the findings to a much broader set of systems and ownerships.

The results from this research also address the relationship between corporate social responsibility and interest group pressure in promoting forest certification. Corporate responsibility and strategic reasons were ranked much more important than pressure from interest groups by almost all respondents, leading us to doubt that certification is only an unwanted system foisted upon unwilling or dissatisfied owners by external groups. However, such market pressure may be more intense at the retail level than for forest owners. Certified owners do feel that certification provides many benefits, and ranked those benefits relatively highly. And in the list of disadvantages, the need to adopt forest certification just as a means to prevent attacks by green groups, and its adverse impacts on forest management practices or discretion were considered only somewhat important at most. Thus the negative view of forest certification as only preventive medicine seems too strong or at least oversimplified, especially compared to the positive responses for most of its potential benefits and for corporate responsibility or being the right thing to do.

The strong support for forest certification was even more apparent in the personal interviews than in the survey forms. There might be some bias since we interviewed and surveyed senior managers responsible for forest certification and environmental programs, not field personnel having to implement new practices and management controls. Nevertheless, the managers interviewed in South America, and many of the written questionnaire responses received, exhibited considerable enthusiasm for forest certification and its overall merits for the company or government organization. The experience of the organizations in North Carolina indicates that commitment of senior management or decision makers is crucial also in keeping forest certification, because field personnel often prefer less controls and responsibilities associated with certification, but do implement certification well if management so decides.

Clearly the largest perceived disadvantages of certification were its costs, especially for small landowners, and its apparent lack of market benefits that offset those costs. Many respondents felt that certification had achieved their objectives, but qualified those statements by noting they had not captured more market share or received higher timber or product prices. And the greatest disappointment in anticipated versus realized certification benefits was with the lack of a price premium for certified timber. However, there did seem to be more perceived market share and access advantages in South America than in North America to date. Perhaps the larger share of export markets there are instrumental. The experience reported by Daniels and Caulfield (2008) also pointed out the instrumental role for certification by investors in Latin America to procure international financing, convey a commitment to environmental stewardship, and sell timber in some South American markets.

Implementation

The personal interviews and the experience in North Carolina organizations also indicate that the distribution of benefits and costs are important. For all the interviewed firms in South America, the direct costs of certification were simply paid for the company, at no cost to the forest managers. This surely contributed to their broad support for forest certification. Each organization in North Carolina essentially paid for the certification from their own forest management budget, which led to lack of support and eventually some who dropped one or both of their FSC and SFI certifications. Thus payments for direct certification costs from corporate or central offices seem important for retention of forest certification. The forest managers seemed much more willing to incorporate any indirect costs of management changes.

There were some differences among forest certification systems and countries as well. Median certification average total costs seemed different among size classes, but did not vary significantly among systems or countries in the regression results. The small sample may have prevented statistical significance, but greater average certification costs in South America could deter more adoption there. Certification was viewed more favorably by the respondents in South America, however. There also was a more favorable view of the environmental and social/worker components of certification in Argentina, Brazil, and Chile in South America. The group systems and American Tree Farm System still are apt to reduce costs more in North America as well, which could provide more "northern" competitive advantage. All systems had many perceived benefits ranked as important, without a lot of difference in these among systems.

Overall, this research provides a large amount of empirical evidence about the costs, benefits, and merits of forest certification in the Americas. This chapter is our first attempt to examine and synthesize several years of research on the subject, and provides a useful summary of those results. We will extend these analyses of current data, and intend to perform further surveys of other forest certification systems as well.

Forest certification does seem to have substantial benefits that are perceived by certified forest organizations, at small to significant costs, depending on the size of the forest ownership and other factors. Organizations in our survey recognized the costs and benefits of forest certification, and feel that it has achieved their objectives. Most intend to remain certified, and hope to improve their forest, social, environmental, and economic performance.

Forest certification has reformed the rhetoric and practice of forestry. Firms that have adopted it recognize the implicit benefit:cost calculus associated with its adoption, and have largely dismissed the negative social critiques of the systems. The expansion of certification will eventually depend on increasing benefits, especially markets and prices, or decreasing direct costs. All systems are working to achieve this objective, which should foster more economic benefits as the well recognized social, environmental, and strategic benefits.

References

Anderson, R.C., D.N. Laband, E.N. Hansen, and R.D. Knowles. 2006. Price premiums in the mist. *Forest Products Journal* 55(6):19-22.

Aquilar, F. X. and R.P. Vlosky. 2007. Consumer willingness to pay price premiums for environmentally certified wood products in the U.S. *Forest Policy and Economics* 9(8):1100-1112.

Araujo, Michelle. 2007. *Forest certification in Brazil: Choices and Impacts.* M.S. Thesis. University of Toronto.

Bass, S. K. Thornber, M. Markopoulos, S. Roberts, M. Grieg-Gran. 2001. *Certification's Impacts on Forests, Stakeholders, and Supply Chains.* Earthprint Limited. Hertfordshire, England. 134 p.

Brown, R. and D. Zhang. 2005. The Sustainable Forestry Initiative's impact on stumpage markets in the US South. *Canadian Journal of Forestry Research* 35(8):2056-2064.

Busby, G.M., C.A. Montgomery, and G.S. Latta. 2007. *The opportunity cost of forest certification on private land in Western Oregon.* Western Journal of Applied Forestry 22(1):55-60.

Carter, D.R. and F.D. Merry. 1998. The nature and status of forest certification in the United States. *Forest Products Journal* 48(2):23-28.

Cashore, B., G. Auld, and D. Newsom. 2003. Forest certification (eco-labeling) programs and their policy-making authority: explaining divergence among North American and European case studies. *Forest Policy and Economics* 5(3):225-247.

Cashore, B., G. Auld, and D. Newsom. 2004. *Governing through Markets: Forest Certification and the Emergence of Non-State Authority.* Yale University Press. New Haven, Connecticut. 327 p.

Cashore, B., G. C. van Kooten, I. Vertinsky, G. Auld, and J. Afforderbach. 2005. Private or self-regulation? A comparative study of forest certification choices in Canada, United States and Germany. *Forest Policy and Economics* 7(1):53-69.

Cubbage, F., S. Moore, J. Cox, L. Jervis, J. Edeburn, D. Richter, W. Boyette, M. Thompson, and M. Chesnutt. 2002. Implementing forest certification in North Carolina: systems, costs, and forest management implications. In: *Proceedings, Southern Forest Economics Workers* (SOFEW) Annual Meeting. Available from: Department of Forestry, Virginia Tech, Blacksburg, VA. p. 137-156.

Cubbage, F., S. Moore, J. Cox, L. Jervis, J. Edeburn, D. Richter, W. Boyette, M. Thompson, and M. Chesnutt. 2003. Forest certification of state and university lands in North Carolina. *Journal of Forestry* 101(8):26-31.

Cubbage, F. J. Cox, S. Moore, J. Edeburn, D. Richter, M. Chesnutt, H. Rohr, and T. Henderson. 2008. Long-Term management impacts and costs of forest certification in North Carolina: the experience of the Southern Center for Sustainable Forests Partners. In: *Southern Forest Economics Workers Meeting (SOFEW) Proceedings.* University of Tennessee, Knoxville.

Daniels, Charles and Jon Caulfield. 2008. Investment strategies in timberland. Presented at: *Timberland Investing Latin America Summit.* March 3-5. São Paulo.

Dogwood Alliance. 2005. *Don't buy SFI campaign.* Accessed at: http://www.dontbuysfi.com. April 26, 2005.

Federation of Nordic Forest Owners' Organisations. 2005. Effectiveness and efficiency of FSC and PEFC forest certification on pilot areas in Nordic countries. *Final report.* Savcor Indufor Oy, Helsinki. Mimeo/PDF.

Forest Stewardship Council. 2008. *FSC program summary statistics.* Accessed at: http:// www.fsc.org/en/ . 21 January.

Gan, J.B. 2005. Forest certification costs and global forest products markets and trade: a general equilibrium analysis. *Canadian Journal of Forest Research* 35(7)1731-1743.

Goetzl, Alberto. 2006. Sustainable Forestry Initiative Standard (SFI) ® cost assessment. *Speech presented at the SFI Annual Meeting.* Toronto, Canada. October 3-5.

Gullison, R.E. 2003. Does forest certification conserve biodiversity? *Oryx* 37(2):153-165.

Hagan, John M., Lloyd C. Irland, and Andrew A. Whitman. 2005. Changing timberland ownership in the Northern Forest and implications for biodiversity. Manomet Center for Conservation Sciences, *Report* #MCCS-FCP-2005-1, Brunswick, Maine. 25 p.

Jensen. K. 2003. Market participation and willingness to pay for environmentally certified products. *Forest Science* 49(4):632-641.

Klooster, D. 2005. Environmental certification of forests: the evolution of environmental governance in a commodity network. *Journal of Rural Studies* 21(4):403-417.

Laband, David. 2004. Why I oppose forest certification. *The Consultant.* p. 21-22.

Lemoine, D., J.P. Evans, and C.K. Smith. 2006. A landscape-level geographic information system (GIS) analysis of streamside management zones on the Cumberland plateau. *Journal of Forestry* 104(4):125-131.

Meidinger, E. 2003. Forest certification as environmental law making by global civil society. In: Meidinger et al., Eds. *Social Dimensions of Forest Certification.* Verlag. Remargen-Oberwinter. Germany.

Meridian Institute. 2001. *Comparative analysis of the Forest Stewardship Council© and Sustainable Forestry Initiative® certification programs.* Accessed at: http://www2.merid.org/comparison/. 14 July 2003.

Newsom, D. and D. Hewitt. 2005. The global impacts of SmartWood certification. Final Report. *TREES Program, Rainforest Alliance.* Accessed at: http://www.rainforest-alliance.org/programs/forestry/perspectives/documents/sw_impacts.pdf. 4 May 2006.

Nussbaum, R. and M. Simula. 2005. *The Forest Certification Handbook,* 2nd Edition. Earthscan. London. 300 p.

Overdevest, C., and M. Rickenbach. 2006. Forest certification and institutional governance: an empirical study of Forest Stewardship Council certificate holders in the United States. *Forest Policy and Economics* 9(1):93-102.

Perera, P., R.P. Vlosky, G. Hughes, M.A. Dunn. 2007. What do Louisiana and Mississippi nonindustrial private forest landowners think about forest certification? *Southern Journal of Applied Forestry* 31(4):170-178.

PEFC. 2008. Programme for Endorsement of Forest Certification. 2007. *PEFC program summary statistics.* Accessed at: http://www.pefc.org/. 22 December 2007.

Ramesteiner, E., and M. Simula. 2002. Forest certification—an instrument to promote sustainable forest management? *Journal of Environmental Management* 67:87-98.

Rickenbach, M. and C. Overdevest. 2006. More than markets: assessing Forest Stewardship Council (FSC) certification as a policy tool. *Journal of Forestry* 104(3):143-147.

Sasser, E.N. 2003. Gaining leverage: NGO influence in certification institutions in the forest products sector. In: Teeter, L.; Cashore, B.:, and Zhang, D.:, eds. *Forest Policy for Private Forestry: Global and Regional Challenges.* New York: CABI Publishing. p. 229-244.

Sasser, E.N., A. Prakash, B. Cashore, and G. Auld. 2006. Direct targeting as an NGO political strategy: examining private authority regimes in the forestry sector. *Business and Politics* 8(3):Article 1.

Simpson, H., J. Donellan, and S. Harrington. 2005. Voluntary implementation of best management practices in East Texas: Results from Round 6 of BMP Implementation Monitoring. *Texas Forest Service.* College Station, Texas. Accessed at: http://txforestservice.tamu.edu/shared/article.asp?DocumentID=950&mc=forest. 2 February 2006.

Simula, Markku et al. 2004. Report on financial cost-benefit analysis of forest certification and implementation of phased approaches. *ITTO.* Accessed at: http://www.itto.or.jp/live/Live_Server/969/Annex-D.pdf. April 2006.

Stevens, J. 1998. Forest products certification: a survey of manufacturers. *Forest Products Journal* 48(6):43-49.

Sustainable Forestry Initiative. 2008. *Sustainable Forestry Initiative Program Marks Record growth.* Press release, January 15, 2008. 2 p.

WWF. 2005. The effects of FSC certification in Estonia, Germany, Latvia, Russia, Sweden and the UK. *Summary report & country reports.* Accessed at: http://www.panda.org/about_wwf/what_we_do/forests/publications/index/cfm?uNewsID=18510. 4 May 2006.

In: Natural Resources
Editor: Jeanette B. Pauling

ISBN 978-1-60456-982-7

Chapter 6

NATURAL RESOURCES, INTANGIBLE CAPITAL AND BARRIERS TO ECONOMIC DEVELOPMENT

María D. Guilló[*]
Department of Economics, University of Alicante, Spain

ABSTRACT

The objective of this study is to provide a theoretical framework to jointly analyze the role of natural resources and intangible capital in the process of economic development, addressing a simple mechanism that can explain why natural resource abundance may lower income and welfare. The model extends the development theory of relative incomes of Parente and Prescott to include intermediate goods production which require the use of a natural input. The model relative income predictions are consistent with the economic development observations of some Latin American countries.

1. INTRODUCTION

One of the fundamental questions in economics is why some countries manage to produce systematically so much more output per worker than others. Since the late 1990s this question has been the center of the discussion among theorists of economic growth and historians, pointing out the different and prime roles of endowments, government policies, and institutions. Whether it is endowments, policy, or institutions the fundamental cause of economic development and long-run growth is still at the core of the debate. Yet recent empirical research suggests that this role corresponds to institutions.[1]

In this chapter we want to address the link between natural resource endowments and barriers to economic development in a context where total factor productivity is driven by investments in intangible capital. In doing so we treat the quality of institutions as exogenous

---

[*] E-mail address: guillo@ua.es

[1] See for example Acemoglu et al. (2001,2004) and Easterly and Levine (2003).

but try to quantify the size of its implied barriers to economic development. The framework proposed builds on Parente and Prescott's (1994, 2000) growth model with total factor productivity differentials and barriers to technology adoption. These authors argue that the size of investment in intangible capital (like maintenance and repair, research and development, costs of perfecting new manufacturing processes and products, advertising, purchases of software, training and organizational capital, and so on) is crucial to understand the effects of savings rates on steady state incomes. These authors estimate that these unmeasured investments can represent between 30 and 50 percent of GDP. Since many of these unmeasured investments can affect directly total factor productivity and can be crowded out by natural capital, I propose a framework to jointly analyze the role of natural resources in the process of capital accumulation, both physical and intangible capital, in a model with differences in total factor productivity.

Natural resources are an important source of income in many developing countries, yet post-war experience shows that most of resource abundant countries tend to grow more slowly than resource poor economies. This evidence, called the *curse* of natural resources, has been documented recently in several empirical studies and has inspired a number of analytical frameworks.[2] The reported evidence suggests that natural resources tend to crowd out all kinds of capital (foreign, social, human and physical capital). These studies include, among others, the works by Gylfason and Zoega (2001), Sachs and Warner (2001), and Gylfason (2000). The results are robust to different measures of resource intensity like the shares of primary exports or natural resource exports in GDP, or as the share of natural capital in national wealth. The explanation of the curse in nearly all existing models is that strong natural resource dependence crowds-out some activity which ultimately drives growth. In Sachs and Warner (2001) this activity is manufacturing exports, whereas in Gylfason (2000) is investment in human capital. Gylfason and Zoega (2001) propose a new mechanism by which natural resource intensity affects economic growth through saving and investment: when the income share of natural capital rises, the demand for physical capital falls leading to lower interest rates and less rapid growth. In this model physical capital is affected by an exogenous quality index that can be interpreted as the degree of maturity of institutions. One of the implications of the model is that the larger the income share of natural capital the greater the need for economic and institutional reforms to stimulate investment and to attain sustained growth.[3]

An example of how natural capital abundance per se does not have to be a *curse* is the case of Botswana, as opposed to Sierra Leone. Both African economies export diamonds, Botswana has managed the rents from the natural resource in a way that has contributed to an impressive economic growth since independence in 1966, whereas Sierra Leone has diverted diamond rents towards devastating rent seeking, destroying the infrastructure and social institutions and becoming one the poorest economies in the world. Other examples of resource rich economies with a very poor performance in growth rates are most oil exporting countries. An exception is Norway, though we can argue that by the time Norway became an important exporter of oil it was already developed and had relatively mature institutions that

[2] See Gylfason (2000) and Gylfason and Zoega (2001) for a review of the empirical evidence.

[3] A similar implication arises in Guilló and Perez-Sebastian (2001). In a Hecscher-Ohlin framework they show that if the share of labor in the natural resource specific sector is large, a greater share of the natural endowment in national income (a resource boom) will have a negative effect on capital accumulation in the long run.

favored an effective management of the oil resources.[4] Authors like Woolcok et al. (2001) and Isham et al. (2001) find that institutions are worse in resource rich economies than in resource poor economies. Auty (2001) develops a stylized facts model of industrialization in a poor-resource country with a developmental state, but argues that most resource abundant countries engender a predatory political state.

More generally, sharp contrasts in economic performance between economies with apparently similar endowments constitute an old controversy; they have been the concern of historians for decades. The conventional view points to the importance of institutions in a broad sense, political and legal structures, as well as culture and religion, in shaping the evolution of economies, yet attributes to factor endowments a primary role in the process of economic development.[5]

Many historians of the New World have being trying to explain why societies of the European colonies in the South evolved so differently from those in the North American mainland despite they started off with similar endowments. Both regions of the New World had a relatively abundance of land and other per capita resources by European standards of the time, yet the United States and Canada are nowadays among the richest in the world and many Latin American countries have not yet enter sustained growth. This sharp contrast suggests that factor endowments alone cannot explain such enormous difference in economic performance and that institutions, in a broad sense, must have played a major role in the process of economic development. Although this point has been emphasized by many scholars and historians, and many aspects of institutions have been proposed as responsible of large discrepancies in economic development, including the degree of democracy, the extent of rent-seeking, the structure of property rights, as well as culture and religion, only a few have tried to explore in a systematic way the influences of endowments on the possible paths of economic and institutional development.

Engerman and Sokolow (1997), trying to explain the different paths of growth among New World economies, argue that in environments where crops are most effectively produced using large plantations with slave labor (sugar, coffee, rice, tobacco and cotton), societies generated a very unequal distribution of wealth and political power, and promptly developed political and legal institutions to preserve the rights of the elite (British colonies in the Caribbean and Brazil as well as the Spanish colonies). In contrast, climate and soil conditions in the northern British colonies favored a regime of farming with no economies of scale (mainly grains and livestock) but with a large productivity potential through learning, that gave rise to the formation of small family-size farms. They conclude that 'the circumstances in these latter regions encouraged the evolution of more equal distributions of wealth, more democratic political institutions, more extensive domestic markets, and the pursuit of more growth oriented policies than did those in the former'.[6]

The lesson we draw from the above argument is that, in early stages of political and economic development (or underdevelopment) endowments are important, but no more than the distribution of wealth among productive units. This distribution will shape the evolution of social and economic institutions, which ultimately will protect the output of all individual productive units or the output of selected groups. Furthermore, using the terminology in the

[4] For a discussion see Gylfason (2001).

[5] For a discussion of the importance of institutions in economic growth see North (1990).

[6] Woolcok et al. (2001) find evidence that "point-source" and coffee and cocoa resources are associated with worse institutions compared to "diffuse" resource economies.

natural resource literature mentioned above, can we conclude that the highly productive plantations were a *curse* for most Latin American countries? Or were the set of economic and social institutions in Latin America what hampered economic growth?

Several recent contributions to the growth literature point toward a focus on levels instead of growth rates.[7] For instance, Bloom et al. (2002) find strong evidence of technological diffusion but not full convergence and show that differences in total factor productivity persist even in the long run due to differences in geography and institutions. In previous models of idea flows across countries, like Parente and Prescott (1994), Barro and Sala-i-Martin (1995), Eaton and Kortum (1995), countries also grow at a common rate in the long run because technological diffusion and long run differences in levels are the interesting differences to explain. Parente and Prescott (2000) argue that relative income levels rather than growth rates are the key to understanding the problem of development and propose a theory of economic development. They show that the neoclassical growth model augmented with intangible capital and total factor productivity differentials accounts for the pattern of development; furthermore, they examine the evidence of differences in barriers and in total factor productivity and conclude that, 'although countries have access to the same stock of knowledge, they do not all make equally efficient use of this knowledge because policies in some countries lead to barriers that effectively prevent firms from adopting more productive technologies and from changing to more efficient work practices.'

Hall and Jones (1999) demonstrate that differences in physical and human capital can only explain partially the large variation in output per worker, and that the differences in capital accumulation, productivity, and so output per worker are driven by differences in institutions and government policies. More recently, Easterly and Levine (2003) and Acemoglu et al. (2004) show that it is institutions what matters for differences in economic development. Easterly and Levine (2003) find evidence that differences in endowments affect country incomes only through institutions and that government policies have no effect on income differences once they control for institutions. Acemoglu et al. (2004) show that institutions are the fundamental cause of differences in economic development and propose a theoretical case where institutions are the result of economic and political decisions of individuals.

As in the latter studies the focus in this chapter is on levels of economic development rather than on growth rates.

2. The Model

The model economy builds on Parente and Prescott's (2000) framework with TFP differences and technological constraints. It augments Parente and Prescott's framework to a three sector setting with a natural resource endowment. There is a final good and two intermediate goods sectors of production. The final good can be consumed or accumulated as capital, but intermediate goods can only be used as factors of production. Intermediate good 1 is produced using natural resources and labor, and intermediate good 2 requires only the use of labor. The final good is produced using capital and intermediate goods. With these

[7] Jones (1995) questions the empirical relevance of endogenous growth models.

assumptions we want to capture the idea that intermediate goods are more labor intensive than final goods. We abstract from population growth and assume that there is a measure L of infinitely lived households. Each household is endowed with one unit of labor in each period. The natural resource endowment is in fixed supply over time and it is equally distributed across households. All markets are perfectly competitive.

The Production Sector

The technology to produce the final output, Y_t, is a standard constant returns production function in growth models with intermediate goods:

$$Y_t = K_t^{\theta} H_t^{1-\theta}, \quad 0 < \theta < 1,$$
$$H_t \equiv \left(\varphi X_{1t}^{1-\theta} + (1-\varphi) X_{2t}^{1-\theta}\right)^{\frac{1}{1-\theta}}, \quad 0 < \varphi < 1. \tag{1}$$

Where K_t represents the stock of physical capital employed at period t, and H_t is a composite of the intermediate goods X_{1t} and X_{2t}. The parameter θ represents both the share of physical capital in total output and the elasticity of substitution between intermediate goods. Given the constant returns technology and the assumption of perfectly competitive markets, we shall assume, without loss of generality, that there is only one representative firm operating in the final good sector.

In contrast, we shall assume that the unit of production in the intermediate goods' sectors is a plant. A plant in the x_1 − sector produces output according with the following technology:

$$x_{1t} = A_t n_t^{\alpha} \eta_{1t}, \quad \eta_{1t} \geq \eta_1 \cdot \left(\frac{1+A_t}{A_t}\right), \quad \eta_1 > 0. \tag{2}$$

Where n_t is the amount of the natural resource employed per plant, η_{1t} is the minimum number of workers required to operate a plant to produce good 1 in period t, and A_t is a technology factor exogenous to the x_1 − sector to be specified later. Notice that technological progress implies that the minimum number of workers needed to operate a plant decreases over time. Let us denote by L_{1t} the total amount of labor employed in sector 1 and by N the constant natural resource endowment of the economy. Then, the number of operating plants in this sector is L_{1t}/η_{1t} and so we can express aggregate output in the x_1 − sector as

$$X_{1t} = A_t \left(\eta_{1t} N\right)^{\alpha} L_{1t}^{1-\alpha} \tag{3}$$

On the other hand, a plant in the x_2-sector only needs labor to produce output. It has the following production function:

$$x_{2t} = B_t \eta_2, \quad \eta_2 > 0, \tag{4}$$

Where η_2 is the fixed minimum number of workers needed to operate a plant and B_t is a technology factor that represents a plant's quality in period t. However, a plant in this sector can increase its future productivity by investing current resources in intangible capital. We follow Parente and Prescott (1994) and assume that the amount of resources needed in period t to increase a plant's productivity from B_t to B_{t+1} next period is given by

$$I_{B_t}^{B_{t+1}} = \left(1+\pi_n\right) \int_{B_t}^{B_{t+1}} \left(\frac{v}{W_t}\right)^{\mu} dv, \quad \mu > 0. \tag{5}$$

In the above expression W_t is the world's stock of usable knowledge that grows at a constant g rate per period, and π_n represents the size of the barrier. We shall assume that the barrier is given by

$$\pi_n \equiv \pi \cdot \left(\frac{n}{1+n}\right), \quad \pi > 0. \tag{6}$$

This specification of π_n tries to capture the relation between the quality of institutions, represented by the inverse of π, and the per capita resource endowment, n. That is, the lower π is the more effective institutions are; so the more abundant the resource is relative to labor (the larger n) the more effective institutions need to be to keep barriers low. It follows from the above integral that we can express a plant's investment in intangible capital in a more compact way as follows:

$$I_{B_t}^{B_{t+1}} = z_{t+1} - \left(1-\delta_z\right) z_t, \tag{7}$$

With $z_t \equiv \dfrac{\left(1+\pi_n\right)}{\left(1+\mu\right)} \dfrac{B_t^{\mu+1}}{W_{t-1}^{\mu}}$, and $\left(1-\delta z\right) \equiv 1/\left(1+g\right)^{\mu}$.

The variable z_t is interpreted as the stock of intangible capital at period t since it is the result of past investments in productivity. Given these definitions, we can obtain a plant's productivity as a function of its stock of intangible capital, the world's stock of usable knowledge and the barrier to productivity improvements. Therefore, the output of a plant in sector 2 can be written as follows:

$$x_{2t} = \left(\frac{1+\mu}{1+\pi_n} \right)^{\frac{1}{1+\mu}} W_{t-1}^{\frac{\mu}{1+\mu}} z_t^{\frac{1}{\mu+1}} \eta_2 .$$

Finally, to simplify notation, we define $\gamma \equiv 1/(1+\mu)$, $\mathrm{B}(\pi_n) \equiv 1/(1+\pi_n)^\gamma$ and $\Psi \equiv (1+\mu)^\gamma (W_0/(1+g))^{1-\gamma}$ so that the above expression reduces to

$$x_{2t} = \Psi \mathrm{B}(\pi_n)(1+g)^{(1-\gamma)t} z_t^\gamma \eta_2 . \tag{8}$$

In this expression the term $\mathrm{B}(\pi_n)$ represents the barrier to productivity improvements or technology adoption and so it will be different across countries, whereas the parameter Ψ is a positive constant common to all countries. Notice that as the world's stock of usable knowledge grows, the plant's stock of intangible capital depreciates. If the plant does not undertake any investment in intangible capital, its productivity B_t remains constant and so does its output; that is, the term $(1+g)^{(1-\gamma)t} z_t^\gamma$ does not change if investment in intangible capital is zero. Therefore, productivity growth at the plant's level in the x_2 – sector will be endogenous, but the stock of usable knowledge will be growing at a constant exogenous rate g.

For simplicity we will assume that all plants in the x_2 – sector start off with the same productivity and that new plants have free access to the current technology. However, once a plant is operated cannot benefit from improvements in productivity unless undertakes some investment (think of only one firm with many operating plants). We postpone the discussion of this point to section 3. Under this assumption, aggregate output in the x_2 – sector is

$$X_{2t} = \Psi \mathrm{B}(\pi_n)(1+g)^{(1-\gamma)t} z_t^\gamma L_{2t}, \tag{9}$$

Where the term $\Psi \mathrm{B}(\pi_n)(1+g)^{(1-\gamma)t} z_t^\gamma$ is just the productivity level in period t, B_t, and L_{2t} is total labor employed in the x_2 – sector in that period.

To close the production side of the economy, we shall assume that improvements in productivity in the x_2 – sector spill over to the natural resource sector but with a time lag. That is, $A_t = B_{t-1}$. With this condition and the assumption that only plants in the x_2 – sector invest in intangible capital we want to capture the fact that the sector which is more intensive in the natural input adopts technologies already in use in other sectors of the economy and that the bulk of productivity investments is done outside the resource intensive sector.

The Household Sector

The household sector consists of a continuum of infinitely lived identical households of measure L. Each household is endowed with one unit of productive time each period and does not value leisure. The natural resource endowment of the economy and the initial stock of physical capital are equally distributed across households. The utility of a household is

$$\sum_{t=0}^{\infty} \beta^t \ln c_t, \quad \beta \in (0,1),$$

Where c_t represents consumption in period t. Each period households will perceive rents from the services of labor, physical capital and the natural endowment, as well as dividends from the operating firms. The budget constraint faced by a household is

$$\sum_{t=0}^{\infty} P_t \left(c_t + k_{t+1} - (1-\delta_k) k_t\right) \leq \sum_{t=0}^{\infty} P_t \left(w_t + r_{kt} k_t + r_{nt} n + d_{1t} + d_{2t}\right), \tag{10}$$

$$given \;\; k_0 > 0, \; n > 0 .$$

The term P_t is the Arrow-Debreu price of a unit of the final good in period t; w_t, r_{kt} and r_{nt} are the rental prices of labor, physical capital and the natural resource, respectively; d_{jt} is the per capita dividend of a plant in sector j, $j = 1,2$; and k_t and n represent, respectively, the per capita stock of physical capital and the per capita stock of the natural resource. The parameter $\delta_k \in (0,1)$ is the depreciation rate of physical capital. Thus, the problem faced by the representative household is standard; it will maximize its utility subject to (10) and the usual transversality condition. If we define $P_t / P_{t+1} - 1 \equiv i_t$, where i_t is the interest rate from period t to period $t+1$, the first order conditions to this problem imply then that

$$\frac{c_{t+1}}{c_t} = \beta (1 + i_t), \tag{11}$$

$$r_{kt+1} = i_t + \delta_k . \tag{12}$$

3. Temporary Equilibrium

The representative firm in the final good sector maximizes profits taking as given the rental price of physical capital, r_{kt}, and the prices of intermediate goods, p_{jt}, $j = 1,2$. Everything measured in units of the final consumption good. The solution to this maximization problem yields the following factor demand functions:

$$K_t = \left(\frac{\theta\left(\varphi X_{1t}^{1-\theta} + (1-\varphi) X_{2t}^{1-\theta}\right)}{r_{kt}} \right)^{1/(1-\theta)}, \tag{13}$$

$$X_{1t} = \left(\frac{(1-\theta)\varphi}{p_{1t}} \right)^{1/\theta} K_t, \qquad X_{2t} = \left(\frac{(1-\theta)(1-\varphi)}{p_{2t}} \right)^{1/\theta} K_t. \tag{14}$$

These factor demands imply that capital income and intermediate goods' expenditures represent, respectively, a constant share of the final output, $r_{kt}k_t = \theta y_t$ and $p_{1t}x_{1t} + p_{2t}x_{2t} = (1-\theta) y_t$, and that intermediate goods relative employment will depend only on the relative price of these goods, $X_{1t}/X_{2t} = \left(\varphi/(1-\varphi)\right)^{1/\theta} \left(p_{2t}/p_{1t}\right)^{1/\theta}$.

The representative plant in the x_1 − sector maximizes profits taking as given the natural resource rental rate, r_{nt}, the wage rate, w_t, and the market price of its output, p_{1t}. Then, profit maximization implies that the demand for the natural resource will be determined by

$$\alpha p_{1t} A_t n_{1t}^{\alpha-1} \eta_{1t} = r_{nt}, \tag{15}$$

Which implies that rents paid per plant to households for the natural resource services, $r_{nt}n_t$, represent a fraction α of the plant's revenues, $\alpha p_{1t}x_{1t}$. Free entry into the x_1 − sector implies that the number of plants in equilibrium will be determined by the following zero profit condition

$$(1-\alpha) p_{1t}x_{1t} = w_t \eta_{1t}, \tag{16}$$

Where p_{1t} and w_t are the market clearing prices of good 1 and labor, respectively. We can solve for p_{1t} by equating the final sector's demand for X_{1t} in (14) and its aggregate supply given in expression (3). This solution is

$$p_{1t} = \frac{\varphi(1-\theta) K_t^{\theta}}{\left(A_t (\eta_{1t}N)^{\alpha} L_{1t}^{1-\alpha}\right)^{\theta}} = \frac{\varphi(1-\theta) k_t^{\theta}}{\left(A_t (\eta_{1t}n)^{\alpha} l_{1t}^{1-\alpha}\right)^{\theta}}, \tag{17}$$

Where $l_{1t} \equiv L_{1t}/L$. Substituting this expression into condition (16) implies that the share of labor employed in sector 1 is:

$$l_{1t} = \left(\frac{\varphi(1-\theta)(1-\alpha) A_t^{1-\theta} (\eta_{1t} n)^{\alpha(1-\theta)} k_t^{\theta}}{w_t} \right)^{\frac{1}{\theta+\alpha(1-\theta)}}. \tag{18}$$

A plant in the x_2 − sector has profits in period t given by

$$\upsilon_t = p_{2t} x_{2t} - w_t \eta_2 - I_{zt}, \tag{19}$$

Where $I_{zt} \equiv I_{B_t}^{B_{t+1}}$. At the beginning of each period a plant decides whether stays in the market or leaves. It will stay in the market if revenues cover the plant's operating cost, $p_{2t} x_{2t} \geq w_t \eta_2$, and will leave otherwise. Taking all prices as given, a plant that operates (stays) in period t will decide how much wants to invest in intangible capital by solving the following problem

$$\max_{z_{t+1}} \left\{ \upsilon_t + \frac{P_t}{P_{t+1}} \upsilon_{t+1} \right\}$$

$$\begin{aligned} s.t. \quad & \upsilon_s = p_{2s} x_{2s} - w_s \eta_2 - I_{zs}, \\ & x_{2s} = \Psi \mathrm{B}(\pi_n)(1+g)^{(1-\gamma)s} z_s^{\gamma} \eta_2, \\ & I_{zs} = z_{s+1} - (1-\delta_z) z_s. \end{aligned}$$

The solution to this program will determine the optimal amount of investment in intangible capital for next period production. If $\upsilon_t < 0$, then investment will be financed by issuing debt; and if $\upsilon_t \geq 0$, the plant pays dividends. The first order condition for this investment decision problem is

$$\gamma p_{2t+1} \Psi \mathrm{B}(\pi_n)(1+g)^{(1-\gamma)(t+1)} z_{t+1}^{\gamma-1} \eta_2 = \frac{P_t}{P_{t+1}} - (1-\delta_z).$$

From the right side of this equation we can define the implicit rental price of intangible capital as $r_{zt+1} \equiv i_t + \delta_z$. It follows from this optimality condition that for all plants operating in period t the implicit return on intangible capital satisfies:

$$\gamma p_{2t} x_{2t} = r_{zt} z_t. \tag{20}$$

Next we have to specify under what conditions new plants are created. We shall assume that new plants starting to produce in period $t+1$ must issue equity in period t that it is worth z_{t+1} (next period intangible capital of operating plants). Then, a prospective plant in period t will enter the market if

$$p_{2t+1}x_{2t+1} - w_{t+1}\eta_2 \geq \left(i_t + \delta_z\right) z_{t+1}.$$

That is, there will be entry of new plants if next period's revenues net of labor costs are sufficient to cover the depreciation of intangible capital and interest payments. In equilibrium, free entry will imply that this condition will hold with equality. This together with condition (20) in production implies that labor costs represent a constant fraction $1-\gamma$ of a plant's revenues,

$$w_t\eta_2 = \left(1-\gamma\right) p_{2t}x_{2t}. \tag{21}$$

As before, w_t is equilibrium wage, and p_{2t} is the market clearing price of intermediate good 2. Taking into account the demand for X_2 from the final good sector in (14) and the aggregate supply in (9), this equilibrium price is

$$p_{2t} = \frac{\left(1-\varphi\right)\left(1-\theta\right) k_t^{\theta}}{\left(\Psi \mathrm{B}\left(\pi_n\right)\left(1+g\right)^{(1-\gamma)t} z_t^{\gamma} l_{2t}\right)^{\theta}}, \tag{22}$$

Where $l_{2t} \equiv L_{2t}/L$. Substituting (22) into (21) we find that the share of labor employed in the x_2 – sector is given by

$$l_{2t} = \left(\frac{\left(1-\varphi\right)\left(1-\theta\right)\left(1-\gamma\right) B_t^{1-\theta}}{w_t}\right)^{1/\theta} k_t, \tag{23}$$

Where $B_t = \Psi \mathrm{B}\left(\pi_n\right)\left(1+g\right)^{(1-\gamma)t} z_t^{\gamma}$.

In equilibrium, the shares of labor employed in each sector must be such that the labor market clears:

$$l_{1t} + l_{2t} = 1. \tag{24}$$

Figure 1 illustrates this equilibrium condition. At the beginning of each period the stock of physical capital, k_t, the natural resource endowment, n, and the productivity levels, B_t and A_t, are given. Market clearing requires that w_t must solve (24), which in turn will determine the equilibrium prices of intermediate goods p_{1t} and p_{2t} in expressions (17) and (22). Let $w(k_t, n, B_t, A_t)$ be the equilibrium wage in period t.

Now we can analyze what is the effect of an unexpected rise in period t of the natural resource endowment. First of all note that this increase does not affect productivity levels B_t and A_t. A current increase in n will influence investment in intangible capital and so it will affect productivity in the future but not in the present. Therefore, given B_t, A_t, and k_t, an increase in the natural resource endowment will increase the demand for labor in the x_1 − sector; the $1-l_{1t}$ schedule in Figure 1 will shift to left. As a result, the wage will rise, some plants in the x_2 − sector must shut down and the equilibrium price p_{2t} will rise. The amount of labor employed in this sector will fall exactly in the same amount it raises in the x_1 − sector. The fall in the aggregate demand for intermediate good 2 during this adjustment process responds only to the increase in p_{2t}, since that demand is not affected by the increase in the natural resource endowment.

It is not difficult to show that, in equilibrium, the elasticity of the wage with respect to the natural resource endowment in period t, given B_t, A_t, and k_t, is

$$\frac{\partial w_t}{\partial n}\frac{n}{w_t} = \frac{\alpha(1-\theta)}{1+\left(1+\alpha(1-\theta)/\theta\right)l_{2t}/l_{1t}} \equiv E_{w_t,n}.\text{[8]} \tag{25}$$

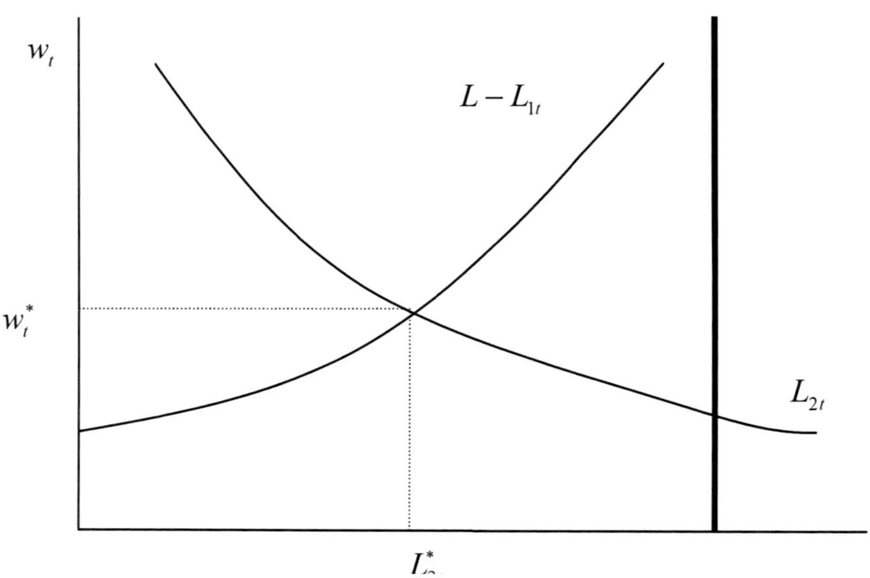

Figure 1. The labor market.

[8] See Appendix.

The ratio l_{2t}/l_{1t} is decreasing in the parameter π, which means that the lower the effectiveness of institutions the larger the share of labor employed in the natural resource sector. In turn, this means that, everything else equal, the rise in wages implied by a resource boom will be higher in economies with low quality institutions.

The next question we want to address in this Section is what happens to current per capita income when there is a rise in the natural resource endowment. Taking into account all the optimality conditions in production and the free entry conditions into the intermediate sectors, total factor income plus dividends per capita is equal to

$$r_{kt}k_t + r_{nt}n + w_t + d_{1t} + d_{2t} = y_t - I_{zt} \cdot l_{2t}/\eta_2, \tag{26}$$

With $d_{1t} = 0$ and $d_{2t} = (r_{zt}z_t - I_{zt})l_{2t}/\eta_2$, where y_t is the final output per capita. Notice that the right side of this equation is measured NIPA income since investment in intangible capital is not included in the national accounts. Given A_t, B_t, and k_t, the key factor that determines the equilibrium effect of a rise in the natural resource endowment on both current final output and factor rents is the response of the composite intermediate good, $H_t/L \equiv h_t$, to changes in n. It can be shown that the effect of rise in n on current output satisfies

$$\frac{dy_t}{dn} > 0 \Leftrightarrow \left(\frac{1-\alpha}{\alpha}\right)\left(\frac{\gamma}{1-\gamma}\right)\left(\frac{\alpha(1-\theta) - E_{w_t,n}}{\alpha(1-\theta)+\alpha}\right) < 1.^{9} \tag{27}$$

Notice that the elasticity of the wage with respect to the natural resource endowment is smaller than $\alpha(1-\theta)$, see expression (25), and so that the third term in brackets is always positive. Therefore, a sufficient condition for a positive effect of the natural endowment on current output is the term $(1-\alpha)\gamma/\alpha(1-\gamma)$ being not greater than one. The key parameter in this expression is γ, which measures the share of intangible capital in the output of intermediate good 2 or, in other words, the importance of intangible capital in total factor productivity. We will show below that this sufficient condition is satisfied for plausible parameter values.

With respect to the effect of a rise in n on per capita income, it is easy to check that total rents from the x_1 – sector will rise and that the effect on physical capital income has the same sign as the effect on current output. While profits per plant in the x_2 – sector will tend to rise because the increase in the price outweighs the increase in the wage, they also can fall because more resources will be needed to increase the future stock of intangible capital. However, since less plants will be operating in this sector, the overall effect on per capita dividends will be very small. As a result, the overall effect of a rise in n on per capita income will be positive for plausible parameter values.

---

[9] See appendix for the proof.

4. Balanced Growth

In this section we will analyze the existence and properties of a balanced growth equilibrium. We define a balanced growth equilibrium as a situation in which per capita variables and productivity all grow at the same rate g, and goods prices and employment shares remain constant over time.

Let us define $k \equiv k_t / (1+g)^t$, $z \equiv z_t / (1+g)^t$, $y \equiv y_t / (1+g)^t$, and $w \equiv w_t / (1+g)^t$.

Then, we can express the equilibrium labor shares of equations (18) and (23) along a balanced growth as follows

$$l_1(\pi_n, z, k, n, w) = \left[\varphi(1-\theta)(1-\alpha)\left(\frac{\Psi \mathrm{B}(\pi_n) z^{\gamma}}{1+g} \right)^{1-\theta} \frac{k^{\theta}}{w} \right]^{\frac{1}{\theta+\alpha(1-\theta)}}, \tag{28}$$

$$l_2(\pi_n, z, k, n, w) = \left[(1-\varphi)(1-\theta)(1-\gamma)\left(\Psi \mathrm{B}(\pi_n) z^{\gamma} \right)^{1-\theta} \frac{k^{\theta}}{w} \right]^{\frac{1}{\theta}}, \tag{29}$$

Where $w = w^*(\pi_n, z, k, n)$ represents the implicit solution to the market clearing condition (24). It is easy to check that any change in the size of the barrier or in the capital stocks implies an overall effect on the labor shares that is fully captured by the response of wages to these changes, so $dl_j / d\pi_n = dl_j / dk = dl_j / dz = 0$, $j = 1,2$. In other words, a change in any of these variables implies a change in the equilibrium wage that totally offsets its effect on l_j. In particular, the effects of n on future productivity and on wages through the barrier, π_n, cancel out. As a result, the overall effect on l_1 of a change in n can be expressed as a function of $E_{w,n}$ alone:

$$\frac{l_1}{n}\frac{dl_1}{dn} = \left(\frac{\alpha(1-\theta) - E_{w,n}}{\theta + \alpha(1-\theta)} \right) \equiv E_{l_1,n}, \tag{30}$$

Where $E_{w,n}$ represents the balanced growth value of the wage elasticity defined in (25).

Therefore, the steady state equilibrium values of the employment shares can be expressed as functions of n alone, $l_j = l_j^*(n)$, which implies that steady state output, $y \equiv y_t / (1+g)^t$, is given by

$$y = \left(\Psi \mathrm{B}(\pi_n) z^{\gamma}\right)^{1-\theta} k^{\theta} \lambda(n),$$

$$\text{With } \lambda(n) \equiv \varphi \left(\frac{(\eta_1 n)^{\alpha} l_1^{1-\alpha}}{1+g} \right)^{1-\theta} + (1-\varphi) l_2^{1-\theta}. \tag{31}$$

Moreover, we can solve for the steady state values of k and z using the first order conditions for physical capital and intangible capital given by equations (13) and (20), respectively. The solution to that system of equations will determine the steady state values of the capital stocks, and so of output, as a function of the natural resource endowment and the barrier to technology adoption:

$$z(n) = \left(\frac{\gamma(1-\varphi)(1-\theta)\eta_2}{r_z l_2^{\theta}} \right)^{\frac{1}{1-\gamma}} \left(\frac{\theta \lambda(n)}{r_k} \right)^{\frac{\theta}{(1-\theta)(1-\gamma)}} \left(\Psi \mathrm{B}(\pi_n)\right)^{\frac{1}{1-\gamma}}, \tag{32}$$

$$k(n) = \left(\frac{\gamma(1-\varphi)(1-\theta)\eta_2}{r_z l_2^{\theta}} \right)^{\frac{\gamma}{1-\gamma}} \left(\frac{\theta \lambda(n)}{r_k} \right)^{\frac{1-\gamma(1-\theta)}{(1-\theta)(1-\gamma)}} \left(\Psi B(\pi_n)\right)^{\frac{1}{1-\gamma}}, \tag{33}$$

$$y(n) = \left(\frac{\theta}{r_k} \right)^{\frac{\theta}{(1-\theta)(1-\gamma)}} \left(\frac{\gamma(1-\varphi)(1-\theta)\eta_2}{r_z l_2^{\theta}} \right)^{\frac{\gamma}{1-\gamma}} \left(\Psi \mathrm{B}(\pi_n)\right)^{\frac{1}{1-\gamma}} \lambda(n)^{1+\frac{\theta}{(1-\theta)(1-\gamma)}}. \tag{34}$$

In these expressions the returns to physical and intangible capital are evaluated, respectively, at their steady state values, $r_k = i + \delta_k$, $r_z = i + \delta_z$, $i = (1+g)/\beta - 1$. Now we are in the position of evaluating the long run effect of natural resources on output.

The model predicts that relative differences in y across countries will be determined by differences in both n and π, provided returns on capital are equalized across countries. Although we can suppose that in the long run there are no differences in the rates of return on physical capital, the implicit returns on intangible capital can be very different due to differences in the depreciation rate δ_z. We shall discuss the point below in the calibration exercise.

The relative endowment n has a direct effect on long run employment shares that is independent of the barrier to technology adoption, and an effect on the barrier itself that influences the productivity level through the term $B(\pi_n)$. Whereas the long run effect of π only influences output through its direct effect on the barrier. Lower values of π imply lower values of the institutional quality index π_n (better institutions), and so higher levels of $B(\pi_n)$.

Formally, taking into account that $dl_1/dn = -dl_2/dn$, we find that

$$\frac{dy}{dn} = \frac{y}{n}\left[-\frac{\gamma\pi_n}{(1-\gamma)(1+\pi_n)(1+n)} + \frac{\gamma\theta}{(1-\gamma)l_2}\frac{dl_1}{dn} + \frac{1-\gamma(1-\theta)}{(1-\theta)(1-\gamma)\lambda}\frac{d\lambda}{dn}\right], \tag{35}$$

Where $\frac{d\lambda}{dn} = \varphi(1-\theta)\left(\frac{(\eta_1 n)^{\alpha} l_1^{1-\alpha}}{1+g}\right)^{1-\theta}\frac{\alpha}{n}\left[1-\frac{\gamma(1-\alpha)}{(1-\gamma)\alpha}E_{l_1,n}\right].$

The first term in the brackets with a minus sign measures the effect of the barrier on output, the second and the third terms are both positive and account for the long run overall effect of n on the composite intermediate input.

5. Calibration of the Model and Relative Incomes

In this section we use US balanced growth observations to identify some of the parameters of the model, but others like γ and δ_z that refer to the investment in intangible capital cannot be identified because productivity investment is not reported in the NIPA. In doing this calibration exercise we follow the methodology proposed by Parente and Prescott (1994, 2000). The key parameter in these previous studies is the share of intangible capital in aggregate output. They demonstrate that this parameter should be large for the model to account for large income disparities; they estimate a value well above 50 percent and show that the model with total factor productivity differentials accounts well for the observed pattern in incomes when the return on intangible capital differs across countries.

In our case, the share of intangible capital in aggregate output is given by $\gamma(1-\theta)$, and its value is also crucial. We find a value of 20 percent for this term, and a total share of capital (physical and intangible) around 40 percent. The reason of this discrepancy with the value reported in the above studies is that we have a natural endowment input in production; this, in turn, entails some additional difficulty to identify the parameters because of the lack in data on natural resource endowments. To overcome this difficulty we will use the natural capital share in national wealth published in Gylfason and Zoega (2001). We will show that our model with natural resources accounts well for the relative income differences between the US and some Latin American countries, even assuming equal returns on intangible capital. For an African economy like Niger or Egypt we conclude that differences in the return on intangible capital must be large.

Calibration

In the US measured investment or investment in physical capital has remained around 20 percent over the last decades, and measured income has been growing on average about 2 percent per year. Assuming a depreciation rate of 6 percent, these growth facts imply a steady state capital/GDP ratio of 2.5. Normalizing per capita GDP to one, this means that $k = 2.5$. Moreover, assuming a long run interest rate of 5 percent (a discount factor of $\beta = 0.97$), it follows from the market clearing condition for the final good and the first order condition of physical capital that $\theta = 0.18$. This calibration results coincide with those of Parente and Prescott's.

To calibrate other key parameters like γ and n is not so straight forward. We take Parente and Prescott's (2000) estimations of unmeasured investment. They find that the amount of resources invested in intangible capital represents between 30 and 50 percent of GDP (measured output). This implies that total (measured + unmeasured) output is between 1.3 and 1.5 times GDP. As in Parente and Presott (2000), we suppose that unmeasured investment is 50 percent of GDP.

Since the minimum number of workers to operate a plant in each sector in the long run is not important for our purposes, we suppose that $\eta_1 = \eta_2 = 1$. The depreciation rate of intangible capital is important to the determine the steady state value of the intangible capital stock; we set $\delta_z = 0.025$ as in Parente and Prescott (2000). Under the assumption that half of the resources of the economy go to unmeasured investment, we get that $(g+\delta_z)z \cdot l_2 = 0.5$; taking into account that per capita GDP is $c+(g+\delta_k)k$ and total output is $y = c+(g+\delta_k)k+(g+\delta_z)z \cdot l_2$, it follows that $y = 1.5$. The share of labor employed in the primary sector has remained steady about 2 percent since 1987.[10] So we set $l_2 = 0.98$ and find that $z = 11.33$, which is very close to the 11.11 estimated by Parente and Prescott. Dividing the steady state solution of z over the steady state solution of k and taking the calibrated values of these capital stocks, it follows that

$$\lambda(n) = 4\gamma(1-\varphi).$$

Next, we need some measure of the share of natural resource rents in total capital rents. We take from Gylfason and Zoega (2001) the US natural capital share in national wealth in 1994 (this is the only year available), defined as the share of natural capital in total capital. Total capital includes natural capital, physical capital and human capital, and the US share of natural capital in that year was 4.1 percent. This is not exactly the participation of natural input rents in our model but we can take it as a good proxy. It is true that we don't have human capital but an important part of the returns on it are contemplated in the returns on intangible capital. Parente and Prescott (2000) report that the amount invested by firms in human capital is about 7.5 percent of GDP, including the resources used up in the process of learning how to use software and the cost of skill training programs; to the extent that on the job training and learning have important returns for firms in terms of productivity, our measure of the natural capital share seems reasonable. Therefore, suppose that per capita rents coming from the natural resource endowment are 4.1 percent of total capital rents. This implies that $r_n n = 0.045$. Taking into account the market clearing condition for the natural

[10] This share corresponds to the fraction of full time –equivalent workers employed in agriculture, forestry, fishing and mining. Source: Bureau of Economic Research..

resource endowment and the first order condition of this input from the plant's problem, it yields

$$\Psi \mathrm{B}(\pi_n) z^{\gamma} n^{\alpha} = \frac{r_n n(1+g)}{\alpha l_1^{1-\alpha}}.$$

The labor income share in primary sector income has remained roughly constant about 58 percent since 1987 in the US. So we set $\alpha = 0.42$. Moreover, we fix the scale parameter Ψ equal to one, and the institutions' index equal to zero, $\pi = 0$, which reflects the assumption that there are no barriers to technology adoption in the US economy. With all these parameter values, the above expression reduces to $(11.33)^{\gamma} n^{0.42} = 1.08$. And the final good market clearing condition reads $(11.33)^{\gamma(1-\theta)} \lambda(n) = 1.28$. Taking into account the expression for $\lambda(n)$ in (31) we are left with three equations and three unknown parameters, γ, φ and n. The solution to this system of equations is $\gamma = 0.25$, $\varphi = 0.24$, $n = 4.08$.

Relative Incomes

In this section we conduct a simple exercise and compute the relative incomes predicted by the model taking as a reference some Latin American economies and two African countries. With respect to intangible capital we presume that in all those countries aggregate unmeasured investment per capita should be smaller than in the US, but we really don't know. Yet we have no reason to suppose that a given industrial plant does not invest in intangible capital as much as the average US plant does, so we shall assume that the stock of intangible capital per plant is the same across countries. The aggregate investment in intangible capital as a share of GDP will be determined by the number of operating plants undertaking improvements in productivity, l_2, and the depreciation rate δ_z. That is, country *j*'s investment in intangible capital will be given by $(g+\delta_{zj}) z l_{2j}$.

We shall assume first that all countries have the same returns on both kinds of capital. Under this assumption, expression (34) implies that the relative US output with respect to country *j*'s is:

$$\frac{y_{US}}{y_j} = (1+\pi_n)^{\frac{\gamma}{1-\gamma}} \left(\frac{l_{2US}}{l_{2j}}\right)^{\frac{\theta\gamma}{1-\gamma}} \left(\frac{\lambda_{US}}{\lambda_j}\right)^{1+\frac{\theta}{(1-\theta)(1-\gamma)}}. \tag{36}$$

Average employment in the primary sector as a share of the labor force for the selected countries during the last decade is 0.1 for Argentina, 0.23 for Mexico, 0.31 for Peru, 0.35 for Egypt, and 0.88 for Niger.[11] Under the assumptions made on intangible capital, these figures imply that the corresponding intangible capital investment shares are 0.45 for Argentina, 0.39

for Mexico, 0.35 for Peru, 0.33 for Egypt and 0.06 for Niger. Let us denote this investment share by s_j. Then, country *j*'s per capita output will be $1+s_j$ times its per capita GDP. Therefore, our model economy predicts that the relative per capita GDP of the US with respect to country *j* should be close to its relative output (36) times $(1+s_j)2/3$.

To complete this exercise we need the measured (reported) investment shares and the natural capital shares for the selected countries.[12] Proceeding as before with the US, we find that physical capital/GDP ratios are 2.8 for Argentina, 2.5 for Mexico, 2.6 for Peru, 2.6 for Egypt, and 1.3 for Niger. Given the stocks of physical and intangible capital, we can compute the implied λ_j's of the model and so the estimated n_j values. Then, we get an estimation of the US relative natural resource income using the natural capital shares reported in Gylfason and Zoega (2001) and our model estimates of capital incomes. With this information and using the first order condition for the natural resource endowment, we can compute the size of the barrier implied by the model as follows:

$$(1+\pi_n)^{\gamma} = (r_n n)_{US,j} \left(\frac{n^j}{n^{US}}\right)^{\alpha} \left(\frac{l_1^j}{l_1^{US}}\right)^{1-\alpha}, \tag{37}$$

Where $(r_n n)_{US,j}$ represents the relative natural capital income of the US with respect to country *j*. The following Table reports the results.

In Table 1 $y_{US,j}$ represents the relative output in (36). The predictions of the model for relative per capita GDP differences are acceptable for Latin American countries, especially for Argentina and Mexico, but they are not for the selected African ones. We should have obtained a different ranking for Egypt and Niger. Nevertheless, recall that these relative incomes have been calculated under the assumption that the return on intangible capital was the same across countries. In view of the results, the discrepancy between these returns must be larger between the US and the African countries than between the US and the Latin American ones. The model also predicts larger barriers in countries with larger natural capital share as reported above (not in Table 1), except for Niger and Egypt, where the predicted pattern seems reversed.

We conclude that the augmented model with natural resources and intangible capital with total factor productivity differentials predicts relative incomes of the order of magnitude consistent with some Latin American countries. Moreover, the relationship between resource dependence, or natural capital share in national wealth, and the institutions quality index tends to have the negative sign found in empirical studies as reported in the Introduction. More generally, for plausible parameter values, the model predicts a positive relation between endowments and per worker income as Easterly and Levine (2003) find in their empirical investigation.

[11] FAO statistics, several years.

Table 1. Model Relative Incomes 1965-1997

	$(r_n n)_{US,j}$	$(1+\pi_n)^{\gamma}$	$y_{US,j}$	**Model** p.c.$GDP_{US,j}$	**1997** p.c.$GDP_{US,j}$
Argentina	0.59	2.3	2.32	2.24	2.49
Mexico	0.79	2.9	3.77	3.49	3.92
Peru	0.61	4.1	5.34	4.80	6.80
Egypt	1.13	8.9	14.3	12.68	9.20
Niger	0.13	1.7	3.40	8.16	35.10

6. Concluding Remarks

We have developed a three sector model with natural resources, intangible capital and barriers to technology adoption. We have followed the methodology proposed in Parente and Prescott (1994, 200) and evaluated the predictions of the model for relative income differentials for a selected group of countries. We have shown that the model predicts pretty well relative incomes between the US and some Latin American countries, but it does a bad job with our selected African economies. Furthermore, for those countries where the model has a good fit, the ranking of the size of the barriers predicted by the model is consistent with the empirical relation between natural resource abundance and the quality of institutions.

Certainly, to fully address whether the proposed model accounts for the observed pattern of economic development we should extend the list of countries and built more complete sets of data, especially for intangible capital investments. The work presented in this chapter is just a first step in that direction.

Appendix 1. Temporary Equilibrium

The equilibrium relation between the wage and the natural resource endowment. The amount of labor employed in each intermediate sector:

$$l_{1t}=\left(\frac{\varphi(1-\theta)(1-\alpha)A_t^{1-\theta}(\eta_{1t}n)^{\alpha(1-\theta)}k_t^{\theta}}{w_t}\right)^{\frac{1}{\theta+\alpha(1-\theta)}},$$

$$l_{2t}=\left(\frac{(1-\varphi)(1-\theta)(1-\gamma)B_t^{1-\theta}}{w_t}\right)^{1/\theta}k_t,$$

[12] For all these observations we use the data reported in Gylfason and Zoega (2001) from the World Bank. The investment shares are averages for the period 1965-98, and the natural capital shares correspond to 1994 (only year available).

Where $B_t = \Psi \mathrm{B}(\pi_n)(1+g)^{(1-\gamma)t} z_t^{\gamma}$ and $A_t = B_{t-1}$. Given A_t, B_t, k_t, and n, the equation $l_{1t} + l_{2t} - 1 = 0$ determines the equilibrium wage w_t^*. Using the implicit function theorem to get $\partial w_t / \partial n$, it follows that

$$\frac{\partial w_t}{\partial n}\frac{n}{w_t} = \frac{\alpha(1-\theta)\theta}{\theta + \left(\theta(1-\alpha)+\alpha\right) l_{2t}/l_{1t}} \equiv E_{w_t,n}.$$

It is easy to check that l_{2t}/l_{1t} is increasing in $\mathrm{B}(\pi_n)$ and so it decreases with π. Therefore, the lower the quality of institutions the larger the elasticity of the wage with respect to the resource endowment, $E_{w_t,n}$.

The effect on current aggregate output of an increase in n. Given A_t, B_t, and k_t, the effect on aggregate output of a rise in n in period t is determined by $dy_t/dn = k_t^{\theta}\, d\left(h_t^{1-\theta}\right)/dn$, where $h_t^{1-\theta} = \varphi\left(A_t(\eta_{1t} n)^{\alpha} l_{1t}^{1-\alpha}\right)^{1-\theta} + (1-\varphi)\left(B_t l_{2t}\right)^{1-\theta}$. To obtain this derivative evaluated at equilibrium, we use the following conditions. From the optimality in the production of the final good we get:

$$(1-\varphi)(X_{2t}/L)^{1-\theta}\Big/\left(\varphi(X_{1t}/L)^{1-\theta}\right) = p_{2t}B_t l_{2t}\Big/\left(p_{1t}A_t(\eta_{1t}n)^{\alpha} l_{1t}^{1-\alpha}\right).$$

From the free entry conditions into the intermediate sectors we have that

$$(1-\gamma)\, p_{2t}B_t = w_t \text{ and } (1-\alpha)\, p_{1t}A_t(\eta_{1t}n)^{\alpha} l_{1t}^{-\alpha} = w_t.$$

And finally, from the labor market clearing condition we have that

$$\frac{dl_{1t}}{dn} = -\frac{dl_{2t}}{dn}.$$

Taking into account all these equilibrium conditions, it follows that

$$\frac{dy_t}{dn} = k_t^{\theta}(1-\theta)\varphi\left(A_t(\eta_{1t}n)^{\alpha} l_{1t}^{1-\alpha}\right)^{1-\theta} \cdot \frac{\alpha}{n}\left(1 - \frac{(1-\alpha)}{\alpha}\frac{\gamma}{(1-\gamma)}E_{l_{1t},n}\right),$$

$$E_{l_1,n} \equiv \frac{dl_{1t}}{dn}\frac{n}{l_{1t}} = \frac{\alpha(1-\theta) - E_{w_t,n}}{\theta(1-\alpha)+\alpha}.$$

Therefore,

$$\frac{dy_t}{dn} > 0 \Leftrightarrow \left(\frac{1-\alpha}{\alpha}\right)\left(\frac{\gamma}{1-\gamma}\right)\left(\frac{\alpha(1-\theta)-E_{w_t,n}}{\alpha(1-\theta)+\alpha}\right) < 1.$$

Recall that $E_{w_t,n} \in (0, \alpha(1-\theta))$ and that the larger π the higher $E_{w_t,n}$. So a positive effect on output of a rise in n becomes more likely the larger π.

APPENDIX 2. BALANCED GROWTH

Let $k \equiv k_t/(1+g)^t$, $z \equiv z_t/(1+g)^t$, $y \equiv y_t/(1+g)^t$, $w \equiv w_t/(1+g)^t$, and let the rest of variables without the time subscript denote simply their stationary values.

The prices of intermediate goods along the balanced growth paths will be determined by

$$p_1 = \frac{\varphi(1-\theta)k^\theta}{\left(\Psi \mathrm{B}(\pi_n) z^\gamma (\eta_1 n)^\alpha l_1^{1-\alpha}\right)^\theta},$$

$$p_2 = \frac{(1-\varphi)(1-\theta)k^\theta}{\left(\Psi \mathrm{B}(\pi_n) z^\gamma l_2\right)^\theta}.$$

The labor shares in each sector along the balanced growth path are given, respectively, by the following functions:

$$l_1(\pi_n, z, k, n, w) = \left[\varphi(1-\theta)(1-\alpha)\left(\frac{\Psi \mathrm{B}(\pi_n) z^\gamma}{1+g}\right)^{1-\theta} \frac{k^\theta}{w}\right]^{\frac{1}{\theta+\alpha(1-\theta)}},$$

$$l_2(\pi_n, z, k, n, w) = \left[(1-\varphi)(1-\theta)(1-\gamma)\left(\Psi \mathrm{B}(\pi_n) z^\gamma\right)^{1-\theta} \frac{k^\theta}{w}\right]^{\frac{1}{\theta}},$$

where $w = w^*(\pi_n, z, k, n)$ is the implicit solution to $l_1(\pi_n, z, k, n, w) + l_2(\pi_n, z, k, n, w) - 1 = 0$. It is easy to check that $dl_j/d\pi_n = dl_j/dk = dl_j/dz = 0$, $j = 1,2$. A change in any of these variables implies a change in the equilibrium wage that totally offsets its effect on l_j. In particular, the effects of n on future productivity and on wages through the barrier, π_n, cancel out. As a result, the overall effect on l_1 of a change in n is determined by the elasticity $E_{l_1,n}$ as defined in the temporary equilibrium:

$$\frac{dl_1}{dn} = \frac{l_1}{n}\left(\frac{\alpha(1-\theta) - E_{w,n}}{\theta + \alpha(1-\theta)}\right).$$

It follows that the steady state equilibrium values of the employment shares can be expressed as functions of n alone, $l_j = l_j^*(n)$. Define $\lambda(n) \equiv \left(H_t / LB_t\right)^{1-\theta}$, evaluated at the balanced growth equilibrium. That is,

$$\lambda(n) = \varphi\left(\frac{(\eta_1 n)^{\alpha} l_1^{1-\alpha}}{1+g}\right)^{1-\theta} + (1-\varphi) l_2^{1-\theta}.$$

Then, we can write per capita output as $y = \left(\Psi \mathrm{B}(\pi_n) z^{\gamma}\right)^{1-\theta} k^{\theta} \lambda(n)$, and obtain from the first order conditions for k and z that:

$$k = \left(\frac{\theta}{r_k}\lambda(n)\right)^{\frac{1}{1-\theta}} \Psi \mathrm{B}(\pi_n) z^{\gamma},$$

$$z = \left(\frac{\gamma(1-\varphi)(1-\theta)\eta_2\left(\Psi \mathrm{B}(\pi_n)\right)^{1-\theta} k^{\theta}}{r_z l_2^{\theta}}\right)^{\frac{1}{1-\gamma(1-\theta)}},$$

where $r_k = i + \delta_k$, $r_z = i + \delta_z$, $i = (1+g)/\beta - 1$. The solution to this system determines the steady state values of the capital stocks, and output, as a function of the natural resource endowment:

$$z(n) = \left(\frac{\gamma(1-\varphi)(1-\theta)\eta_2}{r_z l_2^{\theta}}\right)^{\frac{1}{1-\gamma}} \left(\frac{\theta\lambda(n)}{r_k}\right)^{\frac{\theta}{(1-\theta)(1-\gamma)}} \left(\Psi \mathrm{B}(\pi_n)\right)^{\frac{1}{1-\gamma}},$$

$$k(n) = \left(\frac{\gamma(1-\varphi)(1-\theta)\eta_2}{r_z l_2^{\theta}}\right)^{\frac{\gamma}{1-\gamma}} \left(\frac{\theta\lambda(n)}{r_k}\right)^{\frac{1-\gamma(1-\theta)}{(1-\theta)(1-\gamma)}} \left(\Psi B(\pi)\right)^{\frac{1}{1-\gamma}}.$$

$$y(n) = \left(\frac{\theta}{r_k}\right)^{\frac{\theta}{(1-\theta)(1-\gamma)}} \left(\frac{\gamma(1-\varphi)(1-\theta)\eta_2}{r_z l_2^{\theta}}\right)^{\frac{\gamma}{1-\gamma}} \left(\Psi \mathrm{B}(\pi_n)\right)^{\frac{1}{1-\gamma}} \lambda(n)^{1+\frac{\theta}{(1-\theta)(1-\gamma)}}.$$

$$\frac{dy}{dn} = \frac{y}{n}\left[-\frac{\gamma\pi_n}{(1-\gamma)(1+\pi_n)(1+n)} + \frac{\gamma\theta}{(1-\gamma)l_2}\frac{dl_1}{dn} + \frac{1-\gamma(1-\theta)}{(1-\theta)(1-\gamma)\lambda}\frac{d\lambda}{dn}\right],$$

where $\frac{d\lambda}{dn} = \varphi(1-\theta)\left(\frac{(\eta_1 n)^{\alpha} l_1^{1-\alpha}}{1+g}\right)^{1-\theta} \frac{\alpha}{n}\left[1-\frac{\gamma(1-\alpha)}{(1-\gamma)\alpha}E_{l_1,n}\right].$

REFERENCES

Acemoglu, D. , Johnson, S., and Robinson, J. (2001): "The colonial origins of comparative development: an empirical investigation," *American Economic Review* 91, 1369-1401.

Acemoglu, D. , Johnson, S., and Robinson, J. (2004): "Institutions as the fundamental cause of long-run growth", *NBER WP* 10481.

Auty, R. (2001): "The political economy of resource-driven growth", *European Economic Review* 45, 839-846.

Barro, R., and Sala-i-Martin, X. (1995): "Technological diffusion, convergence, and growth," *NBER WP* 5151.

Bloom, D. E., Canning, D., and Sevilla, J. (2002): "Technological diffusion, conditional convergence, and economic growth", *NBER WP* 8713.

Easterly, W., and Levine, R. (2003): "Tropics, germs, and crops: how endowments influence economic development", *Journal of Monetary Economics* 50, 3-39.

Eaton, J., and Kortun, S. (1995): "Trade in ideas: patenting and productivity in the OECD," *NBER WP* 5049.

Engerman, S., and Sokoloff, K. (1997): "Factor endowments, institutions, and differential paths of growth among new world economies." In: Haber, S.H., (Ed.), *How Latin America fell behind.* Stanford, CA, 260-304.

Guilló, M.D., and Perez-Sebastian, F. (2003): "The curse and blessing of fixed specific factors in small open economies," IVIE, *WP-AD* 2003-36. *Journal of Development Economics, forthcoming 2006.*

Gylfason, T. (2000): *"Natural resources, education and economic development",* CEPR discussion paper No. 2594.

Gylfason, T., and Zoega, G. (2001): *"Natural resources and economic growth: the role of investment,"* mimeo, University of Iceland.

Isham, J., L. Pritchett, M. Woolcock, and G. Busby (2003), "The varieties of the resource experience: how natural resource export structures affect the political economy of economic growth", *World Development Report,* World Bank, Washington D.C.

Hall, R. E., and Jones, C. (1999): "Why do some countries produce so much more output than others?", *The Quarterly Journal of Economics*, February, 83-116.

Jones, C. (1995): "R&D based models of economic growth," *Journal of Political Economy,* CIII, 1127-1170.

Parente, S. L., and Prescott, E. (1994): "Barriers to technology adoption and development", *The Journal of Political Economy*, vol. 102, 2, 298-321.

Parente, S. L., and Prescott, E. (2000): *Barriers to Riches,* the MIT Press, Cambridge, MA.

North, D. (1990): *Institutions, Institutional change, and economic performance,* Cambridge University Press, Cambridge, UK.

Sachs, J. D., and Warner, A. M., (2001): "The curse of natural resources", *European Economic Review* 45, 827-838.

Woolcock, M., Pritchett, L., and Isham, J. (2001): The social foundations of poor economic growth in resource-rich economies. In: Auty, R. M. (Ed.), *Resource abundance and economic development.* UNU/WIDER Studies in Economic Development , Oxford University Press, New York.

In: Natural Resources
Editor: Jeanette B. Pauling

ISBN 978-1-60456-982-7

Chapter 7

ECONOMIC INPUT FOR RESTORATION DECISION MAKING

Éva-Terézia Vesely
Landcare Research, Auckland, New Zealand

ABSTRACT

Restoration is increasingly recognised as an important tool in the resource manager's toolkit. From an anthropocentric view, the restoration of damaged, degraded or destroyed ecosystems aims to reinstate the flow of ecosystem goods and services that contribute to human well being. The application of micro-economic tools can provide input into decision making with respect to ecosystem restoration. This chapter develops a framework that highlights when and how economic input fits into restoration decision making and discusses a series of challenges with the economic analysis of restoration projects. The first elements of the framework links a series of micro-economic tools – ex-ante and ex-post cost–benefit, cost–effectiveness and cost–utility analyses – to the different stages of the adaptive restoration process, while the second element provides guidance for selection among the tools. The practical application of the tools in a restoration context is expected to be challenging from a number of perspectives: lack of costing data, incomplete understanding of ecosystems, substitution and complementarity among restoration projects, non-market multidimensional outcomes, long timeframes, and potential for irreversibilities.

INTRODUCTION

Restoration is becoming an increasingly important intervention as more ecosystems become degraded and demands for their services continue to grow (Clewell 2000, Aronson and Le Floc'h 2000, Cunningham 2002, MA 2005a, Aronson et al. 2007). This chapter investigates when and how micro-economic input focusing on the economic and cost efficiency criteria fits into restoration decision making and how the particularities of restoration projects are reflected in economic analyses. To set the scene, the use of the concept of restoration in the literature is reviewed and motivations for restoration identified. The adaptive restoration process is then introduced with a range of economic tools linked to its different stages accompanied by a process for selection among the tools. This is followed by a discussion of a series of challenges posed by restoration projects for economic analysis. The chapter concludes with a short review of the main findings.

Ecological Restoration

The term restoration is used in a flexible and inclusive manner in the literature (e.g., Aronson et al. 1993, Wyant et al. 1995, SER 2004a, Davis and Slobodkin 2004). The latest definition from the Society for Ecological Restoration defines it as the process of assisting the recovery of an ecosystem that has been degraded, damaged or destroyed (SER 2004a). Bradshaw (1997) argues that, from an ecological point of view, restoration can be applied to ecosystems, habitats, communities, species, water or soil quality, or to some other ecological characteristic of the degraded or damaged area. Often, restoration involves the reconstruction of antecedent physical, hydrologic and morphologic conditions, chemical cleanup or adjustment of the environment, and biological manipulation (USNRC 1992).

There are a number of concepts used to refer to various degrees of restoration: (1) restoration: to restore to a former state or to an unimpaired condition; (2) rehabilitation: to restore to a previous condition or status without the expectation to be in as original or healthy a state as if it had been restored; (3) remediation: to rectify with emphasis on the process rather than on the endpoint reached; (4) reclamation: to bring back to a proper state without the implication of returning it to an original state but rather to a useful one; and (5) reallocation: to impose new uses on the site while disregarding the indigenous ecosystem (Hobbs and Norton 1996, Bradshaw 1997, SER 2004a). Ecological restoration in a holistic sense is the process of assisting the recovery of an impaired ecosystem in terms of species composition and community structure, ecological functioning, self-organisation, and the capacity of self-sustainability (Clewell and Aronson 2007). Ecological fidelity is achieved through the combination of structural replication, functional success and durability (Higgs 1997). However, where it is impossible or extremely expensive to restore composition and structure, alternative goals are appropriate (Hobbs and Harris 2001).

Restoration can be motivated by a range of issues such as the satisfaction of permit conditions that mandate compensatory mitigation, the fostering of biodiversity from genetic to landscape level, the atonement for environmental damage or cultural and spiritual renewal (Clewell and Aronson 2006). Restoration can also be conducted to improve the flow of ecosystem goods and services, thus enhancing human well being (Wyant et al. 1995, Clewell 2000, Aronson and Le Floc'h 2000, SER 2004b, Clewell and Aronson 2006). This is referred to as natural capital restoration (Aronson et al. 2007), renewable natural capital being any stock of natural resources or environmental assets (such as soil, water, atmosphere, and ecosystems) which provides a flow of useful goods and services both now and in the future (Pearce and Turner 1990, Daly 1994). Ecological restoration in a holistic sense, rehabilitation and reallocation can all contribute to the restoration of natural capital and be pursued simultaneously in different landscape units (Aronson et al. 2007). While residents of a few wealthy nations can afford to consider the restoration of ecosystems solely for psychological, humanistic, or biological reasons, Clewell (2000), Aronson et al. (2007) and others argue that, in most regions of the world, an increase in natural goods and services must be the primary rationale for restoration. Indifferent the motivations, the micro-economic tools discussed in this chapter can inform the allocation of resources to restoration and the choice among different restoration options.

MICRO-ECONOMIC TOOLS

Ecological input has traditionally dominated restoration decision-making, but there have been numerous calls for a broadening of the included perspectives (Leiderman 1993, Cairns 1995, Higgs 1997, Holl and Howarth 2000, Lackey 2001, Allen 2003, Davis and Slobodkin 2004, Harris and van Diggelen 2006). Cairns (1995, p.9) justifies such an enlargement of the included perspectives by the amount of funding and resources involved, and the long time frame of restoration projects:

> Not only have nonscientists in a wide variety of field and places undertaken ecological restoration projects, but the field requires the input and cooperation of society to be successful. ... [P]rojects require approval of society or its representatives, significant funding, a long-term commitment to goals, and significant allocation of human, economic, and biological resources. Therefore, communication among disciplines and between scientists, engineers and the general public and its decision makers is crucial.

Lackey (2001), Allen (2003) and Harris and van Diggelen (2006) argue for a broadening of perspectives based on restoration involving societal decisions on appropriate end points. Furthermore, Davis and Slobodkin (2004, p. 2) argue from an opportunity cost perspective and suggest a broad perspective that includes economic arguments as well:

> Restorationists and their supporters must make their cases in the same socio-politico arena as any other advocacy group and justify the merits of their preferences to the various stakeholders in the same way, using social, cultural, economic, health and ethical arguments.

Holl and Howarth (2000, p. 260) give economics a prominent role in the success of large scale restoration initiatives:

> [I]t is essential that insights from ecology and economics be brought together if restoration efforts are to succeed on a large scale.

Traditionally, no economic argument was used in support of restoration despite the lack of funding being identified as the most common obstacle to restoration (King 1991), and the inclusion of economic considerations was slow to progress. Leiderman (1993) pointed out that even the elementary economic aspects of the restoration projects are rarely tackled. The lack of attention to costs in the restoration literature was highlighted by both Edwards and Abivardi (1997) and Holl and Howarth (2000). Potential explanations of the reticence of restorationists to consider the economic aspects of restoration projects included adversity to quantifying environmental values in economic terms due to restorationists' belief in the inherent value of intact ecosystems; the different disciplinary perspectives of economists and ecologists; and the view of restoration and economics as opposing forces (Holl and Howarth 2000).

The concept of natural capital restoration provided a platform for the emergence of an alternative view in which restoration and economics became linked to each other with ecological restoration enabling the increase of natural capital (Clewell 2000, Winterhalder et al. 2004, Aronson et al. 2006, Farley and Daly 2006):

> We must restore impaired ecosystems if we are ever to regain the natural capital necessary to prevent continued economic and social decay and to approach economic and ecological health and sustainability (Winterhalder et al., 2004, p. 3).

Restoration thus can be conceptualized as an investment, while degradation can be thought of as disinvestment in natural capital assets. The decision to restore becomes a resource allocation decision. At the most basic level it involves the allocation of land and the acceptance of the opportunity cost involved (the land allocated to the restoration project is not converted to other land uses that could generate rent). If self-sustaining (autogenic) recovery is possible, then refraining from conversion and extraction might be all that is required. However, often there are a series of indirect and direct threats that cause ecosystem degradation. Restoration involves managing (potentially removing) such threats (e.g. by biological control of invasive species or institution development to deal with open access). Furthermore, the capacity of the ecosystem to recover in a self-sustaining fashion might have been compromised or the ecosystem might have been destroyed. In such cases active restoration involving the allocation of biological, manufactured and human resources is required. Such resources might be scarce and have an opportunity cost. Economics, "the science that explains the choices we make as we cope with scarcity" (McTaggart et al. 2003), with one of its central concepts, efficiency, can inform such allocation decisions. Although markets under highly restrictive conditions will lead to efficient allocation of resources, market failure in a restoration context is expected to be common due to, e.g., lack of property rights and perfect information (and the associated lack of markets and the existence of externalities). Thus for economic (and cost) efficiency considerations to guide restoration decision-making the application of cost–benefit (and cost–effectiveness or cost–utility) analyses will be necessary.

Cost–Benefit Analysis

Cost–benefit analysis is used to identify how the allocation of resources can be made more efficient in the sense of producing net gains in social welfare (Campbell and Brown 2003). It normally proceeds by assuming a preference-satisfaction account of welfare and maximisation of individual utility. Cost–benefit analysis normally proceeds by assuming a preference-satisfaction account of welfare and maximisation of individual utility. The test of efficiency to be used in practical decision making is the Kaldor-Hicks compensation test: situation A is an improvement over B if the gains are greater than the losses, so that the gainers could compensate the losers and still be better off (also referred to as potential Pareto improvement). Cost–benefit analysis compares the costs and benefits of the situation with and without the project. The costs and benefits are considered over the life of the project. This tool can be used as a filter, an evaluation tool or a contribution to an informal and multidimensional information system (Randall 1987).

Cost–benefit (or economic) analysis differs from financial analysis in three primary ways (Enters 1998). (1) Economic analysis considers social costs and benefits, whereas financial analysis considers costs and benefits from the perspective of specific individuals or groups. Distortions induced by regulations, subsidies, managed currencies and market imperfections all give rise to differences in economic and financial costs and reduce the applicability of market prices for valuing inputs and outputs for economic analysis. (2) When discounting is involved in the analysis, the appropriate social and private rates can be different, with social rates typically lower, reflecting a longer term perspective on resource value. (3) Externalities or non-market costs and benefits are typically ignored in financial analysis while they are an integral part of economic analysis.

The complex relationships among natural system inputs, human-controlled inputs, environmental attributes, and the services provided must be understood and quantified if the results of cost–benefit analysis are to be complete and reliable (Randall 1987). This stage of the cost–benefit analysis involves primarily descriptive analyses by natural scientists and natural resource managers. The next step is to assess what the changes in ecosystem goods and services as well as economic activities are worth in monetary terms. Once the magnitude in monetary terms and the temporal occurrence of the costs and benefits associated with a restoration project have been estimated, the net present value of the intervention equals the difference between the present value of the benefits and the present value of the costs (Campbell and Brown 2003). Discounting is used to find the present value (value at the base year) of future costs and benefits. If the net present value is greater than zero, the intervention will be a potential Pareto-improvement and will pass the cost–benefit filter.

There might be uncertainties associated with the identification and measurement of the costs and benefits. The incorporation of risk and uncertainty in cost–benefit analysis means that the net present value will now depend on the realisation of the variables subject to risk and uncertainty. The spreading of risks to many individuals implies, under a number of conditions, that a project can be evaluated only on the basis of its net present value (Arrow and Lind 1977). However, in practice, there are many situations where it is useful to know the distribution of the net present value of a project or policy: when the size or the risk of a project implies that its risks can not be effectively pooled; when the risks are borne disproportionately by some individuals and the affected individuals cannot spread the risks to all individuals by purchasing actuarially fair insurance; or when risks to a large extent have the form of "public bads" (Stæhr 2006). There are a range of options available to include risk and uncertainty in the economic analysis of restoration projects as discussed below.

The theoretically preferred manner of incorporating risk attitudes is to use certainty equivalents, sometimes termed certain monetary equivalents. Certainty equivalents are defined as the minimum amount that an individual would be willing to accept with certainty instead of facing the uncertain outcomes. Estimation of certainty equivalents requires detailed knowledge of (or assumptions about) risk preferences, and analysts are unlikely to have these data. To estimate certainty equivalents one must also be able to assign probabilities to the set of potential outcomes. It is often very difficult or impossible to make these assignments (USEPA 2000).

Probability-weighted sensitivity analysis of the net present value calculation can be carried out using Monte Carlo simulation (Treasury Board of Canada 1998, Campbell and Brown 2003). For each of the uncertain variables there is a density function specified that provides the probability that the variable is within any interval. The Monte Carlo simulation then repeatedly picks values for the uncertain variables as random numbers chosen according to their density function and for each set of values computes the net present value. As the number of repetitions of this process increases, the distribution of the generated set will approach that of the uncertain net present value.

Sensitivity analysis can take into account not only risks, but also to some extent uncertainty. The sensitivity analysis shows what happens to expected net present value when a variable is changed, but the chosen values for the variable need not be drawn from any well-defined distribution. In this sense, the effects of uncertainty in the form of sudden changes in existing variables can be analysed. Such analysis reveals how sensitive the estimated net present value is to given changes in the considered variables. The value of the variable for which expected net present value changes sign is called the switching value (the switching value for a given variable is conditional on all other variables retaining their expected values). The relative change needed to bring about a sign change is sometimes called the switching ratio. In some cases it might be useful to undertake sensitivity analysis changing two or more variables at the same time. This so-called scenario analysis is particularly useful if it is known that the chosen variables are closely correlated. With stress testing or analysis of extremes the worst/best case scenarios are calculated (Treasury Board of Canada 1998).

Cost–benefit analysis makes decision making more transparent and increases accountability (Sunstein 2002a, b, Pearce et al. 2006). It forces a wider view on decision-makers by insisting on all gains and losses of "utility" or "well-being" being counted and it can show the costs and benefits occurring to different social groups of beneficiaries and losers. This tool encourages considering any project or policy as one of a series of options, where the options might include variations in scale and timing. Through the process of discounting, it is explicit about accounting for the temporal distribution of costs and benefits (Pearce et al., 2006). Although the cost–benefit analysis offers a rigorous way of setting out the effects of commissioning an action, it is criticised for its anthropocentric outlook, its fundamentally utilitarian approach, its reliance on discounting and a neglect of questions of justice and rights (Holland 1995, O'Neill et al. 2008). Cost–benefit analysis has been applied, for example, to the restoration of wetlands in Denmark (Dubgaard et al. 2004), subtropical thicket (Mills et al. 2007) and fynbos ecosystems (Holmes et al. 2007) in South Africa, and forage grass in Arid Patagonia (Aguiar and Román 2007).

Cost–Effectiveness Analysis

Cost–effectiveness analysis can be used to find the least-cost means to meet a restoration objective expressed in non-monetary units. It requires cost data for each alternative under consideration and estimates of each alternative's output in the non-monetary unit selected. In practice, cost–effectiveness analysis tends to proceed with indicators of effectiveness chosen by experts (Pearce et al. 2006). By examining the input/output ratio (e.g., \$/ha of wetland restored), it identifies the option which achieves a target outcome at least cost or maximises the outcome measure subject to a cost constraint. For example, Macmillan et al. (1998) used this technique to investigate the cost-effectiveness of government expenditure on the restoration of woodlands in Scotland.

Cost–Utility Analysis

In cost–utility analysis the costs are computed via standard discounted cash flow analysis and the benefits are measured by multiple attributes in different units. For utility measurement the attributes are transformed, weighted and aggregated to derive an overall performance metric. This performance metric allows the effectiveness of unlike activities to be compared. Cost–utility analysis is well established in healthcare economics, and has emerging application in environmental and resource economics (Cullen et al. 1999, 2001). For example, Cullen et al. (2005) use an indicator they call conservation-output protection-years (COPY) for measuring the cost–effectiveness of multiple-species conservation projects in New Zealand. Utility in this case refers to the change that occurs in a species' conservation status. Caution is warranted when the evaluated projects have multiple outputs that are not reflected in the selected performance indicator (Craig and Vesely 2007).

MICRO-ECONOMIC INPUT FOR AN ADAPTIVE RESTORATION PROCESS

The framework proposed in this chapter to identify when and how micro-economic input from the application of the tools described in the previous section fits into restoration decision making has at its core the adaptive management process (Figure 1). Adaptive management (Holling 1978, Walters 1986, Haney and Power 1996) has been recognised as a powerful tool for ecosystem restoration (Murray and Marmorek 2003, Hilderbrand et al. 2005, Clewell et al. 2007). Typically, an adaptive approach emphasizes the use of simple rather than elaborate models, followed by an update of the model based on observation and learning (Failing et al. 2004). It is a problem-solving environmental management approach (Murray and Marmorek 2003). It conceptualises problems from a given local place, and within a multi-scaled system (Norton and Steinemann 2002). It is characterised by high levels of communication between stakeholders, decision-makers and analysts, explicit accounting for uncertainty, active learning from management outcomes and surprises, and frequent adjustment of management controls in response to new information (Iovanna and Newbold 2007).

Adaptive management can be considered either passive or active. While the goal of passive adaptive management is to improve existing management approaches, the goal of active adaptive management is to learn by experimentation in order to determine the best management strategy. With passive adaptive management, as new knowledge is gained, the models are updated and management decisions are adapted accordingly. Active adaptive management involves planned experimental manipulation of a system, using either concurrent or sequential trials, accompanied by comprehensive monitoring and hypothesis testing. Once the monitoring results have confirmed which alternative is better, this is adopted as a management strategy (Failing et al. 2004).

For the purpose of this chapter, the adaptive restoration process is depicted as consisting of (1) context analysis, (2) identification of goals and objectives, (3) identification of strategy option(s), (4) implementation and monitoring, and (5) evaluation and adjustment (see Figure 1).

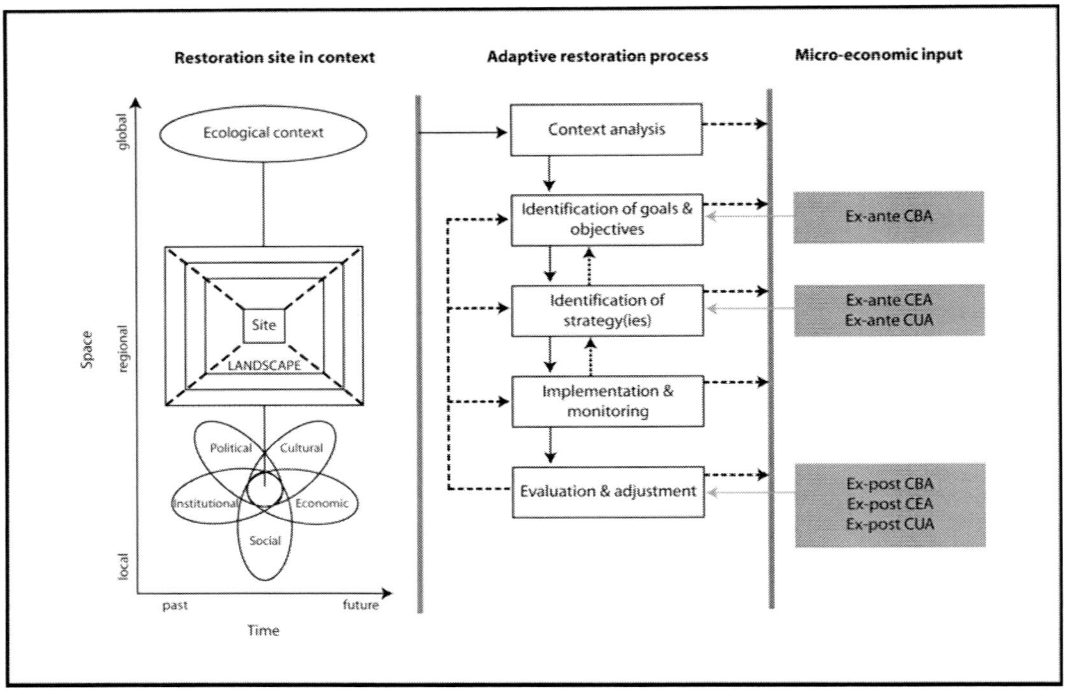

Figure 1. A framework for providing micro-economic input into restoration decision making (CBA: cost–benefit analysis, CEA: cost–effectiveness analysis, and CUA: cost–utility analysis).

The first stage in the adaptive restoration process is context analysis. Many believe that both the ecological and socio-economic contexts in which restoration will occur must be considered in setting restoration project goals; goals for a particular site, or more broadly for a landscape, will need to be determined iteratively by considering the ecological potential for restoration and matching this against societal desires (Wyant et al. 1995, Higgs 1997, Hobbs and Harris 2001, Winterhalder et al. 2004). This extended view of the relevant context is highlighted in Figure 1 by having the restoration site nested spatially and temporally with its specific ecological, social, cultural, economic, political and institutional context. Incorporating such place-specific knowledge in decision making is an important element of an adaptive management strategy (MA 2005a). Analysis of the ecological context includes considerations of the nature of the system being restored, the factors leading to degradation and the current state of the system in relation to biotic and abiotic thresholds (U.S. National Research Council 1992, Hobbs and Harris 2001, Winterhalder et al. 2004). Analysis of the social, cultural, political, institutional and economic contexts can identify enabling conditions and binding constraints for the restoration project. Issues of interest might cover societal desires, political legitimacy, relative power of the different stakeholders, local knowledge, environmental law, property regimes, resource availability, markets, externalities, and capacity for governance and implementation (Aronson et al. 2007). The link in Figure 1 from context analysis to micro-economic input highlights the need for economic assessment to be spatially explicit because both the natural productivity of ecosystems and the value of their services vary across space.

The extended context of the restoration project will impact on the selection of restoration goals and objectives. The clear enunciation of goals is essential for restoration success, and the ability to assess progress toward success (USNRC 1992, Hobbs and Harris 2001, Clewell et al. 2007). The goals and objectives might need to be revised once the costs of the associated restoration strategies are understood. The costs of restoration projects often depend on the objectives both in terms of the expected end product of the restoration and the time frame given for its achievment (Edwards and Abivardi 1997). At this stage economic input from ex-ante cost–benefit analysis is a reflection of having economic efficiency as one criterion in restoration decision making. Ex-ante cost–benefit analysis takes into account both the expected magnitude and temporal distribution of the costs and benefits of the restoration project and investigates whether, from an economic efficiency perspective, this should be undertaken. It can also investigate choice among alternative scales and timings of a project. Furthermore, given a number of mutually exclusive alternatives or a budget, it can identify which restoration project or projects should be undertaken. The tool reflects societal desires albeit weighted by income.

The next element of the adaptive restoration process is identifying the restoration strategy. This will comprise those restoration actions that are expected to lead to the achievement of the restoration objectives given the ecological potential of the site and the enabling conditions and binding constraints identified during the context analysis. Both degradation and self-sustaining (autogenic) recovery are driven by the interconnections and feedback between abiotic (soil stability, hydrology, and nutrient dynamics) and biotic (dynamics of plant resource availability, trophic interactions, pollination etc.) processes (King and Hobbs 2006). The restoration strategy can aim to create as much synergy between these processes as possible and thereby enhance self-sustaining recovery and reduce costs. When the potential for self-sustaining recovery is lacking or its timeframe is considered too long, restorative actions can manipulate both the abiotic and biotic processes. Ex-ante cost–effectiveness and cost–utility analyses can identify the least cost strategy from a set of alternatives for a given restoration outcome or maximise the restoration outcome for a given budget.

If the plan is for active adaptive management there will be a number of potential strategies trialled in order to test for a range of hypotheses (Murray and Marmorek 2003). Failing et al. (2004) argue that in order to determine the value of an experimental approach, four questions need to be considered: How great is the uncertainty about the benefits? Does the experiment have sufficient predictive ability to reduce the uncertainty? Across a plausible range of values, does the uncertainty have the potential to affect a management decision? Do the expected benefits outweigh the costs of the experiment? In their opinion, the first two questions require technical judgments from appropriate experts, while the latter two require value judgments from stakeholders. Consequently, this is another point in the restoration process where cost–benefit analysis can provide input.

During the implementation phase the restoration actions identified in the strategy are carried out. By monitoring the implementation of the restoration actions it is verified whether these were undertaken as prescribed. Further monitoring is usually carried out to measure a range of indicators. The results are evaluated to assess whether predicted outcomes were achieved and to learn which activities best achieved desired objectives during hypotheses testing. Based on the evaluation of the monitoring data, adjustments can be made to all aspects of the restoration project: objectives, strategy, implementation and monitoring.

Traditionally, monitoring had a strong ecological focus. The Primer produced by SER International provides a list of nine ecosystem attributes as a guideline for measuring restoration success from an ecological point of view (SER 2004a). A restored ecosystem is expected to have the following attributes: (1) similar diversity and community structure in comparison with reference sites; (2) presence of indigenous species; (3) presence of functional groups necessary for long-term stability; (4) capacity of the physical environment to sustain reproducing populations; (5) normal functioning; (6) integration with the landscape; (7) elimination of potential threats; (8) resilience to natural disturbances; and (9) self-sustainability. Although measuring the attributes listed in the Primer could provide an excellent assessment of restoration success, few studies have the financial resources to monitor all of these attributes. Furthermore, estimates of many attributes often require detailed long-term studies. In practice, most studies assess measures that can be categorized into three major ecosystem attributes: (1) diversity; (2) vegetation structure; and (3) ecological processes (Ruiz-Jaen and Aide 2005). Diversity is usually measured by determining richness and abundance of organisms within different trophic levels and functional groups. Vegetation structure is usually determined by measuring vegetation cover, woody plant density, biomass, or vegetation profiles. Measures of ecological processes include nutrient pools, soil organic matter, and biological interactions (e.g., herbivory, mycorrhizae, pollination, predation, parasitism). The proposed framework in Figure 1 highlights another aspect to be considered in the evaluation of restoration projects: that of economics. The ex-post cost–benefit analysis can contribute to the evaluation phase by assessing whether a given restoration project should have been undertaken on economic efficiency grounds. Ex-post cost efficiency and cost–effectiveness analyses can evaluate the chosen strategies by assessing cost per outcome.

Collection of cost data during project conception, strategy implementation and follow-up monitoring is a prerequisite for the evaluation of restoration projects from an economic perspective. Furthermore, the ecological monitoring data will provide the basis for estimating the benefits of the restoration project in ecological units, a composite performance metric or monetary measure. This dependency of the economic analysis on data collection during the whole process of restoration is highlighted by the arrows going from the elements of the restoration process to the micro-economic input section.

Given the adaptive character of the restoration process, the micro-economic input will also have a dynamic character. Using actual cost and benefit data in ex-post analysis makes the assessment of the accuracy of any ex-ante analysis and the identification of sources of divergence between the two possible. Ex-post economic analysis is expected to become the basis of future ex-ante analysis in the adaptive cycle.

Selecting an Economic Tool

When selecting which economic tool to apply there is a range of criteria to consider. The flowchart in Figure 2 represents a process for the selection of economic appraisal and evaluation tools and it is followed by a discussion of the suggested criteria.

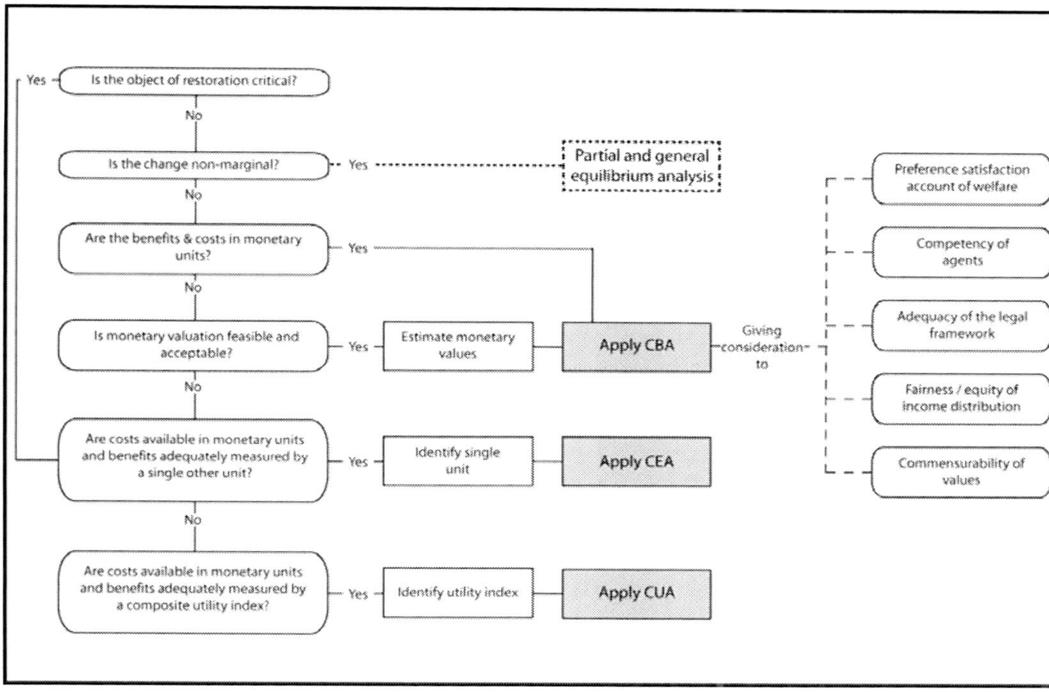

Figure 2. Process for the selection of economic tools to inform restoration decision making.

Criticality

Criticality refers to those natural capital assets that are crucial for human welfare and have no substitutes (Pearce 2006). Criticality arises out of the interaction of ecological and human value systems (Chiesura and de Groot 2003). De Groot et al. (2003) propose two criteria for the criticality of natural capital that complement each other. The first criterion is the ecological, socio-cultural and economic 'importance' of natural ecosystems. The second criterion is the degree of 'threat' based on the quantity and quality of the remaining natural areas in a given region. If one allows a plurality of goods – physical health, particular forms of personal relation, knowledge of the world, aesthetic experience, sensual pleasures, a well-constituted relation with the non-human world – to be constitutive of well-being, then goods might not be substitutable across different dimensions of well-being. Consequently, environmental goods might not be substitutable by other goods because they answer quite distinct dimensions of human well-being (O'Neill et al. 2008).

Criticality can be reflected in preferences and thus in cost–benefit analysis; for capital stocks near the criticality threshold, marginal values are high and fluctuate with small changes in the quantity supplied (Turner et al. 2003, Pearce et al. 2006, Farley and Brown Gaddis 2007). When valuation shows evidence of inelastic demand, the costs of repeated valuations increase, and the costs of small errors could be catastrophic. In such circumstances, Farley and Brown Gaddis (2007) advise a reallocation of resources from valuation to restoration. Even if criticality is not reflected in preferences, the inclusion of criticality as a first tier decision criterion in the proposed framework accommodates the strong sustainability paradigm and allows for the consideration of whether there is a paternal role for decision-makers in providing restoration. For natural capital assets perceived as critical the question will not be whether to restore or not but rather how to restore in the most cost effective way. This approach is similar to the "safe minimum standard", whereby policy-makers follow standard cost–benefit rules unless there is a compelling reason not to, such as to conserve a critical natural asset (Pearce et al. 2006).

The critical natural capital concept is dynamic; depending on the existence of substitutes or a state of knowledge about the perceived importance of certain environmental functions, natural capital may change from being critical to not critical, or vice versa (Ekins 2003). The scope for substitution varies by social, economic and cultural conditions. For some people, especially the least affluent, substitutes and choices are very limited. For those who are better off, substitutability may be possible through trade, investment and technology (MA 2005b). This dynamic character of criticality means that its assessment will rely on the context analysis stage of the adaptive restoration process and will be repeated in consecutive cycles of adaptation.

Marginal Change

Monetary measures capture only exchange values which are the value of one additional unit of service and are not designed to measure non-marginal changes. If the change is non-marginal, the consumer and producer surplus can be measured in a partial equilibrium framework, or the wider response of an economy can be analysed with computable general equilibrium models. Such models use a combination of data on economic linkages between the component sectors of the economy and a series of assumptions about the economic behaviour of households, firms and government. However, Farber (2005) argues that it would not be reasonable to ask what, for example, the economic value of nutrient cycles are, in total, to humans, for without them there would be no humans. What can be asked, he continues, is what the human welfare implications are for small-magnitude or local changes in the nutrient cycle, such as the percentage reduction on nitrogen uptake by plants or the reduction in soil fertility in an agricultural region.

Availability of Cost and Benefit Measures in Monetary Units

The availability of costs in monetary units is a prerequisite for the application of any of the three micro-economic tools identified in the proposed framework. This is an important criterion given that it is difficult to get accurate information upon how much restoration costs (Edwards and Abivardi 1997). Cost–effectiveness and cost–utility analyses do not require the availability of monetary measures for benefits. By using a non-monetary unit or index, these tools can identify the cost efficiency of achieving the specified output. However, neither of the tools can identify whether undertaking a given restoration project is efficient from an economic perspective. Such assessment requires that both the costs and the benefits are expressed in a common numeraire, which in cost–benefit analysis is money. If monetary measures for benefits are not readily available, cost–benefit analysis can be performed only if the application of valuation techniques is feasible and such value estimates are accepted by decision makers. In a restoration decision making context the lack of monetary values might be common due to many of the generated benefits having a public good character and not being traded in markets.

Issues to Consider when Selecting Cost–benefit Analysis

When selecting cost–benefit analysis there are a number of issues to consider. These are listed in Figure 2 and discussed below. The basic value judgement of cost–benefit analysis is that individuals' preferences should count and that preferences are expressed through willingness to pay or willingness to accept compensation. The technique considers preferences as given and assumes fully informed competent agents. With respect to complex environmental issues, full information will possibly be lacking. Furthermore, informing a person can form or reform their preferences. In addition, preferences can be formed by the social context of decision making, by how others behave, by institutions and by social conditioning (Gowdy 2004).

Cost–benefit analysis is consequentialist; whether an action or policy is right or wrong is determined solely by its consequences. Therefore cost–benefit analysis is more acceptable in those situations in which basic human and non-human rights are defended by law. O'Neill et al. (2008) identify two main ethical perspectives offered as alternatives to consequentialism. The first is the deontological perspective which claims that there are constraints on performing certain actions even if they should lead to the most valuable state of affairs. The second is the virtues perspective, which claims that ethical reflection should start with the question of what sort of person one should be, which virtues one should develop, and what vices one should avoid.

Most monetary values are derived from estimated demand curves. Since demand is preferences weighted by income, monetary valuation is based on plutocratic principles, not democratic ones (Farley and Brown Gaddis 2007).

Value commensurability assumes that there is a single measure of value through which we can arrive at policy choices. In neo-classical economics and cost–benefit analysis this measure is money. However, there are alternative deliberative and expressive accounts of rational choice that are consistent with the recognition of value pluralism and value incommensurability (Soma 2006, Trainor 2006, O'Neill et al. 2008). O'Neill et al. (2008) argue that we are faced with a number of reasons or grounds for conflicting options, and we have to judge which reasons count most strongly in a given choice context. Consequently, in their opinion, it is through deliberation rather than measurement that we make decisions.

Challenges with the Economic Analysis of Restoration Projects

The economic analysis of restoration projects is expected to be challenging in a number of ways. There might be difficulties associated with the measurement and attribution of the changes in the flow of ecosystem goods and services, the temporal and spatial scales of the different processes involved, and the multidimensional nature of the outcomes and their valuation.

Challenge 1: Lack of cost data. All restoration interventions have associated costs such as acquisition costs (costs associated with acquiring property rights to a piece of land), management costs (these can be fixed, and therefore independent of the amount of restoration activities pursued, or variable, and therefore proportional to the amount and type of restoration activity), active restoration costs (these are associated with the physical, chemical and biological manipulation of the site being restored) and transaction costs (costs associated with negotiating an economic exchange, e.g., the costs over and above the price of a transfer of property rights to a given piece of land). Furthermore, with restoration, damage costs might also arise; these are associated with damages to economic activities arising from restoration projects (e.g., damages to crops from wild animals living in a restored forest can result in significant losses in income (Langridge et al. 2007). On the other hand, damage costs might also arise in the absence of restoration from the ecosystem 'disservices' associated with the baseline scenario.

There is a lack of attention to costs in the restoration literature (Edwards and Abivardi 1997, Holl and Howarth 2000). Potential explanations include the different disciplinary perspectives of economists and ecologists and the view of restoration and economics as opposing forces (Holl and Howarth 2000). Due to reliable cost data being a prerequisite for any of the 3 micro-economic tools suggested in this chapter, cost data collection is an important element of the proposed framework.

Challenge 2: Incomplete understanding of ecosystems. The quality of the economic appraisal/assessment will be dependent on the comprehensiveness and reliability of models and monitoring protocols used for predicting and measuring the impact of restoration on ecosystem conditions and services. Furthermore, since ecosystems are dynamic, an important issue to be addressed is the definition of the 'baseline' relating to the current condition. In some cases, this will, in itself, vary over time, and it will be necessary to ensure this temporal pattern is accounted for in the economic analysis of restoration projects. There are difficulties in predicting the effect of restoration and its absence on ecosystem structure and function and the associated ecosystem services because ecosystems are complex, self-organising systems nested across temporal and spatial scales (Levin 1999). Despite advances in understanding how different kinds of terrestrial and aquatic ecosystems develop and interact over time, there remain many difficulties in predicting how, in specific cases, they can be expected to respond to intentional interventions (Aronson & van Andel 2006). Predictive errors will result if important variables are omitted, if the relationships between included variables are incorrectly specified, or if stochastic features are inadequately represented.

The identification of appropriate spatial boundaries for an analysis is often fraught with difficulty due to multiple scales of interaction and opposite impacts on different spatial scales. In the temporal dimension, methodological challenges arise from slow-changing variables and substantial lags between actions and the manifestation of their consequences. In addition, the timing of an intervention can also affect its impact. Furthermore, the functions which maintain the basic integrity of natural systems ('functions of' or supporting services) are not easily perceived, and scientific knowledge about them is still uncertain and incomplete. The continued operation of these functions is a prerequisite for the continued performance of those environmental functions which provide direct benefits for humans ('functions for') (Ekins 2003).

There is a range of sources of stochasticity that affects biological assets (van Kooten and Bulte 2000). Such examples may include demographic stochasticity, or accidental variations in birth rates, death rates and the sex ratio (Pindyck 1984); environmental stochasticity, or fluctuations in species abundance due to variations in weather, food supply, predators, parasites and/or competitors (Olsen and Shortle 1996); and genetic stochasticity, or the vagaries by which certain harmful alleles become more common or rare in a population (Quammen 1996).

Due to the evolutionary components, ecosystems exhibit a limited degree of predictability (Costanza et al. 1993). Natural systems are increasingly understood as dynamic constructs that may exist in a number of alternate states ("regimes" or "domains of ecological attraction"). Many ecosystems can persist in a particular state or regime for some time because they exhibit resistance or resilience. Resistance is measured by the capacity to withstand disturbance without significant change, while resilience is indicated by the capacity to return to the original state after perturbation toward an alternate state (Holling 1978, Walker et al. 2004). The concept of alternative states with boundary thresholds is used to explain the nonlinear behavior of natural systems. While understanding of these system dynamics continues to expand, this knowledge can inform assessment of ecosystem functions only if the assessment occurs at appropriate spatial and temporal scales. However, appropriate spatial and temporal scales can be identified only if the dynamics are already understood. In the face of this apparent challenge the practical solution to the need to complete an assessment of ecosystem function and/or provision of services is to proceed with caution. Observations of a system's behaviour through time are an obvious first step, but such monitoring data can only confirm the existence of nonlinear behaviour, not prove its absence.

In some circumstances the abrupt shift, or flip to an alternate regime in state may be part of a hysteretic system behaviour. In this case the recovery threshold differs from the impact threshold such that the state of the system will lag in response to changes in controlling forces. Cascading effects, in which the crossing of a single threshold between alternative regimes often leads to the crossing of multiple thresholds, are another example of ecosystem dynamics that can be difficult to predict (Molles 2002). Such dynamic behaviour of ecosystems makes the prediction of restoration outcomes uncertain.

The efforts to identify and quantify ecosystem services is further hindered by conflicting opinions on the nature of the relationship between biodiversity and ecosystem functioning (e.g., Ulanowicz 1996, Duarte 2000, Ghilarov 2000, Hulot et al. 2000, Schwartz et al. 2000). Uncertainties in this regard make the assessment of the importance of any particular ecosystem's contribution to maintenance of biodiversity, or conversely the role of biodiversity in the functioning of the ecosystem, difficult.

Challenge 3: Substitution and complementarity among restoration projects. The larger 'restoration context' will influence the desirability of individual restoration projects from the economic efficiency perspective. Projects generating benefits that effectively serve as substitutes for each other (e.g. recreation sites) may appear to be welfare enhancing because the interactions with other proposed projects are ignored. Thus, each project may be adopted based on individual assessment, when in fact only a subset of the projects if adopted together are welfare improving. However, individual assessment also can lead to another error in the opposite direction. Due to thresholds or synergistic effects, the benefits of a particular restoration initiative might be contingent on what else has been – and what remains to be – accomplished in terms of addressing environmental problems. In cases where no single project will pass a cost–benefit test on its own, the joint effect of a number of restoration projects might do so, given that multiple projects can act as complements rather than as substitutes. In order to have a significant effect at a regional scale, the restoration of a certain minimum area of a particular ecosystem might be needed. For example, Baker (1992) estimated that a ratio of wetlands to total drainage area of approximately 1:20 was desirable to achieve a reduction of suspended solids in rivers.

Challenge 4: Multidimensional outcomes. The multidimensionality of outcomes means that impact assessment often faces difficult measurement challenges, including very different measurement units and, potentially, the integration of very different natural resource outputs. This multidimensionality extends to those directly and indirectly affecting human beings, and represents a challenge for valuation. Something is considered valuable in an economic sense if it contributes to the goal of maximising welfare, and has negative value if it detracts from this goal. A function like 'maximising human well-being' is deliberately general because it allows individuals to have very different motivations for their preferences such as self-interest, concern for other human beings or for the well-being of the planet. The different motivations do not preclude adding up the resulting preferences because whatever the motive is, this may be revealed through willingness to pay constrained by the present distribution of income or willingness to accept (Pearce et al. 2002, Pearce et al. 2006).

Economists have generally settled for a nomenclature of value, the components of which add up to total economic value (Randall 1991, Freeman 1993, Pearson 2000, Turner et al. 2003). The key distinction is between use values and non-use values, the latter reflecting value in addition to that which arises from usage. Use value may come from both direct use for food and fuel, for example, and from indirect use, which includes ecosystem support functions such as climate regulation, nutrient cycling, soil formation and flood control. The option value is defined as the expected value of future use of the resource. A broader interpretation would consider it as a premium for risk aversion, namely the willingness to pay for maintaining an option to use the resource when future conditions are uncertain. The group of non-use values, the second broad category of the total economic value, comprises altruistic, bequest and existence values. Altruistic value might arise when the individual is concerned that the good or service in question should be available for others in the current generation. Bequest values arise from the benefits individuals derive from knowing a resource will be available for future generations rather than for their own potential future use. Existence values are associated with the benefits derived by individuals as a result of knowing that a resource exists or will continue to exist in a context where the individual expressing the value has no actual or planned use for his/herself or for anyone else. Non-use values may or may not exclude use values, while different usage options may or may not exclude each other. These preclude simply adding up the different components of the total economic value, and expose the inherent trade-offs.

On practical grounds intrinsic value is not part of the total economic value. Philosophers such as Jonas (1966, 1984) dispute whether value is objective or subjective, namely whether it resides 'in' the objects of interest or is conferred 'on' the object by the entity engaging in the act of valuation. Based on the objective point of view, some motivations may be derived from a concern that the object of value has a value 'in itself', i.e. intrinsic value. Intrinsic value does not have a scale of desirability, and this precludes trade-offs. Hence intrinsic value, as an absolute, can not inform decision making that involves trade-offs between various values. Environmental valuation is confined to measuring subjective value, in which there is an entity who engages in the act of valuation (Pearce et al. 2002).

Restorative interventions may result in changes in direct-use values (e.g., increased agricultural production), indirect use values (e.g., increased C sequestration), option values (e.g., the capability of the soil to support crop production is maintained for the future), bequest values (e.g., the service of water purification is maintained in a context when the water drains into an aquifer to be used by future generations) or existence values (e.g., through continued habitat provision). The total economic value framework can help organise the outcomes of restoration interventions, with the next challenge being the valuation of the different elements in monetary terms.

Challenge 5: Monetary valuation. There is a range of techniques available for the valuation of ecosystem goods and services when these are not directly traded in markets (for reviews of these techniques and their strengths and weaknesses see Champ et al. 2003, Shiferaw et al. 2005, Swinton 2005, and Pearce et al. 2006). The valuation techniques can be distinguished by the type of market they use and whether they rely on revealed or stated preferences. Changes in productivity, replacement cost, provision cost and defensive expenditure methods use actual markets. The hedonic pricing and recreational demand models use surrogate markets to value non-tradable goods and services indirectly through marketed goods and services that embody their values. Contingent valuation and choice modelling methods rely on hypothetical markets. Environmental value transfer methods use available value estimates and transfer these to other sites and policies. Characteristics of the non-market good or service, data availability, budget and time constraints as well as acceptability by the decision makers are going to influence whether non-market valuation represents a feasible option and which technique is suitable.

Challenge 6: Long time frames. Restoration projects and their impacts typically have a long timeframe. Therefore, the economic analyses of restoration projects also cover long periods of time, e.g., 20 to 50 years (Aguiar and Román 2007, Holmes et al. 2007, Mills et al. 2007). Individual preferences can be influenced by a variety of factors, including culture and information, which can change over time. In addition, an individual's willingness to trade one good for another will reflect the amounts of the goods and services currently available to him/her, which will in turn depend at least partially on income. If income changes over time, the economic measure of value for an individual can be expected to change as well. For these reasons, the values measured through economic valuation are inherently time- and context-specific (USNRC 2004). With long time frames there is potential for some restoration benefits and costs to attract higher valuation over time relative to the general level of prices. Krutilla and Fisher (1975) suggested that environmental benefits are likely to increase relative to other benefits in the economy because, for example, future richer people will appreciate relatively more environmental amenities if the income elasticity of environmental appreciation is bigger than one.

The costs and benefits of many restoration projects are frequently paid and received at different points over the course of sometimes long time horizons. For projects and policies that require large initial outlays or that have long delays before benefits are realized, the selection of the discount rate can be a major factor in determining whether the net present value is positive (e.g., a benefit that is accrued 10 years from the base year is reduced by 29% if the discount rate is 3.5% per annum but by 61% if the rate is 10%). The theoretical and applied economics literature on discounting from a social perspective is voluminous and technically complex (e.g., Chichilnisky 1996, Weitzman 1998, Dasgupta et al. 1999, Nordhaus 1999, Li and Lofgren 2000). Moreover, in some cases the economics literature by itself does not yield robust discounting rules for practical applications because making such social decisions requires input from other disciplines (e.g., ethics).

The social discounting problem has been divided into intra-generational and inter-generational social discounting to help understand the substantially different contribution economic approaches can offer in each area (USEPA 2000). The intra-generational consumption discount rate represents the weights placed on increments of consumption at different dates and the after-tax returns on savings instruments generally available to the public are considered to provide a reasonable estimate. Whether or not this will need adjustment appears to depend largely on whether the economy in question is assumed to be open or closed and on the magnitude of the intervention or program considered relative to the flow of investment capital from abroad. The inter-generational utility discount rate is intended to represent the relative weights put on present and future utilities. The latter expresses society's preferences for distribution between generations, with a zero rate representing equal weights for all generations, and a positive rate implying less weight to future generations. There is little consensus in the economic literature on the fundamental choice of what moral perspective should guide inter-generational social discounting, e.g., a social planner who weighs the utilities of present and future generations or the preferences of the current generations regarding future generations. USEPA (2000) recommends that economic studies should present a sensitivity analysis of alternative discount rates and for policies with inter-generational effects should generally include a "no discounting" scenario by displaying the streams of costs and benefits over time.

Challenge 7: Potential for irreversibilities. With the crossing of thresholds, ecosystems might experience irreversible changes, so the option of returning them to a historic trajectory or even the recovery of some functions might disappear. If restoration is undertaken to prevent the crossing of such thresholds, irreversible changes might be avoided. In such circumstances the concept of quasi-option value becomes relevant. Quasi-option value is the premium that individuals assign to protecting an ecosystem against uncertain, irreversible damages in order to maintain flexibility and gain more information that will influence future actions.

Conclusion

Given the present trend in ecosystem degradation worldwide, the role of ecological restoration is expected to increase in the near future. This chapter identifies a framework to help address when and how micro-economic input can inform the appraisal and evaluation of restoration projects. The inclusion of economic input in restoration decision making is an expression of having economic and cost efficiency as decision criteria. The inclusion of these criteria do not exclude the application of other decision criteria as well. Furthermore, due to their neglect of equity issues and ecological constraints they should not be considered in isolation.

The framework suggested here is organized around the adaptive management process with ex-ante and ex-post cost–benefit, cost–effectiveness and cost–utility analyses being linked to the different stages of this process. Cost–effectiveness and cost–utility analyses are useful to identify the restoration options which achieve a given restoration outcome at least cost or maximize the outcome measure subject to cost constraint. Cost–benefit analysis can be used to appraise or evaluate whether the allocation of resources to a restoration project would be or was efficient in the sense of producing net gains in social welfare.

A range of selection criteria are listed to help identify in which context the application of economic tools is relevant and to help choose among the different tools. When a given natural resource is considered to be critical, its restoration is imperative and whether such restoration should be undertaken is unlikely to be decided by cost–benefit analysis. However, cost–effectiveness and cost–utility analyses can inform the selection of restoration actions given reliable cost data. Reliable monetary cost data is imperative for the application of all three techniques. Cost–benefit analysis also requires the availability of benefit data in monetary terms, whereas the other techniques can be applied in cases when the restoration output is measured by a single non-monetary unit or index. Given the non-market character of many restoration benefits and, sometimes, costs, environmental valuation becomes often necessary.

The application of economic tools in a restoration context is challenging for a number of reasons. The understanding of ecosystem functioning is incomplete. There are measurement challenges with the costs and multidimensional (and often non-market) outcomes of the restoration projects. Due to the long time frames involved, there is potential for rising relative valuations and sensitivity to the discount rate applied. There might be complementarities or substitutability among restoration projects. Furthermore, the avoidance of irreversible changes might become an issue. The recognition of these challenges and the systematic exposure of the attempts to deal with them means that decision makers will be in a better position to understand and incorporate economic input into restoration decision making.

REFERENCES

Aguiar, M. R. & Román, M. E. (2007). Restoring forage grass to support the pastoral economy of Arid Patagonia. In J. Aronson, S. J. Milton & J. N. Blignaut (Eds.), *Restoring Natural Capital: Science, Business and Practice* (pp. 112-121). Washington: Island Press.

Allen, E. B. (2003). New directions and growth of restoration ecology. *Restoration Ecology, 11*, 1-2.

Aronson, J., Blignaut, J. N., Milton, S. J. & Clewell, A. F. (2006). Natural capital: The limiting factor. *Ecological Engineering, 28*, 1-5.

Aronson, J., Floret, C., Le Floc'h, E., Ovalle, C. & Pontanier, R. (1993). Restoration and rehabilitation of degraded ecosystems in arid and semi-arid lands. I. A view from the South. *Restoration Ecology, 1,* 8-17.

Aronson, J. & Le Floc'h, E. (2000). Restoration of natural capital: Pros and problems. *Restoration Ecology, 8* (3), 214-216.

Aronson, J., Milton, S. J. & Blignaut, J. N. (2007). *Restoring Natural Capital: Science, Business and Practice.* Washington: Island Press.

Arrow, K. J. & Lind, R. C. (1970). Uncertainty and the evaluation of public investment decisions. *American Economic Review, 60*(3), 364-378.

Aronson, J. & van Andel, J. (2006). Challenges for ecological theory. In: J. van Andel & J. Aronson (Eds.), *Restoration Ecology: The New Frontier* (pp. 223-233). Malden, MA: Blackwell Science.

Baker, L. A. (1992). Introduction to nonpoint source pollution in the United States and prospects for wetland use. *Ecological Engineering, 1,* 1-26.

Bradshaw, A. D. (1997). What do we mean by restoration? In K. M. Urbanska, N. R. Webb & P.J. Edwards (Eds.), *Restoration Ecology and Sustainable Development* (pp. 8-14). Cambridge, United Kingdom: Cambridge University Press.

Cairns, J. Jr. (1995) Ecosocietal restoration: reestablishing humanity's relationship with natural systems. *Environment, 37*, 4-33.

Campbell, H. & Brown, R. (2003). *Benefit-Cost Analysis: Financial and Economic Appraisal Using Spreadsheets.* Cambridge, United Kingdom: Cambridge University Press.

Champ, P. A., Boyle, K. J. & Brown, T. C. (Eds.) (2003). *A Primer on Nonmarket Valuation.* Dordrecht: Kluwer.

Chichilnisky, G. (1996). An axiomatic approach to sustainable development. *Social Choice and Welfare, 13,* 231-257.

Chiesura, A. & de Groot, R. (2003). Critical natural capital: a socio-cultural perspective. *Ecological Economics, 44*, 219-231.

Clewell, A. F. (2000). Restoration of natural capital. *Restoration Ecology, 8* (1), 1.

Clewell, A. F. & Aronson, J. (2006). Motivations for the restoration of ecosystems. *Conservation Biology, 20*, 420-428.

Clewell, A. F. & Aronson, J. (2007). *Ecological Restoration: Principles, Values, and Structure of an Emerging Profession.* Washington: Island Press.

Clewell, A., Rieger, J. & Munro, J. (2007). Guidelines for developing and managing ecological restoration projects, 2nd edition. In A. F. Clewell & J. Aronson (Eds.), *Ecological Restoration: Principles, Values and Structure of an Emerging Profession* (appendix). Washington: Island Press.

Costanza, R., Waigner, L., Folke, C. & Mäler, K.-G. (1993). Modeling complex ecological economic systems: toward an evolutionary dynamic understanding of people and nature. *BioScience, 43*, 545-555.

Craig, J. & Vesely, É-T. (2007). Restoring natural capital reconnects people to their natural heritage: Tiritiri Matangi Island, New Zealand. In J. Aronson, S. J. Milton & J. N. Blignaut (Eds.), *Restoring Natural Capital: Science, Business and Practice* (pp. 103-111). Washington: Island Press.

Cullen, R., Fairburn, G. A. & Hughey, K. F. D. (1999). COPY: a new technique for evaluation of biodiversity protection projects. *Pacific Conservation Biology, 5,* 115-123.

Cullen, R., Fairburn, G. A. & Hughey, K. F. D. (2001). Measuring the productivity of threatened species programs. *Ecological Economics, 39,* 53-66.

Cullen, R., Moran, E. & Hughey, K. F. D. (2005). Measuring the success and cost effectiveness of New Zealand multiple-species projects to the conservation of threatened species. *Ecological Economics, 53,* 311-323.

Cunningham, S. (2002). *The Restoration Economy – The Greatest New Growth Frontier*. San Francisco, Ca.: Berrett-Koehler Publishers.

Daly, H. E. (1994). Operationalizing sustainable development by investing in natural capital. In A.-M. Jansson, M. Hammer, C. Folke & R. Costanza (Eds.), *Investing in Natural Capital: The Ecological Economics Approach to Sustainability* (pp. 22-37). Washington D. C.: Island Press.

Davis, M. A. & Slobodkin, L. B. (2004). The science and values of restoration ecology. *Restoration Ecology, 12* (1), 1-3.

De Groot, R., Van der Perk, J., Chiesura, A. & van Vliet, A. (2003). Importance and threat as determining factors for criticality of natural capital. *Ecological Economics, 44*, 187-204.

Duarte, C. M. (2000). Marine biodiversity and ecosystem services: An elusive link. *Journal of Experimental Marine Biology and Ecology, 250*(1-2), 117-131.

Dubgaard, A., Kallesøe, M. F., Ladenburg, J. & Petersen, M. L. (2004). Cost-benefit analysis of the Skjern river restoration in Denmark. In R. Brouwer & D. Pearce (Eds.), *Cost-Benefit Analysis and Water Resources Management*. Cheltenham, United Kingdom: Edward Elgar Publishing.

Edwards, P. J. & Abivardi, C. (1997). Ecological engineering and sustainable development. In K. M. Urbanska, N. R. Webb & P. J. Edwards (Eds.), *Restoration Ecology and Sustainable Development* (pp. 325-352). Cambridge, United Kingdom: Cambridge University Press.

Ekins, P. (2003). Identifying critical natural capital – Conclusions about critical natural capital. *Ecological Economics, 44*, 277-292.

Enters, T. (1998). *Methods for the economic assessment of the on- and off-site impacts of soil erosion. Issues in Sustainable Land Management no. 2*. Bangkok: International Board for Soil Research and Management (IBSRAM).

Failing, L., Horn, G. & Higgins, P. (2004). Using expert judgment and stakeholder values to evaluate adaptive management options. *Ecology and Society, 9* (1), 13.

Farber, S. (2005). The economics of biodiversity in urbanizing ecosystems. In E. A. Johnson & M. W. Klemens (Eds.), *Nature in fragments – The legacy of sprawl* (pp. 263-283). Columbia University Press.

Farley, J. & Brown Gaddis, E. J. (2007). Restoring natural capital: An ecological economics assessment. In J. Aronson, S. J. Milton & J. N. Blignaut (Eds.), *Restoring Natural Capital: Science, Business and Practice* (pp. 17-27). Washington: Island Press.

Farley, J. & Dale, H. E. (2006). Natural capital: The limiting factor: A reply to Aronson, Blignaut, Milton and Clewell. *Ecological Engineering, 28*, 6-10.

Freeman, A. M. III. (1993). *The Measurement of Environmental and Resource Values: Theory and Methods*. Washington, D.C.: Resources for the Future.

Ghilarov, A.M. (2000). Ecosystem functioning and intrinsic value of biodiversity. *Oikos, 90*(2), 408-412.

Gowdy, J. (2004). The revolution in welfare economics and its implications for environmental valuation and policy. *Land Economics, 80* (2), 239-257.

Haney, A. & Power, R. L. (1996). Adaptive management for sound ecosystem management. *Environmental Management, 20* (6), 879-886.

Harris, J. A. & van Diggelen, R. (2006). Ecological restoration as a project for global society. In: A. van Jelte & J. Aronson (Eds.), *Restoration Ecology: The New Frontier* (pp. 3-15). Malden, MA: Blackwell Science.

Higgs, E. S. (1997). What is good ecological restoration? *Conservation Biology, 11* (2), 338-348.

Hilderbrand, R. H., Watts, A. C. & Randle, A. M. (2005). The myths of restoration ecology. *Ecology and Society, 10* (1), 19.

Hobbs, R. J. & Norton, D. A. (1996). Towards a conceptual framework for restoration ecology. *Restoration Ecology, 4*, 93-110.

Hobbs, R. J. & Harris, J. A. (2001). Restoration ecology: Repairing the Earth's ecosystems in the new millennium. *Restoration Ecology, 9* (2), 239-246.

Holl, K. D. & Howarth, R. B. (2000). Paying for Restoration. *Restoration Ecology,* 8(3), 260-267.

Holland, A. (1995). The assumptions of cost-benefit analysis: A philosopher's view. In K. G. Willis and J. T. Corkindale (Eds.), *Environmental Valuation New Perspectives* (pp. 21-38). Wallingford: CAB International.

Holling, C. S. (Ed.) (1978). *Adaptive Environmental Assessment and Management.* Caldwell, NJ: Blackburn Press.

Holmes, P. M., Richardson, D. M. & Marais, C. (2007). Costs and benefits of restoring natural capital following alien plant invasions in fynbos ecosystems in South Africa. In J. Aronson, S. J. Milton & J. N. Blignaut (Eds.), *Restoring Natural Capital: Science, Business and Practice* (pp. 188-197). Washington: Island Press.

Hulot, F. D., Lacroix, G., Lescher-Moutoue, F. & Loreau, M. (2000). Functional diversity governs ecosystem response to nutrient enrichment. *Nature (London), 405*(6784), 340-344.

Iovanna, R. & Newbold, S. C. (2007). Ecological sustainability in policy assessments: A wide-angle view and a close watch. *Ecological Economics, 63*, 639-648.

Jonas, H. (1966). *The Phenomenon of Life: Toward A Philosophical Biology*. New York: Harper & Row.

Jonas, H. (1984). *The Imperative of Responsibility: In Search of an Ethics for the Technological Age*. Chicago: University of Chicago Press.

King, D. M. (1991). Costing out Restoration. *Restoration and Management Notes, 9*, 15-21.

King, E. G. & Hobbs, R. J. (2006). Identifying linkages among conceptual models of ecosystem degradation and restoration: Towards an integrative framework. *Restoration Ecology, 14* (3), 369-378.

Krutilla, J. V. & Fisher, A. C. (1975). The economics of natural environments. Washington D.C.: Resources for the Future.

Lackey, R. T. (2001). Values, policy, and ecosystem health. *BioScience*, *51*(6), 437-443.

Langridge, S. M., Buckley, M. & Holl, K. D. (2007). Overcoming obstacles to restoring natural capital: Large-scale restoration on the Sacramento River. In: J. Aronson, S. J. Milton & J. N. Blignaut (Eds.), *Restoring Natural Capital: Science, Business and Practice* (pp. 146-153). Washington: Island Press.

Leiderman, S. M. (1993). *The Economics of Ecological Restoration: a Preliminary Report.* Durham: University of New Hampshire.

Levin, S. (1999). *Fragile Dominion: Complexity and the Commons.* Reading, MA: Perseus Books.

Li, C. Z. & Lofgren, K. G. (2000). Renewable resources and economic sustainability: A dynamic analysis with heterogeneous time preferences. *Journal of Environmental Economics and Management, 40,* 236-250.

MA (Millennium Ecosystem Assessment). (2005a). *Ecosystems and human well-being: Biodiversity Synthesis.* Washington, D.C.: World Resources Institute.

MA (Millennium Ecosystem Assessment). (2005b). *Ecosystems and human well-being: Synthesis*. Washington, D.C.: Island Press.

Macmillan, D. C., Harley, D. & Morrison, R. 1998. Cost-effectiveness analysis of woodland ecosystem restoration. *Ecological Economics, 27,* 313-324.

McTaggart, D., Findlay, C. & Parkin, M. (4th edition, 2003). *Economics*. French Forest, NSW: Addison Wesley.

Mills, A. J., Turpie, J. K., Cowling, R. M., Marais, C., Kerley, G. I. H., Lechmere-Oertel, R. G., Sigwela, A. M. & Powell, M. (2007). Assessing costs, benefits, and feasibility of restoring natural in subtropical thicket in South Africa. In J. Aronson, S. J. Milton & J. N. Blignaut (Eds.), *Restoring Natural Capital: Science, Business and Practice* (pp. 179-187). Washington: Island Press.

Molles, M. C. Jr. (2002). Ecology: Concepts and Applications. New York: McGraw Hill.

Murray, C. & Marmorek, D. (2003). Adaptive management and ecological restoration. In P. Friederici (Ed.), *Ecological Restoration of Southwestern Ponderosa Pine Forests* (pp. 417-428). Washington D.C.: Island Press.

Norton, B. G. & Steinemann, A. C. (2002). Environmental values and adaptive management. *Environmental Values, 10*, 473-506.

O'Neill, J., Holland, A. & Light, A. (2008). *Environmental Values.* London and New York: Routledge.

Olsen, R. J. & Shortle, J. S. (1996). The optimal control of emissions and renewable resource harvesting under uncertainty. *Environmental and Resource Economics, 7*(2), 97-115.

Pearce, D. (1993). *Economic Values and the Natural World.* London: Earthscan.

Pearce, D.W. & Turner, R.K. (1990). *Economics of Natural Resources and the Environment.* Hertfordshire, United Kingdom: Harvester Wheatsheaf.

Pearce, D., Moran, D. & Biller, D. (2002). *Handbook of Biodiversity Valuation: A Guide for Policy Makers.* Paris: Organisation for Economic Co-operation and Development (OECD) Environment Programme.

Pearce, D., Atkinson, G. & Mourato, S. (2006). *Cost-Benefit Analysis and the Environment.* Paris: Organisation for Economic Co-operation and Development (OECD) Publishing.

Pearson, C. S. (2000). *Economics and the Global Environment.* Cambridge, United Kingdom: Cambridge University Press.

Pindyck, R. S. (1984). Uncertainty in the theory of renewable resource markets. *Journal of Political Economy, 86*, 841-861.

Quammen, D. (1996). The song of the Dodo: Island biogeography in an age of extinctions. London: Pimlico.

Randall, A. (1987). *Resource Economics: An Economic Approach to Natural Resource and Environmental Policy* (2nd edition). New York: John Wiley & Sons.

Randall, A. (1991). Total and nonuse values. In: J. B. Braden & C. D. Kolstad (Eds.), *Measuring the demand for environmental quality* (chapter 10). North Holland, Amsterdam.

Ruiz-Jaen, M. C. & Aide, T. M. (2005). Restoration success: How is it being measured? *Restoration Ecology, 13* (3), 569-577.

Schwartz, M. W., Brigham, C. A., Hoeksema, J. D, Lyons, K. G., Mills, M. H. & van Mantgem, P. J. (2000). Linking biodiversity to ecosystem function: Implications for conservation ecology. *Oecologia, 122*(3), 297-305.

SER (Society for Ecological Restoration International Science & Policy Working Group). (2004a). *The SER International Primer on Ecological Restoration.* www.ser.org & Tucson: Society for Ecological Restoration International.

SER (Society for Ecological Restoration International Science & Policy Working Group). (2004b). Natural capital and ecological restoration. Occasional paper, www.ser.org

Shiferaw, B., Freeman, H. A. & Navrud, S. (2005). Valuation methods and approaches for assessing natural resource management impacts. In B. Shiferaw, H. A Freeman & S. M. Swinton (Eds.), *Natural Resource Management in Agriculture: Methods for Assessing Economic and Environmental Impacts* (pp. 19-52). Wallingford: CAB International.

Soma, K. (2006). *Natura Economica* in Environmental Valuation. *Environmental Values, 15*, 31-50.

Stæhr, K. (2006). Risk and uncertainty in cost benefit analysis. Copenhagen: Institut for Miljøvurdering / Environmental Assessment Institute.

Sunstein, C. R. (2002a). *The Cost-Benefit State: The Future of Regulatory Protection.* Chicago: American Bar Association.

Sunstein, C. R. (2002b). In praise of numbers: a reply. *Georgetown Law Journal, 90,* 2379-2385.

Swinton, S. M. (2005). Assessing economic impacts of natural resource management using economic surplus. In B. Shiferaw, H. A. Freeman & S. M. Swinton (Eds.), *Natural Resource Management in Agriculture: Methods for Assessing Economic and Environmental Impacts* (pp. 155-174). Wallingford: CAB International.

Trainor, S. F. (2006). Realms of value: Conflicting natural resource values and incommensurability. *Environmental Values, 15*, 3-29.

Treasury Board of Canada. (1998). Benefit cost analysis guide, URL: http://www.tbs-sct.gc.ca/fin/sigs/Revolving_Funds/bcag/BCA2_E.asp

Turner, R. K., Paavola, J., Cooper, P., Farber, S., Jessamy, V. & Georgiou, S. (2003). Valuing nature: Lessons learned and future research directions. *Ecological Economics, 46,* 493-510.

Ulanowicz, R. E. (1996). The propensities of evolving systems. In: E. L. Khalil & K. E. Boulding (Eds.) *Social and Natural Complexity*. London: Routledge.

USEPA (United States Environmental Protection Agency). (2000). Guidelines for Preparing Economic Analysis. EPA 240-R-00-003.

USNRC (United States National Research Council). (1992). *Restoration of aquatic ecosystems: science, technology and public policy.* Washington, D. C.: National Academy Press.

USNRC (United States National Research Council, Committee on Assessing and Valuing the Services of Aquatic and Related Terrestrial Ecosystems, Water Science and Technology Board, Division on Earth and Life Studies). (2004). Valuing ecosystem services. Washington D.C.: National Academies Press.

Van Kooten, G. C. & Bulte, E. H. (2000). *The economics of nature: Managing biological assets*. Oxford: Blackwell.

Walker, B., Holling, C. S., Carpenter, S. R. & Kinzig, A. (2004). Resilience, adaptability and transformability in social-ecological systems. *Ecology and Society, 9*(2), 5. URL: *http://www.ecologyandsociety.org/vol9/iss2/art5.*

Walters, C. J. (1986). *Adaptive Management of Renewable Resources.* New York: Macmillan.

Winterhalder, K., Clewell, A. F. & Aronson, J. (2004). Values and science in ecological restoration – A response to Davis and Slobodkin. *Restoration Ecology, 12* (1), 4-7.

Wyant, J. G., Meganck, R. A. & Ham, S. H. (1995). A planning and decision-making framework for ecological restoration. *Environmental Management, 19* (6), 789-796.

In: Natural Resources
Editor: Jeanette B. Pauling
ISBN 978-1-60456-982-7

Chapter 8

INTRODUCING MODELLING TOOLS TO SUPPORT WATER-MANAGEMENT DECISION-MAKING UNDER CLIMATE CHANGE CONDITIONS: A SPANISH EXPERIENCE

Angel Utset Suastegui
Instituto Tecnológico Agrario de Castilla y León Filiberto
Villalobos s/n, 37770 Guijuelo, Salamanca, Spain

ABSTRACT

According to climate change assessments, less precipitations and higher temperatures can be expected in the Iberian Peninsula and other Mediterranean zones. Besides, an increment in droughts and other extreme events can be expected as well. Such climatic conditions require an effort to optimize irrigation technologies and to improve water management efficiency. There are currently available water-use and crop-growth simulation models, which can be combined to climate scenarios and weather generators in order to recommend, through many simulations, the most reliable irrigation management. The Preliminary Assessment of the Impacts in Spain due to the Effects of Climate Change and the National Plan for Adaptation to Climate Change recommend the use of such simulation tools in Spanish climate-change impact assessments. Those tools, however, have not been used yet to support irrigation decision-making in our country. In that sense, the EU-funded proposal AGRIDEMA, leaded by Spain, has been addressed to introduce such tools, connecting the tools "providers" from Universities and high-level research centres, with their "users", located in agricultural technological or applied-research centres. AGRIDEMA comprised courses and Pilot Applications of the tools. Local researchers knew in the AGRIDEMA courses how to access to GCM data and seasonal forecasts, they receive also basic knowledge on weather generators, statistical and dynamical downscaling; as well as on available crop models as DSSAT, WOFOST, CROPSYST, SWAP and others. About 20 pilot assessments have been conducted in several European countries during AGRIDEMA, applying the modelling tools in particular cases.

The AGRIDEMA results are commented, mentioning particularly the Pilot Assessments that were held in Spain and in the Mediterranean area. Furthermore, several "users" opinion regarding the available climate and crop-growth simulation tools are also pointed out. Those opinions can be used as important feedback by the tools "developers". An illustrative example on how modelling tools can help to manage Sugarbeet irrigation under present and future climate conditions in Spain is also shown. Several future research directions are pointed out, as followed from the shown example and the AGRIDEMA results. Those research directions agree with the actions recommended in the Spanish National Plan for Adaptation to Climate Change, as well as in the European and international guidelines. Stakeholder will adopt climate-change mitigation options only if they realize the reliability of such options on their specific cases. To achieve this, the "users" of the modelling tools must develop local demonstration proposals, aimed to model calibration and validation, etc. Particularly, some demonstration proposals should be aimed to recommend productive and efficient irrigation water managements under the adverse climate conditions that Spanish farmers will eventually face in the next years.

1. Climate Change, Agriculture and Water Resources in the Mediterranean Region

The last IPCC (2007) report pointed out clearly the climate variability observed in the last decades, very probably due to the higher concentration of CO_2 and other gases emissions related to human activity. Particularly, the increment in the frequency of extreme event, as droughts and flooding, has been considered also as a climate-change consequence. Despite that temperature rising could be expected all over the world, rainfall changes are different according to the regions. Northern regions might expect increment in yearly rainfall, while total precipitation in other zones, as the Mediterranean regions, could be significantly lower during the second half of the 20 century (IPCC, 2007).

Climate change will bring important consequences to agriculture, perhaps the man activity most dependants on meteorological conditions. According to IPCC (2007), general yield changes, freezing-loosing reductions, increment in crop and livestock damages due to higher temperature and other adverse and positive changes can be expected in the future. Those consequences will be different according to the regions.

The IPCC Working Group II, aimed to assess Climate Change Impacts, Adaptation and Vulnerabilities on natural managed and human systems; reported significant changes on several physical and biological systems in Europe from 1970 to 2004. Most of those changes are consistent with the expected response to temperature rising and cannot explained by natural variability (IPCC, 2007). According to the IPCC Working Group II, Climate Change is expected to magnify regional differences in Europe's natural resources and assets. In Southern Europe, climate change is projected to worsen conditions (high temperatures and drought) in a region already vulnerable to climate variability, and to reduce water availability, hydropower potential, summer tourism and, in general, crop productivity (IPCC, 2007).

One of the main achievements of the IPCC (2007) fourth assessment is its confirmation, through new data and documentary proves, of many previsions that had been already made in the previous IPCC assessments. For instance, the IPCC (2001) report already pointed out the Climate-Change related risks on European and World agriculture.

Olesen and Bindi (2002) studied the climate change impact to European agriculture, considering several regions within Europe. According to them, Mediterranean agriculture will be the most affected, due to precipitation reduction in the zone, which will bring lesser water availability. Water scarcity, combined to higher transpiration rates due to temperature increments, will mean a challenge for irrigated agriculture in Southern Europe. Those conclusions agree with the IPCC (2007) last report. Despite rainfall changes are less confident than temperature rising at the global scale, many of the modelling assessments included in the IPCC (2007) report coincided in predicting less rainfall in the Mediterranean region.

Besides long-term climate-change effects, its related climate variability and the increment in extreme-events frequency (IPCC, 2007) can mean important constraints to agriculture. The higher mean temperature of 2003 summer is a good example of that. Such warm summer brought many agricultural loosing, particularly in France (Seguin et al., 2004).

The European Commission is aware about the Climate Change risks that can be expected in Europe. The European Environmental Agency released a Technical Report aimed to point out the vulnerability and adaptation to Climate Change in Europe (EEA, 2006). The report indicates that Southern Europe, the Mediterranean and central European regions are the most vulnerable to Climate Change. Considering vulnerabilities by issues, the EEA (2006) technical report considered that Climate Change and increased CO_2 atmospheric concentration could bring a beneficial impact on Northern European agriculture, through longer growing season and increasing plan productivity. However, in the South and parts of Eastern Europe the impacts are likely to be negative (EEA, 2006). The EEA (2006) report gives special attention to water resources availability in Southern Europe as one of the most important Climate-Change expected risks. The report remarks the importance of adopting concrete measures and policies on National and EU Adaptation plans to Climate Change, although it is a relative new issue.

Due to the importance of water resources management under Climate Change conditions, the European Environmental Agency released recently a Technical Report addressed to this issue (EEA, 2007). Two main impacts are recognized in the report: Flooding risks in Northern and Central Europe, as well as water scarcity in Southern countries. According to EEA (2007), several adaptation measures have been taken regarding flooding, but few have been addressed to water scarcity. Furthermore, three priorities are pointed out in the EEA (2007) report. The top priority for adaptation in the water sector should be to reduce the vulnerabilities of people and societies to shifts in hydro-meteorological trends, increased climate variability and extreme events. A second priority is to protect and restore ecosystems that provide water resources services. The third priority should be to close the gap between water supply and demand by enhancing actions that reduce demands (EEA, 2007). The report also recognize the need of research on climate-change impacts in water sector, as well as the interactions among European, national and local decision-making levels.

Besides the EEA (2006) and (2007) reports, the European Commission is preparing a "Green Book" regarding Climate Change to be released late 2007. The first draft (EC, 2007) of such "Green Book" identifies also the Mediterranean region as the most risky zone within Europe, due to the combination of temperature rising with precipitation reductions. Concerning the future of European agriculture, the Green Book points out that Climate Change would be one of several challenges, as world-trade globalisation and rural population decrement. Furthermore, the Common Agricultural Policy and several other EU policies and directives can effectively influence in climate-change adaptation issues, as water use efficiency and pollution risks (EC, 2007).

1.1. The Spanish Climate-Change Adaptation Plan

Additionally to the EU concerns, the Spanish government and the National institutions are also ready to introduce Climate-Change adaptation actions, taking into account that Spain is one of the most risky countries within Europe. The huge assessment comprised in the Preliminary Evaluation of Climate Change effects in Spain (Moreno, 2005), including the risks of Spanish agriculture (Minguez et al., 2005), has been an important guidelines to develop Climate-change adaptation strategies at the country level.

In general, the Minguez et al. (2005) assessments agree with the IPCC (2007) and the EEA (2006) reports. They all point out that the increase in CO_2 concentration and air temperature, as well as changes in seasonal rainfall, would have counteracting and non-uniform effects. The positive effect of CO_2 on photosynthetic rates can be compensated by greater temperatures and less precipitation. They also agree that while milder winter temperatures will allow higher crop growth rates if water is sufficiently available, higher summer temperatures can increase evaporative demand and hence irrigation requirements. As highlighted in all the above-cited reports, Minguez et al. (2005) indicated that he expected increase in extreme weather years will difficult crop management and will require more analysis of agricultural systems sustainability.

Minguez et al. (2005) also pointed out that crop simulation models using climate data from Regional Climate Models are nowadays the most efficient tools for impact analysis, as they are able to quantify the non-linear effects of climate change. Furthermore, they indicate the need of identifying regions with different impacts in order to recommend the corresponding adaptation measures.

According to Minguez et al. (2005), short term adaptation strategies can rely on simple management practices such as changes in sowing dates and cultivars. Nevertheless, in the long term, adaptation of cropping systems to future climate conditions is required. Implications on vegetable crops, fruit orchards, olive groves and vineyards should specifically addressed to assess adaptation at minimum cost (Minguez et al., 2005).

Minguez et al. (2005) summarizes that one of the main constraints of Spanish agriculture will be related to water availability for summer-crops agriculture, due to the expected rainfall decrement combined with the temperature rising, particularly in the summer. Furthermore, drought frequency and intensity will be higher in the near future, since it has been observed already from the last 30 years (IPCC, 2007). Along with the IPCC (2007) and the EEA (2006) and (2007) reports, Minguez et al. (2005) point out that weather variability could be the most critical issue in the coming years. The stability and sustainability of Spanish agroecosystems is affected by interannual and seasonal variations in rainfall, water availability for irrigation, the greater or smaller frequency of frost in springtime and the storms that have especial impact on the fruit and vegetable sector. Furthermore, Minguez et al. (2005) indicated also that improving water management efficiency should be a priority.

Minguez et al. (2005) pointed out particularly the influence of the CAP in crop sequences of both dry farming and in irrigation systems. Crop choices are not always the best in agronomic terms, especially in relation to climate and soil, so the sustainability of these agricultural systems is questionable. The progressive reduction of EU subsidies is beginning to affect management decisions, as can be seen in the restructuring and changing geographic distributions of olive groves and vineyards. Therefore, CAP and other European and national policies should be taken into account.

Following the conclusions of the Preliminary Evaluation of Climate Change effects in Spain (Moreno, 2005), the Spanish Climate-Change Office has prepared the National Plan for Adaptation to Climate Change (PNACC, 2006). The Plan comprises action guidelines for the hydraulic resources, the agricultural sector and several other sectors that can be potentially affected by Climate Change.

The PNACC (2006) includes also a Workplan and a Timetable. The first task is to develop Spanish-based Climate-Change scenarios that can be used further for impact assessments at each involved sector. Developing such regional data base was defined as a priority in the EEA (2006) report. The first version of the Spanish Climate-Change scenarios has been already provided by the National Institute of Meteorology (Brunet et al., 2007). Furthermore, due to its extreme importance, assessing Climate-Change effects on the hydraulic resources in Spain is the second commitment included in the PNACC (2006).

Regarding crop agriculture, the PNACC comprises the following guidelines:

- Mapping climate change effects on Spanish agricultural zones.
- Developing crop models to simulate radiation interception, water and nitrogen balances and yields.
- Evaluating irrigation demands according to different scenarios.
- Providing general recommendations for short-term agricultural management under climate change conditions.
- Identifying long term adaptation strategies, particularly in fruits, olives and vineyards.

1.2. Climate Change and Spanish Irrigated Agriculture: The Challenge

Irrigation is largely the main water user in most countries. Worldwide agricultural production in irrigated area is, in average, more than twice the production in rainfed zones, despite that irrigated area is lesser than 25% of the total agricultural area. The increment of world population and their feeding needs point toward an efficient agriculture and therefore irrigation is an absolute need. Irrigated agricultural land means approximately 350 million ha in the world. Irrigated areas are responsible for approximately 40% of the global food production (Smedema et al., 2000).

According to EUROSTAT data, irrigated area comprised 14 807 980 ha in the EU-25 during 2003. It meant 9.5% of the total EU agricultural area. The irrigated area corresponding to the EU Mediterranean countries (i.e. Spain, Italy, France and Greece) is more than 80% of the total EU-25 irrigated area. Particularly, Spanish irrigated area is 30% of the total EU-25 area, which makes Spain as the country with the largest irrigated area in the EU. Irrigated area is about 20% of the total cropped area in Spain, which means more than twice the average EU ratio. Despite their location corresponds to the temperate climate area, solar radiation rates in Mediterranean countries are relatively high. This radiation conditions could lead to higher crop transpiration rates and hence suitable agricultural productions. However, water availability constraints in Mediterranean agriculture are higher than those found in other places of the world. Therefore, rainfed production in those countries of common crops is usually lower than that found, for instance, in Northern Europe.

Table 1 shows the most relevant crops in Spain, according to the Ministry of Agriculture report (MAPA, 2004). Table 1 shows also the total cropped area, as well as the corresponding rainfed and irrigated area. Moreover, the Table depicts the percent of each crop area, regarding the total agricultural area; as well as the percent of irrigated area of each crop, respecting the total crop area. As can be seen in the Table, rainfed cereals as Barley and wheat are the most important crops in Spain, although olives and vineyards represent an important cropped area as well. Maize shows the largest irrigation area, followed by vegetables and olives. Irrigated cereals mean also an important percent of the total Spanish irrigated area. Vegetables, Sugarbeet, Maize, Alfalfa and Potatoes are mainly irrigated crops in Spain, since more than 70% of their cropped area is under irrigation.

Irrigated agriculture in Spain and most of the Mediterranean area was introduced since ancient times and it has been improved through the long farmer' experience. Crops yields under irrigation are indeed quite high. However, irrigation techniques have been kept in the same way for centuries in many Mediterranean countries. Inefficient flooding irrigation systems, for instance, is still the most commonly found in many areas of Spain (Neira et al., 2005) and other Mediterranean countries.

Irrigation is expensive, but assures the farmer productions and keeps rural population in the countryside. It has been shown that farm profitability in Europe is lower than that reported in industrial or technical business. If farming is not profitable then existing farmers will cease their activities, and young people may not be attracted into agriculture. This will mean the long-term decline of the industry and of rural areas. Actually, one of the most important constraints that face European countryside is its continuous depopulation. Most farms are small businesses, often family-run. They are an important local employer in many rural regions and major players in the rural world. Farmers play a positive role in the maintenance of the countryside and the environment by working for secure and profitable futures for themselves and their families. Therefore, to keep good living standards in the European countryside is an important concern of EU authorities, as well as national governs.

A quite large irrigation modernisation is being conducted in Spain (Beceiro, 2003), aimed to replace flooding by sprinkler and other more-efficient techniques with governmental aids. The Spanish program aimed to introduce new engineering irrigation infrastructures in the national agriculture, *Plan Nacional de Regadíos* (MAPA, 2005), is carried out by the Spanish Ministry of Agriculture. The program has been recently revised and its goals comprised not only to increment irrigated areas, but to significantly improve water savings and to avoid groundwater pollution. This kind of effort is in accordance with the Lisbon Strategy and the goals of the EU Commission of Agriculture, addressed to improve farmer's income, to make more competitive their agricultural production and to meet the EU environmental requirements (EU, 2005; Fischer, 2005).

Table 1. Relevant crops in Spain, according to reported rainfed, irrigated and total cropped area (MAPA, 2004)

Crop	Rainfed (ha)	Irrigated (ha)	Total	% of Total	% Irrigated
Barley	2807592	303281	3110873	21.3	9.7
Olives	2056532	383050	2439582	16.7	15.7
Wheat	2024930	195711	2220641	15.2	8.8
Vineyards	1009407	163390	1172797	8.0	13.9
Fruits	987169	271201	1258370	7.6	28.3
Sunflower	699105	87727	786832	5.4	11.1
Maize	96872	464569	561441	3.8	82.7
Oats	462888	33439	496327	3.4	6.7
Vegetables	28897	396866	425763	2.9	93.2
Alfalfa	49441	191239	240680	1.6	79.5
Rye	104789	3283	108072	0.7	3.0
Potato	28466	72635	101101	0.7	71.8
Sugarbeet	17101	82733	99834	0.7	82.9

Irrigation modernisations efforts have been made in non-European Mediterranean countries also, as Egypt. However, there is still a big difference in irrigated agricultural production between European and non-European Mediterranean countries. As can be seen in Figure 1, shown below, rainfed crop production, as wheat, is similar in all the compared countries. However, the yields of a usually irrigated crop, as maize, are much larger in European countries than in non-European Mediterranean countries. The above information is a national average; therefore it includes also non-irrigated maize, as well as irrigated wheat. Nevertheless, the figure depicts clearly the mean yields at each country. Maize yields of the European and non-European Mediterranean countries show a considerable difference. This could be mainly due to the large new engineering irrigation infrastructures, which have been available in European Mediterranean countries since the last 20 years.

Furthermore, Figure 2 depicts the absolute difference in Maize yields (in T/ha) and production (in BT) between Spain and Egypt from 1990 to 2004, following the same FAOSTAT (2005) data. Despite total Egyptian production is higher than that of Spain, the Spanish yields are not only higher than the corresponding Egyptian yields, but their yield differences have been linearly incremented during the last 15 years.

The yield differences between Spain and the European Mediterranean countries as compared to Non-European Mediterranean countries can be due to many reasons, but indeed the new engineering irrigation infrastructures that has been introduced in the European Mediterranean countries, as Spain, during the last 20 years (MAPA, 2005) has a notable influence in this yearly yield increment.

Despite the infrastructures investments in Spain and other European countries, irrigation is still very expensive at the world scale. Water could be not enough under the future-enhanced droughts conditions, particularly considering third-world population rise. However, irrigation must not only been kept, but also enlarged in order to feed the foreseen world population. This contradiction has been pointed out as important concern during the 19th Congress of the International Commission on Irrigation and Drainage (ICID), held in Beijing recently. The ICI Congress focused on the theme of "Use of Water and Land for Food Security and Environmental Sustainability" and they pointed out that: the key to increase future food production lies in expansion of irrigated and drained lands where potential exists; in better water and land management in existing irrigated and drained areas; and in increase in water use efficiency and land productivity, in the Beijing ICID declaration.

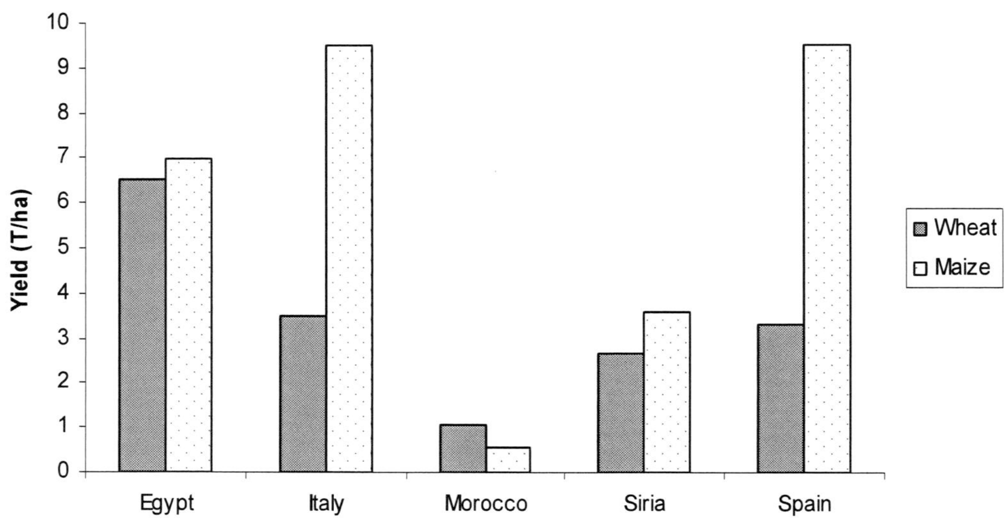

Figure 1. Average yields in 2004 in several Mediterranean countries, according to FAOSTAT data.

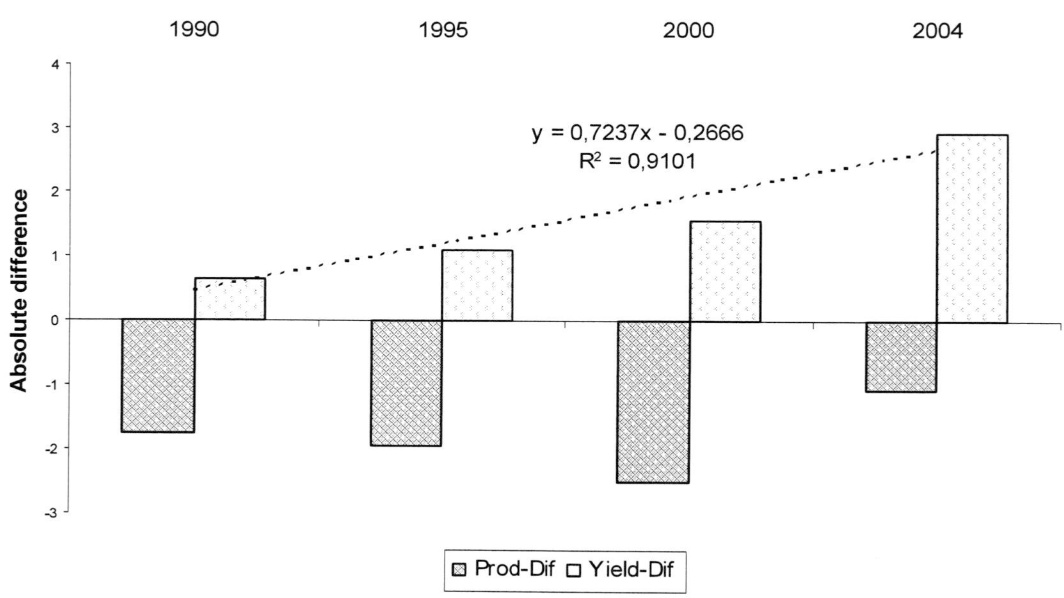

Figure 2. Absolute differences between Egyptian and Spanish Maize productions (in BT) and yields (in T/ha).

Climate change will impose a new challenge to Spanish and Mediterranean irrigation areas. Improving irrigation efficiency is an imperative, although it has been recognized that much water can still be saved in Spanish irrigation systems (Playan and Mateos, 2005). Some climate-change impact assessments have estimated that CO_2 rising will significantly reduce the crop water requirements (Guereña et al., 2001; Villalobos and Fereres, 2004). However, such positive "fertilizing effect" of CO_2 rising seems to have been overestimated according to the FACE results (Craft-Brandner and Salvucci, 2004; Aisnworth and Long., 2005). Hence, Spanish irrigated agriculture might be affordable in the future only by reducing the water consumes. Furthermore, the globalisation of the world market and the "cost recovering principle" included in the EU Water Framework Directive (2000/60/EC) would lead to prices reductions in the future, while incrementing water costs.

Several examples can be pointed out on the challenge that climate change, combined with WFD and other future policies, could bring to the affordability of irrigated agriculture in Spain. Perhaps the most updated situation concerns Sugarbeet cropping. The EU Commission of Agriculture has proposed a reform to current EU sugar production conditions, which has been strongly rejected by Spanish sugar-beet farmers and producers, as well as those from other countries. The reform implies a substantial reduction of current EU prices. Sugar-beet is mainly an irrigated crop in Spain and other Mediterranean countries; hence the production costs are relatively high due to irrigation. Farmers who use groundwater to irrigate sugar beet are the ones facing the highest problem, due to the increment of oil costs. Furthermore, drought conditions, as that found during 2005 in Spain, can be strengthen in the near future, due to global change. Therefore, farmers need to reduce irrigation costs while cropping Sugarbeet under these new prices and climate conditions. They need help in order to find a reliable irrigation management. This is particularly important in those farms where irrigation modernisation or any irrigation investment in new technologies is expected, due to the amortization of the investment costs.

2. Climate Scenarios, Seasonal Forecasts and Downscaling Issues

Complex Models regarding general atmospheric circulation (GCM) have been developed to predict the future earth climate. Those models are able to simulate the energy and mass exchanges between the atmosphere and the earth surface, according to several man-due scenarios of greenhouse gases emissions (IPCC, 2007). The HadCM3 model, developed by the United-Kingdom Meteorological Office, and the German ECHAM4 model were considered in the IPCC (2007) report, among other non-European GCM's.

On the other hand, seasonal time-scale climate predictions are now made routinely at a number of operational meteorological centers around the world, using comprehensive coupled models of the atmosphere, oceans, and land surface (Stockdale et al. 1998; Mason et al. 1999; Kanamitsu et al. 2002; Alves et al. 2002; Palmer et al., 2004). Particularly, GCM were integrated over 4-month time scales with prescribed observed sea surface temperatures (SSTs) within the PROVOST project (Palmer et al., 2004). Single model and multi-model ensembles were treated as potential forecasts. A key result was that probability scores based on the full multi-model ensemble were generally higher than those from any of the single-model ensembles (Palmer et al., 2004).

Based on PROVOST results, the Development of a European Multi-model Ensemble System for Seasonal to Inter-annual Prediction project (DEMETER) was conceived, and funded under the European Union 5th Framework Environment Programme (Palmer et al., 2004). The principal aim of DEMETER was to advance the concept of multi-model ensemble prediction by installing a number of state-of-the-art global coupled ocean–atmosphere models on a single supercomputer, and to produce a series of 6-month multi-model ensemble hindcasts with common archiving and common diagnostic software. As a result of DEMETER, real-time multi-model ensemble seasonal global predictions are now routinely made at the European Centre for Medium-Range Weather Forecasts (ECMWF).

Palmer et al. (2004) showed some DEMETER applications. Results indicate that the multi-model ensemble is a viable pragmatic approach to the problem of representing model uncertainty in seasonal-to-inter-annual prediction, and will lead to a more reliable forecasting system than that based on any one single model (Palmer et al., 2004). On the other hand, Doblas-Reyes et al. (2006), pointed out the potential of DEMETER predictions of seasonal climate fluctuations to crop yield forecasting and other agricultural applications. They recommend a probabilistic approach at all stages of the forecasting process.

The ENSEMBLES EU-funded proposal (Hewitt, 2005) is an important recent effort to improve the skill of seasonal forecasts and to make them available to stakeholders. The ENSEMBLES proposal uses the collective expertise of 66 institutes to produce a reliable quantitative risk assessment of long-term climate change and its impacts. Particular emphasis is given to probable future changes in climate extremes, including storminess, intense rainfall, prolonged drought, and potential climate 'shocks' such as failure of the Gulf Stream. To focus on the practical concerns of stakeholders and policy makers, ENSEMBLES considers impacts on timeframes ranging from seasonal to decadal and longer, at global, regional, and local spatial scales.

Several useful tools to assess climate-change impacts on agriculture have been developed during the last years. GCM are among such tools. However, GCM estimations of temperature, precipitation and other meteorological variables are usually made for large areas. For instance, Guereña et al. (2001) showed that those estimations are not very useful to Spanish agricultural climate-change impact assessments, due to the notable topographical changes within the Peninsula for relative small distances. Therefore, a "downscaling" of GCM outputs is absolutely needed before using their estimations for agricultural applications.

Wilby and Wigley (2001) summarized the available downscaling techniques; which can be classified as statistical, dynamical and weather generators. A dynamical downscaling method is to apply numerical regional climate models at high resolution over the region of interest. Regional models have been used in several climate impact studies for many regions of the world, including parts of North America, Asia, Europe, Australia and Southern Africa (e.g Giorgi and Mearns, 1999; Kattenberg et al., 1996; Mearns et al., 1997). The regional climate models obtain sub-grid scale estimates (sometimes down to 25 km resolution) and are able to account for important local forcing factors, such as surface type and elevation. Particularly, the regional climate model RegCM was originally developed at the National Center for Atmospheric Research (NCAR), USA and has been mostly applied to studies of regional climate and seasonal predictability around the world. It is further developed by the Physics of Weather and Climate group at the Abdus Salam International Centre for

Theoretical Physics (ICTP) in Trieste, Italy. The PRUDENCE Regional Models Experiment has been developed in Europe under the EU Framework Research Program (Christensen and Christensen, 2007). PRUDENCE project provides a series of high-resolution regional climate change scenarios for a large range of climatic variables for Europe for the period 2071-2100 using four high resolution GCMs and eight RCMs.

Wilby and Wigley (2001) classified statistical downscaling in regression methods and weather-pattern approaches. The regression method uses statistical linear or non-linear relationships between sub-grid scale parameters and coarse resolution predictor variables. Wilby and Wigley (2001) included Artificial Neural Network within the regression-type statistical downscaling. On the other hand, weather-pattern based approaches involve grouping meteorological data according to a given classification scheme. Classification procedures include principal components, canonical correlation analyses, fuzzy rules, correlation-based pattern recognition techniques and analogue procedures; among others (Wilby and Wigley, 2001). Theoretically, dynamical downscaling methods are better than simple statistical methods since they are based on physical laws. However, statistical downscaling method are less computational exigent and can give good results if the relationships between predictand and predictors are stationary (Wilby and Wigley, 2001).

2.1. Weather Generators

Weather generators have been very used in agriculture climate-change impact assessments (Hoogenboom, 2000; Sivakumar, 2001). A weather generator produces synthetic daily time series of climatic variables statistically equivalent to the recorded historical series, as well as daily site-specific climate scenarios that could be based on regional GCM results (Semenov and Jamieson, 2001). The weather generator usually mimics correctly the mean values of the climatic variables, although underestimates their variability (Mavromatis and Jones, 1998; Semenov and Jamieson, 2001; Wilby and Wigley, 2001). Different weather generators are available, but according to Wilby and Wigley (2001), the US-made and the UK-made WGEN and LARS-WG are the most widely used.

LARS-WG is a stochastic weather generator which can be used for the simulation of weather data at a single site (Racsko et al, 1991; Semenov et al, 1998; Semenov and Brooks, 1999; Semenov and Barrow, 2002), under both current and future climate conditions. These data are in the form of daily time-series for a suite of climate variables, namely, precipitation, maximum and minimum temperature and solar radiation.

According to Semenov and Barrow (2002), stochastic weather generators were originally developed for two main purposes:

1. To provide a means of simulating synthetic weather time-series with statistical characteristics corresponding to the observed statistics at a site, but which were long enough to be used in an assessment of risk in hydrological or agricultural applications.
2. To provide a means of extending the simulation of weather time-series to unobserved locations, through the interpolation of the weather generator parameters obtained from running the models at neighbouring sites.

A stochastic weather generator is not a predictive tool, but simply a mean to generate time-series of synthetic weather statistically 'identical' to the observations. A stochastic weather generator, however, can serve as a computationally inexpensive tool to produce multiple-year climate change scenarios at the daily time scale which incorporate changes in both mean climate and in climate variability (Semenov and Barrow, 1997).

The LARS-WG weather generator focused to overcome the limitations of the Markov chain model of precipitation occurrence (Richardson and Wright, 1984). This widely used method of modelling precipitation occurrence (which generally considers two precipitation states, wet or dry, and considers conditions on the previous day only) is not always able to correctly simulate the maximum dry spell length. LARS-WG follows a 'series' approach, in which the simulation of dry and wet spell length is the first step in the weather generation process.

The most recent version of LARS-WG (version 3.0 for Windows 9x/NT/2000/XP) has undergone a complete redevelopment in order to produce a robust model capable of generating synthetic weather data for a wide range of climates (Semenov and Barrow, 2002). LARS-WG has been compared with another widely-used stochastic weather generator, which uses the Markov chain approach (WGEN; Richardson, 1985; Richardson and Wright, 1984), at a number of sites representing diverse climates and has been shown to perform at least as well as, if not better than, WGEN at each of these sites (Semenov et al, 1998).

3. Simulating Crop-Growth and Crop Water-Use

On the other hand, many crop simulation models have been appeared in the last 20 years. Those models are able to estimate crop water-use and growth under any weather and cop management conditions. Those models, combined with downscaled GCM scenarios, can be a reliable approach to support decision-making under climate change conditions (Hoogenboom, 2000). Despite many models are available, Mechanistic models i.e. those based in the physical laws of the soil-water-plant-atmosphere continuum, are the most suitable to climate-change impact assessments (Eatherall, 1997), since the laws are, in principle, valid for al climatic conditions.

According to Tubiello and Ewert (2002), more than 40 assessments of climate-change impact on agriculture have been published up to now. They pointed out that generally models provided accurate results, compared to actual data. The most used models in such assessments are DSSAT (Jones et al., 2003) and those developed in Wageningen (Van Ittersum et al., 2003).

As pointed out above, modelling tools appeared in the eighties, due to computer availability, aimed to simulate crop growth and final yields. Numerous crop growth models have been developed since them. The models can use weather data input, such as short term weather forecast, a season's forecasted weather or climate scenarios to estimate potential or actual growth, development or yield. Historical-production records are useful for assessing the impacts of climate variability on crop yields, but cannot reveal crop response under alternative management strategies, which can be done through modelling simulations.

Bastiaansen et al. (2004) provided an update revision of the modelling applications to irrigation assessments. They pointed out the opportunities lying in such modelling approaches to irrigation and drainage assessments, with more than 40 examples. The simulation examples comprises assessing irrigation supply needs, as well as irrigation designing, scheduling, management and performance; salt-affected soils due to irrigation, groundwater recharge and estimating soil losses, among others.

Models have been usually classified as empirical, functional and mechanistics (Connolly, 1998; Bastiaansen et al., 2004). Mechanistic models, i.e. those based in the physical laws of the soil-water-plan-atmosphere are more suitable to assess climate-change effects on agriculture than empirical models (Eatherall, 1997; Hoogenboom, 2000), since the theoretical mechanistic-model backgrounds is still valid under these new conditions. According to Bastiaansen et al. (2004), concerning suitability to describe irrigation and drainage processes, models can be classified as bucket, pseudo-dynamics, Richards-equation based, SVAT models, multidimensional and crop-production models. However, at the plot and field scale only the bucket, the crop-oriented models and those based on the Richards equation have been significantly used. The Richards equation describes the vertical movement of water within the soil profile and its solutions can, at least theoretically, provide the water distribution under certain initial and border conditions (Kutilek and Nielsen, 1994).

Therefore, concerning irrigation studies at field and plot scales, the most important mechanistic modelling approaches are those mainly aimed to simulate crop-growth and those addressed to physically-based simulation of soil-water movement, through numerical solutions of the Richards equation. These models have been called agrohydrological models, because they combine agricultural and hydrological issues (Van Dam, 2000).

3.1. Crop-Growth Oriented Simulation Models

According to Stockle et al. (2003), the initial crop-growth simulation models, mainly theoretical approaches, appeared in the 1970s (de Wit et al., 1970; Arkin et al., 1976). Applications oriented models appeared during the 1980s (Wilkerson et al., 1983; Swaney et al., 1983). Models such as SUCROS and others associated with the Dutch 'School of de Wit' (Bouman et al., 1996); as well as those produced in the US as the CERES (Ritchie, 1998) and CROPGRO (Boote et al., 1998) families of models had a significant impact on the crop modelling community (Stockle et al., 2003). As pointed out by Brisson et al (2003), the rest of the crop-growth simulating models, although different; generally follow similar guidelines than the originally produced models. Alexandrov (2002) provided a complete summary of the crop models that have been used in Europe.

3.1.1. The DSSAT Models and the "Cascade Approach"

The Decision Support System for Agrotechnology Transfer (DSSAT) was originally developed by an international network of scientists, cooperating in the International Benchmark Sites Network for Agrotechnology Transfer project (IBSNAT, 1993; Tsuji et al., 1998; Uehara, 1998; Jones et al., 1998), to facilitate the application of crop models in a systems approach to agronomic research (Jones et al., 2003).

DSSAT is a microcomputer software package that contains crop-soil simulation models, data bases for weather, soil, and crops, and strategy evaluation programs integrated with a 'shell' program which is the main user interface (Jones et al., 1998). DSSAT originally comprises the CERES models for maize (Jones and Kiniry, 1986) and wheat (Ritchie and

Otter, 1985), as well as the SOYGRO soybean (Wilkerson et al., 1983) and PNUTGRO peanut (Boote et al., 1986) models, among others (Jones et al., 2003).

The decision to make these models compatible led to the design of the DSSAT and the ultimate development of compatible models for additional crops, such as potato, rice, dry beans, sunflower, and sugarcane (Hoogenboom et al., 1994; Jones et al., 1998; Hoogenboom et al., 1999; Jones et al., 2003).

According to Hoogenboom et al. (1999), the DSSAT Cropping System Model (CSM) simulates growth and development of a crop over time, as well as the soil water, carbon and nitrogen processes and management practices. The CSM main components are:

- A main driver program, which controls timing for each simulation,
- A Land unit module, which manages all simulation processes which affect a unit of land
- Primary modules that individually simulate the various processes that affect the land unit including weather, plant growth, soil processes, soil-plant-atmosphere interface and management practices.

Collectively, these components simulate the changes over time in the soil and plants that occur on a single land unit in response to weather and management practices.

DSSAT has a module format. Each module has six operational steps, (run initialization, season initialization, rate calculations, integration, daily output, and summary output). The main program controls the timing of events: the start and stop of simulation, beginning and end of crop season, as well as daily time loops (Hoogenboom et al., 1999).

Ritchie (1998) provided the background of DSSAT models regarding simulation of soil-water movement and crop water-use. The DSSAT simulation of the soil water balance depends on the capability of water from rainfall or irrigation to enter soil through the surface and be stored in the soil reserve.

The "cascading approach" as used in DSSAT is explained by Ritchie (1998). Drainage from a layer takes place only when the soil water content at a given depth is between field saturation and the drained upper limit.

The Priestley-Taylor (1972) equation for potential evapotranspiration is used in DSSAT. Calculation of potential evaporation requires an approximation of daytime temperature and the soil-plant reflection coefficient (albedo) for solar radiation. For the approximation of the daytime temperature a weighted mean of the daily maximum and minimum air temperatures is used. The combined crop and soil albedo is calculated from the model estimate of leaf area index and the input bare soil albedo (Ritchie, 1998).

The root water absorption in DSSAT is calculated using a law of the limiting approach whereby the soil resistance, the root resistance, or the atmospheric demand dominates the flow rate of water into the roots. The flow rates are calculated using assumptions of water movement to a single root and that the roots are uniformly distributed within a layer (Ritchie, 1998).

The potential transpiration and biomass production rates are reduced by multiplying their potential rates by a soil water deficit factor calculated from the ratio of the potential uptake to the potential transpiration. A second water deficit factor is calculated to account for water deficit effects on plant physiological processes that are more sensitive than the stomata controlled processes of transpiration and biomass production (Ritchie, 1998).

The DSSAT models have been indeed the most used simulation tools in agricultural climate-effect assessments (Tubiello and Ewert, 2002) and crop water balance studies (e.g. Eitzinger et al., 2002). They were calibrated and validated at many agricultural regions of the world (Hoogenboom, 2000). DSSAT models have been intensively used also in the framework of the CLIMAG activities aimed to mitigate and estimate agricultural climate-risks (Adiku et al., 2007; Meza, 2007; Singh et al., 2007).

3.1.2. The Wageningen Models

Van Ittersum et al. (2003) provided a complete summary of the family of models made in Wageningen, The Netherlands, during the last 30 years. According to Tubiello and Ewert (2002), these Dutch models have been the most widely used, after DSSAT models, in agricultural climate-risk assessments.

As pointed out by Van Ittersum et al. (2003), the Wageningen group has a long tradition in developing and applying crop models in its agroecological research program, based on the pioneering work of C.T. de Wit. In the 1960s and 1970s the main aim of these modelling activities was to obtain understanding at the crop scale based on the underlying processes. De Wit and co-workers at the Department of Theoretical Production Ecology of Wageningen University, and the DLO Research Institute for Agrobiology and Soil Fertility developed the model BACROS and evaluated components of the model (such as canopy photosynthesis) with especially designed equipment and field experiments (De Wit et al., 1978; Goudriaan, 1977; Van Keulen, 1975; Penning de Vries et al., 1974). These modelling approaches have served as the basis and inspiration for modelling groups around the world (Stockle et al., 2003).

In the 1980s a wide range of scientists in Wageningen became involved in the development and application of crop models. The generic crop model SUCROS for the potential production situation was developed (Van Keulen et al., 1982; Van Laar et al., 1997), which formed the basis of most recent Wageningen crop models such as WOFOST (Van Keulen and Wolf, 1986), MACROS (Penning de Vries et al., 1989), and ORYZA (Bouman et al., 2001). In the 1990s the Wageningen group focused more on applications in research, agronomic practice and policy making (Van Ittersum et al., 2003).

Crop modelling in Wageningen for potential production situations follows the photosynthesis approach in the SUCROS family of models (Van Ittersum et al., 2003). LINTUL (Light INTerception and UtiLisation) models use the linear relationship between biomass production and the amount of radiation intercepted (captured) by the crop canopy (Monteith, 1981), which has been found for many crop species, grown under well-watered conditions and ample nutrient supply, in the absence of pests, diseases and weeds. This relationship sets a finite limit on yield potential (Sinclair, 1994), which thus can be modelled without going into detailed descriptions of the processes of photosynthesis and respiration. Spitters and Schapendonk (1990) developed the model LINTUL with a module for the calculation of crop growth based on the LUE concept.

In the photosynthesis approach in SUCROS (Simple and Universal CROp growth Simulator) models, the daily rate of canopy CO2 assimilation is calculated from daily incoming radiation, temperature and leaf area index (LAI). The model contains a set of subroutines that calculate the daily totals by integrating instantaneous rates of leaf CO2 assimilation (Goudriaan and Van Laar, 1994; Van Laar et al., 1997).

Particularly, the model WOFOST (WOrld FOod STudies) simulates crop production potentials as dictated by environmental conditions (soils, climate), crop characteristics and crop management (irrigation, fertiliser application) (Van Diepen et al., 1989). The model has been continuously modified, and applied for many different purposes (e.g. De Koning and Van Diepen, 1992). WOFOST uses the SUCROS approach for potential production conditions.

WOFOST permits dynamic simulation of phenological development from emergence till maturity on the basis of crop genetic properties and environmental conditions. The cultivar-specific values of thermal time assimilate conversion coefficients, maximum rooting depth, daily root development rate and partitioning fractions are important inputs. Dry matter accumulation is estimated by the rate of gross CO2 assimilation of the canopy. This rate depends on the radiation energy intercepted by the canopy, which is a function of incoming radiation and of crop leaf area. Simulated growth processes and phenological development are regulated by temperature (e.g. the maximum rate of photosynthesis), radiation and atmospheric CO2 content and limited by availability of water. Root extension is computed in a simple way, the initial and the maximum rooting depth as determined by the crop and by the soil and the maximum daily increase in rooting depth being specified prior to the simulation. The daily increase in rooting depth is equal to the maximum daily increase unless maximum rooting depth is reached. The Ritchie (1972) equation is used to separate the evaporation and transpiration terms from the evapotranspiration.

The potential biomass production rate is assumed to decrease in the same proportion as the transpiration so that the actual amount of biomass produced on a given day and consequently during whole season can be calculated.

WOFOST has been used by the European Union's Joint Research Centre (JRC) to develop a system for regional crop state monitoring and yield forecasting for the whole European Union (Van Ittersum et al., 2003). The system comprises winter wheat, grain maize, barley, rice, sugar beet, potatoes, field beans, soybean, winter oil seed rape and sunflower. This system, called crop growth monitoring system (CGMS), generates region-specific indicators of the agricultural season conditions in the current year, on a semi-real time basis. This has been realised by simulating yields from weather and soil data, which serve as crop production indicators. This model output is qualitative in the sense that it is based on comparison of quantified indicators of the current year with those of the past. It provides information on whether in the current season a given crop deviates from the 'normal' growing pattern in terms of biomass and phenological development. These crop indicators are used in combination with regression techniques as a basis for quantitative regional yield prediction for the various crops. The system is operational for the EU and has been installed in various non-EU countries.

According to Van Ittersum et al. (2003), despite that Wageningen has a strong tradition in crop modelling, which has yielded a rich variety in crop modelling approaches and modules; there has not been a strong drive towards integration of research efforts, particularly not for implementation and application purposes.

3.1.3. Other Available Crop-Oriented Models

As pointed out above, besides DSSAT and the Wageningen models, several other models have been developed during the last years, aimed to estimate crop development and yields under different agricultural management conditions. Some of these models have been developed and tested in Europe. Numerous models are now available, with different objectives, and many new models are still appearing. Actually, there is no universal model and it is necessary to adapt system definition, simulated processes and model formalisations to specific environments or to new problems (Van Ittersum et al., 2003). To efficiently manage irrigation systems has been one of the most important issues considered in simulation models since they appear.

Particularly, the European Society of Agronomy (ESA), has a special session dedicated to such modelling tools. Besides, special numbers of the European Journal of Agronomy have been dedicated to promote such models. The CROPSYST model (Stockle et al., 2003), the French model STICS (Brisson et al., 2003) and the Australian model APSIM (Keating et al., 2003) are examples of such other models.

Other available European model is the Czech model PERUN (Dubrovsky et al., 2002, 2003). The model is a computer Windows-based system for probabilistic crop yield forecasting. The system comprises all parts of the process: (1) Preparation of input parameters for crop model simulation, (2) launching the crop model simulation, (3) statistical and graphical analysis of the crop model output, (4) crop yield forecast. The weather data series are calculated by the stochastic weather generator Met&Roll (Dubrovsky, 1999) with parameters that are derived from the observed series. The synthetic weather series coherently extends the available observed series and fit the weather forecast. Wind speed and humidity were added to the standard set of four surface weather characteristics generated by Met& Roll to meet the input data requirements. These two variables are generated separately by nearest neighbours re-sampling. To prepare the weather data for seasonal crop yield forecasting, the weather generator may now generate the synthetic series which coherently follows the observed series at any day of the year.

The crop yield forecast made by PERUN is based on the WOFOST crop model simulations run with weather series consisting of observed series till DAY-1 coherently followed up by synthetic weather series since DAY. The simulation is repeated n times (new synthetic weather series are stochastically generated for each simulation) and the probabilistic forecasts are then issued in terms of the average and standard deviation of the model crop yields obtained in the n simulations. The synthetic part of the weather series is prepared by a two step.

3.2. Agrohydrological Models

Agrohydrological or water-oriented models were significantly developed during the last years (Bastiaansen et al., 2004). The models SWAP (Van Dam et al., 1997), DRAINMOD (Kandil et al., 1995), WAVE (Vanclooster et al., 1994), ISAREG (Teixeira and Pereira, 1992) and HYDRUS (Šimunek et al., 1998) can be considered as agrohydrological models, among others.

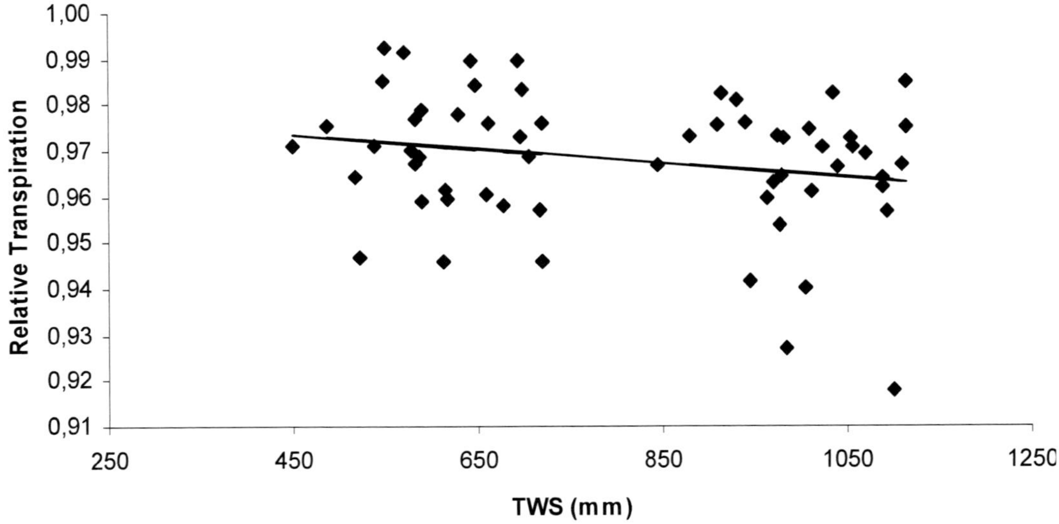

Figure 3. Simulated Maize relative transpirations as a function of Total Water Supply in dry years, considering a shallower water-table at 2-m depth (after Utset et al., 2006).

The unsaturated zone, i.e. the zone between the soil surface and the groundwater, is a complicated system governed by highly non-linear processes and interactions. Flow processes can alternatively be described by means of physical-mathematical models. According to Bastiaansen et al. (2004), unsaturated-zone models can be used to simulate the timing of irrigations and irrigation depths, drain spacing and drain depth, and system behaviour and response. The models have increased our understanding of irrigation and drainage processes in the context of soil–plant–atmosphere systems. Progress in modelling can be attributed to merging separated theories of infiltration, plant growth, evapotranspiration and flow to drain pipes into a single numerical code (Bastiaansen et al., 2004).

According to Van Ittersum et al. (2003) agrohydrological models are more suitable to irrigation and water-use assessments than crop-growth oriented models, although both approaches have been used.

3.2.1. Constraints of Crop-Oriented Models Regarding the Simulation of Soil Water-Movement and Crop Water-Use

Actually, water moves not only down within the soil, but also lateral and even upward, depending on the potential gradients (Kutilek and Nielsen, 1994). Transport phenomena, as water movement into the soil, are driven by potential gradients that depend on gravity, water extraction by roots and water that enters or leaves the profile from top or bottom, causing different soil water suctions in the different layers.

The cascade approach could be appropriate on sandy soils or if the objective is to calculate the amount of water available to the crop over longer periods of time. However, this approach could fail in soils with significant clay and silt content and if the objective is to calculate daily soil-water profiles, as needed in irrigation assessments. A Richards-based approach might be more appropriate in those cases (Van Ittersum et al., 2003).

Several researchers have pointed out the DSSAT limitations regarding soil-water simulations, due to the use of the cascade approach in such simulations (Gabrielle et al., 1995;

Maraux et al., 1998; Mastrorilli et al., 2003). According to Ritchie (1998), there is definitely a need to have better DSSAT simulations of the water balance in very poorly drained conditions where oxygen stresses will impact plant growth. Some attempts to improve DSSAT in that concern have been made already (Yang et al., 2004).

Particularly, since the cascade approach is unable to simulate upward water movement due to capillary rising, DSSAT yield predictions significantly depart from actual yields under heavy rain conditions (Rosenzweig et al., 2002). Particularly, Utset et al. (2006) showed that capillary rising can be an important component of maize water balance, when maize is cropped nearby river and channels, where shallower water tables can be found.

Extreme rainfall conditions will be more frequent in the near future, due to climate change (IPCC, 2007). As pointed out by Rosenzweig et al. (2002), yield loses in the US due to heavy rainfall could be very important in the future and the modelling-based climate-risk assessments should take them into account.

Utset et al. (2006) results also showed that water excess could significantly affect crop production. Figure 3 depicts the maize relative transpiration (ratio between actual and maximum transpiration) as simulated during dry years through SWAP by Utset et al. (2006). RT is depicted in Figure 3 as a function of Total Water Supply (TWS), considering a water table at a 2-m depth. The line shows the obtained regression. As can be seen in the figure, higher TWS gives raise to a reduction in RT rather than to further increments. Since the Feddes et al. (1978) root water-uptake function, included in SWAP, is able to account on water-excess effects on crop water use, the Utset et al. (2006) simulations can estimate the extreme rainfall effect also, whereas other models are unable to evaluate that consequence. Utset et al. (2006) simulation results indicate that precipitation excess could bring a negative effect in flooded irrigated maize, if relatively shallow water tables are found.

3.2.2. SWAP Model. Generalities

Feddes et al. (1978) developed the agrohydrological model SWATR (Soil Water Actual Transpiration Rate) to describe transient water flow in cultivated soils with various soil layers and under the influence of groundwater. The model was further developed to accommodate more boundary conditions (Belmans et al., 1983), crop growth (Kabat et al., 1992), shrinkage and swelling of clay soils (Oostindie and Bronswijk, 1992), and salt transport (Van den Broek et al., 1994). More recently, the model SWAP (Van Dam et al., 1997) was released as a result of a combination of SWATR with WOFOST (Van Keulen and Wolf, 1986). Several improved versions of SWAP were released; the most updated includes also the solute-leaching simulation model PEARL (Kroes, 2001).

SWAP is a computer model that simulates transport of water, solutes and heat in variably saturated top soils. The program is designed for integrated modelling of the Soil-Atmosphere-Plant System. Transport processes at field scale level and during whole growing seasons are considered. System boundary conditions at the top are defined by the soil surface with or without a crop and the atmospheric conditions. The lateral boundary simulates the interaction with surface water systems. The bottom boundary is located in the unsaturated zone or in the upper part of the groundwater and describes the interaction with local or regional groundwater.

Van Dam (2000) provides a detail description of the SWAP theoretical background. SWAP solves Richards's equation numerically, subject to specified initial and boundary conditions and the soil hydraulic functions.

The maximum root water extraction rate, integrated over the rooting depth, is equal to the potential transpiration rate, which is governed by atmospheric conditions. The potential root water extraction rate at a certain depth may be determined by the root length density, at this depth as fraction of the total root length density.

Stresses due to dry or wet conditions and/or high salinity concentrations may reduce The potential root water extraction rate. The water stress in SWAP is described by the function proposed by Feddes et al. (1978), which comprises a coefficient that takes values between zero and one. Under conditions wetter than a certain "anaerobiosis point" (h1) water uptake by roots is zero, as well as the coefficient α. Likewise, under conditions drier than "wilting point" (h4), α is also zero. Water uptake by the roots is assumed to be maximal when the soil water pressure-head is between h2 and h3 and hence α-value is one in that case. The values of α decrease linearly with h for h values lower than h4 but larger than h3. According to Leenhardt et al. (1995), the Feddes et al. (1978) root water-uptake model has the advantage that not only considers the crop transpiration reduction due to lower soil-water contents, but also takes in account the negative effect of water excess in the soil root zone. Utset et al. (2000) showed that the Feddes et al. (1978) model fits better to actual data, obtained in tropical conditions, than the model provided by Van Genuchten et al. (1987). This SWAP feature could be very important, since flooding could be regionally more severe in the future (IPCC, 2000, Rosenzweig et al., 2002; Utset et al., 2006).

For salinity stress the response function of Maas and Hoffman (1977) is used in SWAP (Van Dam, 2000), as this function has been calibrated for many crops.

Besides calculating crop yields through the WOFOST module, a simpler approach to calculate yield reduction as function of growing stage can be used in SWAP (Doorenbos and Kassam, 1979; Smith, 1992). The ratio between actual to potential transpirations is known as "Relative transpiration ratio" (Van Dam, 2000). The relative transpiration reductions can be related to the effects of water stress (De Wit et al., 1978; Van Dam 2000). The relative yield of the entire growing season is calculated as product of the relative yields of each growing stage.

Two different types of irrigation can be specified in SWAP (Kroes et al., 2002). Either a fixed irrigation can be specified, or an irrigation schedule can be calculated for a specific crop according to a number of criteria. A combination of fixed and calculated irrigations is also possible. An example of this is a fixed irrigation (preparation of the seed bed) before planting and calculated irrigations based on soil moisture conditions after planting. Fixed irrigations can be applied the whole year. Irrigation scheduling can only be active during a cropping period. The irrigation type can be specified as a sprinkling or surface irrigation. In case of sprinkling irrigation, interception will be calculated (Kroes et al., 2002).

3.2.3. SWAP Model. The Simple Approach to Estimate Crop Water-Use

Kroes and Van Dam (2003) described the SWAP performance. According to them, the simple SWAP crop-growth approach represents a green canopy that intercepts precipitation, transpires and shades the ground. Leaf area index, crop height and rooting depth must be specified as functions of the development stage. SWAP simulates crop growing on a daily basis. The development stage (DVS) at a given day j depends on the development stage at the previous day and the daily temperature, according to:

$$DVS^{j} = DVS^{j-1} + \frac{T_{eff}}{T_{sum}} \qquad [1.]$$

where T_{sum} is the required temperature sum and T_{eff} is the effective daily temperature, calculated from mean daily air temperature minus a minimum starting temperature (3 °C). DVS reaches 1 at anthesis and 2 at maturity, according to the temperature sums at these two stages.

Van Dam (2000) provided the theoretical SWAP background. SWAP solves the Richards equation numerically, subject to specified initial and boundary conditions and the hydraulic functions of the soil. The maximum root water extraction rate (S_p) at a depth z, considering a uniform root-length density distribution, can be calculated from:

$$Sp(z) = \frac{T_p}{D_{root}} \qquad [2.]$$

Where D_{root} is the root density fraction, integrated over the rooting length density at this depth and T_p is the potential transpiration rate, which is subject to atmospheric conditions.

Actual root water uptake can be estimated through:

$$Sa(z) = \alpha\ Sp(z) \qquad [3.]$$

The α values range from zero (no root-water uptake) to one (maximum water-uptake, no stress) according to the Feddes et al. (1978) function. These values change according to actual soil water-content, but the function is crop-dependent (Van Dam, 2000). Utset et al. (2000) showed that the original parameters of the Feddes et al. (1978) model can be used to simulate potato water-use in conditions that are very different from those existing where the model was originally applied. Therefore, the parameters applied to sugarbeet in the Netherlands have been used in this assessment.

The potential reference evapotranspiration (ETP) is calculated in SWAP by the Penman-Monteith approach, although the user may introduce other ETP calculations (Van Dam, 2000). In addition, the crop coefficients K_c must be introduced to convert reference ETP on maximum crop evapotranspiration.

SWAP first of all separates the potential plant transpiration rate T_p and potential soil evaporation rate E_p and then calculates the reduction of potential plant transpiration and soil evaporation rates. The soil evaporative component can be separated from the total evapotranspiration calculated by the equation:

$$Ev = ETP\, e^{-m.I} \qquad [4.]$$

where m is a crop-dependent coefficient and I is the Leaf Area Index. The transpirative component is therefore calculated from the difference between the total evapotranspiration and the evaporative component. Ritchie (1972) and Feddes (1978) used $m = 0.39$ for common crops.

Secondly, actual transpiration is calculated considering the root water uptake reduction due to water stress, using equation [2]. Actual soil evaporation can be calculated from the Maximum Darcy flow at the soil surface, which depends on actual soil water content and hydraulic conductivity, although several other options for calculating actual soil evaporation are implemented in SWAP (Van Dam, 2000).

The simple SWAP crop-growth approach does not estimate the crop yield. However, the user can define yield response factors (Doorenbos and Kassam, 1979; Smith, 1992) for various growing stages as functions of the development stage. During each growing stage k, the actual yield $Y_{a,k}$ (kg ha-1) relative to the potential yield $Y_{p,k}$ (kg ha-1) during the said growing stage is calculated by:

$$1-\frac{Y_{a,k}}{Y_{p,k}} = K_{y,k}\left(1-\frac{T_{a,k}}{T_{p,k}}\right) \qquad [5.]$$

where $Y_{a,k}$ and $Y_{p,k}$ are the actual and potential yields for the period *k*, $T_{a,k}$ and $T_{p,k}$ are the actual and potential crop transpiration, respectively, and $K_{y,k}$ is a coefficient which depends on the crop and on the crop growing period *k*. Final relative yields, i.e. the ratio between Y_a and Y_p, are calculated as the product of the relative yields of each growing stage *k*.

In SWAP, irrigations may be prescribed at fixed times or scheduled in accordance with certain criteria. According to Kroes and Van Dam (2003), the irrigation scheduling criteria applied in SWAP are similar to those found in CROPWAT (Smith, 1992), IRSIS (Raes et al., 1988) and others. SWAP can therefore be used to select the irrigation management that maximizes crop yield, minimizes irrigation costs, optimally distributes a limited water supply or optimizes production from a limited irrigation system capacity (Kroes and Van Dam, 2003).

3.2.4. HYDRUS Model

An important modelling approach, aimed to simulate water and solute transport through the soil vadose zone is the model HYDRUS-1D (Šimunek et al., 2005). The model consists of the HYDRUS computer program, and the HYDRUS1D interactive graphics-based user interface. According to Šimunek et al. (2005), the HYDRUS program numerically solves the Richards equation for saturated-unsaturated water flow and convection-dispersion type equations for heat and solute transport. The water flow equation incorporates a sink term to account for water uptake by plant roots, as well as in SWAP (see equation 1). The heat transport equation considers movement by conduction as well as convection with flowing water. Salinity is also considered through the Maas and Hoffman (1977) function and the simulation of crop water uptake follows a similar approach than the SWAP model.

The HYDRUS-1D code may be used to analyze water and solute movement in unsaturated, partially saturated, or fully saturated porous media. The flow region itself may be composed of non-uniform soils (Šimunek et al., 2005). Flow and transport can occur in the vertical, horizontal, or in a generally inclined direction. The water flow part of the model considers prescribed head and flux boundaries, as well as boundaries controlled by atmospheric conditions, free drainage, or flow to horizontal drains (Šimunek et al., 2005).

The source code was developed and tested on a Pentium 4 PC using the Microsoft's Fortran PowerStation compiler. Several extensions of the MS Fortran beyond the ANSI standard were used to enable communication with graphic based user-friendly interface (Šimunek et al., 2005). HYDRUS1D comprises an interactive graphics-based user-friendly interface for the MS Windows environment. The HYDRUS1D interface is directly connected to the HYDRUS computational programs. Besides, the HYDRUS program come with several utility programs that make easier the data input process.

HYDRUS1D can be considered as a one-dimensional version of the HYDRUS-2D code. This updated modelling release is aimed to simulate water, heat and solute movement in two-dimensional variably saturated media (Šimunek et al., 1998), while incorporating various features of earlier related codes such as SUMATRA (van Genuchten, 1978), WORM (Van Genuchten, 1987), HYDRUS 3.0 (Kool and van Genuchten, 1991), SWMI_ST (Šimunek, 1992), and HYDRUS 5.0 (Vogel et al., 1996). Indeed, to be able to simulate soil water-movement and crop water-uptake in two dimensions open new possibilities that perhaps make HYDRUS2D the most important currently available model in this concern (Van Genuchten and Šimunek, 2005).

3.2.5. Agrohydrological Models Constraints

Many models comparisons have pointed out that despite mechanistic model yield more accurate and sounder simulations; they require many input parameters that are not always easy to measure or to estimate (Leenhardt et al., 1995; Connolly, 1998; Bastiaansen et al., 2004). Sensitivity analysis of SWAP outputs showed that the simulated water balance are most sensitive to the crop coefficients used for calculating potential transpiration and to the soil hydraulic properties (Van Dam, 2000). This agrees with other analysis made with similar agrohydrological modelling approaches, based on Richards' equation (Clemente et al., 1994; Leenhardt et al., 1995). Unfortunately, the soil hydraulic properties use to show high spatial variability (Warrick and Nielsen, 1980; Van Genuchten, 1994; Leenhardt et al., 1995). Therefore, the SWAP dependence on these properties can be seen as one of the highest constraints when using such modelling approach (Van Genuchten, 1994; Leenhardt et al., 1995; Van Dam, 2000).

3.2.6. Simple Crop Water-Use Simulation Models. CROPWAT

Very often availability of model input data (especially soil input data) is a serious limitation for applications of complex crop water balance models as to be used for irrigation scheduling. This is especially a problem in poor agricultural regions, where input data generation might be a serious cost factor. The limitation on input data quality can lead to the situation that simple models or methods may perform better than the complex models. That is why for all SIRDEM experimental sites the performance of a simple approach will be tested as an alternative option. The test will result in defining limitations and potentials of both simple and complex approaches.

CROPWAT is a free-distributed code from the Food and Agriculture Organization (FAO) and can be downloaded from the FAO web (http://www.fao.org/landandwater/aglw/cropwat.stm). It is meant as a practical tool to help agro-meteorologists, agronomists and irrigation engineers to carry out standard calculations for evapotranspiration and crop water use studies, and more specifically the design and management of irrigation schemes. CROPWAT allows the development of recommendations for improved irrigation practices, the planning of irrigation schedules under varying water supply conditions, and the assessment of production under rainfed conditions or deficit irrigation. It simulates crop water-requirements on a monthly, 10-days period or daily basis with a simplified soil water balance (cascade approach). Actually, the cascade approach can yield same results than the physically-based approach, based on numerical solutions of Richards's equation, as shown by Eitzinger et al. (2004).

3.3. Models Calibration, Validation and Inter-Model Comparisons

Since SWAP simulates the soil-water balance; the model outputs include deep drainage, capillary rising and runoff also. The model itself can provide irrigation recommendations, based on the simulated soil water contents and crop evapotranspiration. All these capabilities can be used at the field level to integrate a general farm water-management, trying to help farmers to control water more efficiently and to improve the environmental and economic performance of irrigation systems. SWAP is specifically oriented to water management, but comprises the WOFOST also, which make SWAP able to simulate crop-growth as well. Nevertheless, SWAP simulation outputs should be compared to other similar modelling approach. As shown by Eitzinger et al. (2004); Tardieu (2005) and others, several model approaches can yield the same results. Particularly, DSSAT models have been used for irrigation and crop water-use assessments in Spain (Guereña et al., 2001; Villalobos and Fereres, 2004) and overseas (Hoogenboom, 2000). Therefore, a prior model comparison should be made before selecting the model that can be used to irrigation decision-making. Such comparison should include, at least, some internationally used model as those of DSSAT, based on the "Cascade approach"; as well as an agrohydrological model.

4. Applying Climate and Crop-Growth Simulation Tools to Support Agricultural Decision-Making

Despite the manifold papers addressed to estimate climate-change and climate-variability effects on agriculture, appeared in the last years, few cases can be referred where such tools have been effectively used to provide recommendations to farmers and stakeholders. Some of the current actions regarding such applications are outlined below.

4.1. Previous Experience

Probably, the most important contributions to the use of the available simulation tools to support agricultural decision-making are CLIMAG (Climate Prediction and Agriculture) activities. The CLIMAG workshops were held in Geneva 1999 and 2005, sponsored by WMO and IRI (Sivakumar, 2001; Sivakumar and Hansen, 2007). The CLIMAG proceedings remain as significant guidelines for using such tools in future studies. However, the assessments of climate-impacts on agriculture made in the framework of CLIMAG were only specially-funding applications. The CLIMAG assessments did not yield to sustainable applications of the simulation tools in the targeted countries.

One of the most important successful applications of climate information, combined to crop-growth simulation models, have been made in Australia (Meinke et al, 2001; Hammer et al., 2001; Meinke et al., 2006). Rainfall and many other meteorological variables strongly depend on El Niño behaviour. Since ENSO occurrence can be forecasted several months in advance, this information can be used to support agricultural decision-making, through crop-growth modelling exercises (Hammer et al., 2001). A "participatory process" (Meinke et al., 2001) comprising researchers, stakeholders and extension facilities has been pointed out as a way to provide sustainable and sounder support to Australian agriculture.

Another important application of climate information and crop-growth models can be found in the South East Climate Consortium (SECC), as described by Hoogenboom (2007). Seasonal forecasts at the county level, using ENSO phases, are combined with DSSAT modelling results in order to provide estimations of final yields, water and fertilizer requirements and several other outputs very useful to farmers. The forecast and the whole system are only reliable in El Niño years, although current researches aim to enlarge the system reliability to other years (Baigorria, 2007).

El Niño signal is not very strong over Europe, which limits the applicability of ENSO-based forecasts. Marletto et al. (2005) showed that WOFOST simulations of winter wheat yields, based on the available seasonal forecasts, departed significantly from the recorded data. However, using spatial and temporal aggregated data, as usually done by JRC when providing recommendations to the EU Commission of Agriculture, might be not the right approach to capture the relationships between weather variables and crop growing.

Hansen et al. (2006) provided an insight view of current advances and challenges while translating climate forecasts into reliable agricultural decision-making. They describe several methods used up to now to spatially and temporal downscale the forecasts, recommending methods comparisons and evaluations at local scales. Likewise, Alexandrov (2007) provided an update revision of current state on applying climate scenarios and seasonal forecasts to support agricultural decision-making. Alexandrov (2007) points out that improved climate prediction techniques are growing faster and finding more applications; hence close contacts between climate forecasters, agrometeorologists, agricultural research and extension agencies in developing appropriate products for the user community are needed. Furthermore, feedbacks from end users are essential identifying the opportunities for agricultural applications (Alexandrov, 2007).

4.2. The Role of Local Agricultural Research and Extension Services

As pointed out above, negative climate-variability impacts could be reduced by following adaptation options, which can be obtained from crop-model simulations combined with climate scenarios. The usefulness of such simulation tools has been proved in manifold papers, usually produced in Universities or similar centres. However, despite of the considerable public concern about climate change, European stakeholders and farmers are not yet using these scientific results for agricultural decision-making. Actually, the most reliable climate-change mitigation options depend on each specific situation.

While experts and researchers at high-level centres in Europe and other places ("developers") have established significant Know-How and produced relevant of the above-cited tools for such climate-impacts studies; practical experts at local agricultural-research or extension centres as well as agricultural advisers ("users"), those who should apply these tools for agricultural decision-making, are often not aware about the available tools or their access to such tools is quite limited due to several reasons, as financial issues or lack of user-friendly design of tools.

A connection is needed between the "developers" and "users", to improve decision making by better implementing the climate and crop-growth simulation model tools. Furthermore, feedback from low end-users to the tool-provider researchers is a prerequisite for improving these tools for their practical use e.g. by providing background information, setting up the actual input data needs, fitting time and spatial scales as required by specific applications and other similar issues.

In that context AGRIDEMA, a Specific Support Action (SSA), has been funded by the EU Sixth Framework Program from January 2005 to June 2007. The SSA aims to promote a research network, linking European modelling tool-providers and developers with the potential users of their research results (Utset et al., 2007a). AGRIDEMA general objective is to establish initial contacts and to conduct primary collaborations between "developers" and potential "users", basically researchers and experts at agricultural services.

4.3. The AGRIDEMA Proposal. General Description

AGRIDEMA comprises the following specific objectives:

1. To identify European human resources that developed, improved and tested simulating tools such as GCM, seasonal forecasts, regional downscaling techniques and agricultural-impact simulation models; inviting them to participate in the SSA proposal activities for implementing their tools and Know-How.
2. To identify and to invite attending the SSA activities to potential users of the European-provided modelling tools.
3. To conduct short courses, where the invited "developers" will present the particularities of their developed or validated tools to the invited "users".
4. To perform pilot collaborations between "developers" and "users".
5. To disseminate the obtained results and to build up a wider consortium, comprising both, the "developers" of the simulating tools and the potential "users" of such tools (e.g. experts from regional agricultural-oriented research centres, advisers and farmers).

According to these objectives, several tasks or "work packages" were scheduled. The tasks can be seen in Figure 1. Following the AGRIDEMA timetable, three Workpackages were finished during the 1st period, i.e. "Identifying and Contacting developers", "Identifying and contacting users" and "Courses on climate and crop-growth modelling tools".

4.3.1. Identifying and Contacting Developers

The AGRIDEMA consortium created an initial list of which developers should be contacted. The list was based mainly the partners experience and previous contact. The use of European-made simulation tools was encouraged.

The following Table shows the simulation tools that were contacted by the AGRIDEMA consortium, as well as the corresponding European institution and relevant person.

Table 2. Models, institutions and "developers" included in the AGRIDEMA activities

Model	Institution	Contact
REGCM3	ICTP, Italy	J. Pal
LARS-WG, SIRIUS	Rothamsted Experimental Station, UK	M. Semenov
Met&Roll	Inst. Atmos. Physics, Czech Republic	M. Dubrovsky
Statistical downscaling	BOKU, Austria	H. Formayer
DEMETER	ECMWF, UK	F. Doblas-Reyes
LAPS	Agrometeorological Institute Novi Sad, Serbia	D. Michailovic
SWAP	Wageningen Agricultural University, The Netherlands	J. Kroes
WOFOST	Wageningen Agricultural University, The Netherlands	K. Van Diepen
PERUN	Mendel University Brno, Czech Republic	M. Trnka
ROIMPEL	Romanian Foundation on Global Change, Romania	C. Simota
CROPSYST	ISCI, Italy	M. Donatelli
STICS	INRA, France	F. Ruget
DSSAT	University of Madrid, Spain	A. Iglesias

Several work agreements were achieved between the AGRIDEMA consortium and most of the contacted "developers", pointing out the "developers" participation in the AGRIDEMA courses, as well as their future support of the "Pilot Assessments" to be conducted by the "users" in the framework of AGRIDEMA.

4.3.2. Identifying and Contacting Users

Mediterranean countries could face the highest negative consequences of global warming within Europe, through water-shortage and crop-water requirements increments. Besides, since climate-change and extreme events effects could be more serious in countries with less-developed agriculture, the EU associated countries from Central and Eastern Europe, with relative reduced technological capacities, would be more affected than Northern-European countries. Therefore, AGRIDEMA focuses on "users" coming from Southern, Central and Eastern Europe, as well as from the countries of the Mediterranean area.

The members of the AGRIDEMA consortium released a call to "users" applicants since April 2005. Relevant institutions were contacted, according to AGRIDEMA partner's experience, as well as official centres depending on the Countries' Ministries of Agriculture or similar institutions.

The call was published also using all the available means, including email lists and internet facilities. As pointed out by the three AGRIDEMA partners during their first meeting, the basic criteria for selecting the "users" institutions to be involved in the proposal were:

i. To be able to communicate in English and to be able to work with data management software (Windows, Excel, etc.).
ii. To be involved with local agricultural decision-making, advising and farming.
iii. To be aware about the potential benefits of agricultural decision modelling tools, being able to identify which agricultural management options should be change and how to optimise management and reduce climate risk of local agricultural production.
iv. To have available data for the training course and for the potential conducting the SSA pilot assessments (crop growth and yields, meteorological variables, soil properties, irrigation and crop management scheduling, etc).

Additionally, users conducting PhD studies in the same subjects of AGRIDEMA activities will be especially considered for invitation.

4.3.3. The AGRIDEMA Courses on Climate and Crop-Growth Simulation Tools

The Courses were held in Vienna in November-December 2005, as scheduled in the proposal. Since many applications to the AGRIDEMA courses were received from "users" out of the targeted countries, the AGRIDEMA partners decided to include these applicants also without any course fee, if they were able to support their trips and lodging expenses. Finally, 44 "users" were present in total, from more than 15 different countries. Sixteen "users" were fully supported by AGRIDEMA and other eight were partially supported by the SSA. A picture showing all the participants in the AGRIDEMA courses is depicted in Figure 2.

Institutions from several countries decided to support additional participants in AGRIDEMA courses. Particularly, the participation of five Spanish researchers was supported by the INIA AC05-008 complementary action. Besides, several students and researchers from BOKU, Austria, were in the courses too.

The AGRIDEMA web page (www.agridema.com) shows all the details of Courses held in Vienna; as the lectures program, time schedule, invited developers, participant users, etc. The courses on Climate tools comprise lectures on climate change scenarios, dynamical and statistical downscaling, as well as weather generators. The details and work-performance of quite known crop-growth models as SIRIUS, DSSAT, CROPSYST and WOFOST; among others, were shown too.

4.3.4. The Agridema Pilot Assessments

The AGRIDEMA pilot assessments were basically applications conducted by some of the "users" that attended the AGRIDEMA courses on climate and crop-growth simulation tools that were held in Vienna ending 2005. Assessments were made using existing data and were addressed to relevant issues concerning climate risks and agricultural decision-making in their respective countries and institutions.

The following issues were considered in the Assessments propositions:

- Local modelling comparisons and validations using available data will be encouraged as the agreement subjects.

- All the collaborations must identify clearly the potential benefits of these modelling applications for local agricultural decision-making. Particularly, those applications which include farmers from regional medium and small enterprises, as potential users of the tested tools, will be better considered for funding.
- Educational outputs, such as Ph. D. studies connected to the work agreements are highly desirable.
- Only original and different propositions can be supported.

The selection of the pilot assessments was based on the propositions that the "users" made at the end of the AGRIDEMA courses. The selection was geographically made. The AGRIDEMA consortium partners considered the available budget and the agreements among them during their first meeting.

Eight assessments were selected in the Mediterranean area, although only six were funded (those not leaded by ITACyL). Five assessments were conducted in Central Europe and three in Eastern Europe. The SSA coordinator gave priority to cooperation and exchange among the Mediterranean "users", as well as funding dissemination activities, rather than to support ITACyL researches that have other funding possibilities. Furthermore, ITACyL received additional funds from the Spanish government to strength the cooperation with the Spanish institutions working in AGRIDEMA Pilot Assessments (Complementary Action CGL2006-26211-E) as well as with the Mediterranean countries involved (International Complementary Action PCI2005-A7-0105).

The Pilot assessments were conducted from March to October 2006. The AGRIDEMA support was based on agreements to be signed between each "user" conducting Pilot assessments and the corresponding partner of the AGRIDEMA consortium. The Pilot assessments information can be seen in the AGRIDEMA web page: www.agridema.org.

The complete lists of the funded AGRIDEMA Pilot assessments can be seen below.

Table 3. Pilot Assessments conducted in the framework of AGRIDEMA Mediterranean area (under the responsibility of the Spanish partner)

Title	Presenter Name	Institution
Full irrigation estimates and palliative measurements for coping with climate change in vineyard and peach orchards in Spain: a past tendency towards a future perspective	Jordi Marsal	IRTA, Spain
Optimizing irrigation water management on the global change context in a Mediterranean region	Jose A. Rodriguez*	DAP, Andalusia, Spain
Estimating climate-change effects on Sugarbeet irrigation efficiency in the Spanish Northern Plateau	Blanca del Rio	ITACyL, Spain
Adaptations of irrigated cropping systems of Southern Italy as affected by climate change at field/farm scale	Domenico Ventrella	CRA-ISA, Italy
Assessment of the Impact of Climate Change on Water Productivity in Rainfed Wheat Systems in the Mediterranean region	Fatema Mosseddaq	IAV Hassan II, Morocco
Assessment of the Impact of Climate Change on Water Productivity in Irrigated potatoes in the Southern Mediterranean region	Mahmoud Medany	CLAC, Egypt
Estimation of water availability for annual crops at Tree – Crop ecosystems	Dimos Anastasiou	NAGREF, FDA, Greece

* Conducting a Ph D in this issue.

Central Europe (under the responsibility of the Austrian partner)

Title	*Presenter Name*	*Institution*
Modelling of the maize production and the impact of climate change on maize yields in Croatia	Visnja Vucetic	Meteorological Service of Croatia
Irrigation in different Climate conditions using crop models	Blaz Kurnik	EARS (Met. Office, Slovenia)
Introducing crop modeling tools into a Serbian crop production	Branislava Lalić	University of Novi Sad, Novi Sad, Serbia and Montenegro
Determination of the water demand and use of various crops in the region Lake Neusiedl and Seewinkel	Ildikó Dobi Gerhard Kubu	Hungarian Meteorological Service; Univ. of Natural Resources and Appl. Life Sciences, BOKU
Modelling of crop yields in the present and future climatic conditions in WIELKOPOLSKA REGION (POLAND) with and without irrigation management practices	Jacek Leśny	Agricultural University of Poznań

Eastern Europe (under the responsibility of the Bulgarian partner)

Title	*Presenter Name*	*Institution*
Impact of climate factors on grain yield of spring barley in Latvia	Jelena Korolova*	Latvia University of Agriculture (LUA)
Climate variability and change over the Balkan peninsula and related impacts on crops	Stanislava Radeva	NIMH, Bulgaria
Complex assessment the efficiency of adaptation of agricultural ecosystems to climate change in the European part of Russia based on integration with European crop models	Vladimir Romanenkov	All-Russian Institute for Agrochemistry

* Conducting a Ph D in this issue.

The reports of the AGRIDEMA Pilot assessments, which can be downloaded from the AGRIDEMA web, comprise an excellent collection of many different applications from several European and Mediterranean countries, all of them addressed to local potential climate-risks. The strategic AGRIDEMA goal, which aims to promote a research network, linking European modelling tool-providers and developers with the potential users of their research results, has been already partially fulfilled.

4.4. The Agridema Pilot-Assessments Results

According to the AGRIDEMA goals, the Pilot assessments should comprise the two following tasks:

1. Downscaling the provided GCM-outputs and/or seasonal-forecasts.
2. Simulating impacts (such as crop growth and yield, drought stress level etc.) under the locally-obtained climate scenarios, evaluating several management options, which might mitigate the probable climate impact.

Scientific quality of the assessments is quite variable, which can be expected from the wide irregularity of AGRIDEMA applicants. Furthermore, the applicability of the obtained results varies among the assessments as well. Generally, those assessments conducted by researchers located in agricultural stations are closer to stakeholder goals, but unclear regarding climate analysis. Objectives were too ambitious sometimes and could not be fulfilled with a simple application. Moreover, the use of the climate and crop modelling tools shown in the AGRIDEMA courses was mainly related to the user' previous experience and not to the tool reliability for the expected goal. Comparisons between modelling tools were not conducted in most of the cases. In spite of all the above, the AGRIDEMA results constitutes perhaps the most important collection of independent climate-change agricultural assessments that have been made in Europe.

The following table shows the climate and crop-growth simulation tools that have been used in the AGRIDEMA pilot assessments. The downscaling method is clearly identified in all the reports. However, the GCM data source is not always pointed out. In some cases, the assessment was very simple due to the lack of data or relevant knowledge on the crop model.

Table 4. Climate and crop-growth tools used in the AGRIDEMA Pilot assessments

Assessment Conductor	Institution	Climate	Crop
Jordi Marsal	IRTA, Spain	CCMA -LARS	CROPSYST
Jose A. Rodriguez	DAP, Andalusia, Spain	CCMA -LARS	DSSAT
Blanca del Río	ITACyL, Spain	CCMA -LARS	SWAP
Domenico Ventrella	CRA-ISA, Italy	CGM-LARS	SWAP
Fatema Mosseddaq	IAV Hassan II, Morocco		DSSAT
Mahmoud Medany	CLAC, Egypt	MAGICC	DSSAT
Dimos Anastasiou	NAGREF, FDA, Greece	CCMA -LARS	SWAP
Visnja Vucetic	Meteorological Service of Croatia	ECHAM4-CSIRO-HADCM3-M&R	DSSAT
Blaz Kurnik	EARS (Met. Office, Slovenia)	REGCM3-LARS	CROPSYST
Branislava Lali	University of Novi Sad, Novi Sad, Serbia and Montenegro	M&R-LARS	SIRIUS-PERUN(W)
Ildikó Dobi	Hungarian Meteorological Service	LARS-WG	PERUN(W)
Jacek Lezny	Agricultural University of Poznan	M&R	PERUN(W)
Jelena Korolova	Latvia University of Agriculture (LUA)		
Stanislava Radeva	NIMH, Bulgaria	HADCM3-REGCM3	ROIMPEL
Vladimir Romanenkov	All-Russian Institute for Agrochemistry	HADCM3-CLIMGEN	CSY+CROPSYST-ROIMPEL

As can be concluded from the above Table, the most used GCM outputs were the Canadian CCCMa (4 times) and HADCM3 (3 times). The ECHAM and CSIRO GCM outputs were used in one assessment, where a GCM output comparison was performed. The LARS-WG appeared in 8 of the AGRIDEMA pilot assessment, which makes this weather generator as the most frequently used climate-tool in the framework of AGRIDEMA. According to Wilby and Wigley (2001), LARS-WG is one of the most used weather generators. The AGRIDEMA results confirm this conclusion. The Met&Roll weather generator was found in 3 assessments, including one comparison with LARS-WG. The Regional ReGCM3 model was used in 2 assessments and the MAGICC model in one.

Regarding the crop models considered in the Pilot assessments, the Wageningen model WOFOST was the most used, but in its SWAP (3 times) and PERUN (3 times) versions. DSSAT models were employed in 4 Pilot Assessments, while CROPSYST was used 3 times, ROIMPEL was considered 2 times and SIRIUS was used in one assessment, which performed a model comparison with PERUN. The frequency of using crop models in the AGRIDEMA Pilot assessments is similar to that found in climate-change impact assessments all over the world, reported by Tubiello and Ewert (2002) as well as in Europe, as pointed out by Alexandrov (2002).

An important AGRIDEMA conclusion is that DSSAT, SWAP-WOFOST and CROPSYST are the most relevant crop-growth simulation models that are being used in Europe for climate-change risk assessments. Furthermore, SWAP has been the most used agrohydrological model within the AGRIDEMA Pilot assessments.

4.5. A Pilot Assessment Example: Managing Sugarbeet Irrigation in the Spanish Northern Plateau under Present and Future Climate Conditions

Castilla y Leon, with 94 000 km^2, is the largest Spanish Autonomic Community and one of the major administrative regions of Europe. Castilla y Leon is basically a large plateau, with an important agricultural production. The region involves more than 20% of the cultivated area of Spain, 22.7% of grassland area and 31.9% of the cereals-cropping area. Even though Castilla and Leon comprises only 6% of Spanish population, they mean about 12% of the reported farm-workers in Spain, almost twice the country mean (7.7%) and higher than the European mean (9.0%).

Castilla y León is, after Andalusia, the Spanish Autonomic Community with higher irrigation surface. According to the last Ministry of Agriculture report (MAPA, 2004), Castilla y León irrigated-agriculture produces 57% of Sugarbeet, 38% of maize and 30% of potatoes of the whole country. The investment in irrigation infrastructures in Castilla y León is the second highest in Spain. However, such investment must be joined to applied researches aimed to improve water-management efficiency, particularly in eventual prices diminishing or severe droughts.

The recent reform of the European Sugar Market (EC Council Regulation 318/2006) will bring important reductions on the Sugarbeet prices. Irrigation means about 35% of the total Sugarbeet production costs in Northern Spain. Sugarbeet water requirements will be higher in the future, according to Climate-Change predictions, while water availability will diminish in the Castilla y León zone. Furthermore, EU Water Framework Directive (EC Directive 2000/60), through its "recovering costs" principle, will very probably increment the water prices. The combination of all these factors could yield that Sugarbeet becomes an unaffordable crop in Castilla y León in the near future.

According to the above, an AGRIDEMA Pilot assessment was conducted in order to calibrate and validate the SWAP model for Sugarbeet water-use simulations, as well as to estimate Climate Change effects on water use efficiency, considering a typical irrigation management. Utset et al. (2007b) provided the calibration and validation of the SWAP model. The assessment was conducted at Valladolid, Northern Spain (41°39'N, 4°43'W). The regional climate is Mediterranean Semiarid with an annual average precipitation of 531 mm. According to the local soil map (JCYL, 1987), Sugarbeet is cropped mainly in Cambisols and Fluvisols.

4.5.1. SWAP Calibration and Validation. The Assessment Data

The SWAP calibration comprised data of experiments addressed to study water-shortage effects on sugarbeet growth, made during 1992, 1993, 1994 and 1995 in a clayey Fluvisol and in a Cambisol (Velicia, 1998). The water-stress effect on sugarbeet yields depends on the growing period (Brown et al., 1987; Groves and Bailey, 1994; Fabeiro et al., 2003). Accordingly, water shortages were applied at the beginning and end of sugarbeet development. Four irrigation start and end dates were considered (Velicia, 1998), based on non-restrictive irrigation management with typical considerations (Morillo, 1993; Allen et al., 1998), which provides all the sugarbeet water requirements from seeding to harvest. Four plots were dedicated to each irrigation design at each soil type. The plots were separated from each other by at least 20 m in other to avoid water redistribution among them.

Sugarbeet roots can reach up to 2 m in length (Brown et al., 1987; Velicia, 1998). The root distribution in depth depends on soil and moisture conditions. However, according to Velicia (1998), about 60% of the roots is usually found in the first 30 cm, whereas 90% could be found at depths shallower than 90 cm. Therefore, a non-linear root distribution was assumed.

Potential evapotranspiration was calculated by the Penman-Monteith approach, using meteorological data available from stations at distances of 1.2 and 2.3 km from the plots. Maximum crop evapotranspiration was calculated considering the Kc coefficients estimated for the zone (Morillo, 1993). Daily temperature values were also recorded. The SWAP FCS stage was considered as the date when sugarbeet covers soil completely under non-restrictive irrigation water-management conditions (Velicia, 1998). The maturity date was assumed as the harvest.

The sugarbeet (Ramona cultivar) germination date was May 15 and the average harvest date was October 15. The said dates were considered for computing the temperature sums at FCS and maturity and can be considered as typical dates for spring-sown sugarbeet (Morillo, 1993). The irrigation water applied at each plot was measured weekly. Final sugarbeet yields were measured at each plot.

The leaf area index (LAI) was measured monthly at each plot. The length and width of all the green leaves on each plant in 1-m rows were measured. LAI was indirectly estimated according to a regression equation obtained from previous studies (Velicia, 1998). Root lengths and weights were also measured (Velicia, 1998) from three randomly selected plants, removed entirely from the ground at each plot on a monthly basis. Soil water content was measured weekly by a neutron probe (Velicia, 1998). The actual crop evapotranspiration was estimated by water balance (Allen et al., 1998).

The actual crop transpiration was separated from total evapotranspiration considering the experimentally-measured LAI values (Ritchie, 1998). Final yields were measured and total crop transpiration was computed as the cumulative sum; the Ky coefficients (Doorenbos and Kassam, 1979; Kroes and Van Dam, 2003) were then calculated. The hydraulic properties of the soil were estimated from the physical soil data taken at each plot (Velicia, 1998) through a pedotransfer function (Shaap et al., 2001). SWAP simulations were performed at each plot, considering the parameters obtained in the calibration and free drainage at the bottom of the 1-m soil layer. A regression between relative yields and actual yields was conducted in order to find which maximum yield adapted better to the experimental conditions.

An independent data set was used for SWAP validations. Two sugarbeet plots, corresponding to a Cambisol (Plot Z) and a Fluvisol (Plot A), were selected in the Valladolid area. The plots were separated from each other by a distance of approximately 15 km.

Sugarbeet was seeded in the two plots in March 2005. Emergence dates were April 5 (A) and April 25 (Z). Undisturbed soil samples were taken at 20-40 cm depth in ten randomly-selected sites within each plot. The soil water retention curves were determined at each sample through a sand-kaolin box and a Richard membrane (Klute, 1986). The saturated hydraulic conductivity of each sample of soil was measured in a laboratory permeameter. The soil field capacity and the wilting point were considered as the water contents at 33 and 1500 kPa, respectively. The parameters of the Van Genuchten model for the soil-water characteristic curve were estimated through the RETC code (Van Genuchten et al., 1991).

Access tubes were placed at the same places where soil samples were taken at each plot. Soil water contents were measured weekly during July and August 2005 at 0-20, 20-40 and 40-60 cm depths by a Trime TDR [IMKO Micromodultechnick GmbH]. Actual crop evapotranspiration was computed using the balance method from the measured water contents and neglecting any possible capillary rising, runoff and/or percolation. Daily precipitation, global radiation, maximum and minimum temperature, wind speed and relative humidity values were recorded at two agrometeorological stations located near the selected plots.

Irrigation was applied traditionally in a way similar to that used by farmers to manage sugarbeet water applications at each plot. The irrigation water supply at each plot was measured through a water counter. Sixteen irrigations were applied on the Z Plot from June to August, comprising a total water application of 508 mm. Likewise, 556 mm of water were applied by irrigation on the A plot in the same period over eighteen irrigations. Precipitations are scarce in the Mediterranean summer. Accordingly, the total rainfall recorded was 41 mm on the Z Plot and 25 mm on the A Plot during the 2005 sugarbeet cropping season.

Actual SWAP simulations were conducted using the measured soil and meteorological data and considering the model calibration performed. Free drainage at the bottom of the 1-m simulated soil layer was considered, which is consistent with the soil descriptions (JCYL, 1987). Correlation and determination coefficients between simulated and estimated actual evapotranspirations were calculated, as well as the same coefficients between the SWAP-simulated actual evapotranspirations and the sugarbeet water requirements, calculated from Penman-Monteith computations of the reference evapotranspiration and the sugarbeet coefficients in use, as provided by Morillo (1993). Furthermore, Root Mean Square Errors (RMSE) were calculated between the simulated ETC and the water-balance estimated ETC, as well as between the simulated ETC and the maximum ETC, estimated from weather data. The RMSE has been considered as the most effective method of comparing simulated and actual values in evaluation model performance (Willmott et al., 1985; Timsina and

Humphreys, 2006). The normalized RMSEn is used to compare modelling performances and can be calculated as:

$$RMSEn = \frac{\left[n^{-1} \sum_{i=1}^{n} (P_i - O_i)^2 \right]^{0.5}}{n^{-1} \sum_{i=1}^{n} O_i} \qquad [6.]$$

where P_i and O_i are the predicted and observed values, respectively, and n is the number of observations.

Table 5. Average temperature sums, Leaf Area Index, Root Lengths and Root Length Densities; as well as K_C and K_y coefficients as function of development stages (DVS) under Mediterranean conditions and those values originally considered in the SWAP calibration provided for Northern Europe (after Utset et al., 2007b)

Function		Locally-obtained		SWAP original	
Temperature Sum (°C)	Anthesis	1141		365	
	Maturity	2008		1622	
Leaf Area Index LAI		**DVS**	**LAI**	**DVS**	**LAI**
		0.55	0.4	0.56	0.13
		0.75	0.6	0.74	0.44
		0.77	0.6	1.00	1.47
		0.80	0.9	1.27	4.48
		0.89	1.2	1.52	5.04
		0.92	1.6	1.76	4.69
		0.98	2.1		
		1.00	1.7		
		1.01	2.1		
		1.02	3.1		
		1.02	2.4		
		1.08	3.2		
		1.10	2.7		
		1.15	3.3		
		1.16	3.2		
		1.17	2.5		
		1.22	2.3		
		1.28	5.5		
		1.79	3.8		
		1.85	4.9		
		1.88	3.5		

Table 5. Continued

Function	Locally-obtained		SWAP original	
Root Length (cm) RL	**DVS**	**RL**	**DVS**	**RL**
	0.55	46	0.56	58
	0.75	71	0.74	70
	0.77	81	1.00	87
	0.80	77	1.27	118
	0.89	81	1.52	120
	0.92	72	1.76	120
	0.98	115		
	1.00	95		
	1.01	81		
	1.02	104		
	1.02	107		
	1.08	112		
	1.10	125		
	1.15	118		
	1.16	107		
	1.17	129		
	1.22	131		
	1.28	125		
	1.79	123		
	1.85	135		
	1.88	126		
Root Length Density (RLD) as a function of Relative Root Length (RRL)	**RRL**	**RLD**	**RRL**	**RLD**
	0.25	0.60	0.0	1.0
	0.70	0.90	1.0	1.0
	1.00	1.00		
Crop Coefficients K_C	**DVS**	**K_C**	**DVS**	**K_C**
	0.40	0.4	0.0	1.0
	0.50	0.5	2.0	1.0
	0.60	0.7		
	0.80	1.0		
	1.80	1.1		
	2.00	0.9		
Yield response factors K_y	**DVS**	**K_y**	**DVS**	**K_y**
	0.33	1.00	0.0	1.0
	0.80	1.50	2.0	1.0
	1.00	1.50		
	1.50	1.00		
	2.00	0.90		

4.5.2. SWAP Calibration. The Results

Table 5 summarizes the calibration results; comparing the experimentally-obtained temperature sums at FCS and maturity, as well as the LAI and K_y values at several development stages with the corresponding values of the original SWAP calibration for Northern Europe.

Average FCS, i.e. maximum foliar development, corresponds to 71 days after germination in the irrigation managements that provide all the sugarbeet water requirements (Velicia, 1998). Therefore, development stage (DVS) reaches one at that date. The temperature sum at this development stage is 1141 °C, which is much higher than the 365 °C originally considered in SWAP. Indeed, average temperatures in Southern Europe after May are higher than the temperatures usually recorded in the Netherlands and other sites of Northern Europe, where SWAP has been previously calibrated. However, temperature sums from germination to FCS similar to those shown in Table 5 for Mediterranean conditions have been found in France (Durr and Mary, 1998) and the UK (Werker and Jaggard, 1997). Furthermore, the difference between the temperature sums at FCS and maturity is lower under Mediterranean conditions than in Northern Europe, which indicates a faster growing rate during summer. Estrada (2001) pointed out the influence of direct sun radiation on sugarbeet growing while cropped under Mediterranean conditions with unlimited water supply. Such direct radiation influence could determine that the temperature sums needed for sugarbeet maturation under Mediterranean conditions is lower than that required in Northern Europe.

The experimentally-measured Leaf Area Indexes are also shown in Figure 4 as a function of the DVS calculated from the temperature sums shown in Table 5. The original SWAP values are included in the figure as a continuous line. Furthermore, Figure 4 also shows the measured and SWAP-original sugarbeet root-lengths as functions of the crop DVS. As the figure shows, the sugarbeet LAI development under Mediterranean conditions follows a pattern similar to that measured in Northern Europe. Therefore, the original function included in SWAP could be considered as still valid in a warmer environment.

The sugarbeet leaf area and root lengths show faster growing rates and higher averages in Mediterranean conditions than those anticipated in the original SWAP functions, particularly before FCS. This is in accordance with the temperature sum differences shown in Table 5.

Figure 5 compares the experimentally-measured sugarbeet root-lengths with those originally considered in SWAP as functions of the crop development stages. The SWAP function might slightly underestimate the sugarbeet root development as grown under Mediterranean conditions. However, the measured values behave in a way that is similar to the original SWAP function. Furthermore, there is a considerable dispersion of the measured values, which can be due to the different soil types considered.

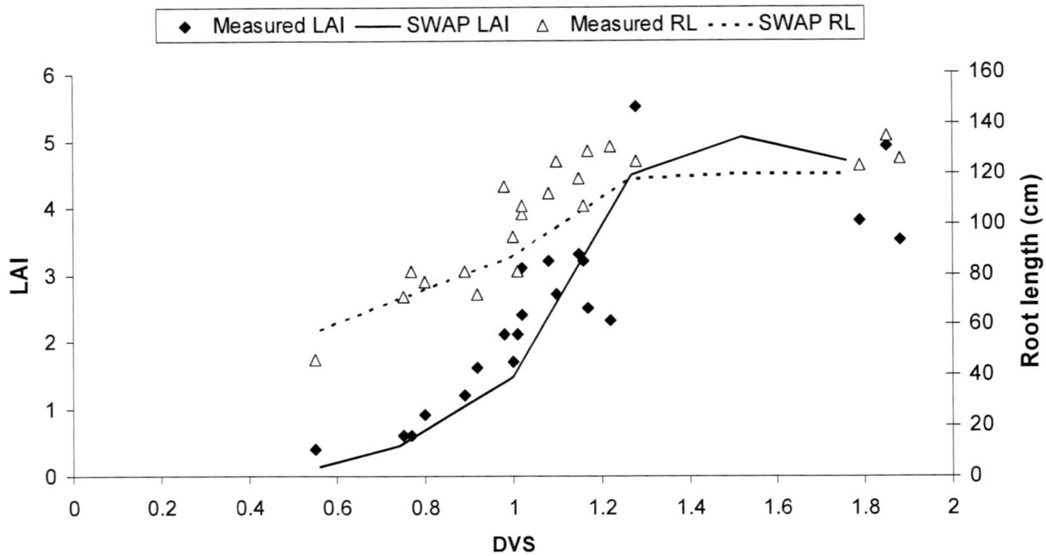

Figure 4. Measured sugarbeet Leaf Area Indexes (LAI) and Root Lengths (RL), as functions of the crop development stages (DVS). The continuous and dashed line shows the respective SWAP original functions (after Utset et al. 2007b).

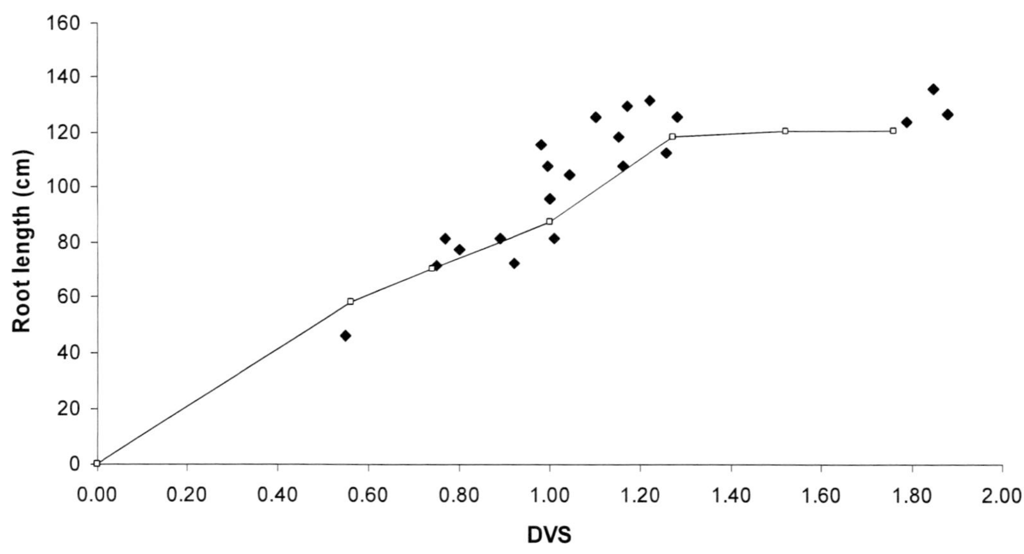

Figure 5. Measured Sugarbeet root lengths under several water managements as function of the crop development stages (DVS). The continuous line shows the SWAP original function (after Utset et al. 2007b).

Likewise, Figure 6 depicts the Mediterranean-considered and the SWAP-original K_C and K_y coefficients as functions of the development stages. Unlike the original SWAP value, which sets the same K_C coefficient for all the sugarbeet crop development, we consider a variable K_C. Velicia (1998) showed that sugarbeet water requirements are lower than the maximum reference evapotranspiration during the initial growing period. However, sugarbeet water needs increase significantly after completing foliar development and starting the root-growing period (Velicia, 1998), which might be considered for a DVS of around 0.8. Crop water needs are reduced close to maturity. Furthermore, the relationships between sugarbeet transpiration and root yield should not be considered as linear, as originally in SWAP. A reduction of actual sugarbeet transpiration regarding its potential transpiration may imply no serious yield reduction during initial leaf development, but such a reduction has significant consequences on final yields at the beginning of the root growing period (Velicia, 1998). The K_y coefficient, as well as the relative importance of water shortage in Mediterranean sugarbeet yields, can be linearly reduced after the initial root-growing period (Velicia, 1998).

Figure 7 depicts the relationship between the measured yields and the simulated relative yields, as well as the corresponding regression line. The data in Figure 10 comprise all the pairs of simulated-actual yields, regardless of water managements or soil types. As shown in Figure 7, lower actual yields start notably at the 1:1 line, while yields of above 50 t/ha generally correlate well with the simulated relative yields. Indeed, SWAP only takes into account the yield reductions due to water shortage. However, final yields rely on many other issues besides water availability, such as weed infections, diseases or nutrient deficiency. Furthermore, relative yields are always estimated as one if irrigation water is sufficient, whereas actual yields are variable. That is why the dispersion shown in Figure 10 is higher around the highest simulated relative yields.

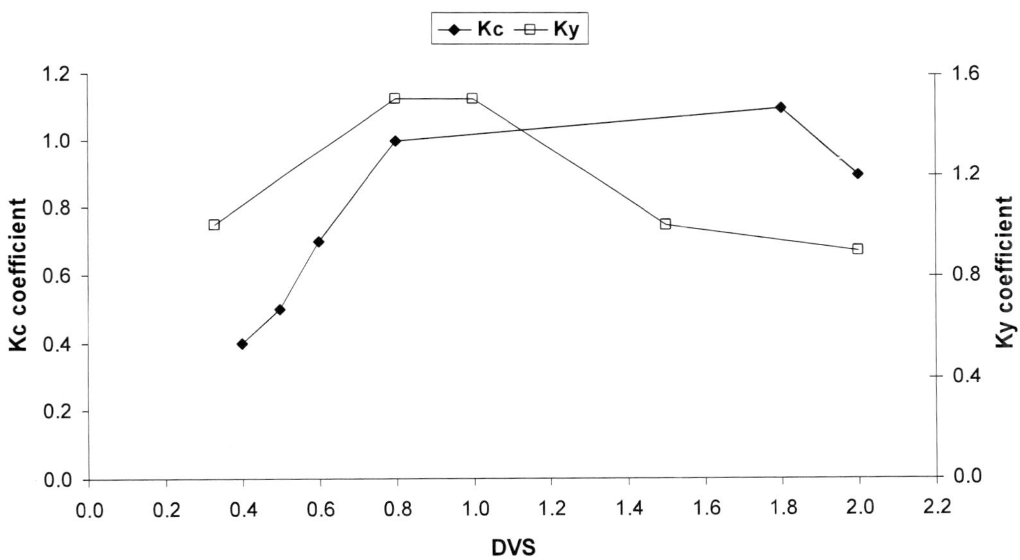

Figure 6. Sugarbeet Crop (KC) and yield factor (Ky) coefficients considered for SWAP simulations under Mediterranean conditions, as functions of the crop development stages (DVS) (after Utset et al. 2007b).

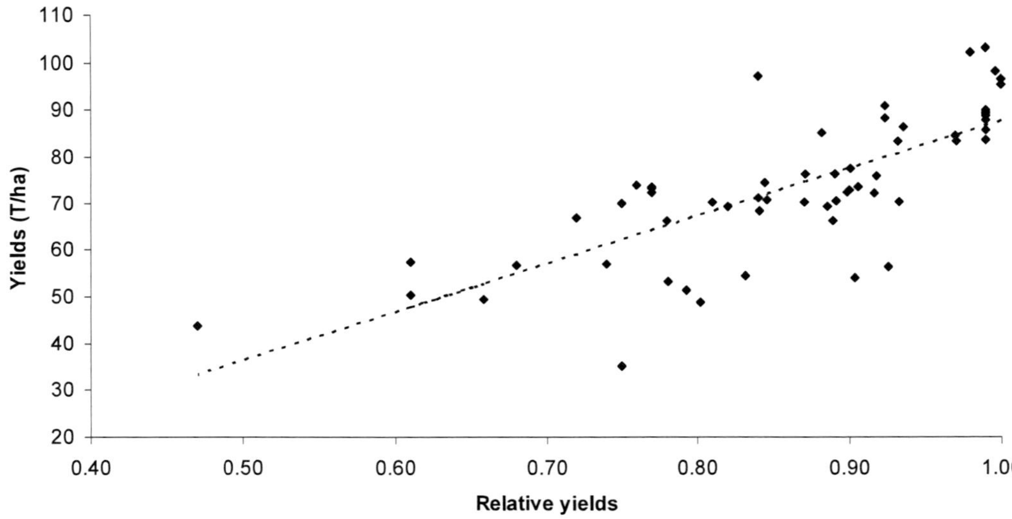

Figure 7. Experimentally obtained sugarbeet yields vs. SWAP simulated relative yields. The dashed and the solid lines show the regressions considering all the data and fitting-reduced data, respectively (after Utset et al., 2007b).

The correlation coefficient between simulated relative yields and the actual sugarbeet yields was 0.71. According to the regression obtained, the average maximum yield to be used in equation [5] should be 87.5 t/ha. The regression is statistically significant at the 99% probability level and explains more than 50% of the yield variability. However, the simulated relative yields are not normally distributed, since they are skewed to their highest value. Therefore, statistical comparisons between simulated relative yields and actual yields are limited. Despite this, the relatively high correlation coefficient and the level of statistical regression confidence would allow this simple SWAP approach to simulate water management effects on sugarbeet yields.

The average sugarbeet yield corresponding to simulated relative yields higher than 0.95 was 90.8 t/ha. Taking into account both results, a potential maximum yield for sugarbeet of around 89 t/ha can be used in SWAP simulations to estimate the effects of water availability on the final yields during crop seasons.

4.5.3. SWAP Validation. The Results

The soil water contents at the average depth of 0-60 cm in the Cambisol and Fluvisol plots, measured during the sugarbeet irrigation season, are shown in Figure 8. The water contents are generally close to the field capacity, shown in the figure by a dashed line. Water contents much higher than the field capacity would indicate an excess of water in the root zone and eventual water percolation. Furthermore, water contents much lower than the field capacity would indicate potential water excess and inefficient irrigation management. The results shown in Figure 8 indicate that, despite their non-technical approach, farmers usually know how to manage irrigation in an acceptable way (Utset et al., 2006).

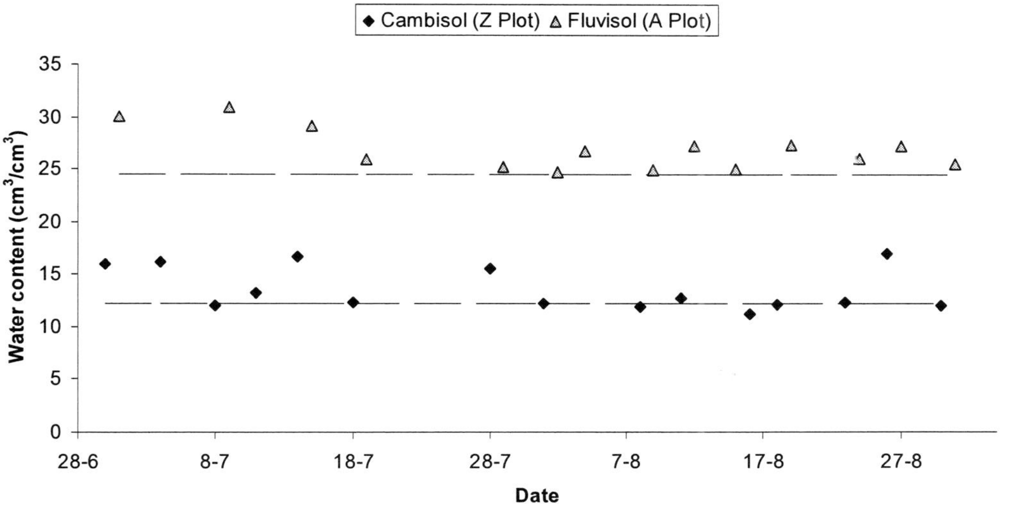

Figure 8. Average soil-water contents at the 0-60 cm depth in the Cambisol and Fluvisol plots during the 2005 Sugarbeet irrigation season. The dashed lines show the corresponding Field Capacities (after Utset et al., 2007b).

However, water contents are higher than the field capacity at the earlier stages of sugarbeet development, when the sugarbeet roots are not long enough and crop water use is lower. The results suggest that water application might be excessive at this stage. The difference between the measured soil water contents and the field capacity is higher in the Fluvisol, where clay contents are higher and water moves slowly across the soil profile.

Figure 9 shows the actual SWAP-simulated sugarbeet evapotranspiration, the maximum sugarbeet evapotranspiration, calculated using the Penman-Monteith reference evapotranspiration and the K_C coefficients shown in Table 5, as well as the actual crop evapotranspiration estimated from water balance and the water content measurements shown in Figure 8. The evapotranspiration values given in Figure 9 comprise both the Cambisol and the Fluvisol data and were calculated on a weekly basis.

As shown in the figure, simulations can follow the temporal changes of both measured ET_C values and those computed from reference evapotranspirations. The measured ET_C values are higher than the simulated and maximum rates computed from weather data at the beginning of the irrigation season. The water balance was calculated neglecting the percolation and capillary rising components of the balance. However, at these earlier sugarbeet stages, irrigation excess might yield to significant water loss by percolation, which is in accordance with the water contents being higher than the field capacity for the same period, as shown in Figure 8. The simulated evapotranspirations are lower than the maximum, as expected.

All the computed evapotranspirations indicate that sugarbeet water use at the end of the cropping season is lower than at the beginning of the root growing period, as pointed out by Velicia (1998).

The correlation coefficient between the actual SWAP-simulated evapotranspiration and the maximum weather-dependent sugarbeet evapotranspiration was 0.81; whereas the correlation coefficient between the simulated and actual estimated water-balance evapotranspirations was 0.75.

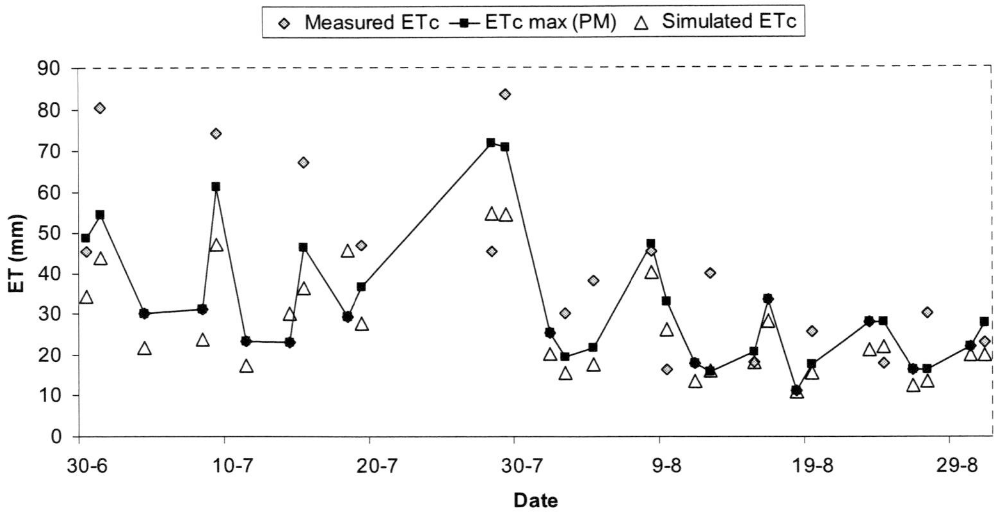

Figure 9. SWAP-simulated sugarbeet actual evapotranspiration (Simulated ETc), sugarbeet maximum evapotranspiration calculated from the Penman-Monteith reference evapotranspiration (ETc Penman-Monteith) and actual evapotranspiration estimated by water balance from the measured soil water contents (after Utset et al., 2007b).

Figure 9 also shows that simulated ET_C values correlate better with the maximum evapotranspiration than with the measured ET_C. In practice, irrigation management at both plots was able to keep soil water contents above field capacity throughout the sugarbeet growing season. Therefore, actual crop evapotranspiration must be close to the highest possible maximum, since water requirements were mainly satisfied. This can explain the good ratios between the SWAP simulations and the weather-based maximum ET_C.

However, ET_C calculations by water balance were made ignoring any eventual percolation. However, water loss by percolation seems to be significant at the beginning of the irrigation season, since the water contents measured during the said period were higher than the field capacity, as shown in Figure 8. SWAP estimates that all the components of the water balance and the simulated evapotranspirations do not comprise percolation. This could explain the relatively lower correlation between SWAP-estimated and measured ET_C.

Figure 10A shows the ratios between sugarbeet evapotranspirations estimated by water balance and the SWAP-simulated evapotranspirations.

As the figure shows, simulated and field-measured evapotranspirations are close to the 1:1 line, particularly for the lower rates of the measured ETc. As indicated below, sugarbeet ET_C could be overestimated by water-balance estimations. Figure 10B shows the absolute differences between ET_C values simulated by SWAP and the ET_C estimated by water balance. Absolute differences depend on the measured ET_C values. Differences are much higher for the water-balance measured ET_C that is higher than 30 mm. This value is higher than the Readily Available Water usually computed for sugarbeet (Morillo, 1993). Therefore, actual sugarbeet evapotranspiration could hardly reach such high values (Allen et al., 1998).

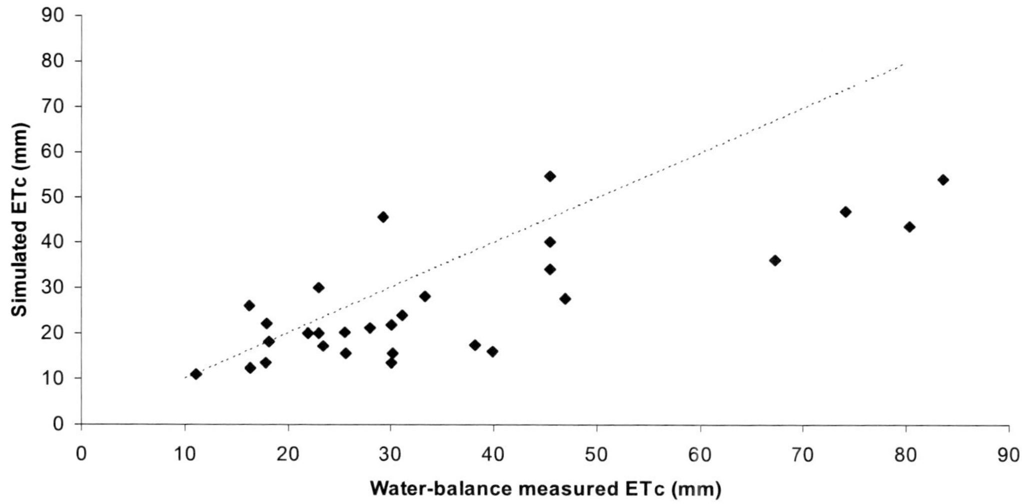

A. Simulated and water-balance measured ETc. The dashed line shows the 1:1 relaticnships.

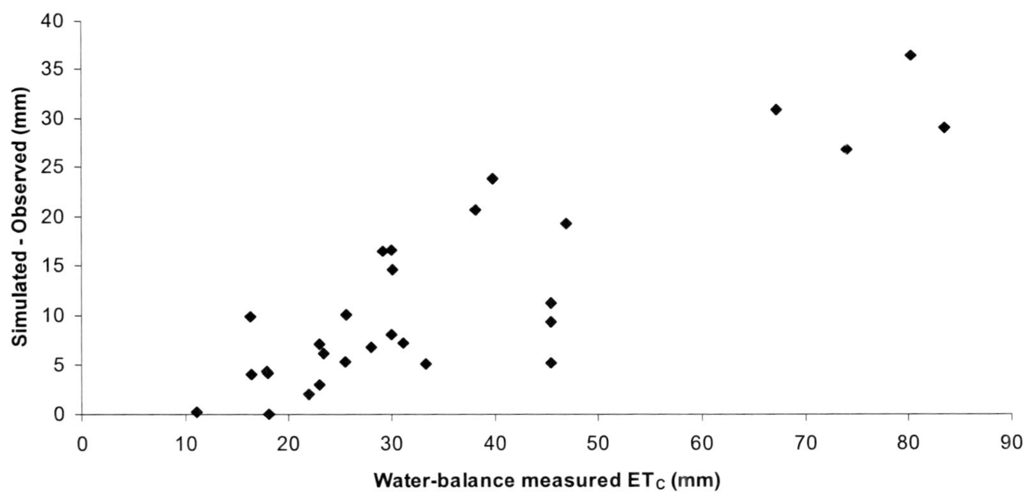

B. Absolute differences vs. Water-balance measured Etc.

Figure 10. Comparison between water-balance measured and SWAP-simulated ETc (A) as well as absolute differences between water-balance measured and SWAP-simulated as functions of water-balance measured evapotranspirations (B) (after Utset et al., 2007b).

Despite these differences, the regression line between simulated and water-balance measured ETc has a gradient of 1.14. The regression is statistically significant at the 99% confidence level. Simulated ETc values can explain up to 56.8% of the variability of water-balance ETc estimates. Furthermore, Table 6 shows the summary statistics of the water-balance measured ETc, the SWAP simulated ETc and the paired differences. As shown in the Table, both ETc data can be considered as distributed normally. According to a t-test for difference between means, considering non-equal variances, there is no statistical difference between the water-balance measured and the SWAP simulated sugarbeet ETc at the 95%

confidence level. The same result was achieved by comparing the probability distributions of the water-balance measured and the SWAP simulated ETc values through a Kolmogorov-Smirnov test. However, according to a variance-comparison F-test, the water-balance measured ETc is significantly more variable than the SWAP simulated ETc at the 95% confidence level.

Calculations of normalized RMSE, as computed by equation [6], yielded 1.8 and 2.3 when comparing SWAP-simulated ET_C with weather-based maximum ET_C and water-balance based ET_C. According to Timsina and Humphreys (2006), the values for normalized RMSE can be considered as relatively high, indicating unreliable modelling performance. Considering only simulated and observed pairs with the water-balance measured ET_C below 30 mm yields a normalised RMSE of 0.9, almost three times lower than considering the higher ET_C values.

According to the simulations, actual sugarbeet evapotranspiration was close to maximum evapotranspiration throughout the crop season. Furthermore, the irrigation managements at both plots were enough to keep the soil water content above the field capacity, as pointed out above. Accordingly, the simulated relative yields were 0.98 at the A plot and 0.92 at the Z plot. This means that the yields obtained with the said irrigation managements are close to the maximum, i.e. 87 and 82 t/ha on the A and Z plots, respectively. However, the simulated water loss due to percolation was relatively high: approximately 10% of the irrigation water applied. This over-irrigation could be useful in the case of saline soils. However, soil salinisation is not a main concern in the Duero basin (JCYL, 1987). The results indicate that sugarbeet irrigation management can still be improved in the area, as pointed out by Playan and Mateos (2005) and many others.

4.5.4. Simulating Current and Future Sugarbeet Water-Use

The baseline 1960-1990 and the 2010-2040 Climate Change scenarios were taken from the CGCM2 model outputs, provided by the Canadian Centre for Climate Modelling and Analysis (Flato et al., 2000; Flato and Boer, 2001). The IPCC SRES A2 scenario for greenhouse gases emissions (IPCC, 2001) was considered. Despite other global circulation models, CGCM2 provides free internet access to daily simulation data in a text format. Hence, this model is more suitable for simple agricultural applications anywhere. According to Merrit et al (2006), results considering CGCM2 are similar than those obtained through other general circulation models.

Table 6. Summary statistics of the water-balance measured and SWAP simulated sugarbeet evapotranspirations (after Utset et al., 2007b)

	Water-balance ETc	Simulated ETc	Difference
Mean	35.1	26.5	11.9
Standard deviation	19.4	12.8	9.9
Minimum	11.1	10.9	0.0
Maximum	83.5	54.8	36.6
Skewness	1.311	0.937	1.035
Kurtosis	1.015	-0.192	0.163

A historical meteorological series of Valladolid (41.7° N, 4.85° W), comprising daily data from 1970 to 2005 of maximum and minimum temperatures, sunshine hours and precipitation; was used in combination with the LARS-WG weather generator (Semenov and Barrow, 2002) to generate 100 realizations of local weather corresponding to 2025, approximately.

The weather generator realizations were perturbed according to the CGCM2 results corresponding to the study site, i.e., Northeast of Iberian Peninsula. The relative change in wet and dry series lengths, as affected by global change, was done following the approach recommended by Semenov and Barrow (2002), based on the daily CGCM2 outputs for each ten-year range. The relative changes in temperature standard deviations, as well as relative changes in mean temperature, precipitation amount and solar radiation were obtained from the CGCM2 daily estimations, as suggested by Semenov and Barrow (2002).

Besides, 100 realizations were also obtained, without perturbing the weather generators. Such data was representative of current climate conditions, for the 1970-2005 period. The Priestley and Taylor (1972) equation for computing the maximum evapotranspiration was used instead of the recommended Penman-Monteith approach. Penman-Monteith computations involve meteorological variables that are not included in GCM and downscaling assessments. The Priestely and Taylor approach, however, needs only maximum and minimum temperatures, as well as global radiation. Those variables can be obtained from GCM and are usually considered in the available weather generators. Besides, many crop-growths oriented models, as DSSAT, uses this approach to compute evapotranspiration (Ritchie, 1998) and most of the studies addressed to estimate climate-change effects on Spanish agriculture (Guereña et al., 2001; Minguez et al., 2005). Furthermore, according to Utset et al. (2004), both approaches are statistically equivalent when considered to simulate water managements through SWAP.

Both climate data, representing current and 2025 climate conditions, were used as input in the SWAP model, considering the sugarbeet calibration parameters described above and shown by Utset et al. (2007b). A typical irrigation management, as conducted by farmers in the zone (Utset et al., 2007b) was considered. The soil hydraulic properties estimated for a Cambisol at Valladolid province were used in SWAP simulations.

Figure 11 depicts the average components of the simulated water balance in the sugarbeet plot, according to the irrigation management considered, for the current and the 2025 climate conditions.

The water balance analysis comprises the Priestley and Taylor maximum evapotranspiration, as well as the simulated sugarbeet actual evapotranspiration, the simulated bottom flux under the 1-m soil layer considered for simulations and the effective rain.

As can be seen in the figure, the considered irrigation management is able to cover the sugarbeet irrigation management at current conditions, since the crop actual evapotranspiration is almost equal to the maximum evapotranspiration. The irrigation water-management was correct from the crop water-use point of view, since soil water contents were over or close to field capacity as can be seen in Figure 8. However, water use efficiency is low, since the simulated bottom flux is very large. The considered irrigation management could still be improved, changing the irrigation frequency and the water depth in order to minimize water looses keeping soil water contents close to filed capacity. Playan and Mateos (2005) pointed out also that despite irrigation managements in Spain are generally able to fulfil crop water requirements; water use efficiency can still be largely improved.

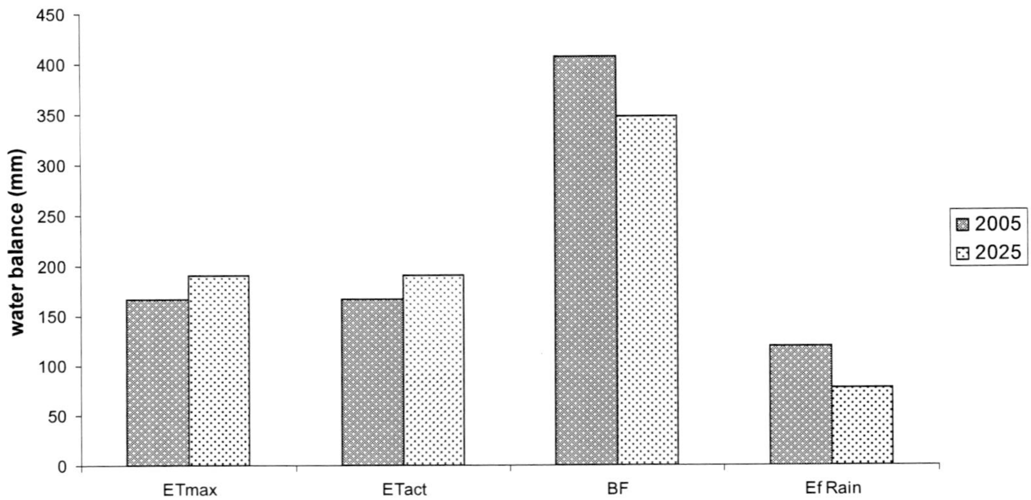

Figure 11. Water balance components in a sugarbeet irrigated plot at current and 2025 climate conditions.

The maximum evapotranspiration in 2025 is higher and the effective rain is lower than in current conditions, which agrees with the Climate Change assessments. However, the considered irrigation management is still able to fulfil the sugarbeet water requirements, in average. Accordingly, the water use efficiency is higher since the water looses by percolation are lower.

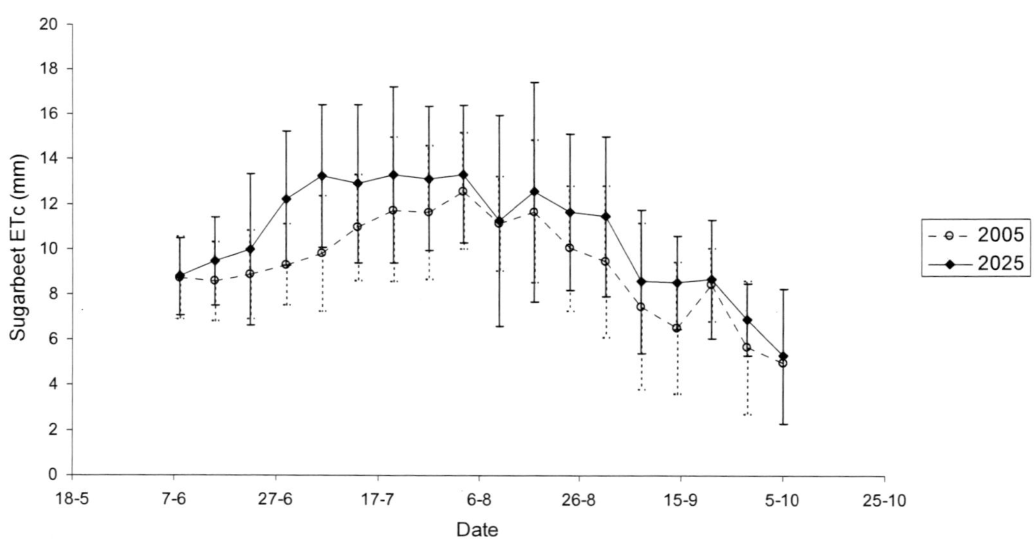

Figure 12. Sugarbeet actual evapotranspiration (ETc) during the crop irrigation period at current and 2025 climate conditions. Vertical bars indicate ETc variability.

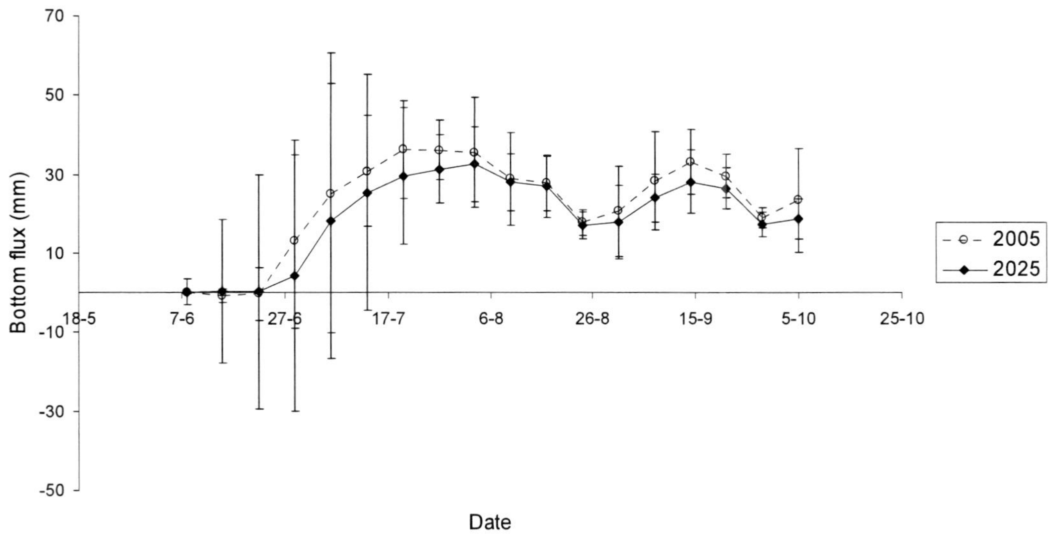

Figure 13. Bottom water flux (positive downwards) during the crop irrigation period at current and 2025 climate conditions. Vertical bars indicate ETc variability.

Besides the average results shown in Figure 11, Figure 12 depicts the simulated actual sugarbeet evapotranspiration under the irrigation period for the current and the 2025 climate conditions.

The sugarbeet actual evapotranspirations in 2025 are higher, or at least similar, than the corresponding evapotranspiration in the current climate conditions, as expected. Furthermore, the variability of actual evapotranspiration is also very high in 2025. It means that the considered water management might be not enough to satisfy the sugarbeet water requirements in several years around 2025. The success probability of the considered water management is much higher under current conditions. Weather variability has been internationally estimated as the most important climate-change risk in agriculture (Katz and Brown, 1992; Mearns et al., 1996; Riha et al., 1996; Rosenzweig et al., 2002). The European approach and the Spanish assessments agree also with these estimates (Minguez et al., 2005; EC, 2007). Our results indicated also that the enhancement of weather variability around 2025, associated to Climate Change, could significantly affect the reliability of the currently considered sugarbeet irrigation-management.

Furthermore, Figure 13 shows the simulated water flux (positive downwards) under the whole irrigation campaign.

As shown in Figure 11, average water looses in 2025 are lower than in current conditions. Sugarbeet maximum evapotranspirations will be higher in the future and hence the crop will use some of the water that is currently percolating. This relative increment of the water-use efficiency of the current irrigation management would be more evident during the first crop growing stages, as well as during the tuber formation period.

However, in the same way than the actual evapotranspiration shown in Figure 12, the water loosing variability will be much higher in the future. The variability is extremely large during the first crop-growing phases. Rainfall variability and temperature extremes are expected one of the most important consequences of Climate Change for the first half of the

XXI century (IPCC, 2007; EC, 2007). It would have a significant effect in the water-use efficiency of the currently considered irrigation water managements.

Introducing Climate and Crop-Growth Simulation Tool to Support Agricultural Decision-Making: The "Users" Point of View

"Users" and "Developers" were invited to the final AGRIDEMA workshop, which was held in Valladolid, Spain, middle 2007. The results of the assessments report were presented, focusing on the "users" points of view regarding the limitations of the available climate and crop-growth modeling tools. Hence, the "developers" received a feedback on how to improve the corresponding tools. Furthermore, the "developers" also pointed out the current development of the tools. Some representatives of farmer organizations, insurance companies and policy makers were also present.

AGRIDEMA interactions between "Users" and "developers" yielded some interesting results. Regarding the GCM outputs, "users" complained on the data format and the time scale. Only the Canadian CCCMa model provides daily data in an easily-converted format, through a Web service. This became such model as the most used in the AGRIDEMA framework. Besides, "Users" request to the national meteorological services to provide statistical (and/or) dynamical downscaled data of the most relevant GCM and emission scenarios. Such data can be used at each country in climate-change agricultural applications. Some of the "Users" and particularly the farmer representatives argue about the utility of RCM data, since the 2070-2100 seems to be extremely far for practical medium-term assessments. Farmers are mainly interested on seasonal or short-term applications. Furthermore, market prices, CAP, WFD and European or national policies can significantly influence farmer decision, besides of climate conditions. Particularly, CAP cross-compliance and the rural development funds can be an important instrument to introduce and evaluate climate-change adaptation measures in the European agriculture.

Concerning the weather generators, "Users" from the Mediterranean region pointed out that the main current approach, based on generating the variables needed for Priestly and Taylor evapotranspiration approach might not be useful. The Penman-Monteith approach has been largely recognized as the most adequate in dry conditions. "Users" took note about the facilities provided through the EU proposal ENSEMBLES. The availability of downscaled data from seasonal forecast and decadal scenarios could be an important encouragement for climate-risk agricultural assessments.

According to the AGRIDEMA results, DSSAT, WOFOST and CROPSYST are the most relevant crop-growth simulation models that are being used in Europe for climate-change risk assessments. The utility of crop models to support agricultural decision-making has been recognized. However, the "cascade approach" considered in many models to simulate soil water balance might be not adequate. This approach ignores capillary rising, which might be important in rainfed or deficit irrigation crop systems.

The AGRIDEMA participants strongly encouraged Universities and Educational politicians to held courses of current climate and crop-growth simulation tools. These tools are still unknown by most of their potential "Users", which has been considered as the main current limitation to introduce them in practice. Besides, they encourage also conducting demonstration proposals, addressed to calibrate and validate the simulation tools in several farm conditions. FP7 cooperation program aims to increase private investment rates in R+D in Europe. The demonstration proposals, funded by FP7, could count on farmers and agribusiness since they are interested in adopting reliable measures in order to reduce climate risks. The participation of agricultural applied-research or extension services in those proposals is crucial.

REFERENCES

Adiku, S.G.K, Mawunya, F. D., Jones J.W., et al. (2007). Can ENSO help in agricultural decision making in Ghana?. Sivakumar, M.V.K., Hansen, J. (Eds.) *Climate Prediction and Agriculture, Adavances and Challenges Proceedings of the START/WMO International Workshop held in Geneva, Switzerland,* 11-13 May 2005, Washington D.C. USA, International START Secretariat, 205-212.

Ainsworth, E.A. & Long, S.P. (2005). What have we learned from 15 years of free-air CO_2 enrichment (FACE)?. A meta-analytic review of the responses of photosynthesis, canopy properties and plant production to rising CO_2. *New Phytologist* 165, 351-372.

Alexandrov, V. (2002). Summarizing Crop Growth Simulation Models in Europe with Potential for Operational Assessment of Crop Status and Yield Prognosis. In: Dunkel, Z., V.Alexandrov, Z. Gat, R. Guerreiro, A. Kleschenko and Y. Ozalp (eds.), *Report of the RA VI Working Group on Agricultural Meteorology.* CAgM Report No.89, WMO/TD No.1113, Geneva, Switzerland, 119-214.

Alexandrov, V. (2007). *Current Climate Forecasting as a Helping Tool for Agricultural Decision Making.* AGRIDEMA, FP6-EC contract No 003944, Deliver 8, 11.

Allen, R., Pereira, L.A., Raes, D., et al. (1998). Crop Evapotranspiration. *FAO Irrigation and Drainage Paper 56,* Rome, 293.

Alves, O., Wang, G., Zhong, A., et al. (2002). POAMA: Bureau of Meteorology operational coupled model seasonal forecast system. *Proc. ECMWF Workshop on the Role of the Upper Ocean in Medium and Extended Range Forecasting,* Reading, United Kingdom, ECMWF, 22–32.

Arkin, G.F., Vanderlip, R.L. & Ritchie, J.T. (1976). A dynamic grain sorghum growth model. *Trans. ASAE* 19, 622-626, 630.

Baigorria, G.A. (2007). *When there is no El Niño: Approaches for crop yield forecasting.*

Bastiaansen, W.G.M., Allen, R.G., Droogers, P., et al. Inserting man's irrigation and drainage wisdom into soil water flow models and bringing it back out: How far we progressed?. In R.A. Feddes, G.H. de Rooij & J.C. Van Dam (eds). *Unsaturated-zone modelling: Progress, challenges and applications*. Kluwer Academic Publishers, Wageningen.

Beceiro, M.S. (2003). Legal considerations of the 2001 National Hydrological Plan. *Water Int.* 28 (3), 303–312.

Belmans, C., Wesseling, J. & Feddes, R.A. (1983). Simulation function of the water balance of a cropped soil: SWATRE. *J. Hydrol.*, 63:271-286.

Boote, K.J., Jones, J.W., Hoogenboom, G., et al. (1998). The CROPGRO model for grain legumes. In: Tsuji, G.Y., Hoogenboom, G., Thornton, P.K. (Eds.), *Understanding Options for Agricultural Production.* Kluwer Academic Publishers, Dordrecht, The Netherlands, 99-128.

Boote, K.J., Jones, J.W., Mishoe, J.W., et al. (1986). Modeling growth and yield of groundnut. *Agrometeorology of Groundnut: Proceedings of an International Symposium,* ICRISAT Sahelian Center, Niamey, Niger. 21-26 Aug, 1985, ICRISAT, Patancheru, A.P. 502 324, India, 243-254.

Bouman, B.A.M., Kropff, M.J., Tuong, T.P., et al. (2001). *ORYZA2000: Modeling Lowland Rice* (ISBN 971-22-0171-6*)*. International Rice Research Institute/Wageningen University and Research Centre, Los Banos (Philippines)/ Wageningen, 235.

Bouman, B.A.M., van Keulen, H., van Laar, H.H., et al. (1996). The 'School of de Wit' crop growth simulation models: a pedigree and historical overview. *Agric. Syst.* 52, 171-198.

Brown, K.F., Messem, A.B., Dunham, R., et al. (1987). Effect of drought on growth and water use of Sugarbeet. J. *Agric. Sci.* 109:421-435.

Brunet, M., Casado, M.J., de Castro, M., et al. (2007). *Generación de Escenarios Regionalizados de Cambio Climático para España.* Instituto Nacional de Meteorología, Ministerio de Medio Ambiente, Madrid, 145.

Christensen, J.H. & Christensen, O.B. (2007). A summary of the PRUDENCE model projections of changes in European climate by the end of this century. *Climatic Change,* 81: 7-30.

Clemente, R., De Jong, R., Hayhoe, H., et al. (1994). Testing and comparison of three unsaturated soil water flow models. *Agric. Water Manag.* 25: 135-152.

Connolly, R.D. (1998). Modelling effects of soil structure on the water balance of soil-crop systems: A review. *Soil Till. Res.* 48:1-19.

Craft-Brandner, S.J. & Salvucci, M.E. (2004). Analyzing the impact of high temperature and CO2 on net photosynthesis: biochemical mechanisms, models and genomics. *Field Crop. Res.* 90:75-85.

De Koning, G.H.J. & Van Diepen, C.A. (1992). Crop production potential of rural areas within the European communities. IV. Potential, water-limited and actual crop production. *Working document W68,* Netherlands Scientific Council for Government Policy, The Hague, The Netherlands, 83.

de Wit, C.T., Brouwer, R. & Penning de Vries, F.W.T. (1970). The simulation of photosynthetic systems. In: Setlik, I. (Ed.), Prediction and measurement of photosynthetic productivity. *Proceeding IBP/PP Technical Meeting Trebon 1969.* Pudoc, Wageningen, The Netherlands, 47-50.

de Wit, C.T., et al. (1978). *Simulation of Assimilation, Respiration and Transpiration of Crops* (Simulation Monographs). Pudoc, Wageningen, The Netherlands, 141.

Doblas-Reyes, F.J., Hagedorn, R. & T.N. Palmer. (2006). Developments in dynamical seasonal forecasting relevant to agricultural management. *Climate Res.* 33:19-26.

Doorenbos, J. & Kassan, A.H. (1979). *Efectos del agua sobre el rendimiento de los cultivos.* Roma, FAO, (Estudios FAO: Riego y Drenaje). 33.

Dubrovsky M., Zalud Z., Eitzinger J., et al. (2003). *PERUN system and its application for assessing the crop yield potential of the Czech Republic.* XXVIII General Assembly of EGS, 6-11 April 2003; Nice, France.

Dubrovsky M., Zalud Z., Trnka M., et al. (2002). PERUN - The System for the Crop Yield Forecasting. in: *XIV Czecho-Slovak Bioclimatological conference*, 2-4. September 2002, Lednice, Czech Rep.

Dubrovsky, (1999). Met&Roll: The weather generator for crop growth modelling. In: *Proc. International Symposium Modelling Cropping Systems,* 21-23 June 1999, Lleida, Spain, p.291-292

Durr, C. & Mary, B. (1998). Effects of nutrient supply on pre-emergence growth and nutrient absorption in Wheat (*Triticum aestivum* L.) and Sugarbeet (*Beta vulgaris* L.). *Annals of Botany,* 81:665-672.

Eatherall, A. (1997). Modelling climate impacts on ecosystems using linked models and a GIS. *Climatic Change* 35: 17-34.

Eitzinger, J., Stastna, M., Zalud, Z., et al. (2002). A simulation study of the effect of soil water balance and water stress on winter wheat production under different climate change scenarios. *Agric. Water Manage.* 2003. 61:195-217.

Eitzinger, J., Trnka, M., Hosch, J., et al. (2004). Comparison of CERES, WOFOST and SWAP models in simulating soil water content during growing season under different soil conditions. *Ecological Modelling.* 171:223-246.

Estrada, M. *Influencia de la radiación solar sobre el desarrollo y la producción de la remolacha azucarera.* Ph D. Dissertation, University of Leon, 189.

European Commission (EC). 2007. Green Paper from the Commission to the Council, the European Parliament, the European Economic and Social Committee and the Committee of the Regions. *Adapting to Climate Change in Europe – Options for EU Action.* COM(2007) 354, Brussels, 27.

European Environment Agency (EEA). 2006. Vulnerability and adaptation to climate change in Europe. *EEA Technical Report No 7/2005.* EEA, Copenhagen, 84.

European Environment Agency (EEA). 2007. Climate change and Water adaptation issues. *EEA Technical Report* No 2/2007. EEA, Copenhagen, 114.

Fabeiro, C., Martín de Santa Olalla, F., López, R., et al. (2003). Production and quality of the sugar beet (Beta vulgaris L.) cultivated under controlled deficit irrigation conditions in a semi-arid climate. *Agric. Water Manag.* 62:21-227.

Feddes, R. A., Kowalik, P. & Zaradny, H. (1978). Simulation of field water use and crop yield. PUDOC, Wageningen, *Simulation Monographs,* 189.

Fischer M. B. 2005. *Rural development and the Lisbon Strategy.* SPEECH/05/22. European Parliament Agricultural Committee. Brussels.

Flato, G.M. & Boer, G.J. (2001) Warming Asymmetry in Climate Change Simulations. *Geophys. Res. Lett.*, 28, 195-198.

Flato, G.M., Boer, G.J., Lee, W.G., et al. (2000). The Canadian Centre for Climate Modelling and Analysis Global Coupled Model and its Climate. *Climate Dynamics,* 16, 451-467.

Gabrielle, B., Menasseri, S. & Houot, S. (1995). Analysis and field evaluation of the Ceres models water balance component. *Soil Sci. Soc. Am. J.* 59:1403:1412.

Giorgi, F. & Mearns, L.O. (1999). Introduction to special section: Regional climate modeling revisited. *Journal of Geophysical Research,* 14(D6): 6335-6352.

Goudriaan, J. (1977). *Crop Micrometeorology: A Simulation Study. Simulation Monographs.* Pudoc, Wageningen, The Netherlands, 257.

Goudriaan, J. & Van Laar, H.H. (1994). Modelling potential crop growth processes. Textbook with exercises. In: *Current issues in Production Ecology,* vol. 2. Kluwer Academic Publishers, Dordrecht, The Netherlands, 238.

Groves, S.J. & Bailey, R.J. (1994). Strategies for the sub-optimal irrigation for sugar beet. *Aspects Appl. Biol.*, 201–207.

Guereña, A., Ruiz-Ramos, M., Díaz-Ambrona, C.H., et al. (2001). Assessment of climate change and agriculture in Spain using climate models. *Agron. J.* 93:237-249.

Hammer, G.L., Hansen, J.W., Philips, J.G., et al. (2001). Advances in application of climate prediction in agriculture. *Agricultural Systems.* 70:515-553.

Hansen, J.W., Challinor, A., Ines, A., et al. (2006). Translating climate forecasts into agricultural terms: advances and challenges. *Climate Res.* 33:27-41.

Hewitt, C.D. (2005): The ENSEMBLES Project: Providing ensemble-based predictions of climate changes and their impacts. *EGGS newsletter,* 13, 22-25.

Hoogenboom, G. (2000). Contribution of agrometeorology to the simulation of crop production and its applications. *Agric. For. Meteorol.* 103:137-157.

Hoogenboom, G., Fraisse, C.W., Jones, J.W., et al. (2007). Climate-based agricultural risk management tools for Florida, Georgia and Alabama, USA. Sivakumar, M.V.K., Hansen, J. (Eds.) *Climate Prediction and Agriculture, Adavances and Challenges Proceedings of the START/WMO* International Workshop held in Geneva, Switzerland, 11-13 May 2005, Washington D.C. USA, International START Secretariat, 273-278.

Hoogenboom, G., Jones, J.W., Wilkens, P.W., et al. (1994). Crop models. In: Tsuji, G.Y., Uehara, G., Balas, S. (Eds.), *DSSAT Version* 3, vol. 2. University of Hawaii, Honolulu, HI, 95-244.

Hoogenboom, G., Wilkens, P.W., Thornton, P.K., et al. (1999). Decision support system for agrotechnology transfer v3.5. In: Hoogenboom, G.,Wilkens, P.W., Tsuji, G.Y. (Eds.), *DSSAT version 3*, vol. 4 (ISBN 1-886684-04-9). University of Hawaii, Honolulu, HI, 1-36.

International Benchmark Sites Network for Agrotechnology Transfer. (1993). The IBSNAT Decade. Department of Agronomy and Soil Science, College of Tropical Agriculture and Human Resources, University of Hawaii, Honoluly, Hawaii.

IPCC (2007) Summary for Policymakers. In: *Climate Change 2007: The Physical Science Basis.* Contribution of Working Group I to the Fourth Assessment Report of the Intergovernmental Panel on Climate Change [Solomon, S., D. Qin, M. Manning, Z. Chen, M. Marquis, K.B. Averyt, M.Tignor and H.L. Miller (eds.)]. Cambridge University Press, Cambridge, United Kingdom and New York, NY, USA.

IPCC (2001). Impacts, Adaptations and mitigation of climate change: Scientific-Technical analysis. *Cambridge University Press*, 879.

Jones, C.A. & Kiniry, J.R. (1986). CERES-Maize: A Simulation Model of Maize Growth and Development. *Texas A&M University Press,* College Station, Texas.

Jones, J. W., Tsuji, G.Y, Hoogenboom G., et al. (1998). Decision support system for agrotechnology transfer: DSSAT v3. En: G. Tsuji, G. Hoogenboom and P. Thornton (Eds), U*nderstanding options for agricultural production,* Kluwer Academic Publishers, Dordrecht, 157-178.

Jones, J.W., Hoogenboom, G., Porter, C.H., et al. (2003). The DSSAT cropping system model. *Eur. J. Agron.* 18:235-265.

Junta de Castilla y León (JCYL), Consejería de Medio Ambiente & Ordenación del Territorio (1987). Mapa de suelos de Castilla y León. Dirección General de Urbanismo y Calidad Ambiental, Valladolid, 98.

Kabat, P., Van dem Broek, B & Feddes, R. (1992). SWACROP: A water management and crop production simulation models. *ICID Bulletin* 41 (2):61-84.

Kanamitsu, M. & Coauthors (2002). NCEP dynamical seasonal forecast system 2000. *Bull. Amer. Meteor. Soc.,* 83, 1019–1037.

Kandil, H.M., Skaggs, R.W. & Abdel-Dayem, S.A. (1995). DRAINMOD-S: water management model for irrigated arid lands, crop yield and applications *Irrigation and Drainage systems* 9:239-258.

Kattenberg, A., F. Giorgi, H. Grassl, G.A. et al. (1996). Climate models - projections of future climate. In: Climate Change 1995. *The Science of Climate Change.* Contribution of Working Group I to the Second Assessment Report of the Intergovernmental Panel on Climate Change. [Houghton, J.T., L.G.M. Filho, B.A. Callander, N. Harris, A. Kattenberg, and K. Maskell (eds.)]. Cambridge University Press, Cambridge, 285-357.

Katz, R. & Brown, B. (1992). Extreme events in a changing climate: variability is more important than averages. *Climate Change.* 21. 289-302.

Keating, B.A., Carberry, P.S., Hammer, G.L., et al. (2003). An overview of APSIM, a model designed for farming systems simulation. *Eur. J. Agron.*, 18, 267-288.

Klute, A. (1986). Methods of Soil Analysis. Part 1. *Agronomy Monograph.* Series No 9 (2nd Edition). ASA and SSSA, Madison, Wiscosin.

Kool, J.B. & Th. van Genuchten, M. (1991). *HYDRUS - One-dimensional variably saturated flow and transport model, including hysteresis and root water uptake*, Version 3.3, Research Report No. 124, U. S. Salinity Laboratory, USDA, ARS, Riverside, CA.

Kroes, J.C., Van Dam, J., Huygen, J., et al. (2002). *User's guide of SWAP,* version 2.0. Report 81, Wageningen University, 138.

Kroes, J.G. & Van Dam, J.C. (2003). *Reference Manual SWAP version 3.0.3.* Alterra-rapport 773, ISSN 1566-7197, 211.

Kroes, J.P. (2001). *Summary on the Swap model. COST ACTION 718 "Meteorological Applications for Agriculture".* Report of WG2 group.

Kutilek, M. & Nielsen, D. (1994). *Soil Hydrology.* Cremlingen-Destedt, Catena Verlag, 370.

Leenhardt, D., Voltz, M. & Rambal, S. (1995). A survey of several agroclimatic soil water balance models with reference to their spatial application. *Eur. J. Agron.* 4 (1), 1-14.

Maas, E.V. & G.J. Hoffman, (1977). Crop salt tolerance-current assessment. J. *Irrig. and Drainage Div.*, 103: 115-134.

Maraux, F. & Lafolie, F. (1998). Modeling soil water balance of a maize-sorghum sequence. *Soil Sci. Soc. Am. J.* 62:75-82.

Marletto, V., Zinoniu, F., Criscuolo, L., et al. (2005). Evaluation of downscaled DEMETER multi-model ensemble seasonal hindcasts in a northern Italy by means of a model of wheat growth and soil water balance. *Tellus*, 57:488-497.

Mason, S.J., Goddard, L., Graham, N.E., et al. (1999). The IRI seasonal climate prediction system and the 1997/98 El Niño event. *Bull. Amer. Meteor. Soc.,* 80, 1853–1873.

Mastrorilli, M., Katerji, N. & Nouna, B.B. (2003). Using the CERES-MAIZE model in a semi-arid Mediterranean environment. Validation of three revised versions. *Eur. J. Agron.* 19:125-134.

Mavromatis, T. & Jones, P.D. (1998). Comparison of climate scenario construction methodologies for impact assessment studies. *Agric. For. Meteor.* 91:51-67.

Mearns, L.O., Rosenzweig, C. & Goldberg, R. (1996). The effect of changes in daily and interannual climatic variability on CERES-Wheat: A sensitivity study. *Climatol. Change* 32:257-292.

Mearns, L.O., Rosenzweig, C. & Goldberg, R. (1997). Mean and variance change in climate scenarios: methods, agricultural applications, and measures of uncertainty. *Climatic Change,* 35, 367-396.

Meinke, H., Baethgen, W.E., Carberry, P.S., et al. (2001). Increasing profits and reducing risks in crop production using participatory systems simulation approaches. *Agricultural Systems.* 70:493-513.

Meinke, H., Nelson, R., Kokic, P., et al. (2006). Actionable climate knowledge: from analysis to synthesis. *Climate Res.* 33:101-110.

Merritt, W.S., Younes, A., Barton, M., et al. (2006). Hydrologic response to scenarios of climate change in sub watersheds of the Okanagan basin, British Columbia. *J. Hydrol.* 326:79-108.

Meza, J. (2007). Use of ENSO Driven Climatic Information for Optimum Irrigation Under Drought Conditions: Preliminary Assessment Based on Model Results. Sivakumar, M.V.K., Hansen, J. (Eds.) *Climate Prediction and Agriculture, Adavances and Challenges Proceedings of the START/WMO International Workshop held in Geneva,* Switzerland, 11-13 May 2005, Washington D.C. USA, International START Secretariat, 79-88.

Mínguez, M.I.T., Ruíz, A. & Estrada, A. (2005). Impacts on the Agrarian Sector. In. Moreno J. M. (Ed) *A Preliminary General Assessment of the Impacts in Spain Due to the Effects of Climate Change.* ECCE Project - Final Report. Spanish Ministry of Environment – University of Castilla La Mancha, Madrid, 30.

Ministerio de Agricultura y Pesca (MAPA) (2004). *Anuario de Estadística Agroalimentaria.* http://www.mapa.es/es/estadistica/pags/anuario/Anu_04/indice.asp?parte=7&capitulo=34

Ministerio de Agricultura y Pesca (MAPA) (2005). Plan Nacional de Regadíos. http://www.mapa.es/es/desarrollo/pags/pnr/principal.htm

Monteith, J.L. (1981). Evaporation and surface temperature. *Quarterly J. Royal Soc.*, 107, 1-27.

Moreno J. M. (Ed). (2005). A Preliminary General Assessment of the Impacts in Spain Due to the Effects of Climate Change. *ECCE Project - Final Report.* Spanish Ministry of Environment – University of Castilla La Mancha, Madrid, 786.

Morillo, R. (1998). Necesidades hídricas de la remolacha. En Morillo, R. (Eds) *El riego de la remolacha azucarera en Castilla y León.* AIMCRA - Caja Duero, Zamora, 190.

Neira, X.X., Alvarez, C.J., Cuesta, T.S., et al. (2005). Evaluation of water-use in traditional irrigation: An application to the Lemos Valley irrigation district, northwest of Spain. *Agricultural Water Management* 75:137–151.

Oficina Española de Cambio Climático (2006). Plan Nacional de Adaptación al Cambio Climático (PNACC). S. G. para la Prevención de la Contaminación y del Cambio Climático. Ministerio de Medio Ambiente, Madrid, 59.

Olesen, J.E. & Bindi, B. (2002). Consequences of climate change for European agricultural productivity, land use and policy. *European J. Agronomy.* 16:239-262.

Oostindie, K. & Bronswijk, J.J.B. (1992). FLOCR - a simulation model for the calculation of water balance, cracking and surface subsidence of clay soils. Report 47, Alterra Green World Research, Wageningen.

Palmer, T.N., Alessandri, A., Andersen, U., et al. Development of a european multimodel ensemble system for seasonal-to-interannual prediction (DEMETER). *American Meteorological Society,* 853-872.

Penning de Vries, F.W.T., Brunsting, A.H.M. & Van Laar, H.H. (1974). Products, requirements and efficiency of biosynthesis: a quantitative approach. *Journal of Theoretical Biology* 45, 339-377.

Penning de Vries, F.W.T., Jansen, D.M., Ten berge, HF.M., et al. (1989). Simulation of eco-physiological processes of growth of several annual crops. Simulation Monographs, PUDOC-IRRI, Wageningen, the Netherlands.

Playan, E. & Mateos, L. (2005). Modernization and optimization of irrigation systems to increase water productivity. *Agric. Water Manag.* 80:100-116.

Priestley, C.H.B. & Taylor, R.J. (1972). On the assessment of the surface heat flux and evapotranspiration using large-scale parameters. *Mon Weather Rev* 100: 81-92.

Rackso, P., Szeidl, L. & Semenov, M. (1991). A serial approach to local stochastic weather models. *Ecological modelling.* 57:27-41.

Raes, D., Lemmens, H. van Aelst, P., et al (1988). *IRSIS (Irrigation Scheduling Information System), reference manual.* Laboratory of Land Management, K.U. Leuven, Belgium.

Richardson, C. & Wright, D. (1984). WGEN: A model for generating daily weather variables. USDA-ARS ARS-8.80.

Richardson, C.W. (1985). Weather simulation for crop management models. *TRANSACTION of the ASAE* 28(5):1602-1606.

Riha, S.J., Wilks, D.S. & Simoens, P. (1996). Impact of temperature and precipitation variability on crop model predictions. *Climatic Change* 32:293-311.

Ritchie J. & Otler, S.(1985). Description and performance of CERES wheat: a user-oriented wheat yield model. En: W. Willis (Ed) ARS. *Wheat yield Project.* U.S. Dept. of Agric. Res. Serv. ARS-38, 217.

Ritchie, J.T. (1972). Model for predicting evaporation from a row crop with an incomplete cover. *Water Res.* 8: 1204-1212.

Ritchie, J.T. (1998). Soil water balance and plant water stress. In: G. Tsuji, G. Hoogenboom and P. Thornton (Eds), Understanding options for agricultural production, *Kluwer Academic Publishers,* Dordrecht, 41-54.

Rosenzweig, C.; Tubiello, F.N.; Goldberg, R.; et al. (2002). Increased crop damage in the US from excess precipitation under climate change. *Global Environmental Change.* 12:197-202.

Schaap, M.G., Leij, F.J., van Genuchten, M.Th. (2001). Rosetta: a computer program for estimating soil hydraulic parameters with hierarchical pedotransfer functions. *J. Hydrol.* 251:163– 176.

Seguin, B., Baculat, B., Baret, F., et al. An overview of the consequences of the 2003 summer for agriculture in France. In Jacobsen, S.E., Jensen C. R. & J.R. Porter (Eds) *Proceedings of VIII Congress of the European Society of Agronomy.* KVL, Copenhagen, 355-356.

Semenov, M.A. & Barrow, E.M. (1997). Use of a stochastic weather generator in the development of climate change scenarios. *Climatic Change* 35: 397-414.

Semenov, M.A. & Brooks, R.J. (1999). Spatial interpolation of the LARS-WG stochastic weather generator in Great Britain. *Climate Research* 11: 137-148.

Semenov, M.A. & Jamieson, P.D. (2001). Using weather generators in crop modelling. In Sivakumar, M.V.K. (Ed.) Climate Prediction and Agriculture, Proceedings of the START/WMO International Workshop held in Geneva, Switzerland, 27-29 September 1999, Washington D.C. USA, *International START Secretariat,* 322.

Semenov, M.A. & Barrow, E.M. (2002). LARS-WG. A stochastic weather generator for use in climate impact studies. *User Manual.* Rothamstead Research, Hertfordshire, 27 pp.

Semenov, M.A. & Barrow, E.M. (2002). LARS-WG. A stochastic weather generator for use in climate impact studies. *User Manual.* Rothamstead Research, Hertfordshire, 27.

Semenov, M.A., Brooks, R.J., Barrow, E.M., et al. (1998). Comparison of the WGEN and LARS-WG stochastic weather generators in diverse climates. *Climate Research.* 10:95-107.

Simunek, J., Sejna, M. & Van Genucheten, M.T. (1998). The HYDRUS-1D software package for simulating the one-dimensional movement of water, heat and multiple solutes in a variable-saturated media: version 2.0. *International Ground Water modelling Center,* Colorado School of Mines, Golden, Report No. IGWMC-TPS-70.

Šimunek, J., Vogel, T. & Th. van Genuchten, M. (1992). *The SWMS_2D code for simulating water flow and solute transport in two-dimensional variably saturated media,* Version 1.1, Research Report No. 126, U. S. Salinity Laboratory, USDA, ARS, Riverside, CA.

Šimůnek, J., van Genuchten, M. Th. & Šejna, M. (2005). *The HYDRUS-1D Software Package for Simulating the One-Dimensional Movement of Water, Heat, and Multiple Solutes in Variably-Saturated Media.* Department of Environmental Sciences University Of California Riverside, Riverside, California, 270.

Sinclair, T.R. (1994). Limits to crop yield? In: Boote, K.J., Bennett, J.M., Sinclair, T.R., Paulsen, G.M. (Eds.), *Physiology and Determination of Crop Yield.* ASA, CSS

Singh, K.K., Raji, D., Kaushik, S., et al. (2007). Application of Seasonal Climate Forecast for Sustainable Agricultural Production in Telangana sub-division of Andhra Pradesh, India. Sivakumar, M.V.K., Hansen, J. (Eds.) *Climate Prediction and Agriculture, Adavances and Challenges Proceedings of the START/WMO International Workshop held in Geneva,* Switzerland, 11-13 May 2005, Washington D.C. USA, International START Secretariat, pp 111-128.

Sivakumar, M.V.K. (Ed.) *Climate Prediction and Agriculture, Proceedings of the START/WMO International Workshop held in Geneva,* Switzerland, 27-29 September 1999, Washington D.C. USA, International START Secretariat, 322 pp.

Sivakumar, M.V.K. & J. Hansen (Eds). (2007). Climate Prediction and Agriculture, Adavances and Challenges *Proceedings of the START/WMO International Workshop held in Geneva,* Switzerland, 11-13 May 2005, Washington D.C. USA, International START Secretariat, 288.

Smedema, L.K., Abdel-Dayem, S. & Ochs, W.J., (2000). Drainage and agricultural development. *Irrigation and Drainage Systems,* 14 (3), 223-235.

Smith, M. (1992). CROPWAT, a computer program for irrigation planning and management. *FAO Irrigation and Drainage Paper* 46, Rome, 60.

Spitters, C.J.T. & Schapendonk, A.H.C.M. (1990). Evaluation of breeding strategies for drought tolerance in potato by means of crop growth simulation. *Plant and Soil* 123, 193-203.

Stockdale, T.N., Anderson, D.L.T., Alves, J.O.S. et al. (1998). Global seasonal rainfall forecasts using a coupled ocean–atmosphere model. *Nature*, 392, 370–373.

Stockle, C.O., Donatelli, M. & Nelson, R. (2003). CropSyst, a cropping systems simulation model. *Eur. J. Agron.* 18:289-307.

Swaney, D.P., Jones, J.W., Boggess, W.G., et al. (1983). Real-time irrigation decision analysis using simulation. *Trans. ASAE* 26, 562-568.

Tardieu, F. (2005). Crop simulation models as a research and a dryland farming tool. In *Proceedings of InterDrought-II Congress,* Roma.

Teixeira, J.L. & Pereira, L.S. (1992). ISAREG: an irrigation scheduling simulation model. *ICID Bulletin* 41:29-48.

Timsina, J. & Humphreys, E. (2006). Performance of CERES-Rice and CERES-Wheat models in rice–wheat systems: *A review. Agric. Syst.* 90:5-31.

Tsuji, G. Hoogenboom & Thornton, P. (1998). Understanding options for agricultural production, *Kluwer Academic Publishers*, Dordrecht.

Tubiello, F.N. & Ewert, F. (2002). Simulating the effects of elevated CO2 on crops: approaches and applications for climate change. *European J. Agron.* 18:57-74.

Uehara, G. (1998). Synthesis. In: Tsuji, G.Y., Hoogenboom, G., Thornton, P.K. (Eds.), *Understanding Options For Agricultural Production. Kluwer Academic Publishers,* Dordrecht, The Netherlands, 389-392.

using Global and Regional Circulation Models. In *Proceedings of II International Workshop on Climate Change and its impact on agriculture,* Viçosa, Brasil.

Utset, A., Eitzinger, J. & Alexandrov, V. (2007). AGRIDEMA: An EU-funded effort to promote the use of climate and crop simulation models in agricultural decision-making. Sivakumar, M.V.K., Hansen, J. (Eds.) *Climate Prediction and Agriculture, Advances and Challenges Proceedings of the START/WMO International Workshop held in Geneva,* Switzerland, 11-13 May 2005, Washington D.C. USA, International START Secretariat, pp 259-264.

Utset, A., Farre, I., Martínez-Cob, A., et al. (2004). Comparing Penman–Monteith and Priestley–Taylor approaches as reference-evapotranspiration inputs for modeling maize water-use under Mediterranean conditions. *Agric. Water Manag.* 66:205-219.

Utset, A., Martínez-Cob, A., Farré, I., et al. (2006). Simulating the effects of extreme dry and wet years on the water use of flooding-irrigated maize in a Mediterranean landplane. *Agric. Water Manag.* 85:77-84.

Utset, A., Ruiz, M., Garcia, J., et al. (2000). A SWACROP-based potato root water-uptake function as determined under tropical conditions. *Potato Research* 43:19-29.

Utset, A., Velicia, H., del Rio, B., et al. (2007). Calibrating and validating an agrohydrological model to simulate sugarbeet water use under Mediterranean conditions. *Agric. Water Manag.* (in press)

Van Dam, J.C., Huygen, J., Wesseling, J.G., et al. (1997). *Theory of SWAP version 2.0. Report 71.* Technical Document 45, Wageningen, 167.

Van Dam, J.C. (2000). Field-scale water flow and solute transport. SWAP model concepts, parameter estimation and case studies. *Doctoral Thesis, Wageningen University.* ISBN 90-5808-256-3, 167.

Van den Broek, B.J., van Dam, J.C., Elbers, J.A., et al. (1994). SWAP 1993, input instructions manual. Report 45, Subdep. *Water Resources,* Wageningen University.

Van Diepen, C., Rappoldt, C., Wolf, J. Et al. (1989). CWFS. *Crop growth simulation model WOFOST documentation version 4.1 Staff Working paper SOW-88-01.* Centre for World Food Studies, Amsterdam.

Van Genuchten, M. (1978). Calculating the unsaturated hydraulic conductivity with a new closed form analytical model. *Research Report 78* WR 08 Dept. of Civil Eng., Princeton, New Jersey, 63.

Van Genuchten, M. (1994). New issues and challenges in soil physics research. In Proceedings of 15th World *Congress of Soil Science*. Volume 1: Inaugural and state of the art conferences, Acapulco, México.

Van Genuchten, M. Th. & Šimůnek, J. *Advanced modelling of water flow and contaminant transport in the vadose zone and groundwater.* Department of Earth Sciences, Utrecht University, The Netherlands, 165.

Van Genuchten, M. Th., (1987). A numerical model for water and solute movement in and below the root zone. *Res. Report,* US Salinity Lab., Riverside, CA.

Van Genuchten, M., Leij, F. & Yates, S. (1991). *The RETC Code for quantitying the hydraulic functions of unsaturated soils*. EPA/600/2-91/065.

Van Ittersum, M.K., Leffelaar, P.A., van Keulen, H., et al. (2003). On approaches and applications of the Wageningen crop models. *Eur. J. Agron.* 18:201-234.

Van Keulen, H. (1975). *Simulation of water use and herbage growth in arid regions. Simulation Monographs*. Pudoc, Wageningen, The Netherlands, 184.

Van Keulen, H., (1982). Crop production under semi-arid conditions, as determined by nitrogen and moisture availability. In: Penning de Vries, F.W.T., Van Laar, H.H. (Eds.), *Simulation of Plant Growth and Crop Production.* Simulation Monographs. Pudoc, Wageningen, The Netherlands, 234-249.

Van Keulen, H. & Wolf, J. (1986). *Modelling of agricultural production: weather, soils and crops.* Pudoc Wageningen Simulation Monographs.

Van Laar, H.H., Goudriaan, J. Van Keulen, H. (1997). SUCROS97: Simulation of crop growth for potential and water-limited production situations. *Quantitative Approaches in Systems Analysis,* No. 14. C.T. de Wit Graduate School for Production Ecology and Resource Conservation, Wageningen, The Netherlands, 52.

Vanclooster, M., Viane, P. & Diels, J. (1994). WAVE: a mathematical model for simulating water and agrochemicals in the soil and vadose environment. *Reference and User's Manual* (release 2.0). Katholieke Universiteit Leuven, Leuven.

Velicia, H. (1998). Efecto del estrés hídrico sobre la producción y calidad de la remolacha azucarera (Beta vulgaris L.) de siembra primaveral en diferentes momentos del cultivo en las condiciones de la Cuenca del Duero. *PhD Dissertation,* Agricultural Eng. Dept., Higher School of Agronomy, Polytechnic University of Madrid, 284.

Villalobos, F.J. & Fereres, E. (2004). Climate change effects on crop water requirements in Southern Spain. II. Contrasting meteorological and agronomic viewpoints. In Jacobsen, S.E., Jensen C. R. & J.R. Porter (Eds) *Proceedings of VIII Congress of the European Society of Agronomy.* KVL, Copenhagen, 349-350.

Vogel, T., Huang, K., Zhang, R. et al. (1996). The HYDRUS code for simulating one-dimensional water flow, solute transport, and heat movement in variably-saturated media, Version 5.0, *Research Report No 140,* U.S. Salinity laboratory, USDA, ARS, Riverside, CA.

Warrick, A. & Nielsen D.R. (1980). Spatial variability of soil physical properties in the field. In: D. Hillel (ed.) *Applications of Soil Physics Academic Press,* New York, 319-314.

Werker, A. R. & Jaggard, K.W. (1997). Modelling asymmetrical growth curves that rise and then fall: applications to foliage dynamics of sugarbeet (*Beta vulgaris* L.). *Annals of Botany*, 79:657-665.

Wilby, R.L. & Wigley, T.M.L. Down-scaling general circulation issues in climate prediction. In Sivakumar, M.V.K. (Ed.) Climate Prediction and Agriculture, *Proceedings of the*

START/WMO International Workshop held in Geneva, Switzerland, 27-29 September 1999, Washington D.C. USA, International START Secretariat. 39-68.

Wilkerson, G.G., Mishoe, J.W., Jones, J.W., et al. (1983). Within-season decision making for pest control in soybeans. *ASAE Paper No. 83-4044,* St. Joseph, MI.

Willmott, C.J., Ackleson, S.G., Davis, R.E., et al. (1985). Statistics for the evaluation and comparison of models. *J. Geophys. Res.* 90 (C5), 8995–9005.

Yang, H.S., Dobermann, A., Lindquist, J.L., et al. (2004). Hybrid-maize A maize simulation model that combines two crop modeling approaches. *Field Crop Res.* 87:131-154.

In: Natural Resources
Editor: Jeanette B. Pauling
ISBN 978-1-60456-982-7

Chapter 9

THE WATER MANAGEMENT APPROACHES: TOWARDS WHERE WE GO?

***Sandra Martinez*[1,*], *Oscar Escolero*[2,†], *Leif Wolf*[3,‡]**
[1]Posgrado en Ciencias de la Tierra, Instituto de Geologia, Universidad Nacional Autonoma de Mexico, Ciudad Universitaria, Coyoacan 04510, Mexico City, Mexico
[2]Departamento de Geologia Regional, Instituto de Geología, Universidad Nacional Autonoma de Mexico, Ciudad Universitaria, Coyoacan 04510, Mexico City, Mexico
[3]Department of Applied Geology, University of Karlsruhe, Kaiserstr.12, 76128 Karlsruhe, Germany

ABSTRACT

This chapter reviews three approaches to water management i) supply-side, ii) demand-side and, iii) integrated. Tools and applications for each approach are reviewed in order to understand their reach in the solution of water-related problems. The paper focuses on management tools which are also applicable on the scale of urban areas.

Recent formulations take into account a holistic understanding of water resources that provides environmentally and socially acceptable solutions. The solutions proposed explore a combination of technologies and strategies, depending on the aims of projects, their local and national context, and the available data. The involvement of decision-makers, stakeholders and other end-users is essential for the specification of relevant issues and the development of useful tools to support decisions.

The challenges that face central and northern Mexico are reviewed. The limitations of conventional practices of water management in Mexico point to the need for a paradigm change, from increasing supply to reducing demand. The change toward more integrated management is a complex and difficult task, given the traditional dominance of centralized and technocratic management. The benefits of holistic management approaches are discussed, as are the obstacles that have limited their adoption so far.

---

* seddam2002@yahoo.com.mx
† escolero@geologia.unam.mx
‡ wolf@agk.uka.de

1. Introduction

Three major driving forces lay behind the development of water resources in the last century: i) population growth, ii) industrial development and iii) the expansion of irrigation agriculture. In Mexico, these driving forces have been concentrated in the center and north of the country, where arid and semi-arid conditions prevail and groundwater is the main source of water supply. Estimates for the year 2030 indicate that Mexico's population will grow by 84 percent, and that 50 percent of the population will be mainly concentrated in cities located in these regions. As a result, future urban water demand will rise inexorably until it eventually exceeds available sources of supply, so increasing competition for water.

Historically, water management has been driven by the need to maximize the amount of water available to meet growing demand by the construction of physical infrastructure, the development of aquifers and transfers from neighboring basins. This conventional approach is facing increasing environmental constraints and competition for water. In order to meet the current challenges, an integrated approach to water management is proposed so as to increase the range of opportunities available, reduce environmental impacts and achieve more sustainable development.

We review approaches to water management and the usefulness of tools with which to explore solutions to problems currently faced by a great part of Mexican territory. The review concentrates on the management of groundwater and strategies with which it can be integrated. Mexico's management approach is discussed, as are the barriers that so far have limited the adoption of integrated water management (IWM).

2. Approaches to Water Management

Water management has developed in relation to population growth, increasing demand, the degradation of resources, deterioration of water quality, and extensive environmental concerns. For several decades, water managers and policy makers were driven to maximize the volume of water available in order to meet growing demand for direct use (Al Radif, 1999). But in order to overcome the limitations of that approach, demand-driven and integrated strategies were developed, along with new technologies.

Approaches to water management can thus be divided into three categories: i) supply-side, ii) demand-side, and iii) integrated.

2.1. Supply-side Management

Simulation models have been widely used as tools to explore options for groundwater management and will continue to be essential. Traditionally, groundwater system simulation models have been used to test response to water withdrawals, the interaction of groundwater and surface water, and the migration of contaminants. A model is executed repeatedly under different scenarios to achieve a particular objective (Sakiyan and Yazicigil, 2004).

An essential aspect of management modeling is to determine the proper objective function that relates to physical and operational restrictions. This is unlikely to be achieved using simulation techniques alone. Management models that combine simulation and optimization techniques have been developed to consider the behavior of a groundwater system and to determine the best operating policy under the objectives and constraint dictated by the water manager (Gorelick, 1983). The optimization model identifies an optimal management strategy from a set of feasible alternatives while the simulation model ensures that the strategy is physically acceptable.

Two methods are generally used to incorporate the simulation model within a management model: i) embedding and, ii) response matrix. The embedding method directly uses the finite difference or finite element form of the groundwater flow equations as part of the constraint set of an optimization model. Other physical and managerial constraints can be incorporated. The response matrix approach uses an external groundwater simulation model to build unit response, which describes the response of the aquifer system to unit perturbations in the pumpage and/or recharge point in the system. The simulation model is resolved several times, each with a unit stress (pumping/recharge) at a single node (Das and Datta, 2001). The assembled unit responses are used to construct the response matrix, which is included in the optimization model.

These models treat the hydraulic heads, and recharge and pumping rates, as decision variables. They may also include economic considerations. Physical decision variables, such as pumping rates, may be interpreted as surrogate economic variables or even as explicit economic factors. In order to solve optimization-based groundwater management models, use is made of such mathematical programming techniques as: i) lineal programming, ii) non-lineal programming, iii) mixed integer programming, iv) differential dynamic programming, v) stochastic programming, vi) combinatorial optimization, and vii) multiple objective programming. The technique used depends on the particular problem under consideration and the assumptions made in resolving it. The optimizations technique attempts to optimize an objective, such as minimizing the cost of achieving a goal or maximizing well production, and is subject to constraints that limit or define the decision variables, such as drawdown, hydraulic gradient and water demand. Detailed reviews of the use of optimization and simulation in groundwater management have been developed by Gorelick (1983, 1990), Wagner (1995), Das Gupta and Onta (1994) and, Das and Datta (2001).

Simulation and optimization techniques, when used in combination, have been shown to be useful in determining planning and management strategies for the optimal development and operation of groundwater systems. A management model was developed by Finney et al (1992) to identify the pumping and recharge policy that would minimize saltwater intrusion in the Jakarta Basin, Indonesia. The trade-offs between water demand and saltwater volume were evaluated to demonstrate that increased water demands would lead to a significant degradation of the basin if historical policies continued to be pursued. An optimized policy was suggested that redistributes pumping and introduces artificial recharge to significantly reduce the saltwater volume.

Varljen and Shafer (1993) determined pumping rates for a well field in Pekin, Illinois, in order to minimize the risk of withdrawing contaminated water. A simulation model was used to determine the pumping of each well as a function of well-field pumping policy. The groundwater management model evaluated the impact of variations in pumping policy on capture zones and identified a pumping strategy to meet water demand while reducing the risk of contamination by 50 percent.

An operational groundwater management model with an economic objective, incorporating both pumpage and recharge, was developed by Das Gupta et al (1996). The model was formulated for a situation in which the available surface water was inadequate to meet demand and the deficit would be equivalent to the minimum groundwater supply requirement. Maximum groundwater withdrawal was limited to avoid adverse environmental consequences. The objective was to obtain an optimal pumping and recharge policy by maximizing relative net benefit or minimizing operational cost, subject to a specified allowable drawdown, a minimum pumping requirement and a maximum allowable recharge. Analysis of optimum pumping distributions satisfied certain defined minimum potentiometric heads as well as economic criteria.

McPhee and Yeh (2004) have developed a multi-objective management model for groundwater resources on a basin-wide scale. The model was formulates for to estimate the tradeoff between the exploitation of groundwater and the conservation of ecosystems that depend on interaction between groundwater and surface water. The basin has seen significant population growth, which has increased the demand for groundwater that constitutes the San Pedro River base-flow. Intensive abstraction has become intermittent along several reaches of the river. Three management objectives were considered in the formulation: minimizing the net present value of mitigation costs, maximizing aquifer yield, and minimizing drawdown al selected locations. The management model defined a set of best policies for groundwater pumping rate and recharge. Decision makers face the task of selecting among them the one that best reflects their preference.

Magnouni and Treichel (1994), Mueller and Male (1993), Feyen and Gorelick (2004), Barlow et al (1996), Reinelt (2005) have demonstrated the use of simulation models combined with optimization techniques in mathematical programming to study a variety of aquifer management problems. Groundwater management models are capable of determining optimal pumping/recharge rate and optimal well locations, subject to restrictions on drawdowns, gradients and water demands. It must be noted that a number of the studies identified strategies for the operation of reservoir systems that were superior to those currently in operation. However, most of the groundwater management models developed have been applied to ideal and hypothetical conditions. There is an absence of published reports describing the implementation of groundwater management strategies derived from the combination of simulation and optimization models. These applications would provide research into elements concerning the practical limitations and the improvements that are needed in groundwater management techniques.

2.2. Demand-side Management

Water-related challenges are attributable to i) increasing demand as a result of population growth and economic development, ii) lower real availability due to pollution, iii) inefficient use, iv) competition among agricultural, urban and environmental demand. In order to face these challenges, a change of the water resources management paradigm has been promoted. Instead of aiming to increase supply, the new paradigm – which is widely considered to be more economically efficient (Gleick, 2000) – strives to curtail demand. From both technological and economic perspectives, water authorities and utilities are beginning to explore improvements in efficiency, options for managing demand, reuse, and reallocation of water among users (Hanemann, 1998).

The complexity of selecting efficient water management options from a set of feasible alternatives suggest that a more integrated approach is needed in order to complement existing simulation-based planning (Jenkins et al, 2004). Optimization techniques are used to identify optimal management strategy to resolve complex problems of water allocation that involve economic objectives. These management models are referred to as policy evaluation and allocation models.

A set of publications describes the application of optimization techniques to design management strategies on a regional scale (Bredehoeft et al, 1995). Lall and Lin (1991) developed a groundwater management model for Salt Lake Valley, Utah. The model was formulated from the perspective of a water authority seeking to meet the demands of competing supply agencies. The objective was to minimize the annual cost of municipal and industrial groundwater supply, subject to drawdown, water rights and water quality restrictions. The model was applied to a variety of groundwater demand scenarios. The results suggested that the redistribution of pumping within the boundaries of the agency supply areas could reduce basin-wide pumping costs by more than 50 percent. In addition there were potential advantages to transferring water between agencies, but the capital cost of the new infrastructure was not evaluated in the analysis.

Watkins and McKinney (1999) evaluated a number of structural and institutional alternatives to meet environmental and economic goals under a range of hydrologic conditions. The model evaluated a combination of demand-side and supply-side strategies. The supply-side alternatives included new water supplies i) construction of surface-water reservoirs, ii) water transfer from a neighboring basin, iii) enhancement of aquifer recharge, and iv) development of the neighboring aquifer. The demand-side alternatives included i) conservation of irrigation and urban water, ii) wastewater re-use, and iii) direct regulation of pumping during the dry season. The urban water conservation program emphasized plumbing retrofits and conservation landscaping that was aimed at reducing municipal water demands, while the use of more efficient irrigation technologies could lower demand for irrigation without sacrificing crop yields. Options were identified for the use of reclaimed wastewater for irrigation or aquifer recharge, thus effectively reducing net withdrawals from the aquifer. Water market was studied as a means of mitigating the economic effects of pumping limits and as a dry-year option. Groundwater and surface water simulation models were incorporated as constraint. The objective function of the model included municipal and agricultural water supplies, riparian habitat, endangered species, commercial fisheries, recreation, and others. These management objectives were expressed in environmental and economic terms using multi-objective programming. The model allowed evaluation tradeoffs, identified alternatives for further study and eliminated inferior alternatives without finding an optimal solution. The combination of water conservation, reuse, and dry-year options appears to be a good solution to the problem of water resources. However, any water management plan requires acceptance by stakeholders.

An economic-engineering optimization model that integrates surface water, groundwater and water demands in California's supply system was presented by Jenkins et al (2004). The results show the value of optimization modeling in order to integrate information needed to manage a complex water system. The model identified significant improvements in performance through water transfers and exchanges, conjunctive use, and various operational changes to increase flexibility. These changes also greatly reduced the costs to agricultural and urban users of meeting environmental requirements. Model results also suggested benefits for the expansion of selected conveyance and storage facilities.

An integrated hydrologic-agronomic-economic model for irrigation-dominated river basins was presented by Cai et al (2003). This model includes multiple-source nodes (reservoirs, aquifers, river reaches, etc) and multiple demand sites. The model's main advantage is its ability to reflect the interrelationships among essential hydrologic, agronomic, and economic components while exploring the economic and environmental consequences of various policy choices. The model's components included the integration of elements that ranged from the crop root zone to the river system. The model was applied to problems of water management in the Syr Darya River basin of Central Asia, providing environmental and economic information regarding reservoir operations, infrastructure improvement, economic incentives, and economic evaluation of irrigation water use. The model was mainly used for short-term analysis; the issue of groundwater quality degradation could not, therefore, be dealt with.

Optimization techniques applied to the development of regional systems with varied water quality, have been dealt with by Brimberg el at (1993). The model's purpose was to determine the optimal distribution of a limited high-quality water supply and plan the optimal development of marginal sources, such as wastewater, runoff and saline groundwater. The objective was to minimize operational and capital cost of the development of marginal sources while simultaneously allocating a conventional regional supply among a set of local sites. Constraint of water quality at each demand site was imposed. In this way an optimal investment strategy for marginal water source development and use was obtained while satisfying quality requirements at the individual sites. An important conclusion is the feasibility and economic viability of saline groundwater production over a wide range of energy prices and required quality levels. Use of this water source could be increased considerably by immediate investments in new capacity.

Management models using optimization techniques for policy evaluation and allocation have been widely developed by academic researchers, but only a few models are currently applied in real-life water management due to the complexity of the issues involved. These models provide means by which to understand the interaction of hydrological, political, and socio-economic factors with the allocation of water resources. They permit the evaluation of the environmental, economic and social benefits of demand management options such as prices, taxes, economic incentives, market-based regulation, infrastructure improvement, and the development of marginal sources, among others. In terms of water supply, the models offer an alternative for the joint management of complex systems of interrelated water supplies and demands, using a wide variety of options over a wide range of hydrologic conditions.

Water demand forecasting models are useful tools for policy-markers who consider demand-side solutions. A computer model based on scenarios of future water use has been designed in order to assess the impact of global change and management measures on water use on a regional scale (Döll and Hauschild, 2002). This model combined two methods, a water use model NoWUM, and the development of scenarios. The NoWUM model was applied to compute two reference scenarios of municipality-specific water uses by various sectors (irrigation, livestock, household, industry and tourism), summarize the story lines of the two reference scenarios and show the assumed developments to the main driving forces of water use. This approach was applied in order to support regional planning in two semi-arid Brazilian states suffering from water scarcity. The results show the impact of certain interventions, such as appropriate water pricing, in controlling the increase in domestic and industrial water use.

The IWR-MAIN water demand analysis program is a tool for estimating future water demand and evaluating demand management measures in urban areas. IWR-MAIN includes a cost-benefit module for evaluating water demand management measures and an advanced user-interface that facilitates the handling of data files and the processing of forecast results. This model requires the user to select and specify a water forecasting methodology (Davis, 2003), dependent on the specific objective and available data. The model is designed for i) translating demographic, housing, and business statistics into estimates of existing water demands, and ii) using projections of population, housing and employment to derive baseline forecasts of water use (Opitz et al 1997). The total urban water consumption may be disaggregated in spatial, temporal and sectoral components, so obtaining projections of water demand by sector, area y time period. Several possible scenarios for water use, supply and management are estimated by specifying the factors that affect demand: i) population density, ii) population distribution, iii) per capita income, iv) commercial activity and mix, v) industrial activity and mix, vi) naturally occurring conservation, vii) urban water use efficiency resulting from the implementation of best management practices (BMPs), and viii) climate change (Davis, 2003). This tool has been widely used in water demand and conservation studies for water utilities and authorities in the United States.

Water demand management allows for the exploration of measures of conservation, efficiency improvements and reallocation among users, in order to reduce potential gaps between water supply and demand. Additionally, tools applied in this approach can be useful for i) assessing the extent and cost of additional water supply infrastructure, ii) showing where conflicts might occur over use and, iii) assessing the problem of scarcity by comparing use with availability.

2.3. Integrated Water Management

IWM seeks to find join solutions to a wide range of management objectives and interests, including supply, quality, flood control, the conservation of aquatic ecosystems, user conflicts, recreation and fisheries (GWP, 2004; Heinz et al, 2007). These include the establishment of multi-disciplinary teams at various levels (local, regional, and national) to discuss different perspectives on water resources and build consensus. The stakeholders, such as farmers, industries, municipalities, households, authorities and NGOs, are incorporated in order to ensure that their experiences and views form part of the development and management plans. The tools employed within IWM include a combination of physical and social technology and strategies (Desa, 2006) that permit a multiplicity of situations to be tackled.

The IWM approach-based water cycle includes the development of alternative resources (stormwater, wastewater, and saline groundwater) in order to increase the range of opportunities available, reduce environmental impacts and achieve more sustainable development (Pinkham, 1999; Niemczynowicz, 1999; Mitchell and Diaper, 2004; Thomas and Durham, 2003). The water sensitive urban design concept in the framework of integrated urban water management (IUWM) to link land development, water-cycle management and the protection of aquatic ecosystems as part of the same management challenge (Lloyd, 2004). Within this concept, a wide range of tool sets are explored and evaluated as management solutions. Case studies in Australia demonstrate practical management applications (Mitchell, 2006). Sites such as Figtree Place and Heritage Mews use rainwater tanks, infiltration trenches and a central basin where treated stormwater enters the unconfined aquifer for retention and retrieval (Coombes et al, 1999; Boubli, 2002). These devices assist in the control of both the quantity and the quality of runoff, potable supply substitution and rainwater harvesting.

IWM can also be addressed from a concept of cleaner production. Cleaner production interventions have been extremely successful in the industrial sector and could be translated to the water sector in order to minimize freshwater consumption and wastewater generation (Nhapi and Hoko, 2004). Nhapi and Gijzen (2005), proposed three intervention steps, focusing on sewage management, but also considering water supply, nutrient use and other material flows associated with the urban water cycle. The first step is to minimize wastewater generation by drastically reducing water consumption and waste generation. The second step is the treatment and optimal reuse of nutrients and water at the lowest possible level. Afterwards, the remaining waste flows may be safely discharged into the environment. The third step involves enhancing the self-purification capacity of receiving water bodies.

The paradigm of IUWM promotes the concept of the total urban water cycle for a more holistic and integrated evaluation (Hardy et al, 2005). Typical representations of the urban water cycle either consider the man-made and natural systems as separate entities or the modeling approach only concentrates on one of the two aspects (Mitchell et al, 2003). One of the recent advances in modeling is the proposed urban volume and quality (UVQ) model. This is a conceptual hydrological model that simulates an integrated urban system at a daily time step (Mitchell and Diaper, 2004). It estimates the volume of water flowing throughout the system and the associated contaminant loads, from source to discharge point. UVQ represents i) a variety of types of land use, such as residential, industrial, commercial, parks and rural open space, ii) different water infrastructure, such as combined sewers, septic tanks, separate stormwater systems, and groundwater wells, and iii) a variety of local climatic conditions. The evaluated area is represented in three spatial scales: land block, neighbourhood and study area. Data requirements for UVQ are demanding. Parameters such as indoor and outdoor water demands, infiltration and exfiltration of pipes, as well as information on occupancy, lot size, gardens, roofs, paving, roads and public open areas, are required for each spatial scale. The model allows estimates to be made of the impact of alternative scenarios that include the performance of a wide range of non-conventional demand- and supply-side management techniques for water collection, infiltration, treatment and reuse on a scale based on the land block, neighbourhood and study area.

IWM has posed challenges to traditional methods based on models that simulate physical systems and on technocratic and centralized decisions. IWM is multidisciplinary and requires the participation of users, planners and policy makers at all levels. Given the increasing complexity and disciplinary breadth of water management problems, decision support systems (DSSs) have become necessary to make models more useful. The enormous advances in computing and information technologies allow individual computer models to be linked with data sets created for different individual problems in a DSS. A DSS for IWM is an integrated, interactive computer system, consisting of analytical tools and information management capabilities, designed to aid decision-makers in solving relatively large, unstructured water resource management problems (McKinney, 2004). The use of technology such as databases and graphic user interfaces permits the creation of inputs and results that are readily understandable to analysts and decision-makers. Three main subsystems must be integrated in an interactive manner in a DSS: i) a user-interface for dialog generation and management of the interface between the user and the system, ii) a model management subsystem, and iii) an information management subsystem. A review of water resources DSSs has been developed by McKinney, (2004). Simulation and optimization models are the most used in water resources DSSs; these include Aquatool, CALSIM and DELFT-TOOLS, among others.

Research models funded by the European Union have been integrated into an interactive DSS addressing physical, economic and social aspects of land degradation on a regional scale (Oxley et al, 2004). MODULUS was built to enable end-users to understand the processes that cause, and are caused by, land degradation, and to provide appropriate tools for the design and evaluation of policy options. MODULUS integrates ten models through a graphic user interface. These include: climate and weather, hill-slope hydrology, plant growth, natural vegetation, groundwater, surface water, crop choice, irrigation, and land-use models. The models operate on very different spatial and temporal scales and utilize different modeling techniques and implementation languages. The system and its models were applied and tested in the Argolida (Greece) and Marina Baixa (Spain) regions in collaboration with local decision- makers and researchers with experience in these regions.

Burn et al (2006) present a DSS for IUWM that integrates a number of complex models with data transfer and handling via a GIS development platform in which stormwater, wastewater, water supply, groundwater and contaminants are simultaneously considered. The principal model is the above-mentioned UVQ. Information on the pipe network is fed into the network exfiltration and infiltration model (NEIMO) that estimates the amounts of exfiltration from, or groundwater infiltration into, sewers. The output is then forwarded to unsaturated zone models calculating water flows and travel times to the water table and the combined effects of absorption and the decay of contaminants. All upstream water and contaminant flows are then gathered to feed numerical groundwater flow and transport models such as MODFLOW® or FEFLOW®, which, based on the selected scenario of water use, will allow for the prediction of impacts to the urban aquifer, such as variations in the level or volume of groundwater with quality deterioration. The DSS supports the selection and comparison of predefined scenarios, allowing the end-user to choose preferences for a best-practice response decision e.g. groundwater treatment, or system improvements that prevent contamination. These scenarios are then used in a separate socio-economic model to assess the socio-economic implications of the different methodologies. The DSS has been applied to four case-study cities located on different aquifers (Klinger et al, 2006). In all case studies, the scenarios were specified by local stakeholders.

A great deal of knowledge, as well as new tools, has been generated by research carried out worldwide. However, only a small amount has been made available to support practical decisions. The involvement of decision-makers, stakeholders and other end-users is essential for the specification of relevant issues and the development of useful interactive support tools. Limitations to the development and application of DSSs to water resources management include, among others, i) lack of effective communication between scientists and end-users of the DSS, ii) the multidisciplinary nature of DSSs and their theoretical underpinnings, iii) lack of available methods to measure the effectiveness of DSSs, iv) lack of case studies in which the performance of DSSs has been evaluated in appropriate institutional settings.

3. Water-Related Problems in Mexico

There have been three mayor driving forces for the expansion of water use in central and northern Mexico, where arid and semi-arid conditions prevail: i) population growth, ii) industrial development, and iii) the expansion of irrigation agriculture. These forces have been associated with speedy processes of urbanization, industrialization and economic transformation, modifying forms of land and water use. The problems that have accompanied this development are:

i. An increase in the extraction of groundwater as a secure source of supply in quantity and quality. Some 70 percent of the volume of water supplied to cities comes from groundwater that supply about 75 million inhabitants (PNH, 2002). The aquifers situated near or below urban areas are subject to intensive extraction, often exceeding the natural recharge rate by more than 40 percent. Significant social, economic and environmental impacts can be observed (Escolero, 1993[a]; Carrillo-Rivera et al, 2007). These include i) the disappearance of springs, lakes and wetlands, ii) a reduction in groundwater discharge, iii) loss of ecosystems, iv) a decline of the water-table and increasing pumping costs, v) land subsidence and surface fracturing, vi) undesirable water quality due to pumping.
ii. Contamination of water sources by wastewater discharge and waste disposal. Seventy-three percent of surface water and some 40 aquifers suffer varying degrees of contamination as a result of anthropogenic activity (PNH, 2002). As a result, indices of diarrheic illnesses are very high, with children the most vulnerable group. Chemical changes in abstracted groundwater due to uncontrolled withdrawal are also an important issue. Most of the wells located in the arid and semi-arid zone of Mexico capture water with fluoride concentrations higher than 1 mg/l, and it is estimated that about 5 million people are affected by fluoride in groundwater (Ortiz et al, 2006).
iii. Increasing competition among different users and uses as a result of scarcity and legislation that has prohibited new groundwater extractions since 1960-1980 in over-exploited aquifers. The 1992 opening of the water market promoted the transfer of water rights, mainly from the farm to the urban and industrial sectors. Irrigation with raw wastewater constitutes a common practice around urban areas as a consequence of the competition for water resources.
iv. Change in the natural drainage pattern. Runoffs are disrupted as ground is sealed during urbanization, by highway construction, and as watercourses are diverted or paved. This has increased flooding and generated a negative environmental and economic impact in urban areas and their surroundings.
v. Lack of economic resources for the construction and maintenance of supply, drainage and sanitation infrastructure have led to deficiencies in services. Even though the coverage of water supply systems in major urban centers is high (more than 95

percent), physical and economic efficiency are low (about 60 and 35 percent, respectively). Municipal water utilities have gained much more independence within the last decade, but pricing is still a political issue. Thus, capital is lacking for investment in obsolete infrastructure, and most utilities barely cover their operational costs.

These problems affect the sustainability of development in central and northern Mexico, where 77 percent of the population lives and the most important industrial infrastructure, irrigation land and principal cities are to be found. Almost 85 percent of the nation's gross domestic product is generated in central and northern Mexico, but it accounts for just a third of the country's water resources (Conagua, 2006).

Urban water supply has been identified as one of the main challenges that will determine the future growth of Mexican cities. Estimates for 2030 indicate that the nation's population will grow by 84 percent compared with its present level of some 110 million inhabitants, and that 50 percent will be concentrated in 31 cities of more than 500 000 inhabitants (Conagua, 2006). To make matters worse, nearly 75 percent of these cities lie in central and northern Mexico, where natural water availability is 32 percent and 104 aquifers that supply 60 percent of the groundwater employed for all uses are over-exploited.

4. Management in Mexico

The technocratic and centralized approach to water management in Mexico promoted policies and technical tools that aimed to maximize the volume of water available in order to meet growing demand. Solutions were focused on the supply side, and the management of water resources was synonymous of optimization of reservoir operations. Simulation models have been widely applied to reservoir management with intensive extraction. Conagua (1996), CEASG (1998), Navarro de León (2004), Garfias et al (2006), Hernández-G and Huizar-A (2006) Escolero and Torres-Onofre (2007) evaluate the historical and future effects of groundwater extraction on the hydrogeologic regime and productive thickness by means of simulation models. Future demand is analyzed in accordance with different climatic scenarios, and trends in population growth and economic development. The results suggest the need for urgent action to reduce the intensive extraction. A review of the use of optimization and simulation in groundwater management in Mexico was developed by Escolero (1993[b]). The models reviewed were applied to determine optimal pumping rate and well locations, subject to specified drawdown, maximum pumping capacity and water demand. More recently, Aldama et al (2006) presented a simulation and optimization model for the Lerma-Chapala basin. A basin simulation model integrating the components – river, aquifers, reservoirs, irrigated areas, urban centers and industrial zones – was linked with optimization. The objective was to achieve maximum well production for irrigation while minimizing the deficit, subject to constraint of allowable drawdown in order to avoid damage to the environment. This model allowed for a consensus to be built around the policy for optimal operation of the basin's water resources.

Policies have favored the construction of new physical infrastructure (dams, wells, channels), the development of aquifers and water transfers from neighboring basins to meet ever-increasing water demand. But the traditional means of supply augmentation are facing increasing environmental constraints and competition for water. The international literature contains examples of adverse economic and environmental impacts associated with this approach. Imbalances between demand and supply, resource degradation, and competition among sectors call for sustainable management of water resources using new methods and innovative approaches. As an indication of progress toward a new vision, a paradigm change from increasing supply to reducing demand was proposed in Mexico by the National Water Commission as a central element of policy (Conagua, 2006).

It is now well established that traditional supply-side water management has reached a limit. However, the inertia built up by ingrained forms of technocratic institutional power and expertise, values and leadership, perpetuates traditional practices and impedes change to integrated management. Until now, technical engineering has been the dominant source of knowledge, decisions and power within the local and national water institutions. These institutions have been responsible for providing water supply and flood protection, but have lacked a vision of a sustainable water future. The political focus is still on drinking water provision; non-traditional resources, including shallow aquifers and stormwater, are not a priority. The change of paradigm clearly requires the reorientation of authorities so that they work to improve cooperation with utilities, planning agencies and water users, and also to promote understanding of the totality of resources involved in management.

Researchers have an important role in assisting planners and policy-makers to lower the barriers that so far have impeded IWM. Researchers can spread knowledge and awareness of the tools that are available. They can generate models and promote debate with decision-makers about the practical limitations of management techniques and the ways in which these can be overcome.

In Mexico, the water market is restricted to the aquifer's administrative limits and bound by the regulations that local authorities dictate. Simulation and optimization models may be useful technical instruments in the promotion of more rational regulations. These models provide scenarios of water allocation, transfers and exchanges that allow decision-makers to explore their economic and environmental consequences, and to consider other economic instruments as complementary measures. This will be particularly useful in aquifers where social and economic forces have failed to interact widely with the allocation of water resources. However, before they can be adopted as instruments of management policy, optimal water allocations must agree with the perspectives of users as well as planners and policy-makers. This often requires that models be calibrated not only with respect to the physical parameters of the system, but also to its decision-making processes. This aspect is often overlooked in the development and design of models, and leads to poor acceptance in practice.

Urban stormwater and wastewater may be used for irrigation and/or recharge of aquifers. Stormwater may be harvested and stored or treated for less demanding uses. Shallow urban aquifers have been neglected because they are commonly considered to be polluted and unusable for drinking water purposes. Tools and methods that can assess the use, and ascertain the demand for, alternative water resources may be applied in the framework of a common urban system. For such applications, the collection and availability of data is critical. Before any calculations are made, it is important to assess and analyze the available data. The selection of the tools to be applied is driven in part by data can be made available through collection. Time and money will be needed in order to identify and compile existing data that may support a first application, and additional costs will be incurred in order to generate new information for future applications.

5. Conclusion

This paper makes reference to the IWRM concept as outlined in GWP (2004) but focused on urban areas as a subset problem.

The development of the management of water resources has been linked with increased demand, the degradation of resources, the deterioration of water quality, and extensive social and environmental concerns. Until recently, water resources management was driven by the need to maximize the volume of water available in order to meet growing demand. The current challenges, however, require the promotion of a paradigm change in water resources management along with the development and application of new technologies.

The Integrated Water Management (IWM) approach includes i) water resource management (including alternative sources and protection), ii) water supply management, iii) water demand management and allocation, and iv) wastewater system and sanitation management. The solutions proposed explore a combination of technologies and strategies in order to assure economic and environmental sustainability as well as social acceptance. However, the development and implementation of IWM is a complex and difficult task. In Mexico, where a centralized and technocratic management has been dominant, IWM still requires wider institutional acceptance of the need to decentralize decision-making by involving the views of farmers, industries, municipalities, households, authorities and NGOs in plans for development and management.

A broad range of tools is available for IWM. These tools include optimal water allocation; optimal development and operation of systems; water-sensitive design, including urban layout and landscaping; utilization of non-conventional sources, including stormwater, wastewater, shallow and saline groundwater; stormwater and wastewater source control and pollution prevention; stormwater flow and quality management; the use of mixtures of soft (ecological) and hard (infrastructure) technologies; and nonstructural tools such as education, pricing incentives, regulations, and restriction regimes. Given the increasing complexity of water management problems, the solutions require a mix of these tools, depending on the aims of projects, their local and national context, and the availability of data. Researchers may assist in the selection and application of the appropriate tools for each particular case.

The challenges that face central and northern Mexico require i) a clear understanding of the regional water cycle and its relation with the urban water cycle, ii) an improvement in public awareness of the main issues that relate to water management and of the risks of unplanned development, iii) an understanding of the interdependency of urban water systems (supply and drainage) and urban groundwater resources as a part of the same cycle, so requiring assessment within a common framework. Alternative sources may complement – or even replace – traditional supply sources, so reducing the volume of drinking water that cities need to import, as well as of the stormwater and wastewater that they export to surrounding areas.

Acknowledgements

The authors gratefully acknowledge the UNAM's General Direction of Postgraduate Studies for their support.

References

Aldama, A.; Güitrón, A.; Aparicio, J.; et al. La Cuenca Lerma Chapala y los modelos de simulación. *Rev Cien Desar.* CONACYT, México, Marzo 2006, pp.36-41.

Al Radif, A. Integrated water resources management (IWRM): an approach to face the challenges of the next century and to avert future crises. *Desalination.* 1999, 124, 145–153

Barlow, P.M.; Wagner, B.J.; Belitz, K. Pumping strategies for management of shallow water table: the value of the simulation-optimization approach. *Ground Water.* 1996, 34(2), 305-317.

Boubli, D. (2002) Heritage Mews, *Castle Hill: a case study in delivering water sensitive urban design.* http://www.wsud.org/downloads/Info%20Exchange%20&%20Lit/Heritage% 20Mews% 20Castle%20hill.pdf Cited April 2007.

Bredehoeft, J.D.; Reichard, E.G.; Gorelick, S.M. If it works, don't fix it: benefits from regional ground water management. In *Groundwater models for resource analysis and management;* El-Kadi, A.; Ed.; CRC Press/Lewis Publishing Co., 1995, pp 101-121.

Brimberg, J.; Oron, G.; Mehrez, A. A model for the development of marginal water sources in arid zones: The case of the Negev Desert. Israel. *Water Resour Res.* 1993, 29(9), 3059-3067.

Burn, S.; De Silva, D.; Ambrose, M.; et al. A decision support system for urban groundwater resource sustainability. *Water Practice & Technology. 2006,* 1(1), http://www. iwaponline.com/wpt /001/0010/0010010.pdf doi: 10.2166/WPT.2006010.

Cai, X.; McKinney, D.C.; Lasdon, L.S. Integrated hydrologic-agronomic-economic model for river basin management. *J Water Resour Plan Manag.* 2003, 129(1), 4-17, doi: 10.1061/(ASCE)0733-9496(2003)129:1(4).

Carrillo-Rivera, A.; Cardona, A.; Huizar-Alvarez, R. et al. Response of the interaction between groundwater and other components of the environment in Mexico. *Environ Geol.* 2007. doi 10.1007/s00254-007-1005-2.

CEASG – Comisión Estatal del Agua y Saneamiento de Guanajuanto. *Estudio hidrogeológico y modelo matemático de los acuíferos del estado de Guanajuato.* Elaboró Guysa, S.A. de C.V., 1998.

Conagua – Comisión Nacional del Agua. Estudio de simulación hidrodinámica y diseño óptimo de las redes de observación de los acuíferos de Calera, San Luis Potosí y Toluca, *Informe técnico,* Contrato No. GAS-012-PRO-96. Elaboró Ariel Consultores SA., 1996.

Conagua - *Comisión Nacional del Agua. Water in Mexico,* Document printed for 4th World Water Forum. 2006.

Coombes, P.J.; Argue, J.R.; Kuczera, G. (1999) *Figtree Place: a case study in water sensitive urban development.* http://www.wsud.org/downloads/Info%20Exchange%20&%20Lit/FIGTREE%20LAST21.pdf. Cited April 2007.

Das Gupta, A.; Onta, P.R. Ground-water management models for Asian developing countries. *Water Resour Devl.* 1994, 10(4), 457-474.

Das Gupta, A.; Nobi, N.; Paudyal, G.N. Groundwater management model for an extensive multi-aquifer system and an application. *Ground Water.* 1996, 34 (2), 349-357.

Das, A.; Datta, B. Application of optimization techniques in groundwater quantity and quality management. *Sadhana.* 2001, 26(4), 293–316.

Davis, Y.W. (2003) Water demand forecast methodology for California water planning areas. Work plan and model review. *Report submitted to: California Bay-Delta Authority.* http://www.waterplan.water.ca.gov/docs/technical/Water_DemandForecast_Methodology .pdf . Cited May 2007.

Desa, M.N. (2006) Integrated urban water management and modeling approach: an overview. Paper presented at the national conference, water for sustainable development towards a developed nation by 2020. *Nigeria Sembilan,* 13-14 July 2006, http://jps.selangor. gov.my/NC/Integrated%20Urban%20Water%20Management.pdf. Cited June 2007.

Döll, P.; Hauschild, M. Model-based scenarios of water use in two semi-arid Brazilian states. *Reg Environ Change.* 2002, 2, 150–162.

Escolero, O. Panorama del agua subterránea en México. In El agua, recurso vital. *Universidad Tecnológica de la Mixteca,* Mexico, 1993[a], pp:37-52.

Escolero, O. Manejo óptimo de un acuífero. Tesis Maestría, Facultad de Ingeniería, Univ Nac Aut México, México, 1993[b], p 68.

Escolero, O.; Torres-Onofre, S. Análisis de la intrusión de agua de mar en el acuífero de La Paz (México). *Bol. Geol Min.* 2007, 118(núm esp), 637-648.

Feyen, L.; Gorelick, S.M. Reliable groundwater management in hidroecologically sensitive areas. *Water Resour Res.* 2004, 40 W07408, doi:10.1029/2003WR003003.

Finney, B.; Samsuhadi, A.; Willis, R. Quasi three-dimensional optimization model of Jakarta basin. *J Water Resour Plan Manag.* 1992, 118(1), 18-31.

Garfias, J.; Navarro de León, I.; Llanos, H. Gestión integral de recursos hídricos con arreglos a distintas modalidades de utilización. *Paper presented in VIII Congreso latinoamericano de hidrología subterránea,* ALHSUD, Asunción, Paraguay, Septiembre 2006.

Global Water Partnership – GWP. Catalyzing Change: A handbook for developing integrated water resources management (IWRM) and water efficiency strategies. 2004. http://www.gwpforum.org/gwp/library/handbook.pdf Cited June 2007.

Gorelik, S.M. A review of distributed parameter groundwater management modeling methods. *Water Resour Res.* 1983, 19(2), 305-319.

Gorelick, S.M. Large scale nonlinear deterministic and stochastic optimization: Formulations involving simulation of subsurface contamination. *Mathematical Program.* 1990, 48, 19-39.

Gleick, P.H. The changing water paradigm: a look at twenty-first century water resources development. *Water International.* 2000, 25(1), 127–138.

Hanemann, W.M. Determinants of urban water use. In *Urban water demand management and planning;* Baumann, D.D.; Boland, J.J.; Hanemann, W.M. Eds.; McGraw-Hill Professional, 1998, pp: 31-76.

Hardy, M.J.; Kuczera, G.; Coombes, P.J. Integrated urban water cycle management: the urban cycle model. *Water Science & Technology.* 2005, 52(9), 1–9.

Heinz, I.; Pulido-Velazquez, M.; Lund, J.R.; et al. Hydro-economic modeling in river basin management: Implications and applications for the European water framework directive. *Water Resour Manage.* 2007, 21, 1103–1125, doi 10.1007/s11269-006-9101-8.

Hernández-García, G.; Huizar-Alvarez, R. Evolución de la extracción de agua subterránea en la región de Zumpango-Pachuca, México central, sus efectos ambientales. *Paper presented in VIII Congreso latinoamericano de hidrología subterránea,* ALHSUD, Asunción, Paraguay, Septiembre 2006.

Jenkins, M.W.; Lund, J.R.; Howitt, R.E.; et al. Optimization of California's water supply system: Results and insights. *J Water Resour Plan Manag.* 2004, 130(4), 271-280, doi 10.1061/(ASCE)0733-9496(2004)130:4(271).

Klinger, J.; Morris, B.; Souvents, P.; et al. Application to real world problems. In *Urban water resources toolbox: integrating groundwater into urban water management,* Wolf, L.; Morris, B.; Burn, S., Eds; IWA Publishing, London UK, 2006, pp 100-250.

Lall, U.; Lin, Y.W.H. A groundwater management model for Salt Lake County, Utah with some water rights and water quality considerations. *J. Hydrol.* 1991, 123, 367-393.

Lloyd, S.D. (2004) *Quantifying environmental benefits, economic outcomes and community support for water sensitive urban designs.* http://www.wsud.org/downloads/Info Exchange & Lit/Lloyd 2004 _final paper.pdf. Cited April 2007).

Magnouni, S.E.; Treichel, W. A multi-criterion approach to groundwater management. *Water Resour Res.* 1994, 30(6), 1881-1895.

McKinney, D.C. International survey of decision support systems for integrated water management. *Technical report.* Support to enhance privatization, investment, and competitiveness in the water sector of the romanian economy. IRG Project No 1673-000. 2004. p 65.

McPhee, J.; Yeh, W.W.G. Multiobjective optimization for sustainable groundwater management in semiarid regions. *J Water Resour Plan Manag.* 2004, 130(6), 490-497.

Mitchell, V.G.; Diaper, C.; Gray, S.R. et al. UVQ: modelling the movement of water and contaminants through the total urban water cycle. Paper presented at the 28th international hydrology and water resources symposium, Wollongong 2003.

Mitchell, V.G.; Diaper, C. (2004) UVQ: a tool for assessing the water and contaminant balance impacts of urban water development scenarios. *Paper presented at the IWA world water forum.* http://www.urbanwater.de/results/publications/mitchell-diaper-uvq-iwa-2004.pdf. Cited June 2007.

Mitchell, V.G. Applying integrated urban water management concepts: A review of Australian experience. *Environ Manag.* 2006, 37(5), 589–605.

Mueller, F.A.; Male, J.W. A management model for specification of groundwater withdrawal permits. *Water Resour Res.* 1993, 29(5), 1359-1368.

Navarro de León, I. *Análisis de estrategias de manejo integral del agua subterránea mediante modelación de flujo: Cuenca de la Independencia,* Guanajuato, México. Universidad Nacional Autónoma de México, Tesis doctoral, 2004.

Nhapi, I.; Hoko, Z. A cleaner production approach to urban water management: Potential for application in Harare, Zimbabwe. *Phys Chemy Earth.* 2004, 29(15-18, SPEC.ISS.), 1281-1289.

Nhapi, I.; Gijzen, H.J. *A 3-step strategic approach to sustainable wastewater management.* Water SA. 2005, 31(1), 133-140.

Niemczynowicz, J. Urban hydrology and water management: present and future challenges. *Urban Water.* 1999, 1, 1–14.

Opitz, E.M.; Langowski, J.F.; Dziegielewski, B., et al. Forecasting urban water use: models and application. In *Urban water demand management and planning;* Baumann, D.D.; Boland, J.J.; Hanemann, W.M.; Eds.; McGraw-Hill Professional, 1997, pp: 95-136.

Ortiz, P.M.; Bocanegra, S.M.; Landín, R.L. Evaluación de la contaminación por flúor y arsénico en el agua de pozo para consumo humano de las zonas centro, altiplano y media del estado de San Luis Potosí. Universidad Autónoma de San Luis Potosí. 2006.

Oxley, T.; McIntosh, B.S.; Winder, N. et al. *Integrated modelling and decision-support tools: a Mediterranean example, Environ Model & Software.* 2004, 19, 999–1010, doi: 10.1016/j.envsoft.2003.11.003.

Pinkham, R. (1999) *21st century water systems: scenarios, visions and drivers.* https://www.rmi.org/images/PDFs/Water/W99-21_21CentWaterSys.pdf. Cited April 2007.

PNH - Plan Nacional Hidráulico 2002 -2006, *Comisión Nacional del Agua,* México. 2002.

Reinelt, P. Seawater intrusion policy analysis with a numerical spatially heterogeneous dynamic optimization model. *Water Resour Res.* 2005, 41 W05006, doi 10.1029/2004WR003111.

Sakiyan, I.; Yazicigil, H. Sustainable development and management of an aquifer system in western Turkey. *Hydrogeol J.* 2004, 12, 66-80, doi 10.1007/s10040-003-0315-z.

Thomas, J.S.; Durham, B. Integrated Water Resource Management: looking at the whole picture. *Desalination. 2003,* 156, 21-28.

Varljen, M.D.; Shafer, J.M. Coupled simulation-optimization modeling for municipal ground-water supply protection. *Ground Water.* 1993, 31(3), 401-409.

Wagner, B.J. Recent advances in simulation-optimization groundwater management modeling. *Rev Geophys.* 1995, 33 (Suppl American Geophysical Union). http://www.agu.org/revgeophys /wagner01 /node2.html

Watkins, D.W.; McKinney, D.C. Screening water supply options for the Edwards Aquifer Region in Central Texas. *J Water Resour Plan Manag.* 1999, 125(1), 14-24.

INDEX

A

B

C

D

G

H

I

J

L

M

Q

R

S

T

U

V

W

Y